OVERLOAD

Russ Shipton

**Too much of what we *want*
– too little of what we *need***

Published by New Generation Publishing in 2014

Copyright © Russ Shipton 2014

First Edition

The author asserts the moral right under the Copyright, Designs and Patents Act 1988 to be identified as the author of this work.

All Rights reserved. No part of this publication may be reproduced, stored in a retrieval system or transmitted, in any form or by any means without the prior consent of the author, nor be otherwise circulated in any form of binding or cover other than that which it is published and without a similar condition being imposed on the subsequent purchaser.

www.newgeneration-publishing.com

 New Generation **Publishing**

Acknowledgements

I would firstly like to thank Larry Tomscha for bringing the wisdom of Victorian and Edwardian self-help authors to my attention. Their willingness to challenge the prevailing orthodoxy inspired me to re-appraise my lifestyle and initiate beneficial changes that ultimately led to this book.

I would also like to thank Anne Moir and Kate McNeilly for their advice regarding the book's structure, ambition and scale, Shan Rees for her views on the "tone" of the material, and my brother, Chris Shipton, for his numerous insightful suggestions – particularly those that served to clarify the information provided in the awareness section.

I am especially indebted to Mike Herbert, who stoically and graciously listened to my views about the world over a period of at least 5 years. I am grateful for the continued interest and enthusiasm he showed throughout our regular discussions about the pros and cons of today's way of life. His open-mindedness, common sense, balanced criticism – and unflagging encouragement – proved invaluable in the honing of my analysis.

This book is dedicated to the memory of my late wife, Terry Tomscha. I believe her consistent example of kindness and concern for others, throughout our 27 happy and productive years of life together, made me a better person.

CONTENTS

Acknowledgments   3
About the Author   6
How This Book Came About   8

INTRODUCTION   18

PHYSICAL OVERLOADS   23
Self-Appraisal   24
Food   27
Caffeine   44
Alcohol   53
Tobacco   63
Illegal Drugs   71
Pharmaceutical Drugs   81
Supplements   95
Pollution (water, air, soil and food)   100
Disease and Illness   123

MENTAL OVERLOADS   147
Self-Appraisal   148
Social Pressure   151
Work   170
Speed   182
Information   194
Technology   202
Entertainment   214
Education   224
Alienation   234
Pollution (visual and aural)   258
Fear and Anxiety   269
Mental Illness   285

AWARENESS	297
The Master Key	298
Self-Awareness	301
Breaking Out of Prison	304
Self-Responsibility	309
Needs	312
Motivation	316
Morality	321
Willpower	324
Risk, Probability and Prevention	329
Balance	336
Appreciation	343
Detachment	346
Self-Development	351
Contentment	354
THE WAY AHEAD	357
References	360
Source Books	423
Quote Authors' Biographies	425

About the Author

Before reading a self-help book, I like to know something about the author – what might qualify him (or her) to write such a book, what's his background, and what kind of person is he? And in particular, does he practise what he preaches?

I attended a military boarding school for 7 years, where amongst other things I learnt to shine shoes, fire guns, play rugby, march and salute. 5 more years were spent before and after university pushing pens in accountancy offices. I've also worked on a building site, swept floors and cleaned toilets at the crack of dawn. I took up guitar at the age of 23 and travelled to Australia as a "£10 Pom". After returning to the UK, I taught guitar, toured Europe with a theatre group, and ran *Bunjies*, a folk club/vegetarian restaurant in central London. Somehow I've managed to make a living out of music most of my life – by performing, writing songs and teaching.

Okay, I'll come clean. Do I have a sociology degree? No (though I admit to one in economics). Am I a trained psychologist with letters after my name? No. Am I a recognised philosopher? No. Am I a medical doctor or nutritionist? No and no again. But I believe that the very absence of these kinds of qualifications has enabled me to look at human behaviour and lifestyle matters with a fresh, unbiased and truly open mind – and thereby to see the wood from the trees. I did something similar in the music area some time ago.

In the late 1970s I persuaded a well-known company to distribute my guitar tuition books (for non-classical music), and about 2 million have now been sold. The approach I took then is analogous to the one I used for this book. Because I had not been trained classically and had started playing relatively late in life, I observed other guitarists with a keen eye, fresh pair of ears and an open mind. I realised that instruction books then had two major flaws: they included no modern material and concentrated almost entirely on the left hand, i.e. the notes and chords. It became clear to me that the rhythmic side of music – particularly for non-classical accompaniments – was of at least equal importance to pitch. So my tuition books provided 6 distinct rhythm styles and modern songs as examples. These proved to be extremely useful for beginners to play a whole variety of songs with just a handful of chords.

When I looked at lifestyle, I became aware of an apparent paradox: the significant increase in our material wellbeing had been accompanied by an equally significant increase in our physical and mental problems. On the following pages you'll find an abundance of persuasive statistics as well as the analyses and conclusions of experts who have studied the excesses and stresses in the developed world. Taken together they provide a convincing explanation for this phenomenon – convincing enough for me to alter my diet, exercise more, simplify my life, and to view myself and the world in a different, more positive and constructive way.

Do I practise what I preach in this book? Yes, I believe I do, though that's perhaps for others to judge.

How This Book Came About

What you're about to read emerged after extensive research led me to make significant adjustments to my lifestyle, which in turn resulted in positive developments in my bodily health, mental clarity and overall approach to life. Of the several changes I made over a number of years, the first was an adjustment to my diet. Sadly, my wife developed breast cancer some time before I understood the possible consequences of certain dietary habits and other lifestyle factors that might have prevented this from happening. In fact her diagnosis, suffering, chemotherapy, and premature death in her early fifties, a nightmare that dominated our lives for over three years, was the catalyst that precipitated my first stumbling steps along the road to greater awareness – though it wasn't till several years after she died that I began to understand not only the importance of maintaining a high level of physical and mental health, but also what really matters in life.

Various nuggets of information concerning health had crossed my path over the decades, but like most people I was always too concerned with the usual things in a busy life to examine them in detail and recognise their potential significance – apart from a hard-to-ignore visual message during the 1960s. Intended to frighten smokers, huge posters of blackened, diseased lungs appeared on billboards in London. I am grateful to *The British Medical Association* for standing up to the powerful tobacco lobby because their warnings convinced me to give up my twenty-five a day habit, though I do recall that it took considerable willpower – and up to 18 months after I stopped smoking I had a recurrent nightmare where I would be taking a large drag on a cigarette and then wake up in a cold sweat.

"The Diet"

Most people who become aware of my diet view it as "extreme", and for a while my friends loved to joke about it. I play squash regularly and comments like "You need a good piece of steak!" would occasionally ring out from the gallery if I missed a shot.

Though I didn't know it at the time, a change in the food and drink I consumed was just the first but key move in what would later metamorphose into a quest for awareness – to learn how to increase my daily wellbeing as well as achieve greater fulfilment and long-term contentment. A few more years on and before I actually recognised it myself, that personal quest had mysteriously expanded into an attempt not only to understand the problems caused by the excesses in the Western world – or "overloads", as I call them – but also the even more challenging task of discovering what might be done to counteract them.

My decision to experiment with my diet came about during a visit to my wife's relatives in the States, several years after her death. At the end of my trip I stopped off in New York to see one of her brothers who kindly allowed me to stay at his flat in Manhattan. He happens to be one of those interesting people who are inclined to experiment with ways of doing things that most would consider somewhat left-field. He has a penchant for searching out old, self-help material and happened to have just bought two second-hand books on diet and fasting, written by a certain Professor Arnold Ehret in the early 20th century. I remember that one was called somewhat bizarrely, *The Mucusless Diet*. The author claimed that radical dietary changes had cured serious health conditions that he and many others had suffered from. I spent an interesting and enjoyable evening discussing both the material in these books with my brother-in-law as well as the effects of dietary experiments he himself had made. I resolved to find out more about the health implications of diet on my return to the UK – and then to undertake some personal experiments.

Although I was beginning to regain my shattered equilibrium after my wife's death, I was feeling a little jaded and somewhat world-weary. Perhaps I was just ready for a change in my life and sensed I wanted to do something different – and diet seemed a good place to begin. Partly because my wife had died of cancer and partly because so many people were suffering from one form of the disease or another, I first investigated whether diet had anything to do with this much feared and widespread illness. The information led me to examine the possible link between diet and other health problems. After much research I was convinced that diet did indeed have a significant impact on our health. Though I was confident that a wiser choice of the food and drink I consumed would make it far less likely that I would suffer from cancer or dementia, have a heart attack or become diabetic, I wondered whether it would also make me lose some weight. Would my energy level increase? And would my outlook on life be affected?

Many people have great ideas but don't necessarily see them through to some form of completion. I happen to be someone who is not much of an ideas person but who has always been a "finisher", almost to the point of obsession. I guess I never liked the idea of putting effort into something without seeing some sort of "successful" conclusion, and would otherwise consider that I had somehow wasted my time – though now I know that's not necessarily true. In any case, I felt just about strong enough – and young enough – not to be too concerned about any unfortunate repercussions that a radical diet change might produce. Once I had made the decision, I was determined to be resolute for whatever time it took to make a fair assessment of the results.

Not long before I began my dietary experiment the "caveman diet" was highlighted in the media. Our ancestors from long ago ate grass-fed, pasture-raised meats, fish, vegetables, fruit, roots and nuts. They didn't eat grains, legumes, dairy products, added salt, refined sugar or processed oils, because they weren't available then. The discussion about the possible merits of "natural" food made me think about the way my body felt an hour or so after consuming highly processed, sugary things like sweets, toffee, ice-cream, fizzy drinks or biscuits – my mouth didn't feel quite right, my digestion was disrupted, and my energy level dropped. On balance, having mulled this over for a while, I came down on the side of the small minority who believed it likely that our bodies would function better with simple food provided by the natural environment. This hunch caused me to take what I now strongly believe to be the most important lifestyle decision of those I made – to eliminate virtually all processed food.

Lifestyle Choices

Like almost everybody else in the developed world, I had been touched by the suffering of close family members who experienced serious illnesses. My wife's sister was also diagnosed with breast cancer in her forties, my father had dementia in his eighties while my mother had a mild heart attack in her sixties and a stroke in her early seventies, and died soon after. One of my aunts suffered from dementia and another had a stroke, while two uncles died in their sixties from heart attacks and another was prescribed blood thinner. Various friends and associates had suffered health problems too, including cancer, diabetes, high cholesterol, heart attacks, an under- or over-active thyroid, depression, schizophrenia, and allergies. The idea came to me that perhaps everybody was under par physically and didn't know it until they were diagnosed with an illness. I began to observe people more closely and noticed that so many adults – and sadly many children too – looked physically unhealthy to a greater or lesser extent. And the facial expressions of these city dwellers suggested they were also experiencing a great deal of stress and anxiety merely going about their daily activities.

After trawling through a multitude of statistics and talking to others, it seemed that illness and debilitation had been increasing significantly. Why was this happening? Occasionally governments or charities informed the public that certain dietary or other lifestyle changes were "advisable", yet the prevailing wisdom seemed to be that illness was somehow normal when people reached a certain age. The story went, and still generally goes, that our greater longevity, supposedly resulting from the miraculous advances of modern medicine, inevitably meant more illness as we aged. And it was just the luck of the draw – in particular the genetic blueprint we are born with – if health problems were avoided.

Further research, reinforced by the results of changes to my lifestyle, led me to the firm conclusion that far from being inevitable, the ill-health that people experienced, usually from middle age on, was largely due to lifestyle factors. Whilst acknowledging that there could well be a small number of exceptions – where extremely powerful genetic or environmental forces might not be countered successfully by any positive lifestyle choices – a person's health is in his or her hands. Certainly it goes against conventional wisdom and is quite contentious, but it gradually became clear to me that the majority of physical and mental problems suffered by adults of *all* ages are caused by the choices they make in the conduct of their lives – though our incredibly strong and adaptable bodies do not break down easily. It may well take several decades before symptoms become obvious and illnesses are diagnosed. Study after study showed that obesity, poor diet, lack of exercise and stress were the main contributory factors to the significant increase in ill-health.

Motivations

My research into physical health inevitably inspired me to look into the more subtle area of mental health. I suspected that physical and mental health were closely linked. I have a natural disposition to introspection – probably induced by my incarceration in a military boarding school from a young age – and though extremely important, it seemed that good physical health was only part of the answer to a fulfilling and content life. I also knew that too much of my energy and time was expended being irritated, angry, jealous and frustrated, and that I occasionally became over-confident in my abilities, or had a eureka moment of pure joy, believing that all would be well from then on. Inevitably I would come down with a bump. So I started reading books that explored the workings of the human mind.

It sounds obvious, but I learnt that the very first question I needed to ask was: "What actually makes me content?" Experts agree that indulgence, possessions, wealth, power or status do not bring long-term contentment. In fact they can often prevent it. I came to understand that the essential ingredients for our wellbeing are good health, appreciation and a sense of purpose, supportive relationships with family and friends, and self-respect – which is built from personal integrity, an open mind, humility, application, self-development, together with respect for other people, other creatures, and the natural world. The various psychological and philosophical concepts I gathered from many sources are presented in the "awareness" section.

Unfortunately, in this world of immediacy and "quick-fix" mentality, my personal experience and the accounts of others suggests that *at least six months to a year* of persistence and consistency with any major change in lifestyle is necessary to be sufficiently aware of the true benefits that can be achieved. There is no doubt that doing something not fully supported by mainstream belief and that yields no significant rewards in the short term will make it very difficult for people to persevere. Though it was certainly not easy, my obdurate inclination combined with a strong interest in the subject matter and my love of a challenge helped to maintain my resolve. I am a squash player, after all, for which persistence is vital, and I was the schoolboy – and arguably "fool" in this case – who slept all night upright in a clothes cupboard because I was dared to.

Discussions about my research and views on lifestyle have made me realise that people are either unaware of the facts, or they understand the potential negative ramifications of their actions yet are still unwilling to make positive changes – perhaps due to fear of change, the perceived difficulty to do so, or just inertia. A small number of people claim to be aware but unwilling to change because "life should be fun", but perhaps when they inevitably confront serious ill-health at some point in the future they would most likely have regrets…

Back to "The Diet"

As I was saying before discussing lifestyle choices and motivations, I avoided virtually all processed food. I now prepare and eat savoury meals only, some of which are cooked, though I do eat out occasionally. I eschew cakes, biscuits, sweets, pre-packaged meals and anything else that industrial man has concocted – apart from tea and the occasional beer. The only sweet food I eat is fruit. I consume no fizzy drinks, no honey, no sugar, no puddings or anything else with sugar in it. Complete abstinence is necessary because I know I can't have just one biscuit or a couple of sweets – a problem it seems that many others with a sweet tooth have. Sweet things weren't quite as addictive for me as cigarettes had been, but almost. I also don't consume bread, milk, cheese and eggs because my research and personal experience have led me to believe they are "clogging agents", and at the least not conducive to efficient digestion.

I had given up meat in my twenties because of digestive problems, but continued to eat fish. There had been – and still is – a lot of controversy about eating animal flesh, and I was unsure whether it was either healthy or necessary to do so. I did, however, have strong feelings about the way we treat the animals we eat, so as part of my dietary experiment I decided to become vegan, in other words have no animal product whatsoever. *The British Medical Society* and dietary experts advise that as little as 10% of our daily diet needs to be protein, and for me that would be nuts of various kinds plus occasional legumes – as well as the smaller amounts of protein from fruits and vegetables. Eating nothing of animal origin gives me cause for concern about my body lacking the vitamin B12, so I don't preclude the possibility of eating some fish again in the future, but my diet now consists almost exclusively of porridge made with just water and oat flakes, fresh vegetables (raw or cooked), fresh fruit, nuts, beans and pulses, and brown rice.

Exercise

For some years before and after embarking on my new diet, I would often feel stiff and began to have muscle pulls and lower back problems. Another nugget of information that I had registered but not acted upon was the importance of stretching – particularly after squash games. The frustration I felt from being unable to play because of injuries was the impetus to approach the fitness coach at my club. I remember not being able to even get near to touching my toes at the time, but he showed me a variety of stretching exercises, and after a few months I not only felt generally more flexible, I also just managed to bridge that ten-inch gap.

Apart from stretching, the trainer showed me how to use various machines to tone up different muscles. The initial gain in flexibility and toning inspired me to stretch after every squash game and do an hour-and-a-half fitness session in the gym once a week. Like most people, I find that gym sessions are not exciting or even interesting. For some time in fact the thought of another session looming didn't exactly fill me with joy. But after the benefits became clear I was able to approach the workouts with greater equanimity, if not exuberance. As my body became more supple, I no longer felt stiff – particularly noticeable when getting in and out of a car. Twisting and turning my body on the tennis and squash court – and in general – became much easier. My long gym workout included running and cycling, and so my stamina and aerobic capacity also gradually increased.

The Results

The results of my radical diet change were interesting and a little surprising, but mostly positive. Over three months I lost about 1lb a week, my weight stabilising at what I had been at the age of about twenty. I no longer had to count calories and worry about getting heavier. I can now eat – and enjoy – as much "natural" food as I want and always stay the same weight. Because I was so used to the incredible variety of food and drink that we all take for granted, however, my mind as well as my body took some time to get used to the new regimen. In the first few weeks I had one or two minor headaches, and for a number of months I did hanker after "comfort" food. This included bread, butter, cheese and sweet stuff (my penchant used to be for liquorice and mint choc chip ice-cream, though not at the same time). After about six months, however, my desire for the strong taste sensations of processed food lessened and I became more accustomed to my much simpler diet.

The huge reduction in the range of food selection had another positive effect – it freed up time and energy for other things. After about 18 months the new diet felt completely normal to me, though socially meals could be a little awkward. A number of friends naturally asked why I was doing what I was doing, some felt a little put out, though I tried to be flexible, while others felt it was an inherent criticism of their eating habits. Some results were rather unexpected. My approach to life was more positive and I felt my concentration and clarity of thought had significantly improved. I had become calmer and more appreciative of what I had and what I could do. And though I had been a little apprehensive about the effect on my physical energy – particularly on the squash and tennis courts – if anything it seemed that I had slightly more stamina. I could certainly move faster because I was lighter. I now feel that I am the "right weight". It's hard to describe the benefit that flows from this exactly. It may sound unusual or seem like an exaggeration, but not carrying any excess weight at all contributes considerably to a feeling of wellbeing in my daily life.

And after consistent stretching and workouts, I fully understood the importance of exercise, something I had only vaguely recognised before – how necessary it was for our bodies to be put through their paces. Many years of gym sessions have resulted in a higher level of stamina, aerobic capacity, muscle power and flexibility than I had 25 years ago. I now believe that not only would everybody gain by exercising regularly, aerobically in particular, but that contrary to what most laymen believe and many doctors advise, as people get older they should do *more* exercise, not less. When the body is young, everything – the muscles, skeleton, tendons, sinews – will normally be flexible and working smoothly. As the body ages, the skeleton loses support from muscles that become flaccid and tendons that become stiffer.

How far have I travelled along the road to optimum health, greater awareness and peace of mind? Well, that's for those who know me to assess. Though I'm sure I'll never achieve perfection, my efforts to put the advice given on the following pages into practice continue…

INTRODUCTION

*"The tragedy of life is not that it ends so soon
but that we wait so long to begin it."*

(Anonymous)

Over the past 200 years the scientific and technological advances of the Industrial Age have worked wonders for the lot of the average person. Incredible changes for the populations of Western countries have occurred in all areas of life, whether personal comfort, health and lifespan, work, travel, diet, information and education, or news and entertainment.

Today we live longer, we have access to health care of a high standard (though far too little attention is given to prevention), we don't go hungry, we're better clothed and housed than our predecessors, and we are formally educated. Most of us are able to find employment and are protected from exploitation, and the rights of minorities are better recognised and respected. And we have a democratic system that accords all adults the opportunity to vote for who governs them (though it does have serious flaws).

Instant communication between people, whether close or distant and whatever the time, is now possible online or by mobile phone, and local and global news can be gleaned in various ways and 24 hours a day. Though much of the material presented by the seemingly "free" media actually serves the agenda of vested interests, people can use the internet to check the accuracy of the information provided and find more details should they wish to attain a more balanced viewpoint.

The leisure industry offers a wide choice of activities, high-speed travel to a whole host of exotic holiday destinations, and a huge variety of entertainment on radio and television and in cinemas and theatres. Over the last 20 years people have been able to access an ever-increasing volume of material in their homes – and more recently on the move – with millions of websites offering games, music, videos and films.

Despite the impressive technological progress and huge rise in the material standard of living, however, most people in the rich countries of the world are still not satisfied. In fact a strong case could be argued that contentment is actually lower overall than 50 years ago. Even if you don't accept that contention, our quality of life could certainly have been much greater had our priorities been different. The importance accorded to money, possessions, comfort, image and status has placed a heavy burden on us.

Today's frenetic pace of life leaves little time to pause and question the wisdom of our perpetual struggle to keep up with the Joneses. We are under constant pressure to do so much and maintain the high level of consumption that we now perceive as normal. In this maelstrom of activity, quantity is often confused with quality, speed with achievement, action with purpose, qualifications with education, titillation with entertainment, consumption with meaning, and daily short-term gratification with long-term contentment.

Overload

"If you realise you have enough,
you are truly rich."

(Lao Tzu) *

The word "overload" represents the first part of my hypothesis in its simplest form: that people in developed countries are finding life difficult to cope with today. And health statistics provide the irrefutable proof – cancer, obesity, high blood pressure, heart attacks, strokes, diabetes, anxiety, depression, and dementia, are now endemic. Though conventional wisdom says that much physical illness is occurring because we are living longer, the rapid rise in ill-health is in fact mostly the result of lifestyle factors. The level of both physical and mental illness has been increasing considerably and this trend is expected to continue, along with the already huge cost of health care.

* Short biographies of the quote authors are provided at the end of the book.

Why are we getting ill? Well, the underlying cause is the stress we experience in our daily lives – because we are being overloaded. Compared to the pace of life up to perhaps 60 years ago, we now function at breakneck speed, and the speed of change is accelerating. We have so much more to deal with that there is too little time or energy to actually ruminate on, absorb, or appreciate what we have and do. We have come to equate greater quantity with greater quality, but the contrary is invariably true – and though we already have too much, we forever hanker after yet more.

And what steps do we take to deal with the daily stress we're under? We attempt in vain to alleviate the pressure through short-term gratification – but rich food and drugs inevitably lead to further problems. Most of us are addicted to processed food to some degree and are consequently overweight by at least 6 or 7 pounds, and the number of people classified as obese continues to rise. Alcohol consumption has become excessive and pharmaceutical drugs are now accepted as a normal part of life – no matter the person, the problem, or situation, some kind of drug is touted as a solution.

Thus stress has led to excess, which leads to more stress and yet more excess – it's a vicious circle. Increased urbanisation, central control and gigantism, the disintegration of families, friendships and community, the 24/7 deluge of news, information, marketing and entertainment, and the growing inequality of income and wealth, have all added to our stress and contributed to the huge rise in mental illness.

To make the analysis clearer and easier to follow, physical and mental overloads are dealt with separately, though they are in fact inextricably interlinked and can sometimes overlap. At the end of each overload segment, suggestions are given as to how that particular overload might be avoided, or at least reduced.

Awareness

> *"The world is not a problem;*
> *the problem is your unawareness"*
> (Bhagwan Shree Rajneesh)

Though it may sound a little melodramatic, I believe that society is exhibiting all the signs of a kind of a collective, obsessive compulsive disorder. We spend much of our time in artificial, densely packed conurbations like rats in a cage, convinced that yet more consumption and growth will solve our problems. Passively accepting that this surreal existence is all that life can offer, it seems we are living in a dream world rather like that depicted in the film *The Matrix*.

It would be easy to blame politicians, scientists, industrialists, advertisers and the media for the current state of affairs, but that would not be very fair, accurate, or constructive. So is there a solution? Can the pressure we are experiencing today be relieved without adding to our problems? Yes, it can be. It is highly unlikely to happen from the "top down" through changes in laws and regulations, because much of the societal framework would have to change first, but it can certainly occur from the "bottom up". Which brings me to the second part of my hypothesis: that the individual can take steps to eliminate his or her "overload" through greater awareness and self-responsibility.

To rid ourselves of the daily stress we feel, we need to increase both self-awareness and our awareness about how the world works. We have to escape from our cultural "prison" and view life and ourselves in a different way. We need to understand and control our emotions, act with more humility and regain the moral sensibilities we seem to have lost. Having long since satisfied our material needs, we must focus our attention on what *really* matters to us.

If we reduced our consumption and led simpler, less hectic lives, we could enjoy near-optimum health as well as achieve far greater fulfilment and long-term contentment. Unfortunately a number of in-built human traits prevent us from making changes – we are creatures of habit, we succumb to peer and marketing pressure, we are inclined to go to excess, we are often irrational, we take things for granted, we are masters of excuses and self-delusion, and most of us blindly trust the "experts" and follow our leaders.

The awareness section examines those subtle psychological and philosophical insights – rarely taught by either parents or teachers – that can provide a guide for us to make wiser lifestyle choices. The prevailing "quick fix" mentality, however, obliges me to point out that understanding yourself and exploring the nature of existence takes time. And once grasped, it will take yet more time to put this knowledge into practice in your daily life.

I believe that we can all make positive changes, but this will be less likely to happen and more difficult to do without a change in how we actually view life. Otherwise changes – like fad diets – will last for just a short period and not be of benefit for a lifetime.

PHYSICAL OVERLOADS

SELF-APPRAISAL

*"Our body has this defect, that the more
it is provided care and comforts,
the more needs and desires it finds."*

(Saint Teresa of Avila)

Look at your face in the mirror. You may well see dark patches and bags under your eyes. You might also notice a furred up, mottled tongue, dry or blotched skin, blood-shot eyes or a flaky scalp. And have you developed a paunch and sagging folds of flesh? Perhaps you feel stiff and unsteady when walking and moving about. Check how out-of-breath you get when climbing stairs, or even just by walking.

A couple of years ago I went for a Christmas stroll in the rolling hills of Gloucestershire with a number of friends and relatives of various ages – and an aging dog. As we walked up a small hill to a ridge I was suddenly aware of much puffing and panting. I expected the old dog to find it hard going, but was taken aback to see the twenty-somethings struggling too.

If in your busy life you can find the time or be bothered to look at other people more carefully, you'll see that most are either overweight or physically ill to some degree – or both – and many are struggling to move around. Whether you're young, middle-aged or of pension age, nature designed human bodies to be flexible and dynamic, not stiff and sluggish; they should be contoured and smooth, not puffy and blotchy.

You Are Not Alone

We all experience at least some degree of "overload" on many different fronts on a regular basis, which means our wellbeing can be considerably diminished. This section of the book details the numerous ways our bodies are being physically overloaded. The scale, resulting problems, and causes of each overload are explained, followed by various suggestions on how you might avoid experiencing excess and suffering ill-health. Some of this advice is simple and common sense, and you might well have heard it before, but it needs to be reiterated.

Food is arguably the major influence on our physical health, so that is looked at first – together with exercise, because they are inextricably linked. After detailing the many drugs of various kinds that we use – legal and illegal, pharmaceutical or not – the types of pollution that affect the air we breathe, water we drink, and soil in which we grow our food, are examined. The final segment of the physical overloads section shows the many diseases, illnesses, and conditions that are the unhappy results of the food, drug and pollution overloads to which most of our long-suffering bodies are subjected.

To present an analysis that is both clearer and easier to follow I have in the main provided data on the population of the UK, though the current situation and trends in most developed countries will be similar – with the Americans often leading the way. Statistics are important and necessary for me to present a convincing case that people are experiencing a whole variety of overloads – and *you* will probably be in at least a few of those statistics somewhere. Of course numbers and averages can never show the full picture, the exact situation, the whole truth, but they are strong indicators of what is happening now and what is likely to happen in the future.

Here are some figures taken from the analysis of physical overloads, and you'll see that most of us are in this together. You are certainly not alone:

- 68% of men and 58% of women in England are either overweight or obese.

- The average Briton's sugar intake per year is about 34 kg. The figure was just 2 kg in 1704.

- There are still 10 million Britons who smoke. About 50% of all regular cigarette smokers will eventually be killed by their habit.

- 37% of British adults (18 million) exceed the "safe" *daily* alcohol limit.

- 7% of those aged 19 to 59 in England and Wales – over 2 million people – are cannabis users, 700,000 take cocaine, and 500,000 take ecstasy. And there are over 300,000 registered heroin addicts in the UK.

- More than 50 chemicals in common usage have been identified as "hormone disrupters", which scientists say may be the cause of a 33% decline both in sperm counts and healthy sperm.

- We use an average of 9 personal-care products daily, containing about 126 chemical ingredients.

- 42% of Britons will be diagnosed with cancer during their lifetime, up over 10 years from 33%. And 64% of these will die from the disease.

- Almost 1 million Britons have dementia, and the number is predicted to keep rising.

FOOD

"What we eat and drink affects our mind-body
equilibrium more than anything else...
taken to excess in quantity or time worrying
or enthusing about it can lead to sickness or obsession."
(Jon Wynne-Tyson)

Consuming food is of course an essential human activity in order to stay alive, but many other important positives apply to eating – the sheer enjoyment of it, the social aspect, the artistry of creating meals, and the huge employment and income generated by the food industry. Unfortunately the deleterious effect on our health from the amount and type of food we have been eating over recent decades has to be set against the various short-term pleasures we gain. Food is of paramount importance in determining the level of both our physical and mental health. And the better our health is, the better our body and mind will function, thus enabling us to appreciate and enjoy life all the more – a simple and obvious fact that is so often overlooked. There is truth in the old saying "We are what we eat".

Over the long period of human evolution, our bodies were "programmed" to guard against starvation, not to deal with too much food. Just like primates in the wild and members of so-called primitive societies today, early humans would never have been obese, or even overweight. Though they might well have gorged themselves during occasional times of plenty, they rarely had the opportunity to overeat – and certainly not day after day for most of their lifetime, as those in the affluent countries now do. Many people are eating too much fast and processed food in particular, and the resulting "food overload" is clear for all to see in overweight and obesity statistics. The negative effect of this excessive food consumption on our health – and sadly involving ever younger children – has even prompted some health professionals to warn that life expectancy rates could fall for the first time.

The Scale of Food Overload

Researchers found that the average American gains about 1lb per year in adulthood and listed the foods that caused the most weight gain. Chips and crisps topped the list, followed by sugary drinks and meat. Though the situation is even worse in the USA, the latest overweight statistics for the UK are worrying:

- Among English men, 68% (about 17 million) are either overweight or obese; 26% (6.5 million) are obese. The figures for women are 58% (16 million) and 26% (7 million).

It is now expected that 80% of men and 70% of women in the UK aged 20 to 65 will be overweight by 2020, with obesity levels at around 40% and 35% respectively. If we take in more energy than we expend, the excess is stored as fat. Even a little daily indulgence and not quite enough exercise will gradually increase our weight. *The World Health Organisation* uses BMI (body mass index) measurements for weight classifications. According to these, 2006 was the year when the number of overweight people in the world – one billion – exceeded the number of undernourished – 800 million – for the first time.

Over a period of just 50 years "fat" has become the norm in most Western countries, and overweight problems are now fast turning into obesity problems. To marginally different degrees, all developed countries are following the same trend, and obesity has recently increased in developing countries. Weight gain is now becoming more common in children as well as adults, which does not augur well for the future. The most recent statistics should be a cause for concern:

- Among English children aged 2 to 15, 30% (4.5 million) are overweight or obese.

- 55% of boys and 70% of girls in the UK are predicted to be overweight or obese by 2050.

Too Much Meat, Fat, Sugar and Salt

Not only has there been a global shift from vegetable protein to animal protein, but the much larger proportion of processed food in people's diet has also resulted in a greatly increased consumption of fat, sugar and salt. 90% of food consumed in the USA comes in a box, can, bag or carton – from stores and fast-food restaurants.

- Only 10% of food bought by Americans consists of raw products, i.e. fruit, vegetables, fresh meat and fish.

- Even in France, ranked much lower in the obesity league of countries, the figure is just 20%. (No statistic is available for the UK, but it probably lies somewhere between America and France.)

In medical literature *The Western Pattern Diet* (or *The Meat-Sweet Diet*) is the name used to describe the diet that more and more of us are consuming today: high-calorie convenience food, high intakes of red meat, sweet desserts, high-fat foods, refined grains, high-fat dairy products, eggs, and sweetened drinks. *The Western Pattern Diet* is often contrasted with *The Prudent Diet*, which consists largely of fruits, vegetables, whole-grain foods, poultry and fish.

Together with a high level of salt, trans-fats, starch and sugar, scientists expertly blend colourings, artificial sweeteners and other unnatural additives to make their products more enticing in appearance, texture and taste. The food industry consistently refuses to admit any responsibility for consumers' weight gain – despite the incessant advertising and marketing of its fast food, soft drinks, and other high-calorie, low-quality products.

- The average person in the UK eats almost 80 kg of meat per year, double the level it was 50 years ago.

- The average daily fat intake for a British man is 102g and 74g for a woman, representing 40% of the energy of the total food consumed. In the 1930s the figure was 30%.

- The average Briton's sugar intake per year is at least 34 kg. It was just 2 kg in 1704. It increased by 31% in the 20 years to 2002.

The huge increase in sugar consumption is largely due to highly refined sugars in the forms of sucrose (table sugar), dextrose (corn sugar) and high-fructose corn syrup being used in so many processed foods. These include bread, breakfast cereals, mayonnaise, peanut butter, ketchup, spaghetti sauce and microwave meals.

- Just 25% of men and 27% of women in England eat the recommended 5 daily portions of fruits and vegetables.

- 92% of British children consume more saturated fat than recommended, 86% consume too much sugar, 72% consume too much salt, and 96% don't eat enough fruits and vegetables.

Too Little Exercise

Food and exercise are inextricably linked – the first adds calories to our bodies and the second removes them. Some sports authorities have suggested that inactivity may be a more significant factor in the development of obesity than overeating. The amount of exercise recommended by the UK government is 30 minutes of moderate activity 5 times a week, or 20 minutes of vigorous activity 3 times a week. The latest statistics show that:

- 61% of British men and 71% of women don't meet exercise guidelines.

- 68% of English boys and 76% of girls aged 2 to 15 don't meet exercise guidelines.

The Resulting Health Problems

Research has shown that what and how much we eat and drink affects our health. Those extra unwanted pounds not only make daily life generally more uncomfortable, harder work, and maybe cause a loss of self-confidence and difficulties in relationships, they also contribute significantly to numerous health problems. It has been estimated that obesity can reduce lifespan by 3 to 12 years. Disturbingly, more children admitted to hospital – including toddlers and even babies – are reported to be suffering from obesity-related conditions.

Researchers are finding increasing evidence of a link between diet and many health problems – more information is provided in the disease and illness segment at the end of this section on physical overloads. These are the diseases and conditions that are now known to have a close correlation with food consumption and being overweight:

Cardiovascular Disease

Cardiovascular disease means problems of the heart and circulation, including heart attacks and stroke. High blood pressure (hypertension) is the main reason for cardiovascular disease, and research has shown that as well as too much stress, an unhealthy diet can lead to high blood pressure. Smoking, alcohol, too much salt, too many refined sugars and other refined carbohydrates, as well as too much fat and cholesterol from meat and dairy foods, have all contributed to the huge growth in heart disease. Conversely, research has shown that eating fruit, vegetables and whole grain cereals can significantly reduce the risk of heart problems.

Diabetes

A diabetes diagnosis means the body cannot control the level of glucose in the blood, and a major symptom is fatigue. There are two kinds of diabetes. Type 1 is largely due to hereditary and genetic factors and represents just 10% of diabetes cases in North America and Europe. There is no known preventative measure against it. Obesity, refined sugar consumption, and lack of exercise are the main causes of Type 2 diabetes. A radical change of diet and regular exercise can significantly ameliorate the symptoms of Type 2 diabetes, and in some cases correct the condition.

Cancer

Most forms of cancer are "sporadic", meaning that only in a small minority of cases does the disease have an inherited, genetic cause. The main factors that cause cancer are either lifestyle or environmental factors, or both. It was finally accepted that smoking tobacco could result in lung and other cancers, and now it has been recognised that being overweight raises the risk of cancer, and that poor diet plays a significant role in many types of the disease.

To lower the risk of cancer, people are advised to give up smoking, exercise more, stay slim, and abstain from too much fast food, red meat, refined sugar and alcohol. Eating too much red and processed meat has been linked to breast, colorectal, stomach, lymph, bladder, and prostate cancer. Research has found that women who regularly eat a lot of fat – saturated fats in particular – are far more likely to develop breast cancer. These are found mostly in full fat milk, butter, cheese, meat, and processed food like biscuits and cakes. Studies have shown that an increase in cereals, fruits and vegetables can significantly reduce the risk of cancer of the lung, prostate, pancreas and bowel.

Gallstones

Gallstones are lumps of solid material that form in the gall bladder – the reservoir for bile. Overweight people and those with diabetes are more likely to develop gallstones – a high-fat diet means they are more likely to form. If they block the normal flow of bile it may cause an attack of biliary colic, with upper abdominal pain, nausea and vomiting. Inflammation, infection of the gall bladder and bile ducts, jaundice, and acute pancreatitis might then occur. GPs normally advise a healthy, balanced diet and weight control to reduce the symptoms.

Infertility

Research has shown that consuming a lot of easily digested carbohydrates, such as white bread, potatoes and sugared drinks, increase the odds of infertility, while slowly digested carbohydrates – that contain a lot of fibre – improve fertility. Whole grains, beans, vegetables and whole fruits, and getting more protein from plants and less from animals, improves ovulation and the chance of getting pregnant, while the more trans-fat in the diet, the greater the likelihood of developing ovulation infertility. For men, obesity has a greater negative effect on fertility than smoking and drinking.

Sleep Problems

45% of the UK population have occasional sleep problems from snoring, but an estimated 25% are habitual snorers, which can reduce the quality of the snorer's sleep and perhaps that of his or her partner. Fatty tissue around the throat area impairs the movement of air and can cause the airway to vibrate, so losing weight will not only lead to an improvement of health in general, but might also reduce snoring.

Digestive Problems

Constipation is uncomfortable and often results in haemorrhoids (piles), just one of many different ways that our bodies tell us we are overeating, eating the wrong foods, or often both. An estimated 1 in 10 adults suffer from heartburn every day – usually smokers, pregnant women, heavy drinkers and overweight people. The main causes of indigestion and heartburn seem to be alcohol, tobacco, coffee, tea and other drinks that contain caffeine, chocolate, fried and fatty foods, tomatoes and tomato-based products, citrus fruits, and juices – or very large meals.

Teeth and Gum Problems

Sugar, prevalent in the modern diet, is the main cause of dental problems. Most young children are eating more sugary foods and drinking more sugary drinks, and their teeth are suffering. Avoiding processed foods and regular brushing will prevent most deterioration of the teeth and gums.

The Reasons for Food Overload

There are many reasons why we eat and drink too much:

More Addictive Foods

Processed food is intended to excite our taste buds, and there are ever more tasty and "more-ish" products available. Some commentators contend that food manufacturers deliberately create concoctions that are addictive. There is such a huge variety of temptations that almost everybody finds it hard to resist at least a few of them. And because so many different kinds of things are available to eat and drink, it's easier to switch from one to another and keep consuming till we get bloated. Studies have shown that repeated over-consumption of high-fat or high-sugar foods like ice-cream may alter how the brain responds to these foods in a way that perpetuates further intake, that animals eat more when food contains artificial sweeteners instead of sugar, and that the strong taste of fast and processed food (and drink) can result in children being unable to enjoy the more subtle tastes of natural food.

Overeating natural foods doesn't happen. We might eat just one apple, for example, possibly two if particularly hungry, and we would be unlikely to consume huge amounts of salad in one sitting. When we eat processed food, however, we will often consume far too much – because of the lure of the strong taste sensation, the "comfort" we get from it, and the inability of the body to recognise when it has had enough.

Fast Food

People eat fast food not only for its strong taste but also for convenience, to save time and for social reasons. Unfortunately this kind of food allows the consumption of a much larger calorific load in one sitting or a period of time. Unlike animals who chew all day long on large quantities of berries, shoots, leaves and nuts, many of us now eat cooked, softened food of high caloric density, and we might take in as much as 2,000 calories in less than an hour.

Food is Inexpensive

Our incomes are now much higher, and in proportion to our income our food bill has dropped substantially – despite recent rises – from 25% in the 1930s to around 10% today.

Marketing

The food industry's primary objective is to make more profits for shareholders, so it is unlikely to discourage people from getting fatter – larger people need more food to sustain themselves. We are enticed by ever more advertising and sophisticated marketing ploys, as well as simple ones like supermarkets putting junk food like crisps and sweets next to the check-out. Companies make far more money on food that's processed, so "added value" means they will continually invent new products and aggressively market them, rather than highlight the health benefits of raw fruit and vegetables. Junk food is also cleverly advertised to exploit "pester power". A study found that 70% of British 3-year-olds recognised the *McDonald's* arch symbol, and when children were given different types of food, some in plain and some in *McDonald's* packaging, they said the latter tasted better – even when it was milk.

Larger Portions

Larger portions make us eat more. Plates, portions and containers have become ever larger. The cost of ingredients like sugar, fats and water is trivial, so manufacturers can make more money while customers perceive the larger amount as delivering greater value. Originally one serving of *Coke* was six and a half fluid ounces – now the average plastic bottle contains five times that. The *McDonald's* hamburger was 260 calories, now the standard order of *Double Cheeseburger* is 444 calories, while the *Big Mac Extra Value Meal* contains 1250 calories.

Eating Faster

The pace of life today means most of us get through our meals more quickly. It takes around 15 minutes for our brains to register that we've eaten enough, and eating fast means we often go past that point and eat too much. Eating a meal too quickly curbs the release of hormones in the stomach that signal the brain to stop eating.

Stress

Our hectic lives cause many of us to continually comfort ourselves with small "rewards" or sops to keep our emotions up, such as crisps, biscuits, chocolate bars, sweets, tea, coffee and fizzy drinks. Today the perpetual self-rewarding culture is viewed as normal and has become endemic. The stress of modern life plays an important part in our unhealthy eating habits, contributing to eating disorders like anorexia and bulimia as well as obesity.

Insufficient Exercise

The more calories taken in by children and adults, the more must be expended to maintain the same weight. We are far more sedentary today, and technology has largely removed the "built in" exercise that used to be part of people's daily lives. Children are eating more and not exercising as much as they used to, and most adults do less exercise as they age.

Childhood Weight Gain

Over-indulgence is starting younger and sets the pattern for life. Parents are not controlling their children's diet – some obese children in the UK have even been taken into care by social services.

Normalisation

Peer pressure encourages us to eat junk and processed fast food, and now overeating and weight gain has become normalised. Many believe themselves to be moderate in their habits because they compare themselves to the ever growing number of obese people. When a bare midriff was the fashion for girls in the summer, even fat stomachs were deemed acceptable because so many girls were overweight by the time that particular trend emerged.

Eating and Drinking in Public

One factor that might cause more of us to gain weight is the social acceptance of eating outside the home. We eat while working, watching TV or at the cinema, or travelling by cars, train, bus and foot. Not that long ago it was considered ill-mannered to eat or drink in public places not designated for that purpose.

Inadequate Sleep

Our modern life seems to encourage us to sleep less – in 1960 Americans slept an average of 8.5 hours per night, but now the average has fallen to under 7 hours.

- 70% of Britons sleep 7 hours or less a night, with 33% getting by on 5 to 6 hours. The average is 6 hours and 35 minutes.

Studies have shown that sleep loss affects key appetite hormones. It reduces the level of leptin – which signals when you've eaten enough – and increases that of ghrelin – the hormone that tells you that you want to eat more. This could lead to excessive caloric intake when food is freely available.

Less Smoking

In recent decades a large number of people have given up smoking. Despite the considerable advantages of stopping, ex-smokers might well gain weight because for many, smoking suppressed the appetite.

Medicine Bias

The focus of orthodox medicine on germs and chemicals has led doctors to ignore or vastly underrate the importance of diet. Lifestyle changes are not emphasised anywhere near enough. This is not surprising because pharmaceutical companies make huge profits from their products and pressurise doctors to prescribe drugs for all ailments, whether major or minor.

Confusion

Despite recent governmental efforts to inform the public about the necessity to eat fruit and vegetables, and despite the fact that the packaging of processed food now has more information on it, there is still a lack of awareness about what constitutes a healthy diet. Food manufacturers are naturally keen to promote their products and will do what they can to muddy the waters and confuse people. The public may well be unaware that an "expert" expounding his views in the media is funded by an organisation with a financial interest, and doubt will be sown in their minds.

Dieting

Paradoxically, the fad for diets has led to many people becoming more overweight. It's been shown that after losing weight on a diet, many people become heavier than they were before. And research has shown that the more children and teenagers diet, the more likely they are to become obese adults.

We Don't Listen to Our Bodies

The overload of too much food and the wrong kind of food has meant our bodies have lost their natural balance – unlike animals in the wild, we are no longer able to instinctively feel what is good or bad for us.

How to Avoid Food Overload

Processed food has far less nutritional worth than fresh food because processing removes much of the vitamins, minerals and fibre and is designed for maximum shelf-life. And many products involve ingredients such as artificial sweeteners, colouring or preservatives which are unnatural and difficult for the body to deal with – and maybe even harmful. I avoid processed food for those reasons, but for another as well – unlike natural food, it can lead you to overeat. Manufacturers make processed food addictive, especially with fat, dairy, sugar and salt. In her book *What to Eat*, Joanna Blythman advises that our diet should be based on "real", unprocessed food, and that we should eat organic produce where possible and affordable.

Most experts would agree with these suggestions:

- Try to eat only when you're hungry, and drink only when you're thirsty. Because much of what we do is habitual, we often don't follow this common sense. This will be far easier if you avoid processed food.

- Easy to say, but for various reasons – discussed above – difficult for many to do, you should eat a moderate quantity of food. This is more likely to happen if you eat slowly, avoid doing something else while eating, and appreciate what you eat. If you've been "trained" when young to finish what's on your plate, as I was, use smaller plates and portions. And if you eat raw or freshly cooked, natural food, you're far less likely to overeat.

- Try to reduce the unhealthy food you eat i.e. that which includes salt, fat, and sugar. Most processed food comes into this category. You should in particular severely limit the sugary snacks, cakes, biscuits and sweets you consume. Virtually everybody is addicted to something or other, so avoid having any unhealthy food at home that you can't resist. A study listed the top 12 foods that caused the most weight gain: French fries (chips), potato chips (crisps), sugar-sweetened soda (fizzy drinks), processed and unprocessed meat, trans fats (in deep fried, shortening and processed foods), potatoes, sweets and desserts (cakes, pies, biscuits and sweets), refined grains (white flour, white bread, spaghetti, white rice), fried foods, fruit juice, and butter. Though butter is at least more "natural" than its unhealthy substitutes, you should keep butter – and other dairy products like milk and cheese – to a minimum.

- Children's relationship with food is very important because it could have a significant influence in their adult life. Though it's understandably difficult for parents when virtually all children are consuming too much of the wrong kinds of food and beverages, as the responsible adults they should severely limit the processed food in their children's diet – and sweets and fizzy drinks in particular. Perhaps a reasonable compromise would be to allow children to decide what they eat and drink once a week. And if they are encouraged to make simple but healthy meals in the home, they can be weaned off fast food. Many enjoyable and nutritious meals can be made without too much expense, trouble or expertise.

- Advice on a healthy diet is given by the charity *Cancer Research UK* on their website. They recommend that we severely limit our consumption of red and processed meat, salty foods and fatty foods (like meat, biscuits, crisps, cheese, butter, full cream milk and fried food), and suggest that our diet should include a high proportion of fruit, vegetables and other fibre-rich foods (like wholemeal bread and wholegrain cereals). A recent study found that eating whole grain foods like porridge and brown bread can reduce the risk of suffering a stroke as effectively as taking drugs that lower blood pressure.

- "Diets" are supposed quick fixes and are better avoided. They may involve some weight loss in the first weeks, but usually lead to disillusion and weight gain in the long term. What is required is a new way of viewing food and life in general to engender *a change of lifestyle*. Common sense, backed by numerous studies, suggests the body (and mind) will fare much better on natural food.

- Also avoid slimming pills, another supposed "quick fix". They are drugs, and drugs don't deal with underlying problems and inevitably have side effects.

- Drastic "solutions" – like stomach surgery, liposuction, stomach clamps or balloons, lap banding and gastric bypasses – should be avoided unless it's a matter of life and death. Apart from being extremely expensive for taxpayers to fund, they may well not provide a long-term solution, because they again do not deal with the underlying problems.

- Regular exercise is a vital part of a balanced life, and is to some extent an antidote to overeating. Aerobic exercise is particularly important. We need to sweat. It seems, however, that just as giving up tasty and comforting food is difficult for many people, so is doing regular exercise. If you are overweight and don't do any exercise, I suggest you start by getting into a habit of walking a mile or so every day, at your normal pace. After a few weeks try increasing the pace and distance so you get a sweat going.

If you can reduce your weight a little by reducing the fattening food and drinks you consume, and get to enjoy walking, after a number of months you might try swimming, going to the gym, or taking up a sport. Once you feel the benefits of regular exercise, this should spur you on to do more.

- We are creatures of habit, so we need to get into the *right* habits, though people will do this in different ways. Some may need to cut out certain food from their diet completely, while others may restrict their consumption to, say, only one day a week. Like so many others, I am a "sugarholic", i.e. addicted to sugary food, so I decided it would be easier for me to cut out *all* sweet food from my diet – other than fruit. I also felt that bread and dairy products like cheese and milk gave me digestive problems, so I cut them from my diet as well.

- Seek out someone of like mind. We are social creatures and are strongly influenced by those around us. If your partner, family or friends eat an unhealthy diet, it will be difficult for you to make changes. Conversely it will be easier to alter your diet and start exercising if you can co-opt someone else who also wants to change their lifestyle.

- Whatever changes you make, you'll need to persevere for some time. It may take 6 months to a year for your body (and mind) to get used to less food and healthier food, and for you to appreciate the advantages of how you feel. My craving for processed products gradually decreased and I became accustomed to less variety. And now I'm no longer tempted by processed food. It is worth noting that the more natural food you eat, the less you'll need to count calories to maintain a healthy weight.

- If some overriding psychological or environmental reason somehow prevents you from being able to change an unhealthy relationship with food by yourself or together with a friend, partner, or slimming club, then try a counsellor or dietician. You may well need professional help in the short term if you have a deep-seated depression or are really struggling to cope with life.

- However hard it is to accept and put into practice initially, it is necessary to get into a different way of thinking, to realise that a *permanent* change of lifestyle is necessary.

CAFFEINE

"If they took all the drugs, nicotine, alcohol and caffeine off the market for six days, they'd have to bring out the tanks to control you."

(Dick Gregory)

Psychoactive drugs were used just occasionally in older "primitive" societies, to induce trances for initiations or other ceremonies, for medicinal purposes, and maybe for seasonal celebrations. Today, however, there is regular, widespread, and increasing consumption of all kinds of mind-altering, legal and illegal drugs. Whether legal or illegal, any drug, to a greater or lesser degree, will be considered by the human body to be an unwelcome invader, an unnatural substance – in fact, a poison. We need to seriously question the wisdom of subjecting ourselves to tobacco, alcohol, marijuana, cocaine, heroin, over-the-counter or prescribed pharmaceutical concoctions, or indeed any other type of drug – even caffeine.

Of the huge array of drugs that modify human consciousness, there are three widely, regularly and heavily used legal drugs in the West – tobacco, alcohol, and caffeine. Caffeine is in fact the world's most widely used psychoactive substance. It is found in certain leaves, seeds, and fruits of over 60 plants worldwide, but is sometimes produced synthetically. We consume caffeine in coffee, tea, soft drinks, and energy drinks, but also – perhaps not widely realised – in some food products and over-the-counter drugs. Caffeine is a metabolic stimulant and (mildly) addictive, and must be shown on product ingredient labels – though manufacturers are not required to show the amount.

Used both "recreationally" and medicinally to reduce physical fatigue and restore mental alertness when weakness or drowsiness occurs, caffeine has been shown to significantly increase the capacity for mental or physical labour. It stimulates the central nervous system, resulting in greater wakefulness, faster and clearer flow of thought, increased focus, and better general body co-ordination. Once in the bloodstream, it takes about 15 minutes for the effects to be felt. The brain is stimulated in the same way as with cocaine and heroin. The adenosine reception – which suppresses arousal – is blocked, adrenaline injected into the system, and dopamine production manipulated, making you feel good and more alert. Particularly in coffee, caffeine has become an accepted "pick-me-up" that gives people a boost in the morning and helps people cope with their busy lifestyle.

The precise amount of caffeine necessary to produce effects varies from person to person depending on body size and their degree of tolerance to it. A mild dose wears off in 3 to 4 hours. It doesn't eliminate the need for sleep, it just temporarily reduces the sensation of being tired. The more caffeine a person has daily will increase the stimulation, but those who regularly consume a lot will soon develop less sensitivity to it, which means they will need more to achieve the same effect.

The Scale of Caffeine Consumption

The consumption of caffeine has increased in recent years, partly because it has found its way into a whole range of drinks, foods and tablets. So-called "energy drinks" have become popular, and caffeine is now even used in shampoo and other personal cleansing products. Caffeine tablets are also available, with manufacturers claiming that using caffeine of "pharmaceutical quality" improves mental alertness. These are often used by students who are studying for their exams and people who work or drive for long periods. Global sales of beverages containing caffeine are huge, earning commensurate profits for the manufacturers and distributors. Global coffee production is about 9 million tonnes per year (150 million bags), with the average American drinking 3 cups of coffee a day. Global tea consumption is about 4 million tonnes, and though Britons are now the biggest consumers of instant coffee in Europe – the UK retail sales of coffee having topped the £1 billion mark – and their tea consumption is declining, tea is still the most popular beverage.

- The British use about 114 million kg of standard teabags annually, with an average per capita consumption of almost 2 kg. In 2000 the average consumption was 3.5 cups per day.

Filter coffee has the highest caffeine content of the various coffee drinks, and espresso has more caffeine per millilitre than a regular brew. Tea contains about half as much caffeine per serving (about 50 mg) as coffee (about 100 mg), depending on the strength of the brew. Some teas, like the pale Japanese green tea *Gvokuro*, contain far more caffeine than others like *Lapsang Souchong*, which has very little.

Tea and coffee are not the only drinks with caffeine. There are many soft drinks which contain about 10 to 50 mg of caffeine per serving, and so-called "energy drinks" like *Red Bull* have about 80 mg per can − some contain as much as 160 mg.

- About 500 million litres of "energy" and "sports" drinks are consumed in Britain each year, a market worth around £1 billion.

The Health Problems from Caffeine

Some people avoid caffeine and other drugs because they consider them to be unnatural substances and harmful to both body and mind. Others steer clear of mind-altering drugs – including caffeine – because they want to "remain in control". Certain religions advise against the consumption of all drugs because they claim that their god wishes them to be free of all addictions. Hindus generally abstain from caffeine because they believe it clouds the mind and over-stimulates the senses. Having banned alcohol, the Muslim world, however, uses coffee as a substitute.

How much is consumed is the crucial factor regarding the health consequences of using caffeine. Its effects on individuals vary. Some people can consume substantial amounts without apparent ill effects, while others are quite sensitive to it, and no one knows for sure what the long-term effects may be. Some experts believe a low to moderate intake is in the range of 130 to 300 mg per day, while others think a "heavy" consumption is over 6,000 mg per day. Just 100 mg has been suggested as a daily maximum for teenagers, and even less for younger children. Most consider between 250 and 500 mg spread over the day is "safe", but there are possible dangers:

Inability to Conceive

Various studies have found that drinking several cups or more of coffee a day can significantly reduce the chance of pregnancy.

Danger to the Foetus

The development of the foetus may be affected by stimulants and drugs taken by pregnant women. They get into the bloodstream and reach the foetus through the placenta. A breast-fed child can also get caffeine from its mother's milk. A recent study concluded that drinking caffeine during pregnancy can increase the chance of miscarriage and the researchers recommended total abstinence.

Urine Stimulation

Caffeine is a diuretic, meaning it causes a person to urinate more. Because of this, perhaps people should reduce intake in hot weather, during long workouts, or in other situations where they sweat a lot.

Stomach Irritation

Those with stomach or digestion problems should avoid caffeine, because it can irritate the stomach and stimulate the excretion of excessive acid, which will aggravate ulcers.

Faecal Incontinence

Caffeine relaxes the internal anal sphincter muscles, so it should be avoided by those with faecal incontinence.

Blood Clot Risk

Red Bull has been banned in Norway, Uruguay and Denmark because of health fears. An Australian study found that drinking just one 250 ml sugar-free can of *Red Bull* could increase the "stickiness" of the blood and raise the risk of blood clots forming. The manufacturer does not recommend its product for children and advises customers not to drink more than 2 cans a day.

Bone Problems

Caffeine may cause the body to lose calcium, which could lead to bone loss over time. It has been associated with a decrease in bone mineral density, increasing the risk of osteoporosis in women.

Addiction

As with cigarette smoking and other drugs, regular caffeine consumption can lead to addiction and weaken the body, making it more difficult to reduce intake or stop using it. Studies have shown that consuming as little as 100 mg of caffeine a day can make a person dependent on it. The body feels good after a shot of caffeine, but when the adrenaline wears off, fatigue and depression may well follow.

Anxiety

Too much caffeine will over-stimulate the nervous system, increase the heart rate and blood pressure, and may produce restlessness, nervousness, anxiety, dizziness, nausea, headache, tense muscles, irregular heartbeat, tremors, and sleep disturbances. In some individuals, large amounts of caffeine can induce anxiety severe enough to necessitate clinical attention. A recent study found that 3 cups of brewed coffee or 7 cups of instant coffee a day can triple the risk of hallucinations, because caffeine heightens the effect stress has on the body. An overdose can cause symptoms similar to organic mental disorders – such as panic or bipolar disorder, or even schizophrenia. Over 750 mg in a day could produce delirium, ringing ears, diarrhoea, vomiting, light flashes, breathing difficulties and convulsions. Caffeine-intoxicated people may be misdiagnosed and unnecessarily medicated when the treatment for caffeine-induced psychosis would simply be to stop more caffeine consumption. A study estimated that "caffeinism" may afflict as many as 1 in 10 people.

Danger to Children

Health campaigners have reported that schoolchildren showed signs of caffeine addiction after consuming energy drinks. *Drugs Education UK* warned that caffeine intake from energy drinks and tablets was an increasing problem in schools. Children stimulated by an energy drink are likely to be agitated during lessons. The organisation advised nurses to look out for pupils complaining of chest pains, headaches, restlessness or sleeplessness. As with adults, children may experience nausea, urinary urgency, nervousness, or other effects from an elevated caffeine intake from products like chocolate milk, soft drinks, cold medicines, tea, and coffee.

Other Potential Health Problems

Caffeine can affect the body's use of vitamins and minerals. It can increase their excretion so the body won't get the full benefits from healthy foods, and can interfere with calcium and iron absorption. It can raise the blood sugar level, producing an insulin response and inevitable drop in energy. It can constrict blood vessels, interfering with digestion, and can irritate the kidneys, causing more urine output. Caffeine may also precipitate asthmatic attacks, contribute to allergies, aggravate certain heart problems, and interact with some medications or supplements.

Caffeine withdrawal might involve headaches, depression, exhaustion, lack of appetite, nausea and vomiting. Withdrawal symptoms may well appear within 12 to 24 hours, peak at about 48 hours, and usually last 1 to 5 days. The blood vessels of the head dilate, leading to an excess of blood in the head, then to a headache and nausea. There may also be feelings of fatigue and drowsiness. The drop in serotonin levels when caffeine use is stopped can cause anxiety, irritability, inability to concentrate and diminished motivation to initiate or to complete daily tasks. In extreme cases it may cause mild depression.

Why Do People Consume Caffeine?

These are some of the reasons:

Cultural Norm

In many countries, caffeine consumption has become a completely normal and accepted part of every day life, though both tea and coffee came to England only in the late 17th century. When others visit, people often offer tea or coffee, but few recognise caffeine as a drug, or even pause to consider it may be doing them some harm.

Peer Pressure

There is probably stronger peer pressure to drink alcohol and smoke, particularly among the young, but when everybody else drinks tea or coffee, it is also difficult not to go along with the majority.

For Energy and as a Sop

Many people drink coffee in the morning in order to "get them moving" for the day, and a cup of tea or coffee is often used to break up daily boredom or as a "reward" for achieving something, however small. Some students use caffeine tablets to stay awake for all-night study, and there are truck drivers who take them to stay alert during long-distance journeys.

For Medicinal Purposes

Caffeine is sometimes used in combination with painkillers to combat migraines and Type 2 diabetes, and in creams to reduce redness and itching in dermatitis.

As an Athletic Stimulant

Athletes often use caffeine as a legal stimulant, though there is a designated limit. Bodybuilders use it to improve their training.

As a Slimming Aid

Though the evidence for its long-term effectiveness is weak, some people use caffeine as a slimming aid.

Lack of Parental Control

Younger children don't normally drink tea or coffee, but they are allowed and even encouraged to drink soft drinks, many of which contain caffeine.

Drug Combinations

More people today consume two or more drugs or go to excess in more than one area, i.e. smoking and eating too much, or drinking a lot of coffee and alcohol. Once people's lives involve too much pressure, they may go to excess – then their bodies could become imbalanced, resulting in them going to excess in other areas.

How to Avoid Caffeine Overload

The information above would suggest that if you aren't willing to give caffeine up altogether, then you should at least be "moderate" with your consumption, though that of course prompts the question "What is moderate?"

- You could try limiting caffeine drinks to just one in the morning to help you into the day.

- Check soft drinks to see if they contain caffeine.

- You could try switching to decaffeinated coffee or tea.

- An appreciation of the simple things in life and a greater awareness of the potential harm of any drug might persuade you that stimulants are not actually necessary. For millennia most people have led lives without daily stimulants, so life without caffeine is perfectly possible, though it could take some time for your body (and mind) to be weaned off it.

ALCOHOL

*"Alcohol is the anaesthesia by which
we endure the operation of life."*
(George Bernard Shaw)

Alcohol has been used as a "social lubricant" for thousands of years. Like caffeine and tobacco it is widely consumed throughout modern, industrial countries. Alcohol allows people to lose their inhibitions and feel more relaxed and sociable, and for many drinkers it also provides a temporary respite from the trials and stresses of their lives. It affects the brain like an anaesthetic – after one or two drinks we become more talkative and our heart rate speeds up a little, resulting in a heady, warm and happy feeling. The alcohol in the blood makes small blood vessels in the skin expand, allowing more blood to flow closer to the surface and lowering blood pressure at the same time.

So many of us enjoy the taste of a large variety of alcoholic drinks, with more than a few drinkers relying on alcohol to get them through the day – but it is poisonous to the human body and can be addictive. The attraction, availability and affordability of alcoholic drinks have in recent decades resulted in large numbers of people suffering from "alcohol overload".

The Scale of Alcohol Consumption

Alcoholic drinks are measured in units. A unit is half a pint of beer, a small, 125 ml glass of 9% proof wine, or 25 ml of spirits. A pint of strong continental lager is 3 units. *The World Health Organisation* suggests a limit of 35 units per week for men and 17.5 for women, whereas British guidelines are 21 and 14. Men are advised to drink no more than 4 units a day, and women no more than 3, with at least two days a week alcohol free. "Binge" drinking is defined as drinking 8 or more units in a day by a man and 6 or more by a woman. There are other (mainly Eastern European) countries that consume even more alcohol than the British, but the *average* weekly consumption of alcohol in

England is 16.4 units for men and 8 units for women. Many drink irresponsibly, as shown by these recent statistics:

- 37% of British adults (18 million) exceed the "safe" *daily* alcohol limit. Around 6% of men drink more than 35 units a week.

- In England more than 1 in 5 young men and 1 in 5 young women binge drink.

- About 9% of British men and 4% of women show signs of alcohol dependence.

- By 2009/10, England's hospital admissions related to alcohol reached a million, an increase of 12% compared to the previous year, and more than twice that for 2002/3.

In England the average age for the first alcoholic drink is 12-and-a-half. 50% of 10 to 19-year-olds drink alcohol just to get drunk. In 2009/10 almost 24,000 under-18s needed professional help for alcohol abuse. Children as young as 11 are treated for alcohol-related illnesses, and experts have warned that thousands of children are at greater risk of early dementia from excessive alcohol.

"Safe" Levels of Alcohol

The populations of most Western and other developed countries drink a lot of alcohol, but some say *any* amount of alcohol is bad for you and therefore an "overload". These include Muslims, Seventh Day Adventists, Mormons, some Protestants and Quakers, and many who practise meditation. Another group avoid alcohol because they don't want to "lose control". And some don't touch alcohol any more because they know they cannot stop once they start i.e. they are addicted (and often members of *Alcoholics Anonymous*).

Many believe there may be a "safe, moderate, sensible" level of alcohol consumption where the risks are low, but that depends on numerous factors including gender, size, and genetics. Medical authorities all say that there is no completely safe limit for alcohol, yet still publish advice on consumption. One of the doctors who drew up the original UK guidelines in 1987 admitted that the figures were "plucked out of thin air". If we drank just small quantities once or twice a month, alcohol would probably do us no significant harm. The cumulative effect of drinking regularly for many years, however, will almost undoubtedly cause health problems. Alcohol affects all kinds of cells in the body, causing changes in some and preventing others from working properly.

The Problems of Alcohol

Apart from increasing the likelihood of accidents, violence, unintended pregnancy, suicide, anti-social behaviour, and work or financial difficulties, alcohol abuse is almost certain to result in severe health problems. Alcohol is the third largest risk factor for disability, loss of health, and premature mortality.

- Globally, alcohol kills over 2.5 million people per year – more than AIDS, malaria or tuberculosis.

- For British men aged 16 to 55, up to 27% of deaths are alcohol related, and up to 15% for women.

Deaths in the UK from liver disease were 16,000 in 2008, an increase of 12% from 2005. Liver experts warned that there could be 250,000 more alcohol-related deaths over the following 20 years unless government action was taken.

Cancer

Research published in 2011 showed that drinking fewer units per week than suggested by NHS guidelines still increases the likelihood of developing cancer. After smoking, alcohol is the second biggest risk factor for cancers of the mouth and throat. Cirrhosis of the liver can lead to liver or mouth cancer.

- Research has found that just 1 glass of wine a day (3 units) increases the chance of getting breast cancer by 20%, and by 50% with 3 glasses a day.

A Europe-wide study of over 350,000 people published in 2011 showed that 1 of 10 cancer cases in men and 1 of 33 in women were caused by past or current intake of alcohol. The study suggested that men who drank more than 2 standard units a day (about a pint of beer or a 125ml glass of wine), and women who consumed more than 1 unit were particularly at risk of alcohol-related cancers.

Liver Cirrhosis and Liver Failure

Consuming 8 or more units of alcohol in a day can damage the liver. The liver makes a special substance that breaks down alcohol and burns it as fuel. Excessive alcohol can exhaust the liver's ability to do this and damage it permanently. Any damage will probably be repaired provided someone doesn't drink too much at any one time and has recuperative non-drinking days. As well as being smaller and producing less of the chemical that neutralises alcohol, women's livers can't repair themselves as quickly as men's when damaged. This means that it takes women longer to recover from a heavy drinking session, and unfortunately women's drinks come in the same measures.

- In 30 years the number of British men and women dying from cirrhosis of the liver increased by 500% and 400% respectively.

An estimated 30,000 Britons are living with cirrhosis of the liver and at least 7,000 new cases are diagnosed each year.

Pancreatitis

Long-term heavy drinkers can develop this painful condition. The pancreas makes insulin and other substances needed to properly digest food. If left untreated, pancreatitis causes malnutrition and can lead to diabetes. In the UK around 500 people die of alcohol-related pancreatitis each year.

Heart Disease

Alcohol can increase blood pressure and damage heart tissue. Though the French drink a lot, a study has shown that they don't suffer from as much heart disease. This may be because they drink a little each day as opposed to drinking heavily on weekends, as happens in Britain.

Strokes

A 20-year study found that men who drank more than 5 units a day were twice as likely to die from a stroke compared with non-drinkers. Over 8 units for men or 6 for women will cause dehydration and make the blood thicker and more likely to form clots, in the brain or elsewhere. Prolonged heavy use of alcohol also raises blood pressure, which is another cause of stroke. In their book *Dynamic Living*, Diehl and Ludington referred to studies which had demonstrated that alcohol intake accounts for 5% to 15% of hypertension (high blood pressure).

Diabetes

Long-term heavy users of alcohol are far more likely to be overweight than the average person, and this raises the risk of developing diabetes – which shortens lives and entails restricted diets and daily insulin injections or medicine. At 7 calories per gram, alcohol has more calories than many foods – the alcohol in a large glass of red wine amounts to 200 calories. Alcohol also stimulates the appetite and reduces self-control, making it easy to eat too much. Prolonged heavy drinking can even lead to the embarrassment of men developing "breasts", popularly known as "man boobs".

Mental Health Deterioration

There is a link between drinking too much alcohol and mental health problems, including memory loss. Not only do people fail to remember what went on during a heavy session, persistent heavy drinkers can develop long-term memory problems. A study found that regular drinking can accelerate the start of Alzheimer's disease, as can smoking, though to a lesser extent. Those who had consumed more than 2 drinks a day prior to diagnosis would on average get Alzheimer's about 5 years earlier.

Osteoporosis

The number of people suffering from porous, weak bones is large and increasing. As well as early menopause and low oestrogen, other factors that cause osteoporosis include a sedentary lifestyle, a high protein diet, cigarettes, caffeine – and alcohol.

Malnutrition

Heavy drinkers can sometimes be overweight yet malnourished, because they replace food with alcohol. Once alcohol has damaged the liver, the body's food processing mechanism will function poorly, meaning it will absorb fewer essential nutrients.

Lowered Fertility

Studies have shown that women who drink a lot are less likely to achieve pregnancy, and that excessive alcohol consumption can cause sperm defects. 5 (and sometimes fewer) drinks every week can decrease a woman's chance of becoming pregnant. Drinking while pregnant can also harm the unborn child – any alcohol in the mother's blood will cross the placenta and get into the bloodstream of the foetus. Over 1,600 London women went to hospital for drink-related miscarriage in 2008, up 10% in 4 years.

Other Health Problems

Alcohol affects the circulation by expanding blood vessels. This causes thread veins, often on the face, and the purple, bulbous "drinker's nose". Excessive and regular intake of alcohol will affect the skin adversely and result in brittle hair and nails. Alcohol can irritate the nasal passages, is a depressant, and can cause muscles to relax far more than usual during an ordinary night's sleep, which all help to cause snoring. Excessive drinking might result in the more serious condition of sleep apnoea (involving pauses in breathing) – which can be far more difficult to treat and keep in check.

The Cost of Alcohol Abuse

Though the focus should naturally be on the health problems caused by alcohol consumption, the financial costs are considerable and rising.

- In 2013 the total cost of alcohol abuse in the UK was estimated to be £6 billion a year – half for health care and half due to premature death, business losses and drink-related crime and accidents.

Why People Drink Alcohol

As well as alcohol's apparent ability to provide temporary relief from the stresses of life and to "oil the cogs of social intercourse", the main reasons why people drink include its legality, its social acceptance, its ready availability, and its relative cheapness.

Innate Human Drive

Andrew Weil in his book *The Natural Mind* argues that humans naturally seek to experience "periodic episodes of non-ordinary consciousness". This may be a factor in why people smoke and drink alcohol, as well as take other drugs.

Availability and Legality

Alcohol is readily available in shops, supermarkets and off-licences, and many people believe that alcohol must be safe to consume, otherwise the authorities would make it illegal.

Alcohol Is Cheap

It is now 65% more affordable than it was in 1980. Though it has gone up in price, wages have risen far more. In recent years supermarkets have been encouraging people to increase their consumption by cutting the price of alcohol as an enticement to shop in their stores. Many young people now drink cheaper alcohol at home before going out

Social Habit

Get-togethers in people's homes are now almost certain to involve alcohol consumption. At the same time, drinking alcohol in public places – once frowned upon – has now become more tolerated in Western countries.

Peer Pressure

People want to conform. For older people drinking wine with meals has become normal, and many young people view binge-drinking as acceptable behaviour.

Escape from Stress

Financial problems, work pressure and family issues cause many people to turn to drugs of one sort or another, often alcohol.

Youthful Drinking

More under-age children are drinking, which is likely to mean they will consume alcohol as an adult. Young people think it's exciting, especially those who have nothing inspiring or useful to do. It has become easier for children to get hold of alcohol because some shop owners serve under-age children, or adults may buy it for them. And more recently new drinks (like "alcopops") have been conjured up by manufacturers and marketed aggressively to young drinkers.

Role Models

Growing up in a household with parents who regularly drink alcohol may well lead to children taking up the habit.

Reward

As with food and other goods, alcohol is used as a "reward" for getting through a working day, or achieving anything, no matter how trivial.

Ignorance

People don't realise the damage alcohol can do to their health, and many still don't understand units and glass sizes.

How to Avoid Alcohol Overload

The possible consequences for your health should make you pause for thought before drinking that extra pint of beer or glass of wine. A greater awareness of your motivations and real needs as well as the potential health problems from drinking alcohol would help you to enjoy a positive social life and other activities without the use of much, if any, alcohol or other drug.

- You might try designating only certain days – weekends for example – or times for drinking, or limit yourself to a lower amount. After a while your body's tolerance is likely to gradually decrease, so the same euphoric and relaxed state can be reached with less alcohol. I drink the occasional half pint of beer, and ignore those who laugh about me not having a "manly" pint.

- If you do regular exercise, it will not only strengthen your body and immune system, keep your blood flowing and your veins clearer, it will also diminish the time, and possibly the desire, for alcohol. Calories will be burnt and bodily systems invigorated to counteract the effects of alcohol.

- If you take up an interesting hobby, there'll be less time to drink or think about drinking. Having a sense of purpose by creating goals and working towards them is vital for a healthy life.

- Associate with those who don't drink too much – the power of peer pressure is strong.

- The support of family and friends might help you with personal and drink problems you may have, but if they remain insurmountable, then you should seek professional help. This could be a counsellor or perhaps a group like *Alcoholics Anonymous*.

TOBACCO

*"A cigarette is a pipe with a fire
at one end and a fool at the other."*

(Anonymous)

Smoking is one of the older and more persistent addictions in both the Western world and elsewhere. Few people – whether smokers or non-smokers – would say anything positive about smoking. Tobacco has been described as "the only legally available consumer product which kills people when it is used entirely as intended". Because of the poisonous ingredients in tobacco, any level of smoking can be considered an overload for the body. Nicotine – the mind-altering ingredient – is strongly addictive, which makes this habit particularly difficult for most people to give up.

The Scale of Tobacco Consumption

There are over a billion smokers in the world, and the number is rising. In 2010 the annual tobacco industry revenue was $664 billion.

- In 2002 about 15 billion cigarettes were sold daily – or 10 million every minute – across the world.

- Between 80,000 and 100,000 children worldwide start smoking every day, roughly half of whom live in Asia.

- 10 million adult Britons are smokers (21% of men and 19% of women).

On average, 1 in 3 male adults in the world smoke, as well as 1 in 5 teenagers aged 13 to 15. Unfortunately many young people still take up smoking. The highest proportion of smokers is amongst 20 to 24-year-olds (34% men and 30% women). Though smoking has been – and still is – falling in developed nations, it is increasing elsewhere. Tobacco companies have been maintaining their profits by encouraging the habit where controls are looser and authorities "more friendly". Tobacco consumption has been rising in the developing countries, with nearly two-thirds of men in the East Asian and Pacific regions now smoking.

The Health Problems Caused by Tobacco

Tobacco smoke contains over 4,000 chemical compounds, which are present either as gases or tiny particles. They include nicotine, tar and carbon dioxide, as well as many toxic substances like formaldehyde, arsenic, cyanide, benzo pyrene, benzene, toluene and acrolein. Nicotine stimulates the central nervous system, increasing the heartbeat rate and blood pressure. It is addictive, and in large quantities is extremely poisonous.

The "average" addict smokes about 15 cigarettes a day. When the level of nicotine in the body falls, the smoker feels the need for another "hit". The tar is brown and treacly in appearance, and consists of tiny particles. It is formed when tobacco smoke condenses, and is deposited in the lungs and respiratory system and gradually absorbed. The carbon dioxide binds to haemoglobin in the bloodstream more easily than oxygen, and this means the blood carries less oxygen round the body.

For those of you who need more encouragement to kick this dangerous habit, here are some calculations made by cancer researchers after studying life expectancy statistics and smoking:

- Roughly every 8 seconds, someone dies from tobacco use.

- On average 1 cigarette costs 11 minutes of a (male) smoker's life, a week of smoking costs one day of life, and smokers are likely to die 6.5 years earlier than non-smokers.

- Approximately 50% of all regular cigarette smokers will eventually be killed by their habit.

Smoking-related diseases kill 1 in 10 adults globally – around 4 million deaths. By 2030, if current trends continue, smoking will be responsible for the death of 1 in 6 people. In the USA, smoking accounts for 87% of lung cancer deaths, 82% of deaths from chronic obstructive pulmonary disease (emphysema and chronic bronchitis), and 21% of all coronary heart disease. Cigarettes cause more than 1 in 5 American deaths and 12 times more British people have died from smoking than were killed fighting in World War 2. About 114,000 people in the UK die of smoking-related diseases each year, roughly 5 times more than the combined deaths from road traffic and other accidents, poisoning and overdose, alcoholic liver disease, murder and manslaughter, suicide, and HIV infection.

Until the late 1950s the tobacco companies claimed that cigarettes were not harmful to human health. Overwhelmed with negative studies, health authorities in Western countries finally campaigned against smoking in the early 1960s. All experts today are agreed that smoking is bad for us, yet polls show that smokers still underestimate the health risks – they not only have a significantly increased risk of dying prematurely, they are also likely to experience a more painful death and spend longer being ill while they are alive. If you do smoke, here are some of the health problems you may well suffer from in due course:

Cancer

Smoking causes about 90% of lung cancer deaths and 30% of *all* cancer deaths. Studies have found that tobacco smoking can also cause cancers of the upper aero-digestive tract (oral cavity, nasal cavity, nasal sinuses, pharynx, larynx and oesophagus), of the pancreas, stomach, liver, lower urinary tract (renal, pelvis and bladder), kidney, uterine, cervix, and in the blood (myeloid leukaemia).

Bronchitis and Emphysema

80% of deaths from these conditions are the result of smoking. There is a risk of gangrene or amputation caused by circulatory problems.

Heart Disease and Stroke

Smoking contributes significantly to illness and death from cardiovascular problems, and is responsible for around 17% of all heart disease deaths. Giving up cigarettes has been shown to significantly lower the risk of suffering a stroke.

Memory Deterioration

Smoking damages blood vessels, including those in the brain. Studies have shown that smoking can destroy memory. It kills nerve cells and quitting won't help them grow back. Research has found that smoking in midlife results in poor memory and makes it harder to think and learn, and it seems that developing cognitive problems in your 30s, 40s, and 50s may speed the onset of dementia. Another study found that smokers between the ages of 46 and 70 have a 70% higher chance of chronic memory loss. Another study showed that smoking 20 cigarettes a day brings the onset of Alzheimer's forward by over 2 years.

Lowered Fertility and Dangers to the Foetus

Studies have shown that smoking reduces levels of fertility, and smoking during pregnancy not only raises the risk of spontaneous abortion, pre-term birth, low birth weight and stillbirths, but also of children having behavioural problems.

Other Health Problems

These include blocked-up airways and lots of coughing, stained teeth, diseased tonsils and gums, and bad breath. A smoker's skin is very likely to become tough, wrinkled, leathery and unhealthy, and researchers have found a connection between moderate to severe baldness and smoking 20 cigarettes a day, probably because tiny vessels that supply blood to the hair follicles become damaged. The habit lowers the overall wellbeing of smokers – they lose strength, fitness, concentration and alertness. Research has shown that workers who smoke take more days off from work for illness than non-smokers

Passive Smoking

Studies have discovered many problems associated with ETS (environmental tobacco smoke). ETS is estimated to result in thousands of non-smokers dying from lung cancer and heart disease, as well as suffering from emphysema, bronchitis, and asthma. Young children's exposure to ETS contributes to the incidence of ear infections like "glue ear", asthma, wheezing, coughs, bronchitis, 'flu and pneumonia. It may also cause slower growth rates and SID (sudden infant death syndrome). Studies estimated that non-smokers who lived with a smoker had a 20% to 30% increased risk of lung cancer and a 15% greater risk of premature death than those in a smoke-free household. Research by *The World Health Organisation* estimated that 1 death in every 100 is caused by passive smoking.

Why Do People Smoke?

Most people start smoking when they are young. As adults they continue to smoke for the same reason as they do other things that are bad for them. Once addicted, they use cigarettes as one of the props to get them through the day. Many claim that smoking relaxes them, or that it helps them keep slim, though these are probably excuses to avoid facing up to the difficult task of giving up. Any addiction can be extremely difficult to fight, and many people struggle – sometimes for years or even decades – to stop smoking. People need a strong enough reason or purpose for quitting, and many find it hard to adopt a sufficiently positive attitude to life. Overwhelmed by today's confusing, frenetic and competitive world, some are unable to find the strength and courage to meet the challenge and make this important change to their lifestyle. These are some reasons why people smoke:

Smoking Is Legal

If a drug is legal, somehow it "can't be that bad". More than 80% of smokers take up the habit as teenagers. Many start at the legal age of 16, but most are younger. In the UK about 450 children start smoking every day.

Smoking Is Grown-up and Exciting

Young people want to experiment with something their parents or other adults are doing that feels a little dangerous. Young women want to emulate models who smoke so they too will look and feel grown-up, cool and sexy.

Peer Pressure

Smoking, like drinking alcohol, is associated with social gatherings – and peer pressure is one of the strongest influences of all. Understandably, young people find it very difficult to resist doing what their friends do, however unwise it may be.

Staying Slim

A more recent reason for smoking amongst young girls seems to be the desire to stay slim, and many of them believe that smoking will help. This belief has undoubtedly been influenced by the media showing famous models smoking.

Idle Minds and Bodies

Children who are not kept fully occupied with study, sport and hobbies are more likely to take up bad habits like smoking.

Bad Role Models

Parents and other older relatives who smoke – or don't advise children about the perils of this addictive habit – probably have a greater influence than even media celebrities.

Immature Attitude

Young people are generally in good physical shape and feel the future is extremely distant – they believe that they will be able to give up any bad habits, including smoking, whenever they need to.

How to Give Up Tobacco

Smoking is so harmful to our bodies that the advice of every health professional is to give up. To help you summon up the necessary willpower, remind yourself of the various health (and other) advantages if you do quit, and of the considerable health risks if you don't. As an ex-smoker myself I remember that it was difficult, but when I knew I would no longer be a smoker, I also remember the wonderful feeling of "release" from being hooked on cigarettes.

- It is difficult to do, but you need to visualise yourself as a non-smoker.

- The health benefits of quitting should be uppermost in your mind, but there's also the financial benefit – put aside what you used to spend on cigarettes each day and that should strengthen your motivation to keep going.

- In 2008 a major long-term study of smoking habits in America revealed that people tend to give up smoking in groups. People were far more likely to quit if one of their siblings had just done so, even more likely if a friend had, and most likely if a spouse had. Find someone else to give up with you.

- If you live with smokers it will naturally make it much harder for you to quit, as would breathing in the second-hand smoke of friends or colleagues.

- You could use distractions to help you quit, particularly those that involve the hands, such as practical hobbies. Strictly as a short-term aid, you could chew gum whenever you feel the urge to smoke. Initially I ate more sweets and put on a little weight.

- If you exercise regularly it will help you quit smoking. A brisk walk for half an hour each day would be a good start. Exercise produces the same kind of chemicals in the brain as nicotine. Both release dopamine, the hormone that makes us feel content.

- Giving up smoking with just willpower alone might well prove very difficult for you. Today there are many outside aids that can help – nicotine gum, patches, or hypnosis, for example. Try *anything* that might help you to quit this lethal habit.

ILLEGAL DRUGS

"A junkie is someone who uses their body to tell society that something is wrong."

(Stella Adler)

The human inclination to be experimental and indulgent, together with our ever-increasing efforts to escape from life's worries, has led to the widespread and regular consumption of illegal as well as legal drugs. Drugs prohibited from private use include cannabis, ecstasy, cocaine, amphetamine, heroin and LSD, though in some places personal use of cannabis is legal. Some of these drugs are sanctioned in certain countries for medical purposes only, but are mainly consumed privately for "recreational" purposes. Cannabis is said to alleviate symptoms of various medical conditions, including cancer, HIV, multiple sclerosis, and glaucoma, but cannot be used legally for medicinal purposes in the UK. Amphetamine, cocaine and morphine are used by doctors and hospitals to treat certain types of illness.

Historical events and cultural factors have influenced which drugs are legal today and which are not. All cultures sanction at least one kind of drug, yet are determined to forbid others. In Western countries alcohol is legal and other substances termed "drugs" are banned, while in many Eastern, Islamic countries some "drugs" are accepted while alcohol is illegal. Tobacco and coffee were more taboo in the West before *The Industrial Revolution*, and as recently as the early 20th century heroin and opium were still legal. There is certainly no clear-cut logic to explain why a drug should be legal or illegal, especially in terms of the potential or actual damage to people's physical or mental health.

How much damage is done by a drug depends on the individual's reaction to it, how much is consumed and over what period. Recent research has analysed the link between the harmful effects of drugs relative to their current classification by law (classes A, B and C). Alcohol, solvents and tobacco (unclassified drugs) have been judged by some experts to be more dangerous than ecstasy and LSD – both Class A drugs, which are supposedly the most harmful.

Despite the determination of most governments to eliminate the taking of illegal drugs for almost a century, their overall availability and consumption continues to increase, along with the associated criminality and almost inevitable deterioration in the physical and mental health of those who take them. Many experts, politicians, and even some top-level policemen, have called for the decriminalisation of all drugs, together with greater education and help for addicts.

The Scale of Illegal Drug Consumption

The level of illegal drug consumption in affluent countries is indicative of the stresses felt by many in those societies today, as well as the ineffectiveness of prohibition. The USA, which influences much of the world's drug research and drug policy agenda, has the highest use of cocaine and cannabis, despite punitive illegal drug policies.

- A survey in 2010/11 found that 36% of adults in the UK had taken illegal drugs, and 9% had used an illegal drug during the previous year.

- 7% of those aged 19 to 59 in England and Wales – over 2 million people – are cannabis users, 700,000 take cocaine, and 500,000 take ecstasy. And there are about 300,000 registered heroin addicts in the UK.

Amphetamines and crystal meth are used "recreationally" in the gay and rave cultures to break down inhibitions, keep dancing, or have sex for prolonged periods. A police report warned that crystal meth was present in almost every town in England and Wales, and was also increasingly found in other drugs such as heroin and cocaine.

The Problems of Illegal Drugs

Illegal drugs might lead to addiction, can have extremely adverse physical and mental health effects, and are certainly the cause of much crime – by addicts to fund their habit as well as dealers. Experimentation with drugs does not necessarily lead to dependence, but the greater the frequency and amount of a substance used, the higher the risk of dependence. Like tobacco and alcohol, all drugs can be addictive and very difficult to give up. Just as with food, short-term highs can lead to long-term lows, though with more pronounced effect.

Cannabis

As well as marijuana, cannabis has many other street names. It was classified in Britain as a class C drug, but more recently was reclassified as class B because some versions of the drug had become much stronger. Though on average it is not as addictive as amphetamines, tobacco or alcohol, cannabis contains more toxic substances than tobacco smoke: 20 times more ammonia, a carcinogen, and 5 times more hydrogen cyanide, which can cause heart disease, and more nitrogen oxides, which can cause lung damage. It also contains more tar, so it can lead to bronchitis, emphysema and lung cancer. It can disrupt the control of blood pressure, increasing the risk of fainting. Cannabis use has been linked to psychosis, short-term memory and attention loss, loss of motor skills and dexterity, and reduced reaction time. Studies suggest that the brains of those younger than 15 can be adversely affected by taking cannabis. There is evidence that some of the effects can become permanent with heavy usage, but no acute lethal overdoses of cannabis are known – in contrast to several other legal and illegal drugs including alcohol, aspirin, acetaminophen, and cocaine.

MDMA (Ecstasy)

MDMA is a synthetic, psychoactive drug. It has a similar structure to stimulants like cocaine and hallucinogenics such as

LSD. It produces feelings of overwhelming euphoria, intimacy, and connectedness with others, and is associated with the "rave" culture. There were only 5 deaths from MDMA alone in the UK during 2010, but many more from a drug mixture that included MDMA. Short-term health risks include hypertension, dehydration and hyperthermia. Heavy or frequent use may precipitate anxiety, lasting depression and addiction in vulnerable users. Possible health problems from continued usage include sleeping difficulties, teeth clenching, blurred vision, acne-like rash, nausea, chills and sweating, liver damage, confusion, anxiety, paranoia, aggression, memory impairment and damage of the central nervous system.

Cocaine

Cocaine is both a stimulant of the central nervous system and an appetite suppressant. The initial signs of stimulation are hyperactivity, restlessness, increased blood pressure, increased heart rate, and euphoria. Sexual interest and pleasure can be amplified. The user experiences increased body temperature, mental alertness, heart rate, and energy, but over time more is required to get the same level of effect. If a cocaine user goes for days without eating, it may lead to cocaine addiction and malnutrition. Cocaine can cause itching, twitching, irritability, restlessness, hallucinations, paranoia, impotence, respiratory failure, heart disease, stroke, heart attack, and gastrointestinal problems.

Amphetamine

Often referred to as "speed", this and related drugs such as methamphetamine, are a group of drugs that act by increasing levels of norepinephrine, seretonin, and dopamine in the brain. The use of amphetamine during strenuous physical activity can be extremely dangerous, especially when combined with alcohol, and athletes have died as a result. Physical effects of amphetamine can include reduced appetite, hyperactivity, headache, increased blood pressure, fever, diarrhoea, constipation, dizziness, insomnia, and numbness. Psychological effects can include anxiety, euphoria, increased concentration and alertness, a feeling of power or superiority, excitability, talkativeness, aggression, and paranoia. Withdrawal can cause depression, fatigue, psychosis, and suicidal thoughts. Tolerance is developed rapidly, so the amount needed to satisfy the addiction quickly increases. Chronic users of amphetamines sometimes snort or use injections to experience the full effects in a faster and more intense way – thereby adding risks of infection and vein damage as well as a greater possibility of overdosing.

Crystal Meth

A type of amphetamine with many street names, crystal meth is a powerful stimulant that even in small doses can cause insomnia, increased physical activity and decreased appetite. Usually in ice-like crystal chunks or in a coarse powdered form, it is made from a highly volatile combination of substances – which can even include household cleaning products. It is smoked, eaten, snorted or injected, and the effects can last anywhere from 2 to 20 hours. It produces sharpened attention, heightened libido, euphoria, and increased activity. The negative effects include loss of appetite, increased heart rate and breathing, heart problems, irritability, self-harm, aggression, anxiety, extreme weight loss, severe insomnia, hallucinations, paranoia, psychosis, stroke, dependence, and an irreversibly damaged immune system. Some people have died after taking small doses of the drug.

Heroin

Heroin is processed from morphine, a naturally occurring substance extracted from the seed pod of the Asian poppy plant. It usually appears as a white or brown powder. Heroin produces an intense euphoria, but this diminishes with increased tolerance. Apart from the risk of contracting infectious diseases – including HIV and hepatitis – regular users may develop collapsed veins from injecting, infection of the heart lining and valves, abscesses, cellulitis, and liver disease. Pulmonary complications, including various types of pneumonia, may result from the poor health condition of the abuser, as well as from heroin's depressing effects on respiration. According to experts and contrary to popular belief, pure heroin, properly handled, is a benign drug. Apparently it is easier to overdose on *Paracetamol* than pure heroin, although heroin is addictive. The illness, misery and death associated with heroin are not the result of the drug itself but the black market on which it is sold as a result of the "war" against drugs. Only since its prohibition in the early 20th century did problems with its use arise.

LSD

In comparison with other illegal drugs, LSD use is low. In the UK well below 1% of the adult population use the drug. Though it rarely causes physical problems and it is almost impossible to overdose on it, LSD is highly hallucinatory. It can cause severe psychological discomfort, even trauma.

Drugs for Athletic Performance

"Lean mass builders" are used to drive or amplify the growth of muscle and lean body mass, and sometimes to reduce body fat. This class of drugs includes anabolic steroids, beta-2 agonists, and the human growth hormone. Side effects of anabolic steroids include water retention (indicated by swelling in the neck and facial areas), acne, gynecomastia (the formation of breasts or abnormally large glands), aggression, hypertension, cardio-vascular disease, palpitations, impotence, and jaundice. Possible side effects of the human growth hormone include nerve, muscle or joint pain, carpal tunnel syndrome, water retention, numbness and tingling of the skin, and high cholesterol levels.

Costs

Addiction to illegal drugs can not only lead to the bankruptcy of the addicts themselves, but can also ruin the finances of their families. And the societal cost of controlling drugs has proved to be enormous.

- Illegal drug use in the UK was estimated to have cost £110 billion in the 10 years to 2008, with £100 billion attributable to drug-related crime and £10 billion to health costs. Each illegal drug addict was estimated to cost the country around £44,000 per year.

Why People Take Illegal Drugs

Psychoactive substances are readily available to the many people who like to experience different, interesting, and pleasurable effects. Their use – as with all "recreational" drugs – is driven largely by peer pressure, with most trying both legal and illegal drugs when young.

Innate Human Drive

It seems from a young age we naturally seek to experience periodic episodes of non-ordinary consciousness.

Appetite Suppressant

Cocaine and amphetamines may be used to reduce appetite.

Education and Parenting

If they don't have good role models or mentors, and if parents and schools fail to inspire them, keep them usefully occupied and supervised, children may be more likely to turn to drugs. Adults must make sure children understand the dangers of drugs to physical and psychological health, and that regular indulgence is likely to create problems in their lives sooner or later.

Lack of Purpose

Children (and adults) who are not inspired by modern life and see a bleak future for themselves, or are suffering mental/physical abuse, are more likely to find ways to escape their reality – and often it is drugs they turn to.

Peer Pressure

The influence friends have, particularly on young people, is incredibly powerful.

Accessibility and Affordability

Today most drugs are easily accessible and relatively inexpensive (until chronic addiction). And now children as well as adults have more money.

Rebellion

Children like to experiment, especially with illegal or dangerous substances and activities that their parents and authorities in general would disapprove of.

Lack of Awareness

Children don't understand the dangers of drugs and think they will live forever.

Sporting Advantage

The potential rewards of success can be huge, so despite huge efforts of various sporting bodies, there are always some competitors who cheat by taking illegal substances.

Genes

Studies have shown that there is a strong genetic influence to addiction in a minority of people. One study found that genetic factors play a part in 70% of cocaine addiction, and 50% for alcohol. Though many addictions – in fact almost any behaviour – could probably be linked to hereditary factors, nurture and lifestyle factors can in most cases override inherited pre-dispositions.

How to Avoid Illegal Drugs

The awareness that they are poisonous to the body should persuade you to avoid the consumption of drugs or other unnatural substances. And you need to realise that the use of a drug, whether legal or illegal, prescribed or over-the-counter, may well be just masking symptoms of a problem, whether physical or mental.

- Escaping reality with drugs is merely a short-term "solution". A short-term "high" could be dangerous and may well lead to long-term "lows".

- Be aware that any drug, legal or not, can lead to addiction – and then possibly financial stress and crime.

- Illegal drugs are likely to be more dangerous than other drugs. They may contain impurities and result in ill-health, or their strength may be difficult to determine, which makes a lethal overdose more likely.

- Taking illegal drugs runs the risk of prison or at least a criminal record.

- To steer clear of illegal drugs it would of course be wise to avoid keeping the company of those indulging or dealing in them.

- An interest or hobby might take your attention away from indulgences, whether legal and illegal drugs or "comfort" food. As mentioned before, a sense of purpose in life and working towards goals is vital for good health and fulfilment.

- Regular aerobic exercise will help to keep your body healthy and mind positive, as well as be a distraction from taking harmful substances.

- With greater awareness you won't consider that mind-altering substances are necessary to achieve inspiration, spiritual "transcendence" or contentment. Once you realise that the world is so extraordinary to be sufficiently awe-inspiring and "mind-blowing", you won't have to rely on unnatural substances. A positive approach to life will enable you to give up destructive habits or addictions. The necessary willpower can be engendered by a strong, inspiring reason to make the effort.

- If you have a problem with illegal drugs that you just cannot deal with yourself, you should seek professional help. This could be a counsellor or perhaps a group like *Narcotics Anonymous*.

PHARMACEUTICAL DRUGS

*"The habitual use of any drug is harmful.
The most eminent physicians are now agreed that
very few drugs have any real curative value.
The essential thing is right habits of life."*

(John Harvey Kellogg)

Pharmaceutical drugs are chemical substances normally used for medical purposes, some prescribed by doctors and others available for sale over the counter. Many pharmaceutical drugs have proved to be of considerable benefit to the human race. Apart from the increase in our wellbeing through the alleviation of pain, they have helped eliminate dangerous diseases like smallpox and malaria from much of the world, and they are extremely effective in emergencies – stabilising patients during operations and after heart attacks and strokes.

The variety and number of pharmaceutical drugs have grown exponentially over the last 50 years, along with the unquestioning acceptance that their use and effects are positive. Though drugs have saved and continue to save many lives, some experts – and a growing number of medical practitioners – believe that they are often unnecessary and even harmful to people's health. Doctors are encouraged by profit-driven companies to prescribe drugs, and people are not sufficiently inclined, informed or exhorted to maintain optimum health in order to prevent illness. There is now a "pill for every ill" mentality, with pharmaceutical drugs used routinely and daily as a substitute for making healthy lifestyle choices.

The Scale of Pharmaceutical Drug Consumption

There are drugs for treating cancer, drugs for lowering cholesterol in the blood, drugs to combat hypertension, drugs for diabetes, drugs for arthritis, drugs for asthma and eczema, drugs for phobias, anxiety and depression, drugs for behavioural problems, drugs for the menopause, drugs to help people sleep, drugs for slimming, constipation and diarrhoea, drugs for earaches, back aches, headaches and migraine, drugs for irritable bowel and restless leg syndrome, and drugs for colds and 'flu, to name just some of the health problems for which we use drugs today. And the upward trend will continue as long as people abrogate responsibility for their health and drug companies put a label on any behaviour or condition and turn it into an illness that we "need" to treat with drugs.

- In 2009 global pharmaceutical sales were about $700 billion, and by 2014 the figure is expected to top $1 trillion.

Though the lion's share of drugs goes to patients in the first world, developing countries are increasingly contributing to the drug companies' profits. In 2011 the UK drugs expenditure was almost £9 billion – up from just £3 billion in 1993.

- During 2010, the number of prescriptions written in England was 961 million, averaging over 18 per person (an increase of 64% from the year 2001).

Millions of drugs are prescribed for high cholesterol and hypertension. About 8 million Britons take statins for high cholesterol. Health authorities have recommended that anyone with a 20% or greater risk of cardiovascular disease within 10 years should be eligible for them. In 2009 almost 7 million British patients were treated for hypertension, involving about 15 million subscriptions. Drugs in huge numbers are taken by patients for depression, sleeping difficulties and pain. Doctors in England issued 43 million prescriptions for anti-depressants in 2010/11, an increase of 28% in just 3 years. And the 15 million sleeping pills prescribed during 2010/11 cost the *NHS* £50 million. In 2011 Britons bought about 6 billion pain relief pills, with sales increasing by 4% year on year.

Between 1993 and 2003, ADHD (attention deficit hyperactivity disorder) prescriptions tripled, with global spending increasing nine-fold. Various drugs are used to treat the condition, including *Ritalin*. In 2007, 400,000 British children between 5 and 19 were taking drugs for behavioural problems. Spending on ADHD rose by 65% over 4 years to 2010 to more than £31 million, and 610,000 *Ritalin* prescriptions were written in 2009. In 2010 the *NHS* spent £37 million on weight-loss drugs – now also being used to combat the growing problem of childhood obesity. Between 1999 and 2006 the drugs use for children rose fifteen-fold. Large numbers of drugs are also taken by the increasing number of asthma sufferers – now over 5 million people in Britain. Drugs prescribed include cortisone drugs (steroids), bronchodilators, corticosteroids, systemic corticosteroids, aerosol drugs, antihistamines and decongestants.

The Problems of Pharmaceutical Drugs

Every pharmaceutical drug will have one or more side effects, which can sometimes be serious. Even something as common as aspirin may cause indigestion, nausea, and irritation of the stomach or bowel. The blood thinner *Warfarin*, prescribed for the many people in danger of heart attacks and strokes, can cause bleeding – from cuts, the nose or gums – as well as easy bruising, dark urine, black stools, headaches and nausea.

- Adverse drug reactions were responsible for more than 6.5% of all UK hospital admissions during 2006, amounting to a million people.

Prescription medications may well be important for treating serious conditions, but they are also the fourth leading cause of death, are responsible for a large number of hospital admissions, and are a major factor in disability and drug dependency. The now widespread treatment of older people with polypharmacy – the use of 5 or more different drugs – can lead to inappropriate prescribing, incorrect usage, and harmful synergistic effects.

These are some of the prescription drugs problems, listed by the condition they are used to treat:

Drugs for Cancer

There are many different cancers and many different drugs used in treating them, so they have a different set of side effects. The common ones are a decrease in blood cell counts, hair loss, nausea, vomiting, a lack of energy, decreased appetite, and mouth ulcers. These will normally be short-term effects that occur just during therapy, though the powerful drugs may well compromise the immune system for life.

Drugs for Hypertension

These include diuretics, beta-blockers and drugs that open blood vessels and decrease the heart workload. They are often used in combination. The potential side effects of drugs used to reduce high blood pressure may be different for each class of drug, but include an irritating cough, dizziness, facial flushing, swollen ankles, constipation, gout attacks, cool hands and feet, poor sleep, tiredness, and impotence.

Drugs for Cholesterol

Statins can significantly reduce the risk of heart disease by lowering cholesterol and other fatty substances in the blood, but a review found that for three-quarters of patients taking them they offered little or no value – thus exposing millions to potential undesirable side effects unnecessarily. And though it is difficult for those with a genetic disposition to high cholesterol levels to reduce them by dietary changes and more exercise, the vast majority could do so. Some say that the widespread use of statins is a clear example of the "mass medicalisation" that drug sellers seek. Side-effects can include fever, nausea, upset stomach, serious liver problems, and severe muscle breakdown, resulting in muscle pain and soreness. Pregnant and nursing women are advised not to take them because of the potential hazards to the foetus and nursing infants. Sexual dysfunction, gastrointestinal issues, memory loss, irritability, anxiety and depression are other potential side-effects.

Drugs for Depression

Drugs have been widely prescribed for depression, but studies have found that they work no better than a placebo for many, and only in cases of severe depression do they seem to be marginally more effective. The official *Prozac* website lists the "common possible side effects": abnormal dreams, decreased sex drive, orgasm and erection problems, decreased appetite, anxiety, weakness, diarrhoea, dry mouth, indigestion, 'flu, sleeping problems, feeling sick, nervousness, sore throat, rash, watery nasal discharge, sweating, tremor, hot flushes and yawning. Studies have also suggested that anti-depressants can increase the risk of suicidal thoughts in children, adolescents, and young adults, and that they cause DNA damage to sperm, impairing fertility.

Drugs for Asthma

The *Asthma UK* website lists sore tongue, sore throat, hoarseness and thrush (a mouth infection) as side effects of inhalers, while steroid tablets can lower resistance to chickenpox, create mood swings and increase hunger. In 2008 two officials from *The Food and Drug Administration* in America found that asthma sufferers risked death if they continued to use four popular asthma drugs, and advised people of all ages not to take them. A third drug-safety official concluded that two of them could be used by adults but that all four drugs should no longer be used by those under 17 years-old.

Drugs for Arthritic Conditions

The *Arthritis Research UK* website lists the possible side effects of non-steroidal arthritis drugs as stomach upsets, heartburn, indigestion, rashes, headaches, wheeziness, fluid retention and a small increase in the risk of heart attack and stroke. *Voltaren* is one of a class of traditional non-steroidal anti-inflammatories and is prescribed to treat osteoarthritis as well as rheumatoid arthritis and spondylitis. Although it can be helpful, the many possible side effects include an increased risk of a heart attack and stroke, inflammation, bleeding, ulceration and perforation of the stomach, liver problems, jaundice and hepatic failure. Kidney problems, anaemia, fluid retention and oedema may also occur.

Drugs for Behavioural Problems

Drugs for treating ADHD help to normalise levels of chemicals in the brain called neurotransmitters. The side effects include decreased appetite, stomach ache, difficulty falling asleep, irritability, nausea, vomiting, dizziness, tics, allergic reactions, weight loss, increased blood pressure, and psychosis. There have been reliable reports of children in nursery and pre-school being prescribed *Ritalin* unnecessarily, with parents putting pressure on GPs. Because young children's brains are still developing, it is particularly dangerous to give them toxic drugs.

Drugs for Insomnia

Studies have shown that those who take sleeping tablets are a third more likely to die prematurely than those who don't. Prescription and over-the-counter medications to induce sleep all have likely side effects, including dependence, drowsiness, constipation and urinary retention, dry mouth and throat, and balance problems. They may also affect reaction time, alertness and co-ordination, which could result in accidents – a study found that sleeping pills more than doubled the risk of having a car accident. *Melatonin* is recommended to help stabilise sleep patterns, but potential side-effects include headaches, nausea, depression, nightmares and vivid dreams, irritability, abdominal cramps and dizziness. A study found that sleeping pills may increase the risk of contracting pneumonia.

Drugs for Pain

Side effects of aspirin include gastrointestinal bleeding, and sometimes for children, Reye's syndrome. For a few people, aspirin can induce an allergic reaction causing hives, swelling and a headache. Used in many pain-alleviating drugs, codeine could lead to dependency, even after just 3 days. Other potential side effects of codeine are euphoria, itching, nausea, vomiting, drowsiness, dry mouth, urinary retention, depression, constipation, erectile dysfunction and rashes. *Ibuprofen* is an extremely popular non-prescription drug used for fever, inflammation and mild to moderate pain, but possible side effects include stomach pain, diarrhoea, heartburn, ulcers, bleeding, ringing in the ears, dizziness, liver or kidney problems, allergic reactions, and increased blood pressure. High doses over a period can increase the risk of heart attack or stroke.

Drugs for Colds and Flu

In spite of the fact that nothing can cure a cold, heavily advertised drugs are bought in huge numbers. These may mask symptoms to some degree but can have various side effects – antihistamines can cause drowsiness, dizziness, headaches and a dry mouth, while decongestants can increase blood pressure and the heart rate, and possibly cause restlessness, insomnia and anxiety. And because the influenza virus grows poorly at temperatures greater than 37 degrees, bringing a fever down might well prolong the condition.

Drugs for Sexual Problems

Viagra is effective for men with erectile problems, but for some there is a risk of hypertension, heart attacks, and even sudden cardiac deaths. More common side effects include headaches, dizziness, blurred vision, flushing, nasal congestion and indigestion. *Viagra* labelling now includes a warning about the rare occurrence of painful, prolonged erections, advising users to call a doctor if their erection lasts longer than 4 hours.

Drugs for Slimming

The possible side effects of weight-loss drugs include increased blood pressure and heart rate, insomnia, dizziness, fatigue, nausea, dry mouth, and constipation. The drug *Alli* can be obtained over-the-counter at chemists in the UK, though only obese people can buy it. If the user doesn't stick to a low-fat diet, they may well experience sudden "embarrassing leakages". Apart from loose stools, there may be other side effects. These include lower back pain, blood in the urine, urinating less, drowsiness, confusion, mood changes, greater thirst, shortage of breath, nausea, stomach ache and vomiting.

Most appetite suppressants contain caffeine and ephedra. Ephedra is a herb that constricts blood vessels and speeds up the heart and nervous system. Side effects include irritability, increased heart rate, nervousness, insomnia and high blood pressure. It has been linked to strokes, seizures and serious heart problems, and can lead to panic attacks, violent behaviour, hallucinations, breathing problems, seizures, coma, and even death. In 2008 the anti-obesity drug *Rimonabant*, linked to depression and suicide, was approved for use by the NHS. It was banned in America because of safety fears, but can now be prescribed for British patients who cannot use other weight-loss drugs.

Drugs for Menopausal Symptoms

HRT (hormone replacement therapy) increases the risk of developing and subsequently dying from ovarian, breast and endometrial cancer. A study of women taking *Prempro* was abruptly halted by the US federal government when it was found that it raised a woman's risk of stroke by 41%, heart attack by 29%, and breast cancer by 26%.

Other Drug Problems

Some people abuse pharmaceutical drugs – they might use a drug purchased on the internet, a drug prescribed to someone else, or take more than has been advised. Many become addicted to them and some overdose on them. Millions of Americans abuse pharmaceutical drugs, and in 2009 it was reported that at least 30,000 Britons were addicted to painkillers. The non-medical use or abuse of prescription drugs has increased exponentially in the last 20 years and has become a major public health issue in the USA, the UK and other developed countries. Hundreds of internet sites sell these drugs without a prescription. They may relieve anxiety and pain, but they can be lethal and just as addictive as illegal drugs like cocaine. People are admitted to emergency rooms in the UK every day with an overdose, some intentional and some not. *Co-proxamol*, a popular painkiller, was withdrawn from the UK market in 2005 because it was too easy to take an overdose – it had been connected to 300 to 400 deaths.

Sometimes drugs can have unintended consequences. Particular anti-schizophrenia drugs have led to obesity and diabetes, and a drug to treat Parkinson's disease caused patients to become sex addicts or pathological gamblers. The possible effects of drug combinations are rarely tested, but the synergistic effect of two or more drugs can have serious and maybe fatal results – studies have found that *Paracetamol* with large amounts of caffeine or alcohol can increase the risk of liver damage, and the combination of hay-fever, pain-relieving and sleep medications could be dangerous.

The overuse of antibiotics has led to bacteria developing greater and greater resistance to them. 17 strains of Staphlococcus have developed resistance to the main antibiotics. In 2011 *The World Health Organisation* issued a warning that resistant bacteria are spreading faster than new drugs are being developed to combat them. In the European Union up to 25,000 people a year die from these bacteria. Hospital-acquired, infectious diseases in Britain cost the NHS £1 billion a year.

The Reasons for Pharmaceutical Drug Overload

Though prevention is by far the best approach to health, medical services become involved with people's health almost exclusively from the point of diagnosis – and drug companies are keen to convince us that their products can cure every disease or illness. In the capitalist system there is far more money to be made treating people with drugs once they are ill, so pharmaceutical companies are quite content to see their sales increase in line with ill-health while lacklustre and futile attempts are made by governmental agencies to promote less indulgent lifestyles. If people ate mainly natural food, exercised more and created a better balance in their lives, they would be far healthier and in need of far less treatment – with drugs or anything else.

Marketing

The pharmaceutical industry has managed to "medicalise" life's problems to such a degree that most people now believe that taking drugs is normal, that they can fix any health problem – as opposed to merely mask symptoms – and that their side effects are minimal. Instead of rest, sleep, or other natural remedies for the stress and minor aches and pains we experience in our daily lives, most of us turn to drugs, even though their ineffectiveness to cure is clear – the ever-increasing drug use over at least 100 years has been more than matched by the rise in the level of ill-health and disease.

The media, together with politicians and mainstream medical opinion, have helped foster the view that the pharmaceutical industry is trying to make us all healthy, when in fact it is primarily concerned with making money. It seems that pharmaceutical companies spend at least as much on marketing their products as on research and development, which helps to make them extremely profitable. Their most recent ploy is to promote some drugs as "prevention". Just in case you are more likely to suffer a heart attack, don't bother to change your lifestyle, just take an aspirin every day. If a high level of cholesterol runs in the family, take statins, and if you're more likely to get breast cancer, take *Tamoxifen*.

The Conventional Medical Approach

During the previous century medicine became allopathic, which involves treating, masking and suppressing symptoms instead of dealing with the real causes of ill-health. Despite irrefutable research findings that diet, exercise and avoidance of stress can prevent most illness, the conventional medical approach continues to blame "outside" agencies such as microbes and viruses for the diseases and conditions we suffer from – and tries to destroy them or hammer them into submission. We have all been conditioned to believe that drugs and surgery are the answer to our health problems, but a headache doesn't mean your body is "deficient in aspirin". It probably means you're tense or you got hopelessly drunk last night. Blocked arteries and thickening blood doesn't mean you have a "deficiency of *Warfarin*". It means you've lived an indulgent lifestyle, and the way to reverse the resulting negative effects is to change it.

Apart from not actually dealing with the underlying reasons for ill-health, all drugs have one or more side effects. And in many cases, illnesses would be self-limiting – suppressing symptoms by taking an over-the-counter medication can in fact make things worse because it doesn't tackle the cause of the problem. Symptoms we often associate with illness are actually the body correcting imbalances and curing us naturally. Fever kills off invading bacteria, coughing gets rid of excess mucus, inflammation protects the injured part while repair takes place, and a rash is the body getting rid of toxins through the skin.

Modern medicine is extremely effective for emergencies and correcting "mechanical" malfunctions of the body, but still at a relatively primitive stage when dealing with the more subtle, systemic problems at the cellular level – like cancer, heart disease, diabetes and dementia. For millennia prior to the allopathic approach, healers used holistic methods with natural therapies. They treated patients mainly with non-toxic substances, dietary changes, exercise, and the empathic healing power of the healer over the patient. This gentler and holistic approach to good health focuses on prevention and works with the body's immune system and its built-in power of healing.

Life Should Be Easy

People have been led to believe that life should be easy, and that they shouldn't have to use self-discipline, effort and patience to maintain good health.

The "Quick Fix"

People have been led to believe that there is a quick, medicinal fix to any health problem, physical or mental.

Ignorance

People have been led to believe it's just the luck of the draw why ill-health occurs, and are not informed about potential "real" cures of their ills. They are not usually given the right or sufficient guidance and psychotherapy for mental problems, or nutritional and exercise advice for physical problems.

How to Avoid Pharmaceutical Drug Overload

Be aware that drugs are unnatural for the body to deal with, mask symptoms and do not address the cause of ill-health. Once you understand that personal choices are the cause of the majority of illness in the developed world, you'll examine your own behaviour and make changes before any health conditions become chronic. Then you will rarely have to take drugs, and if you do, only for a brief period.

- You can improve your health and strengthen your immune system by adopting a moderate diet, doing regular exercise, and having enough sleep to feel refreshed. We all need to avoid harmful habits and instead get into good ones. Try making just small changes at first i.e. walking briskly for at least a mile every day, eating more fruit and vegetables, and buying less fast and processed food.

- If problems at work or in relationships are causing you stress, they need to be faced and discussed. If solutions cannot be found, you must be brave enough to make changes. If you are suffering from lasting depression and are unable to make the necessary changes that will improve your situation and view of life, try visiting a counsellor before taking drugs. Mind-altering substances should be the last resort, and then be taken for as short a time as possible.

- If something needs to be done in the short term, instead of pharmaceuticals, try natural substances. They may take some time to work because their action is much more subtle, so be patient and give your body time to heal, to correct any imbalance. You could use rest, fluids and time to "cure" the common cold, and to help you sleep try a warm bath or cup of herbal tea rather than take a sleeping pill – and stay away from caffeine and alcohol many hours before bedtime. Go for a brisk walk or have a cold shower rather than take a stimulant. In 2007 an American study found that a dose of honey was a more effective remedy for children's coughs than over-the-counter medicines. You might try herbal and other natural substances for various ailments after investigating their efficacy online or elsewhere. And before resorting to surgery or drugs, "alternative" treatments could also be worth trying, such as acupuncture for migraines.

- It is better to do all you can to prevent health problems occurring and thereby keep the use of drugs to a minimum, but their moderate and occasional use for pain relief – and of course for emergencies – is perfectly acceptable. If you sometimes experience severe asthmatic breathing problems, powerful drugs should be on hand – though you could also try changing your diet by limiting acid-forming foods and increasing alkali-forming foods, use ionisers to take allergens and contaminants out of the air, get more fresh air, sun, and water, and do breathing exercises.

- Because of the potential danger to their foetus, pregnant women should be extremely cautious about taking any drugs at all, and parents should avoid giving their children antibiotics or any other drugs except where absolutely necessary. They should be fed well, encouraged to exercise daily, and allowed to go out and "play in the dirt" to develop their immune system. Drugs always have side effects, and children's developing bodies and minds are probably more vulnerable to synthetic substances invading their system. And children, like adults, need to get used to the idea that drugs only mask symptoms, and should only be used in an emergency situation.

SUPPLEMENTS

"The nutritionists and the multi-billion dollar food supplement industry tell people they've got food intolerances, hidden dietary deficiencies or frightening disease risks for which they have a solution in a pill."

(Ben Goldacre)

A sizeable minority of people in developed countries has recognised the limitations and possible dangers of taking pharmaceutical drugs. The growing distrust of the processed food that we eat, the confusion in both the scientific community and the general public about nutrition, together with the suspicion about the pharmaceutical industry's motives and aggressive marketing techniques, have resulted in people turning to herbal medicines and supplements. Patients are often not advised to make lifestyle changes or told about alternative treatments and products because doctors are largely influenced by material published by or sponsored by the pharmaceutical industry. Medical schools concentrate on diagnosis and drugs, so doctors will have little or no training in nutrition and are unlikely to know much about herbs, vitamin and mineral supplements or "alternative" treatments. Along with the most important factors for good health – the right diet and sufficient exercise – they are considered marginal.

Most people do little research before trying products and therapies. Many follow what others recommend and see what happens. It's largely guesswork and hit and miss. Though the best path to tread is that of prevention, many are reluctant to change their lifestyle. Just like others in the "health industry", the herbal and vitamin companies have grown large, driven by the priority to make big profits for their shareholders. They also pander to the public's desire for magic bullets – take one or several of their products and you'll be healthier and live longer. Unfortunately health doesn't work like that. Though drug or vitamin interventions may occasionally be useful – or even vital – for short-term deficiencies or problems, the key to most people's good health is the right lifestyle habits pursued for the long term. The huge sales of vitamin supplements and herbal medicines, especially considering that there is little solid evidence for their efficacy, suggests that there is an "overload" in this area too – though on balance these products are not as potentially harmful as pharmaceutical drugs.

The Scale of Supplements

The burgeoning supplement industry has shown every sign of being as profit-driven and ruthless as the pharmaceutical industry – in the 1990s a vast price-fixing cartel was uncovered amongst firms selling vitamin supplements. And just like the pharmaceutical industry, those in the supplement industry are also quick to issue legal threats when any criticism is made.

- The global vitamin and supplement market was worth $68 billion in 2009.

- Almost a third of Britons took vitamins or other some kind of supplement in 2008. In 2009 the UK market was worth £670 million and is expected to reach £788 million in 2017.

The biggest sellers worldwide were multivitamins, B vitamins, vitamin C, vitamins D and H (biotin), vitamin E and vitamin A/carotenoids. The most popular minerals were calcium, magnesium, iron, chromium, potassium, zinc and selenium. The most popular herbs and botanical products were noni juice, garlic, mangosteen juice, green tea, saw palmetto, echinacea, ginkgo biloba, ginseng, milk thistle and psyllium. The best selling specialties were glucosamine and/or chondroitin, homeopathics, fish or animal oils, CoQ10, probiotics, plant oils, digestive enzymes, MSM and SAMe.

The Problems of Supplements

Many vitamins and supplements are advertised as "natural", but may well contain coal tar, preservatives, artificial colourings, disintegrants (aids to dissolving in liquid), coating materials, and a range of other potentially harmful additives. And under the microscope, natural and synthetic vitamins may look similar to some chemists, but the body doesn't assimilate them in the same way. Studies of vitamins C and E have shown that the naturally occurring forms can be absorbed more readily and are more biologically active.

Common sense would suggest that consuming things in their natural form will be better for our health, because they and humans evolved together. Our bodies need the "life force" in natural vitamins, which involves their synergistic effects – they are biological complexes. It seems that in addition to ascorbic acid, for example, "real" vitamin C needs to include bio-flavonoids along with other naturally occurring compounds like mineral cofactors. A natural vitamin has been described as "a working process consisting of the nutrient, enzymes, coenzymes, antioxidants and trace mineral activators".

Lack of Effectiveness

A standard and consistent criticism of those in "alternative medicine" by those in the orthodox field is that few of their claims stand up to scientific scrutiny. Studies support this view: two types of echinacea provided no benefit in the treatment and prevention of colds, saw palmetto was no better than placebo for treating urinary problems, glucosamine alone or taken in combination with chondroitin did not benefit sufferers of osteoarthritis, the effectiveness of St. John's wort for treating major depression was shown to be questionable, and multi-vitamins don't protect against heart attacks or cancer.

Despite their apparent lack of effectiveness, sales of these "alternative" treatment products remain high. Some standard drugs and procedures, however, have also been shown to be hardly more effective than placebos. Orthodox practitioners should be more concerned with preventative measures and dealing with the whole person, while alternative practitioners should be more scientifically rigorous. In both fields, the power of the mind has not perhaps been recognised, understood, appreciated or analysed sufficiently – it seems, for example, that placebos work even when people *know* they're placebos.

Potential Health Dangers

Some believe that if a particular herb or vitamin might be beneficial, then a lot of it would be much more so. Unfortunately this is not true and sometimes could actually be dangerous, though unlike pharmaceutical drugs, there is a relatively low risk of harm in taking herb and vitamin supplements. There have been concerns that herbs and supplements might reduce the efficacy of orthodox treatment – St. John's wort, for example, seems to interfere with drugs to treat cancer and HIV. A study of the effect of taking dietary supplements published in 2011 showed that some might even result in a slightly higher mortality risk.

Diehl and Ludington suggest that large doses of vitamin and mineral supplements could be dangerous because they may interfere with the absorption of other nutrients. They believe that separating nutrients from food and concentrating anything in the food chain will probably upset the natural balance. There is no documented evidence that vitamin and mineral supplements make people more energetic or have any effect on stress. Energy comes from food fuels – carbohydrates like grains, legumes and potatoes – not from vitamins and minerals. And we need these micro-nutrients in only very miniscule amounts.

How to Avoid Supplement Overload

Vitamins, minerals and herb supplements should not normally be required unless we have a specific health problem from some deficiency or other. Humans and our biped predecessors consumed only what nature provided, living their lives and evolving over millions of years without supplement pills. Don't be influenced by the marketing claims of supplement manufacturers.

- Experiment with changes to your diet and lifestyle before buying vitamins or supplements.

- If you follow a moderate and balanced lifestyle, you shouldn't need to use supplements. You will achieve and maintain good health if you eat well, exercise regularly, rest fully, avoid too much stress, pursue meaningful and satisfying work, and have a sympathetic and supportive family and wider social circle.

- A balanced diet should supply your body with what it needs in the long term. It may well be that a change of diet might help you feel more positive and energetic, and consulting a specialist dietician could prove useful. If you continually feel lethargic or have some other problem that won't go away, you should of course go to your doctor for a check-up. And if a blood test shows a lack of a particular mineral or vitamin, the appropriate supplement should be taken for as short a time as necessary.

POLLUTION

"For the first time in the history of the world, every human being is now subjected to contact with dangerous chemicals, from the moment of conception until death."

(Rachel Carson)

The benefits we enjoy because of science, industry and technology are undeniable. Brilliant entrepreneurs, engineers and scientists have enabled those of us in the developed nations to have comfortable and interesting lives. Unfortunately, however, too little attention was paid regarding the possible detrimental effect of their activities on human health. The result of the machinations of these clever and well-meaning pioneers who believed in "progress", confident that they could conquer and then control nature, is that our environment has been polluted to an ever-increasing degree by dangerous substances. Chemicals and metals that can be toxic to us and other life on Earth have been unleashed through laboratory and industrial activities. In his book *The Hundred-Year Lie*, Randall Fitzgerald puts forward the view that we have been "the unwitting guinea pigs in a dangerous long-term scientific experiment".

Though it is difficult to measure the precise detrimental effect of environmental toxins, and though they are unlikely to debilitate us quickly, studies suggest we should pay more attention to the potential damage they pose to our health. Some experts claim that virtually all of us are in a state of toxic overload, which contributes to the rising level of illness. It seems that small toxic exposures each day can exceed and even incapacitate the body's ability to detoxify, causing these chemicals to accumulate enough to make people sick. According to American scientists from *The Environmental Protection Agency*, in just our daily diet, total toxic residues can exceed 500% of the recommended daily maximum – even if each individual food is within "safe" limits.

Most of us blithely assume our leaders would not allow a situation to occur where contaminants could endanger our health. Thus we are generally unaware of the potential danger and make little effort to avoid them. Without monitoring our behaviour and choosing carefully, we might constantly be eating foods with trace toxins, constantly drinking water with trace toxins, constantly using personal products with trace toxins, and constantly breathing toxic air. And by the end of each day, these contaminants could often reach a dangerous total.

Safety Limits

Over the last 50 years or so, in an effort to reassure the general public, scientists have set safety limits. The rule of thumb for setting public health standards is "the dose makes the poison", i.e. any chemical can be toxic if you eat, drink, or absorb too much of it. Indeed, even chemicals naturally present in our food and drinks are toxic if consumed in sufficiently large quantities. Research suggests, however, that new synthetic chemicals may well be biologically destructive at extremely low levels, and sometimes very low doses of certain compounds can induce stronger toxic responses than much higher doses.

The public's confidence would be dented if they knew that setting a safety standard level is affected not just by health studies, but by the "technical and financial feasibility" of achieving that particular level. Though most physicians and toxicologists assure us that our immune systems and healthy livers and kidneys will keep us safe from nearly all levels of toxic accumulation, *The Health Protection Agency* in the UK has admitted that the long-term consequences of low-level, chronic exposure to chemical and poisons are not well understood. And *The American Institute of Biological Sciences* has expressed concern about chronic effects of long-term exposure to relatively low doses of contaminants. Perhaps of more concern than the arbitrary level of the bar set for negative effects from individual chemicals, the effects of two or more chemicals interacting together are usually unknown – there are too many possible combinations and permutations for the synergistic effects to be calculated.

Setting safety levels is certainly difficult. Different species may respond in different ways to toxic chemicals, some individuals are more sensitive to a particular chemical, and the sensitivity to contaminants varies between life stages. Foetuses, infants and children are often more sensitive to some chemicals than adults. Ideally, all public health standards would be designed to protect the most sensitive sections of the population, but too little is known about the effects of most contaminants to tailor standards in this way. Some chemicals mimic natural hormones produced by our bodies to stimulate or regulate functions such as growth, digestion, reproduction, and sexual function. These "false" hormones can disrupt crucial life functions at doses much lower than those previously thought to be safe, especially in foetuses and children. More research is needed on the potential impacts of chemical exposure on health, growth, reproduction, and behaviour of individuals at various life stages. Scientific uncertainties about chemical toxicity and possible long-term negative effects should persuade us to question safety levels and exercise greater caution.

The Scale of Pollution

So much of what we ingest and utilise regularly today is relatively "unnatural", i.e. has been isolated, modified, purified or synthesised by man rather than being in its original form provided by nature.

- Each year, about 10,000 chemicals are being synthesised by industry and added to the over 1 million already in existence. *The European Commission* has admitted that 99% of these substances are not adequately regulated.

There is not even proper safety information on 85% of them, and only a fraction has actually been tested for human toxicity. So the pollution potential is huge and continually increasing. Because of our industrial activities, all living creatures as well as humans now have to deal with thousands of toxic compounds in the form of inorganic chemicals and toxic metals that are everywhere. The air we breathe will usually be polluted by toxic fumes, the processed food we eat contains synthetic additives, the soil, the oceans, rivers, and lakes – and subsequently the water we drink and the fish and meat we eat – are polluted by heavy metals and chemicals from industrial and personal use, and our bodies and brains are subjected to emissions from our many and ubiquitous entertainment devices and technological aids.

Various studies have found dozens of particular toxic compounds in people's blood and urine, and many chemicals persist in the body because they cannot be broken down rapidly or excreted. They accumulate in fat cells, the liver, kidneys and brain, in the thyroid and adrenal glands, in the central nervous system, and in the bones – and can remain in the body for decades or even a lifetime. In 2010 a US committee was told that the number of cancers caused by toxic chemicals was "grossly underestimated", and that Americans faced grievous harm from largely unregulated chemicals that contaminate air, water and food. Of particular concern were the hundreds of chemicals found in the umbilical cords of newborns. And substantial public costs were associated with toxic exposures, amounting to tens of billions of dollars.

The Dangers of Pollution

Most people probably don't worry about toxins because they blissfully assume that anything on the market for consumption or use "must" be safe. Of those who might be concerned and even investigate, many will make little effort to avoid toxins once they've learnt that the levels have been officially sanctioned. But because small toxic exposures each day may exceed and even incapacitate our body's ability to detoxify, they might cause us to become sick and experience headaches, depression, sleepless nights, fatigue, arthritis and possibly more serious health problems.

- *The World Health Organisation* estimated that globally 2.4 million people die each year from the effects of air pollution, with 1.5 million of these deaths from indoor air pollution.

Most pesticides, herbicides and fungicides accumulate in fatty tissues and tend to settle in the bones, while fluoride builds up in the brain, thyroid, and bones. Eventually they might prevent the body assimilating and utilising essential minerals such as iron, calcium and magnesium. This in turn could cause enzyme dysfunction, nutritional deficiencies, hormonal imbalances, neurological disorders, and could even lead to auto-immune disorders, cancer, and other debilitating chronic conditions. At the very least, the body's immune system has more to deal with, and general health will be lower than otherwise.

Human Fertility

Biologists have become alarmed with the gender aberrations and decline in human fertility by hormone disruption, and some believe a mass extinction of living things may even occur – with man's activities as the main cause. A study on rats suggested that endocrine disruption from chemical exposure during pregnancy could be passed on in some way to future generations. The offspring of males with low sperm counts also had low sperm counts. We know little about the short-term implications of our actions, but even less about those for the long term. We may not only be altering many things in our world, we may also be changing ourselves.

- More than 50 chemicals in common usage have been identified as "hormone disrupters", which scientists say may be the cause of a 33% decline both in sperm counts and healthy sperm.

12% of the US reproductive population is experiencing infertility and the rate is rising overall, particularly among women under 25. Similar effects of infertility, along with demasculation and birth defects, have been documented among wildlife populations. It seems that low levels of exposures to chemical contaminants are causing these changes in humans and animal life, and that we've underestimated the synergistic effects of two or more chemicals.

Studies have found that the fertility of men and women is being disrupted by toxins, resulting in genitalia abnormalities. In American and European boys, problems like abnormal penises and symptoms of feminisation have increased by 40% since the 1960s, in developed countries there has been a decline in male births, and from 1980 to 2000 tubal pregnancies increased by 400%. IVF clinics have reported a large increase in the number of abnormal embryos produced by young, healthy women in their 20s – nearly 80% of the embryos examined. A study published in 2012 showed a huge decrease in the sperm count of French men, which is indicative of the global situation. The recent upsurge in men seeking breast reduction surgery in London may be due to hormones in food and female hormones from contraceptive pills flushed into the sewage system then recycled in tap water. 1 in 6 girls now enter puberty by the time they are 8 years-old, and some authorities believe toxins in food may be one cause – and the earlier onset of puberty seems to increase the risk of breast cancer. Women who live near to where pesticides are sprayed on crops face a large increase in the risk of miscarriage, and toxins in car exhausts has been shown to cause a significant fertility reduction in test animals.

Food Pollution

There are a whole host of additives used in processed food, many of which are synthetic. It could be argued that the greater number used, the further away from "natural" the product becomes, the less nutritious it is likely to be, and probably the more dangerous to human health. The list of food additives is longer than the layman probably realises, and includes acids, acidity regulators, anti-caking agents, anti-foaming agents, anti-oxidants, bulking agents, food colouring, colour retention agents, emulsifiers, flavours, flavour enhancers, flour treatment agents, humectants (to keep food moist), tracer gas and preservatives (to extend shelf life), stabilisers, sweeteners and thickeners.

Colourings

Colourings are found in a wide range of foods and drinks. These include beer, sauces, puddings, sweets, children's food and drinks, chocolate, buns, toothpaste, canned fruit, vegetables and wines. 23 of the current 45 'E' numbered colourings are banned in one or more countries, yet are still available in the UK. A further 21 colourings and 49 other E-numbered food additives (including sweeteners) commonly found in children's foods have been linked to behavioural problems. Colourings have been linked to other conditions such as eczema and asthma.

Artificial Sweeteners

Some people have an allergy or sensitivity to the sucralose molecule in the sweetener *Splenda*, and can suffer from skin rashes and flushing, agitation and panic, dizziness and numbness, diarrhoea and muscle aches, headaches, intestinal cramping, bladder problems, and stomach pain. Nobody knows how the majority is affected. Aspartame is the main ingredient in *Equal* and *NutraSweet*, and though research found that it produced dangerous side effects in rodents, *The Food and Drug Administration* chose not to take these findings into account and approved it for public use in America. The same side effects have increasingly appeared in those vulnerable to the chemical structure of aspartame. Evidence is also emerging that the artificial sweeteners in soft drinks may cause brain tumours and neurological diseases such as Parkinson's and Alzheimer's. Their increased use has been matched by the increased occurrence of these diseases.

MSG

MSG (monosodium glutamate) is a common flavour enhancer in processed and restaurant food – and not just in Chinese establishments. It has been found to be addictive and to cause weight gain. It has been linked to diabetes, migraines and headaches, autism, ADHD and Alzheimer's disease. It was also found to cause infertility problems in animals.

Hormones in Meat and Fish

Growth hormones make livestock gain weight more quickly on less feed and can decrease the amount of fat in meat. They are commonly used in the USA but are banned from use in the European Union because of the difficulties in determining "safe" levels of growth hormone residues in meat. These hormones are known to cause reproductive dysfunction and cancers in humans. In 2010 *The Food and Drug Administration* recommended phasing out of drugs used to foster animal growth.

Antibiotics in Meat

In both America and Europe, agribusinesses regularly treat their livestock with antibiotics to prevent and treat disease and illness caused by their cramped and unnatural living conditions. Pigs and farmed fish reared intensively are routinely given large amounts of drugs to keep them healthy (or at least alive). Not only do residues of these drugs enter our bodies when we eat the meat or fish, they also increase the antibiotic resistance of bacteria that we contend with.

Toxins in Fish

For some time it has been known that certain types of fish, such as swordfish, shark, king mackerel and tilefish, can contain high levels of methylmercury.

- A study reported in 2013 found that 84% of fish have unsafe levels of mercury.

The level of mercury could be dangerous to our health, especially for the developing nervous system of a foetus or infant. PCBs (polychlorinated biphenyls) have also been found in fish, and these too are dangerous. It takes around a year for the body to get rid of mercury, and around 6 years to eliminate PCBs. A study found that chemicals in British waters affect the fertility of fish and may have an adverse effect on those eating them. An American study found that eating fish such as grouper, snapper, amberjack and barracuda – that feed on smaller fish which have eaten toxic marine algae – can cause nausea, vomiting, vertigo and joint pain. Another American study found that river fish were contaminated by chemicals in pharmaceuticals and personal care products via waste water from treatment facilities.

GM (Genetically Modified) Ingredients

At least 70% of the processed foods in American food stores contain one or more genetically engineered ingredient that has never been tested for potential harm. European countries have banned virtually all GM foodstuffs because, as with so many other unnatural substances, nobody knows what the effects of consuming them will be in the long term. Biotech proponents believe GM crops are vital to feed the developing world, while opponents claim that traditional farming methods can be used on integrated farms – combining fish, crops and livestock – to produce abundant food with zero toxic inputs and emissions.

Air Pollution (outside)

Air pollution includes chemicals, particulate matter or biological materials, as well as radiation. Some air pollution can occur naturally, like sand or dust storms created by strong winds, ash and sulphur from an eruption of a volcano, or methane from animals and radon gas from the ground, but the most common air pollution is caused by industry and vehicle exhaust emissions. These can affect people only temporarily by creating repugnant smells, but can be dangerous to human health in the long term. The nuclear industry can pollute the air (and soil or water) with radiation, as may communication technology. Our planet is now bathed in a synthetic chemical soup. Toxic molecules attach themselves to dust which is carried around by wind, particularly to the Arctic Circle. The breast milk of Inuit mothers contains

PCBs and mercury. Children in these colder climes suffer high rates of infectious diseases because their immune systems are compromised even more.

Air pollution can cause difficulty in breathing, wheezing, coughing and aggravate existing respiratory and cardiac conditions. This leads to more medical intervention and even premature death.

- In 2011 it was estimated that air pollution kills 50,000 British people every year, and on average reduces their lifespan by 7 to 8 months. In pollution "hot spots", lifespan reduction rises to about 8 years.

- Health costs of air pollution in the UK are estimated to be as much as £20 billion a year.

Exhaust Emissions

Toxic fumes, whether from factories or traffic, are not good for our health. Most of us, especially in large, urban centres, are breathing in exhaust fumes from cars, vans, lorries and buses on a daily basis. Children regularly exposed to traffic fumes are more likely to develop asthma, and the development of the lungs is hindered in children aged 10 to 18 – researchers suspect that diesel emissions are responsible. Traffic jams create more fumes which can trigger heart attacks from breathing in soot particles emitted from exhausts. German scientists estimate that 1 in 12 heart attacks are caused by traffic pollution, and the risk of suffering a heart attack triples in the first hour of exposure. Tests on people in an enclosed room indicated that the long-term effects of exposure to nanoparticles (extremely small particles) may interfere with normal brain function and information processing. A study found that polluted air can lower children's IQ level. Dense pollution by ground-level ozone raises the risk by 30% of people dying from lung diseases. Ozone, which forms from vehicle exhausts in sunlight, can lead to pneumonia, emphysema and bronchitis.

Nuclear Radiation

Studies have shown that living near nuclear reactors increases the incidence of cancer, including breast cancer and childhood cancers like leukaemia. It has been officially accepted in Germany that children living near nuclear power plants develop cancer more frequently than those living further away.

Water Pollution

Water pollution occurs when pollutants are discharged directly or indirectly into water bodies without adequate treatment to remove harmful compounds. It has been claimed that contamination of oceans, rivers, streams, lakes and groundwater is the leading worldwide cause of deaths and diseases. Water pollution is of particular concern in developing countries, accounting for the deaths of more than 14,000 people per day, but developed countries have problems too.

- In 2013, only 27% of the UK's open water bodies were classified "good status" as set down by the European Union's *Water Framework Directive*.

Farms, industry and homes all contribute to water pollution. When it rains, farm pesticides and fertilisers come off plants and end up in the rivers, lakes or oceans, killing ocean plants and animals. Factory farms also contribute pollutants like pharmaceuticals, antibiotics and hormones. Wastes from industry include mercury, lead, arsenic, and petrochemicals. Oil, heavy metals and various chemicals get into water bodies because of spills and leaks from landfills, dumps and mines.

The residues of what we use in our daily activities are discharged from our homes. These include chemical detergents, batteries, plastics, oil, antifreeze, lawn and other chemicals – as well as sewage. And when sewage pipes share their space with storm water drains and rainfall causes the pipes to overflow, sewage waste mixes with the storm water drain, flowing into lakes or rivers. Lead – which can damage the brain, kidneys, and reproductive system and cause birth defects – may also pollute water. House and car paint, lead batteries, fishing lures, certain parts of bullets, some ceramic ware, water pipes and fixtures all give off lead. Excess petrol from boats' engines pollutes the water, but cars pollute the ocean even more – exhaust materials fall in the form of "acid rain".

Personal care products and drugs also contribute to water pollution. In America, recent testing showed that 60% of rivers and streams contained high levels of *Prozac*, *Ritalin*, and antibiotics. Excess prescription drugs are flushed directly into water bodies or into sewer and septic systems where the chemicals then leach into ground water. And research has shown that musk fragrances (in shampoos, air fresheners and detergents) are not removed by sewage treatment and are absorbed by fish, mussels and other invertebrates – it is highly likely that our natural defences are weakened or compromised when we ingest these chemicals. Pollution directly affects ocean organisms and indirectly affects human health. Toxic waste is passed along the food chain and into our seafood.

Drinking Water

Tap water can be contaminated by industrial waste, the underground disposal of extremely hazardous toxins through injection wells, and leaking underground fuel tanks, plus the agricultural runoff of pesticides, the toxic runoff from streets and rooftops of chemicals used in paving and building materials, and the radioactive contamination of radium, a by-product of the decay of uranium, used in nuclear power plants.

- Though there are controls and tests on water quality, most tap water still contains traces of arsenic, fluoride, chlorine and a host of other unhealthy toxins.

A report found that tap water between 1998 and 2003 in 42 American states contained many contaminants that were dangerous, if not technically illegal. Of the 141 contaminants identified, 52 were linked to cancer, 41 to reproductive toxicity, 36 to developmental toxicity and 16 to immune system damage. An average household uses 18 toiletries and cleaning products a week, and about 10 synthetic chemicals are in each. Tap water not only contains fluoride and chlorine, both possible carcinogens, but usually traces of herbicides and pharmaceutical drugs as well. Chlorine is one of the most discussed contaminants in drinking water. Its purpose is to kill living organisms, so even small amounts ingested every day could build up and cause harm. Many people believe bottled water to be purer than tap water, but 25% of bottled water is in fact tap water – and plastic bottles can leach chemicals into the water. They are often made of PVC (polyvinyl chloride), which is itself an environmental hazard. Independent studies of bottled water have discovered fluoride, phthalates, trihalomethanes and arsenic, either present from the bottling process or from the bottles themselves.

Soil Pollution

Soil contamination can be caused by the rupture of underground storage tanks, the application of pesticides, the percolation of contaminated surface water to subsurface strata, the dumping of oil and fuel, the leaching of wastes from landfills, and the direct discharge of industrial wastes. Arsenic is a dangerous poison, yet it is widely used and therefore a frequent contaminant – the glass industry uses arsenic to eliminate a green colour caused by impurities of iron compounds. Soil pollution from heavy metals occurs when ores are mined to extract metals such as tin, silver, nickel, lead, iron, chromium and copper. Most of these metals occur naturally as ions in the soils, and though some metals, such as copper, iron, and zinc, are necessary for plant growth, high concentrations will render the land unproductive.

The still extensive use of pesticides and herbicides means some degree of soil contamination will in turn find its way into what we eat – though food that is grown "organically" will have extremely low pesticide residues. Another worrying problem of soil pollution is the effect on animals. A study in Florida found that male toads were turning female because of exposure to a number of chemicals in a heavily farmed part of the state. And there appears to be a link between pesticides and children's behavioural problems.

- A study found that pesticide exposure is strongly associated with an increased risk of ADHD in children.

An analysis of children's urine found that those with the highest levels of dialkyl phosphates – the breakdown products of organo-phosphate pesticides – also had the highest incidence of ADHD. Overall, there was a 35% increase in the chance of developing ADHD with every tenfold increase in urinary concentration of the pesticide residues. Another study linked the organophosphate insecticide *Chlorpyrifos*, used on some fruits and vegetables, with delays in learning rates, reduced physical co-ordination, and behavioural problems in children, especially ADHD.

Workplace Pollution

If workers regularly handle substances or face fumes that are toxic, their health may well suffer. Occupations that involve chemicals have been shown to affect fertility and cause birth defects as well as other health problems, some serious like cancer. Those at risk include microelectronics assembly workers (because of chemical solvents used to clean components), nurse anaesthetists, painters, dentists and dental assistants, those working in the aircraft industry who handle paints or chemical solvents, firemen (because of the toxic smoke from the burning of carpets, furniture, paints and plastics), printers, textile workers, dry cleaners, welders, those in the manufacturing of synthetics, and other workers exposed to lead, mercury, cadmium, antibiotics, rubber, formaldehyde, polyvinyl alcohol, benzene, (found in gasoline), cleaning solvents, or adhesives.

Roofers or sheet metal workers who work with rubber and plastic products, or those employed in cleaning businesses, are at greater risk of developing brain cancer. Hairdressers, machinists, textile workers, printers, metal workers, painters, and those in the chemical, rubber and leather industries have a higher risk of bladder cancer, and stained glass workers, lead smelters, and potters may get lead poisoning. High risk industries for bronchial and asthma problems are the construction, rubber, plastics and synthetics, metal, and printing industries.

Studies have shown that those exposed to low levels of pesticides, like amateur gardeners, are 9% more likely to develop Parkinson's disease, while those with high exposure – like farmers – are 39% more at risk. And women with breast cancer were three times more likely to have worked on farms when younger – perhaps because developing breast tissue in teenage girls may be more vulnerable to pesticides and other toxic agents. Breast cancer risk was also particularly high among women who went on to work in car factories or hospitals, where they might be exposed to solvents and hormonally active chemicals.

Home Pollution

You may be surprised to learn that the home environment can be dangerous to your health. The products that surround us in our houses and flats, including the myriad of personal products we use on a daily basis, may well contain toxic substances or emit something toxic. Furniture, carpets, cleaning materials, air fresheners, personal hygiene products, cosmetics, mobile phones and the multitude of machines and gizmos can all contribute to a toxic environment.

Personal Hygiene and Cosmetics

Our bodies contain many toxins, chemicals, parasites, fungus, bacteria and yeast that, if not cleansed from our system, might well cause health problems or even develop into major illnesses. Unfortunately however, the powerful products we use to cleanse ourselves also have potential health dangers.

- We use an average of 9 personal-care products daily, containing about 126 chemical ingredients.

The skin can absorb up to 60% of what is put on it, so we need to be careful about the kind and amount of soaps, deodorants, perfumes and make-up we use. And soaps containing animal fat may cause the pores of the skin to clog, thereby trapping chemicals and toxins in the body. There are about 7 chemicals in deodorants, including aluminium, parabens (a preservative), propylene glycol (a lubricant and suspected cancer agent) and some labelled as "fragrance". Body lotions contain chemicals that drive toxins from other toiletries deeper into the flesh. A study found that women who shave their underarms and use deodorant may be at more risk of getting breast cancer – and the more zealous the underarm regime, the younger the women were when first diagnosed. Previously preservatives used in anti-perspirants and deodorants had been found in some tumours. And research suggested that young boys between 4 and 10 using soap and hair gel products with lavender in them were at risk of growing breasts – lavender seems to have hormone-like properties that mimic the effects of the female hormone oestrogen.

Some toothpaste ingredients may be harmful to human health. Sodium lauryl sulphate is a detergent and suspected gastrointestinal or liver toxicant, and may also increase the risk of mouth ulcers and oral cancer. *Triclosan*, also an irritant, is associated with a rise in "superbugs" that are resistant to many antiseptics and antibiotics. Silica, an abrasive, can build up under the surface of the gums causing small nodules of inflamed tissue, leaving the gums more vulnerable to infection. Fluoride, mentioned above in relation to the water pollution, is highlighted by manufacturers as a reason to buy their toothpaste, but there is little evidence to show it protects teeth. Studies do however link it with allergic reactions and a host of illnesses, including oral cancers, gastro-oesophageal reflux disease, bone problems, diabetes, thyroid malfunction, mental impairment and dental fluorisis, which mottles and discolours the teeth. Research has also suggested that alcohol-based mouthwashes may increase the risk of throat and mouth cancers by changing the pH of the mouth and stripping away the throat's protective mucous membrane. The testing of cosmetic ingredients is a requirement in Europe, and many have been banned. In the USA manufacturers are relied on to vouch for the safety of their own products.

Air Fresheners, Insect Repellents and Home-cleaning Products

A survey of women in and around Barcelona revealed that 12% of domestic cleaners had asthma and chronic bronchitis, compared with 5% of other women, and the likely cause seemed to be the frequent contact with chemicals in cleaning products. Researchers warn that the chemical irritants from the use of aerosols and detergents in the home – even once a week – can cause asthma. Studies found that domestic air fresheners and furniture polish sprays can cause depression, earache and nausea, and in babies diarrhoea and vomiting, and that insect repellents can affect the nervous system, with pregnant women and children particularly vulnerable.

Electromagnetic Fields (EMFs)

Electricity is used extensively in industry and homes and our modern way of life would be severely restricted were it to cease. Electromagnetic forces are unleashed by electricity and there has been much controversy about the potential harm to our health that might be caused from our use of so many devices that involve electric power. EMFs includes electric fields generated by charged particles, magnetic fields generated by charged particles in motion, and radiated fields such as TV, radio, and microwaves. Mobile phones use electromagnetic radiation in the microwave range. Other digital wireless systems, such as communication networks, produce similar radiation. Some experts believe that EMF exposure, like toxic chemical exposure, can result in DNA damage and multi-system failures, and that communications radiation may be a major factor in the epidemics of dementia and autism.

A Swedish study found that a national epidemic of illness and disability had been caused by the wireless revolution in 2005, with around 200,000 people (3% of the population) affected by EMFs. Long periods of sick leave, attempted suicides and industrial accidents all increased simultaneously with the introduction of mobile phone radiation – people were plagued with sleep disorders, recurrent headaches and migraines, chronic fatigue that didn't respond to rest, difficulties with cognitive function, and serious blood problems.

According to some scientists, there is no "safe" level of exposure to radio-frequency current, which now routinely flows through the wiring of our homes, schools and offices. One world-renowned medical scientist has been trying to persuade us that radio frequency/microwave radiation poses a far greater threat than cigarette smoking and asbestos. According to Dr Carlo, gamma waves and RF/microwave radiation are identically carcinogenic and genotoxic to the cellular roots of life. He believes that the safe dose of either kind of radiation is zero. Because the invisible electronic and magnetic radiation causes constant stress, it may be linked to the more recent incidence of many central nervous system and neurological disorders – such as lupus, attention deficit, hyperactivity, memory loss, dizziness, confusion, depression, immune system dysfunction, chronic fatigue, chronic pain, migraine headaches, multiple sclerosis, motor neurone disease, and tinnitus. EMFs could also be linked to diabetes, adult leukaemia, brain tumours, and miscarriages.

In Russia, public exposure standards are far more stringent than in the USA because their scientists believe that at American "safe" EMF exposure levels people develop pathological changes in heart, kidney, liver and brain tissues, plus cancers of all types. Some say that for pragmatic and financial reasons, US exposure limits were deliberately set so high that no matter how much additional wireless radiation was added to America's burden, it would always be "within standards". A European committee concluded, however, that the three lines of evidence – animal, in vitro, and epidemiological studies – indicated that exposure to EMFs was *unlikely* to lead to an increase in cancer in humans.

It appears that to date the evidence of harm to human health from the use of mobile phones is inconclusive, but in 2007 a review of 11 Swedish studies concluded that long-term regular use of a mobile phone might *possibly* increase the risk of cancer. Researchers recommended the use of hands-free sets that emit as little radiation as possible and advised that children, who have thinner skulls and a developing nervous system, shouldn't use mobiles at all. In 2011 a European committee recommended that mobile phones should be banned from all classrooms as a precaution, and called for a "dramatic reduction" in exposure to other wireless devices such as baby monitors and cordless phones.

Though it cannot be said with certainty that the use of mobile phones is harmful, the health of those who work or live near the masts (cell towers) that enable mobile phones to work, could well be at risk. Many of those who worked in the vicinity of these masts without safety equipment became severely disabled from lung damage, blood abnormalities, extreme fatigue, tremors, allergies and other problems. A report found that workers exposed to high levels of RF/microwave radiation routinely had high cancer rates. Across the world there have been reports of cancer clusters and extreme illness in office buildings and multi-tenant dwellings where antennas are placed on rooftops directly over workers or tenants. People living close to masts can suffer extreme sleep disruption, chronic fatigue, nausea, skin problems, irritability, brain disturbances and cardiovascular problems.

"Sick Building Syndrome"

"Sick building syndrome" is normally blamed on poor ventilation. Tightly sealed modern buildings may save energy but could also cause health problems – from formaldehyde in wood products and other chemical fumes from carpeting, copy machines, upholstery, cleaning products and freshly dry-cleaned clothes, or carbon monoxide and nitrogen dioxide from gas ranges, fireplaces and kerosene heaters. These pollutants may produce symptoms like burning eyes, sore throats, coughing and itching, or headaches, sluggishness, nausea, dizziness, exhaustion and depression. Bacteria can also be spread by air-conditioning systems, sometimes causing Legionnaire's Disease – a potentially fatal form of pneumonia. The bacteria can be found naturally in environmental water sources such as rivers, lakes and reservoirs, but also in purpose-built water systems such as cooling towers, evaporative condensers and whirlpool spas.

Other Home Products

In his book, Randall Fitzgerald detailed the huge range of products regularly used in homes that are potentially dangerous because of the chemicals they contain. These include mattresses coated with flame retardant chemicals, synthetic carpets treated with benzene, styrene and several other cancer-causing chemicals, toilet deodorisers that emit benzene fumes capable of causing leukaemia, dry-cleaned clothes that emit fumes and residues of trichloroethylene and n-hexane (chemicals known to cause cell damage, memory loss and cardiac abnormalities), mothballs and toilet deodorisers that contain the carcinogenic pesticide dichlorobenzene, and synthetic fibres in clothes that expose us to gases from a form of plastic. The synthetic material in an energy-efficient home may cause mood swings, feelings of spaciness, headaches and the inability to concentrate. We are exposed to chlorine fumes from the dishwasher, and cleaning solvents, insect spray, and air fresheners can also contaminate the air we breathe.

Sandwich plastic wrap contains vinyl chloride, a carcinogen known to cause liver, brain and lung cancers, and phthalates seem to cause fertility problems. Phthalates are made from petroleum by-products and turn rigid plastic into pliable plastics, and industries round the world use 5 million metric tons of them each year. They are used in children's plastic toys, drugs, cosmetics and insecticides. *Harvard University* scientists tested American men who attended a fertility clinic, and those with the highest levels of phthalates in their urine were up to 5 times more likely to have low sperm counts. A Danish study examined 96 boys, and found that those with abnormally low testosterone had been fed with mother's milk containing high levels of phthalates. Japan and the European Union have banned their use in certain products. Naturally the plastics and chemical industries deny there is any proof of harm from phthalates, but as to be expected, what is described as "safe" or "normal" varies according to whose interests are taken into account.

PFOS (perfluorooctane sulfonate) was the key ingredient in fabric protection for over 40 years – preventing stains by repelling both water and oil. It has now been established that PFOS is a significant health risk to wildlife and people. Extremely resistant to environmental breakdown, PFOS is now a ubiquitous contaminant, found in polar bears in the Arctic, dolphins in Florida, seals and otters in California, albatross in the mid-Pacific, and in people round the world. In 2008, new rules were introduced to restrict the marketing and use of PFOS and substances that break down to it.

How to Avoid Pollution

Scientists understand little about the dangers of low-level chemical exposure. They don't claim that low levels of chemicals in the human body are harmless, but advise us to carry on ingesting a variety of chemicals until it is proved that they are harmful! The many examples of damage to human health – and that of other creatures – from synthetic substances and chemicals should make us question the accuracy of toxicity predictions. *The Precautionary Principle* was an approach developed in Europe in the face of uncertainties of potential harm from products. It calls for the implementation of preventative measures to protect environmental quality and public health.

Each of us would be wise to adopt our own precautionary principle. Because the extent and danger of pollution has proved to be difficult to quantify, and because governments are unlikely to restrict manufacturers in the near future with tighter regulation, we should take some sensible precautions – without going to extremes or becoming paranoid. Where it is financially and practicably feasible, you might consider following the advice below.

- Create your own meals with a high percentage of raw ingredients, or at least natural ingredients.

- Select food and drinks without artificial colours or other potentially harmful ingredients. Avoid tuna and swordfish because they are likely to contain a dangerous level of mercury.

- If you can afford them, buy organic products where they are available.

- Use a good water filter (reverse osmosis filters or water filtration pitchers).

- Ban smoking indoors.

- Improve ventilation. Air out your home at least once a day, and when the temperature outside is not too low, sleep with a window open. Air conditioners and heating systems should be set to bring in at least 35% fresh air – although energy costs may be higher, there will be health benefits. Should you be a city or town dweller, if possible move to, or spend more time in, the countryside. Not only will you feel less stress, you will breathe cleaner air.

- Use house plants – they enrich the air with oxygen, absorb carbon dioxide and remove toxic pollutants, as well as enhance the appearance of homes and offices.

- Make sure all heaters, gas cooking ranges and clothes driers are properly vented.

- Avoid air fresheners and minimise the use of moth balls, toilet cleaners, and dry-cleaned clothes.

- Keep stored paint or gasoline as far from the main house as possible i.e. in a garden shed.

- Those with particular allergies and conditions might find air-cleaning devices useful. Try using an ioniser to create more negative ions. Polluted air is full of positive ions. Air with an abundance of negative ions is beneficial to our health. It is plentiful around lakes, in forests, near rivers and waterfalls, at the seashore, and after a rain storm. Anything that diminishes oxygen to cells is detrimental.

- Furnish your house with materials and products that don't have potentially harmful ingredients, and keep cleaning agents to a minimum. Buy products with more "natural" ingredients. Marketing, peer pressure and custom has perhaps overwhelmed our natural ability to sense what is good or bad for us, whether food, what we breathe in, or what we put on our skin. We could all probably get by perfectly satisfactorily with a fraction of the soap, shampoo and deodorants that we use. I'm convinced that spray deodorants are toxic to some degree and move quickly away when someone uses one in the changing room.

- If you live close to a mobile phone mast, there are ways to shield yourself from exposure. Where possible, reduce your use of computers and avoid too much exposure to Wifi. Use electronic gadgets, particularly mobile phones, less frequently. Take the precaution of limiting the exposure of young children to IMFs.

- The *ezine* website provides advice on avoiding harmful toxins in everyday products.

DISEASE and ILLNESS

"Today, in a socio-economic system that is fundamentally pathogenic, no one should be surprised now by the increases in the chronic and degenerative 'diseases of civilisation' – a 'civilisation' in which millions are the victims of stress, pollution and drug abuse, are overfed and under-exercised, are addicted to cigarettes, alcohol and convenience food, and are expected to thrive on mindless work and passive leisure."

(Jonathan Porritt)

In the developed world we now live longer than in previous centuries, and everybody would agree that in principle a longer life is to be welcomed. During the 20th century the use of vaccinations largely eradicated major and often fatal diseases, including chicken pox, diphtheria, malaria, measles, whooping cough, polio, tetanus, typhoid, yellow fever and smallpox. And the advance in drug treatment and the ability to repair and replace body parts have saved many lives.

While recognising our undoubted medical achievements, however, we need to acknowledge our inadequacy when dealing with systemic health problems, demonstrated by the huge increase in disease and illness that has occurred over the last 50 years, especially amongst the elderly. The undeniable, widespread and still increasing level of suffering should prompt us to ask some key questions: "What has caused these burgeoning health problems?", "What quality of life do we enjoy, especially when older?", and "Could different lifestyle choices result in a better quality of life?"

Gradual Deterioration

In a sense we are all ill to some degree, because few of us can claim to be at or even near to an optimum level of physical and mental health once beyond childhood. It is easy to believe that only those judged to have some condition or another are unhealthy, but our incredibly strong and resilient bodies – for which we should be grateful – will normally delay the fateful moment when ill-health is sufficient for a doctor to diagnose a disease. For most of us it will take 30 or 40 years of adulthood for our lifestyle to gradually weaken, then overload our bodies, until finally our ill-health becomes evident. Partly because our immune system is being compromised, deterioration is occurring long before that moment – the malignant cells of those diagnosed with cancer, for example, have been through several stages of mutation. As time goes on we get accustomed to functioning at a lower level of health. We become overweight, less mobile and more inflexible, prone to colds and flu, have less energy and experience a general loss of vitality. Clarity of thought and concentration may well deteriorate, and many lose the zest for life they had when young.

Conventional wisdom would have us believe that cancer, diabetes, heart disease, dementia and other systemic diseases are almost inevitable because we are living longer. Instead we need to acknowledge the major contribution to our poor health that indulgence, lack of exercise and stress make – plus a difficult to quantify contribution from the pollution of our air, water and food. Research on human migration and lifestyle changes has shown clearly that *The Western Diet* and insufficient exercise are the major causes of the chronic diseases and conditions now experienced by so many in developed countries. Studies have shown that only 20% to 30% of lifespan is related to genetics, with the rest due to behaviour and environment, and that the systemic diseases we suffer from in the developed world hardly occur in poorer countries and so-called "primitive" societies. *We cannot blame the ageing process itself for our health problems.*

Visits to doctors, admittances to hospitals, blood tests, X-rays, surgical procedures, and the use of both prescription and over-the-counter drugs have continued to rise, yet health problems like cancer, heart disease, diabetes, dementia, asthma, allergies, attention deficit disorder, hyperactivity, thyroid malfunction, multiple sclerosis, Parkinson's, lupus, muscular dystrophy, migraines, headaches, backaches, acid reflux, ulcers, stomach aches, menopause problems, pre-menstrual tension, chronic fatigue, insomnia, acne, impotence, infertility, arthritis, constipation, fibromyalgia, herpes, yeast infections, cold sores, colds and 'flu – as well as anxiety and depression, examined later in "mental overloads" – have all been increasing at the same time. Who could deny that we are suffering from an overload of ill-health? And the rise in ill-health and its costs is set to continue.

Life Expectancy

But we must be healthier because we're living so much longer! That is the immediate response to the assertion that our physical and mental health is deteriorating, and indeed the increased life expectancy in the developed world will always be highlighted by health authorities to demonstrate progress in their area of expertise. It is indeed true that *average* life expectancy at birth increased throughout the 20th century, but total life span remained more or less static – the increase in life expectancy being mainly due to far fewer deaths of young children, particularly in the first year of life. Other significant factors were much improved hygiene and sanitation, a better understanding of nutrition, and the elimination of many infectious diseases. Medical advances in the last 50 years have played only a relatively minor role.

Another extremely significant – but never highlighted – fact is that *the last years of more and more people's lives now involve disability and ill-health.* Though assessing "healthy life expectancy" and "disability-free life expectancy" is complicated and fraught with difficulties, these official statistics for 2008-10 indicate that many people suffer from years of ill-health at the end of their lives:

- The life expectancy of a male baby born in the UK today is, on average, 78.1 years. The average life expectancy for a female baby is 82.1.

- "Healthy life expectancy" for the average male baby born in the UK today is 63.5 years. For the average female baby it is 65.7 years.

- "Disability-free life expectancy" for the average male baby born in the UK today is 63.9 years. For the average female baby it is 65.0.

This means that for as long as 14 to 17 years respectively the average person can expect to become a patient, propped up by pills, potions, pacemakers and other paraphernalia, often struggling to cope with discomfort, infirmity, pain, and indignity each day.

The Scale and Types of Disease and Illness

The level of disease and ill-health and its upward trend is evident from health care statistics – the quantity of drugs, the types and number of surgical procedures, and the sophistication of medical facilities are all continually rising, along with the workforce and cost involved.

- The UK National Health Service employs 1.4 million people and since 1949/50 its costs have increased tenfold in real terms to £121 billion in 2010/11 (about £2,000 per person).

Chronic diseases – heart disease, stroke, cancer, major respiratory conditions and diabetes – cause 63% of all deaths globally, but they were all far less prevalent until the latter part of the 20th century. Just 10% to 15% of Americans died from heart disease and strokes a hundred years ago, and less than 6% from cancer. Today the figures are 31% and 23% respectively. No comparable figures are available for the UK and other developed nations, but they would undoubtedly be similar to the USA. The leading causes of death in England are (in order): heart disease, respiratory disease, stroke, cancer and liver disease.

- In 2011, 29% of deaths in England and Wales together were caused by heart disease and circulatory problems, and 30% from cancer.

Cancer incidence rates in the UK have increased by 22% in males and 42% in females since the mid-1970s. There have been large increases in those cancers that are strongly linked to lifestyle choices. There were about 325,000 new cancer diagnoses in 2010. The UK and other developed countries experienced a huge increase in heart disease up to the 1960s, followed by a gradual decrease – which was almost certainly due to greater use of drugs for lowering blood pressure and cholesterol levels rather than lifestyle changes.

- Most Britons over 65 – and 23% of all patients – suffer from 2 or more chronic conditions.

The kinds and degrees of bodily disease and ill-health are listed below. Dementia is included because it is largely connected with physiological factors. Other mental problems that are more psychological in origin, such as anxiety, depression, phobia, anorexia, and attention deficit disorder, are examined in "mental overloads".

Cancer

There are more than 200 types of cancer, each with different symptoms and treatments. The numbers of people diagnosed with the disease has risen substantially over the last 100 years and the trend is expected to continue. It has been estimated that just 1 in 8,000 suffered from cancer in 1900, yet in developed countries it will soon be 1 in 2. Though other factors may sometimes play a role, lifestyle is the major cause of most of them. Cancer can develop at any age, but is most common in older people because it normally takes some time for the body's immune system to be sufficiently compromised – 75% of cases occur in people aged 60 and over, but just 1% in children, teenagers and young adults.

- Globally cancer killed 8 million people in 2010, and about 13 million new cases of cancer are diagnosed per year. The number of new cases is expected to rise to 26 million by 2030.

- 42% of Britons will be diagnosed with cancer during their lifetime, up about a third over 10 years. 64% of these will die from the disease.

- By 2027 in the UK the lifetime risk of developing cancer is expected to be 44% for women and 50% for men, i.e. 1 in 2.

Breast, lung, bowel, and prostate cancer together account for over 50% of all new cancers each year in Britain. The incidence of a few cancers – lung and cervical cancer in particular – is decreasing, but most continue to rise. Testicular cancer in developed countries has risen significantly over the last 40 years. In the UK breast cancer increased by 72% from 1978 to 2010 – when the lifetime risk became 1 in 8. Non-Hodgkin's lymphoma, oesophagus, malignant melanoma (skin), uterine (womb) and kidney cancers have all increased. Thyroid cancer has risen at about 6% a year since 1997, with nearly two-thirds of those diagnosed with the disease between the ages of 20 and 55. Childhood cancers increased on average by about 1% every year from the 1950s to 1990s, but by less since then.

Heart Disease

Heart attacks are the leading cause of death globally. CVD (cardiovascular disease) includes coronary heart disease, myocardial infarction (heart attack), angina pectoris (chest pain), heart failure and stroke. Though cancer has overtaken it by a small margin in England and Wales, CVD is the main cause of death in the UK, the USA and most other developed countries. Coronary Heart Disease (CHD) is usually caused by a build-up of fatty deposits on the walls of the coronary arteries, made up of cholesterol and other waste substances. This build-up process is called atherosclerosis. It narrows the arteries and restricts the flow of blood to the heart. This is far more likely to happen if people smoke, have high blood pressure, have high cholesterol (a 2013 study found that vegetarians had a 32% lower risk of ischemic heart disease), don't take regular exercise, and have diabetes. Other risk factors include being overweight or having a family history of CHD. Major heart attack risk factors include a history of angina or vascular disease, a previous stroke or heart attack, excessive alcohol, the abuse of illegal drugs, smoking, obesity, high levels of stress, high or low cholesterol, high triglyceride levels, high blood pressure, and diabetes.

- Globally 13 million people die from heart disease and strokes, accounting for 1 in 4 deaths.

- About 2.7 million Britons live with CHD. Heart disease in Britain was the cause of even more deaths than cancer, accounting for 20% of men and 17% of women, with strokes as the next leading cause.

1.2 million Britons have survived a stroke, but 43,000 die from a stroke each year. 1.5 million have survived a heart attack, but 191,000 die from heart disease each year – about a third of all deaths. 46% of deaths from CVD are from CHD, and 23% from stroke. CHD by itself is the most common cause of death in the UK, with around 1 in 5 men and 1 in 8 women dying from the disease – around 88,000 deaths per year. 60,000 deaths are caused by other circulatory diseases.

Hypertension (High Blood Pressure)

Hypertension increases the risk of stroke, congestive heart failure, kidney disease, blindness, and coronary artery disease. Over time, hypertension can damage arteries to the point when they cannot deliver enough oxygen to parts of the body. This means that the brain and kidneys can be adversely affected. The factors that can raise the risk of hypertension include a family history of hypertension, too much salt, stress, smoking, excessive alcohol, a lack of exercise, and being overweight. Obesity multiplies the risk of developing hypertension about fourfold in men and threefold in women. Another factor may be too little sleep. Research has shown that those who sleep for less than 7 hours a night are far more likely to develop higher blood pressure.

- A billion people in the world suffer from hypertension.

- In England at least 32% of men and 30% of women have hypertension, amounting to over 16 million people – plus perhaps 5 million more who are undiagnosed. It is the cause of half of all strokes and heart attacks, leading to 62,000 deaths every year.

Diabetes

As mentioned in the food segment, there are two kinds of diabetes, Types 1 and 2. Those with Type 2 make up 90% of sufferers. Type 1 is usually diagnosed when young – the peak age in the UK is 10 to 14. Obesity is the main cause of Type 2 diabetes, so the number of those suffering with this condition is rising most in Western countries where more and more people are becoming overweight. Diabetics are usually prescribed tablets or insulin injections to control their blood sugar levels. Many "alternative" medical practitioners believe that a radical change of diet and regular exercise can cure Type 2 diabetes. Diabetes can lead to serious complications such as heart disease, blindness, kidney failure, stroke and nerve damage – sometimes requiring limb amputation. Life expectancy for Type 2 diabetics is reduced by up to 10 years, and by up to 20 years for those with Type 1.

- In 2011 an estimated 366 million of the world's population (8.5%) suffered from diabetes – more than double the figure in 1980. Globally diabetes kills 1.3 million people per year, twice as many as in 1990.

- Almost 3 million Britons suffer from diabetes (4.6% of the population). It has risen 50% since 2005. There are also about 850,000 undiagnosed diabetics.

In both the USA and UK there has been a large increase in young children's Type 1 diabetes in recent years. Believed to be too fast a rise to be genetic, less breast-feeding, sterility of modern environments affecting children's immune systems, and low levels of vitamin D, have been suggested as possible causes.

Disease of the Liver

As well as cancer of the liver, liver disease includes hepatitis (caused by a viral infection or excessive alcohol), cirrhosis (caused by excessive alcohol) and abscesses. Hepatitis can be treated by anti-viral and interferon drugs.

- Globally over 2 billion people have been infected by hepatitis B some time in their lives, with 350 million of those chronically affected and therefore at risk of dying from liver disease.

- Globally about 150 million people are chronically infected with the hepatitis C virus, causing 350,000 deaths per year.

Deaths from liver disease in England rose by 25% from 2001 to 2009, caused by heavy drinking, hepatitis and obesity. Up to 2 million Britons are suffering from chronic liver disease, many of whom remain unaware of their illness. In 2007, over 13,000 died from liver-related conditions.

- Over the last 30 years, diseases of the liver in the UK have increased 8-fold in men and 7-fold in women aged 35 to 44 – because of the increased and widespread heavy drinking and binge drinking.

Dementia

Dementia is the umbrella term for the huge and rapidly growing problem of brain deterioration in older people. Alzheimer's disease is by far the most common of the many dementia conditions that are diagnosed today, with vascular dementia due to impaired blood flow to the brain (mini strokes) the next. Largely suffered by people aged around 65 or older, dementia is a clinical syndrome of loss or decline in memory and other cognitive abilities from brain cell damage. To be classified as dementia, the syndrome must include a decline in memory and one of various inabilities: to generate coherent speech and understand spoken or written language, to recognise or identify objects, to execute motor activities, and to think abstractly, make sound judgements and plan and carry out complex tasks.

- It is estimated that over 35 million people worldwide have dementia, and the number is expected to reach 65 million by 2030.

- In 2010 there were an estimated 955,000 Britons with dementia, costing £34 billion per year to look after.

Up to 70% of acute hospital beds in the UK are occupied by older people, and about 40% of them have dementia – and they experience many more complications and stay longer in hospital. Sufferers are said to occupy 25% of *all* hospital beds. Around two-thirds of people living in care homes have dementia, which causes about 60,000 deaths a year.

Alzheimer's has a number of possible causes, and usually involves plaque deposits or "protein tangles" in the brain. A growing body of evidence suggests that brain health is closely linked to the overall health of the heart and blood vessels. To lessen the risk of dementia, it would therefore be advisable to avoid high cholesterol levels, Type 2 diabetes, high blood pressure, and carrying extra weight. Research has found that those between 40 and 45 with very high amounts of abdominal fat are 3 times more likely to be afflicted with Alzheimer's disease eventually, that those with diabetes have more than double the chance of developing dementia, that those with high blood pressure face a 60% higher risk, and that smokers between the ages of 46 and 70 are 70% more likely to suffer chronic memory loss.

Conversely, research suggests that together with good social ties and mental stimulation, brain health is helped by a low-fat diet which includes a high proportion of fruit and vegetables. A study found that the stricter that people kept to *The Mediterranean Diet* – one that is rich in fruit, vegetables and cereals, with some fish and alcohol but very little dairy and meat – the less likely they were to suffer from Alzheimer's. It could lower the risk of developing the condition by up to 40%. Another study confirmed that a healthier diet led to less brain shrinkage in old age and much improved performance in mental tests. Research on mice has shown that luteolin – found in celery, green peppers and camomile – reduces the inflammation in the brain that can lead to dementia. Other studies found that a considerable reduction of calories one or two days a week can reduce the chance of suffering from Alzheimer's, and that older people who exercise regularly are up to 40% less likely to develop dementia. Drugs used to treat dementia, on the other hand, can slow deterioration by just 6 months or a year.

Arthritis

Arthritis involves painful inflammation and stiffness of the joints. By far the most common form of the disease is osteoarthritis. Other arthritic conditions include fibromyalgia, gout, and rheumatoid arthritis. The onset of arthritis is much more likely when people are older, and women are affected more than men.

- About 10 million Britons suffer from an arthritic condition. 8.5 million have osteoarthritis, and 400,000 have rheumatoid arthritis. The number of osteoarthritis sufferers is expected to double by 2030.

Research has found that a high intake of protein is linked to inflammatory arthritis – the group who ate the most red meat were more than twice as likely to have the condition. Gout has increased in recent years and can be caused by the consumption of red meat, offal (liver or kidneys for example), game, seafood, beer, lager, port and some red wines – or even sugar-sweetened soft drinks. There is increasing evidence that *The Mediterranean diet* has a positive effect on arthritis. Omega-3 is believed to have an anti-inflammatory effect, which may reduce joint pain – it is found in oily fish, such as sardines, mackerel and salmon, as well as in nuts and seeds, especially linseed or flax seed. Apples, berries, cherries, citrus fruits, leafy green vegetables, and whole grains are also recommended for those with arthritis.

Sufferers are advised to do aerobic exercise to achieve and maintain a lower weight, and to use weights for strengthening muscles in order to support joints. Osteopathic manipulative treatment might also lessen arthritic pain, promote healing and increase mobility. Good posture can protect the joints from further injury. A study found that of many "alternative" products, only fish body oil can reduce joint pain and stiffness, and only capsaicin gel, made from chilli peppers, can relieve pain and joint tenderness. Orthodox medical practitioners prescribe painkillers and other drugs.

Parkinson's Disease

Parkinson's occurs when the balance between two chemical messengers in the brain is upset, affecting a person's ability to co-ordinate movements. Symptoms include shaking, muscle stiffness and slowness of movement. It can affect a person's ability to walk, talk, write, speak, smile, and swallow. PD is not considered to be a fatal disease by itself, but as it progresses it can lead to choking, pneumonia or life-threatening falls. The average life expectancy of a PD patient is generally lower than for people who do not have the disease. The disease is more common in men than in women. The reason for the discrepancy is unclear, but one suggestion is the increased exposure to toxic chemicals and a higher rate of head injuries among men.

- 1 in 200 will get PD during their lifetime, with the risk increasing with age (to 1 in every 100 for those over 60 years old).

- Around 120,000 people in the UK have PD, with 10,000 being diagnosed each year.

Though people are usually diagnosed with PD in their 60s and early 70s, there has been a worrying increase of younger patients. Some experts have estimated that 5% to 10% of those diagnosed with PD are now under the age of 40.

Most people have "idiopathic" PD, meaning there is no specific known cause, though for a small number the disease might result from genetics, head trauma, cerebral anoxia, drug-taking, or toxins. Perhaps some people have a genetic vulnerability to environmental toxins like pesticides and some metals. There has been a rise of 50% in Parkinson's and motor neurone disease in Western countries yet no increase in Japan, so experts have suggested the cause may be chemical pollution from pesticides, industrial effluent and car exhausts, and/or diet – in Japan they eat more fish and fewer dairy products. A family history of the disease and being knocked unconscious several times seem to be stronger causes, increasing the risk of Parkinson's by 350% and 174% respectively. There is no cure, but medications or surgery can provide relief from the symptoms. Broad-based management of the condition includes patient and family education, support group services, physiotherapy, exercise, and a nutritious diet.

Multiple Sclerosis

MS is a disorder of the brain and spinal cord, believed to involve an immune malfunction caused by an initial trigger. Chemicals and cells of the immune system – which normally target bacteria and viruses or other invaders – attack the myelin sheath which surrounds the nerve fibres in the brain and spinal cord. This leads to small patches of inflammation. A virus or another environmental factor may trigger the immune system to act in this way in people with a certain genetic make-up. The inflammation around the myelin sheath stops the affected nerve fibres from working properly. Repeated bouts of inflammation can leave a small scar (sclerosis) which can permanently damage nerve fibres. Symptoms of MS include numbness or tingling in parts of the skin, weakness, tremors, spasms or paralysis of some muscles, reduced mobility, partial loss or blurring of vision, difficulties with balance and co-ordination, dizziness, difficulty in passing urine, erection problems, difficulty with speaking, tiredness, and psychological symptoms such as mood swings and depression.

- About 85,000 Britons suffer from MS.

The prevalence of MS ranges between 2 and 150 per 100,000 people, depending on the country or specific population. It can affect anyone at any age, though it is rare under the age of 10. It usually develops between the ages of 20 and 40 and is the most common disabling illness of young adults in the UK. It is twice as likely to occur in Caucasians as in any other group, and women are twice as likely as men to be affected earlier in life. There is an increased chance of MS developing in close relatives of affected people. The life expectancy of those with MS is reduced on average by 6 to 11 years compared to the general population. The progression of symptoms can take 20 years or longer to be fatal. There is no way to predict what course the disease will take for a particular individual. To some extent the symptoms can be reduced by drugs, but many patients try alternative treatments, including dietary regimens, herbal medicine and cannabis. Tai chi, yoga, or general exercise might mitigate fatigue, but they have no effect on cognitive function.

Thyroid Problems

When this small endocrine gland in the neck is under-active or over-active, it can lead to all kinds of debilitating symptoms, including weight changes, fatigue, constipation, poor memory and concentration, mood swings and migraines. Women face as high as a 1 in 5 chance of developing a thyroid condition, a risk 7 times greater than for men. The risk increases with age and for those with a family history of thyroid dysfunction. The risk is also greater for women who have just had a baby or are menopausal, those who smoke, those who have been exposed to radiation, those who have been treated with lithium, or those who have been exposed to certain chemicals like perchlorate and fluoride. The thyroid function may be affected by eating too many uncooked "goitrogenic" foods – such as Brussels sprouts, cabbage, broccoli, kale, peaches and pears, turnips, radishes, cauliflower, and millet. Consuming insufficient food with iodine may also be a factor.

- Between 4 and 5 million Britons suffer from thyroid problems.

The standard medical treatment for an underactive thyroid involves hormone replacement with drugs. When the thyroid is overactive, surgery or drugs will be used to prevent the thyroid from producing hormones. Radioactive iodine to kill thyroid cells is the most widely recommended permanent treatment. Surgery is not used as frequently as other treatments for this disease. Nutritionists believe that dietary changes can help, and advise sufferers to consume foods rich in vitamin A, iodine, zinc and copper, to avoid refined foods, saturated fats, sugars, and white flour products, and to include at least 50% of fresh food in their diet (preferably organically grown), in order to rebalance and establish a better metabolism.

ME

ME (myalgic encephalomyelitis), sometimes known as "Chronic Fatigue Syndrome", affects many bodily systems and their functions. It is more common in women than in men, and may be more common in certain families. The nervous and immune systems in particular are affected. Symptoms vary from person to person but the most common features include profound, lasting fatigue, which is unaffected by rest, a general feeling of being unwell (which increases after normal physical or mental activity), painful or aching muscles and/or joints, persistent headaches or migraines, concentration problems, sleep problems, digestive disturbances, intolerances and increased sensitivity to alcohol, some foods, and some medications.

- About 17 million worldwide suffer from ME.

- About 250,000 people in the UK suffer from ME, nearly two-thirds of them female.

Most people develop the condition between their early 20s and mid-40s, though it does affect children and young people, generally those between the ages of 13 and 15, but sometimes as young as 5. There is some evidence of factors that can trigger and maintain ME (infections, immunisations, emotional traumas, physical injury, environmental toxins, sleep difficulties, over activity, inactivity, and mood disorders), but its origins are not yet fully understood and there is currently no known cure. Abnormalities have been found in the immune and nervous systems, including the functioning of the hypothalamus (a part of the brain that regulates basic functions like appetite, sleep and temperature control).

ME can last anywhere between a few months and many years. 20% of sufferers are likely to make a full recovery, usually within 2 to 4 years. Around 60% make a significant recovery, but up to 20% remain chronically disabled. Early diagnosis and advice on managing the illness can help with long-term improvement. Sufferers must learn to live within their energy levels and carefully pace their activities. This means discovering their limitations and learning what degree of activity their bodies will tolerate without causing a relapse. Doctors can work with sufferers to tackle some aspects of the condition on a symptom-by-symptom basis.

HIV and AIDS

First identified in the USA in 1981, AIDS (acquired immune deficiency syndrome) is a disease of the immune system caused by HIV (the human immunodeficiency virus). It quickly became a pandemic – to date more than 60 million people have contracted HIV and nearly 30 million have died from HIV-related causes. Most deaths occurred in sub-Saharan Africa, destroying human capital and retarding economic growth, and the spread of the virus is not slowing – Eastern Europe and Central Asia are now experiencing the fastest growth of HIV infection in the history of Aids. HIV is transmitted through direct contact of a mucous membrane or the bloodstream with a bodily fluid containing HIV, such as blood, semen, vaginal fluid, or breast milk. For many years HIV was associated largely with sex between men, but in Africa and now European countries, the infection is increasingly passed between heterosexuals.

HIV progressively reduces the sufferer's immune system and leaves the body susceptible to infections (caused by bacteria, viruses, fungi and parasites) and tumours, which can affect nearly every organ system. The symptoms of AIDS are primarily the result of conditions that do not normally develop in people with healthy immune systems. Although treatments for AIDS and HIV can slow the course of the disease, there is currently no vaccine or cure. Anti-retroviral treatment reduces both the mortality and the morbidity of HIV infection, but these drugs are expensive and routine access to anti-retroviral medication is not available in all countries. Due to the difficulty in treating HIV, preventing infection is a key aim in controlling the AIDS epidemic, with health organisations promoting safe sex and needle-exchange programs for drug addicts to help slow the spread of the virus.

- More than 34 million people are living with AIDS worldwide. 1.7 million died from the disease in 2011 and about 2.5 million were newly infected with HIV.

- At the end of 2011, an estimated 96,000 people were living with HIV in the UK (including 30% who don't know they are infected).

Sexually Transmitted Infections (other than HIV)

The most common STI is Chlamydia, followed by genital warts, herpes, gonorrhoea and syphilis. Those with STIs experience pain, discomfort and embarrassment, but some infections can cause infertility in women and affect the quality and quantity of sperm. Studies have found that there was a lack of awareness of STIs (1 in 10 men thought Chlamydia was a flower), that 75% of women aged 16 to 30 don't practise safe sex in casual relationships, and that sexual health nurses believed levels of promiscuity among young adults would increase STIs considerably. In 2011 doctors called on the UK government to introduce an NHS vaccine for girls against genital warts as this infection had risen by a third in a decade.

- In 2010 there were about 420,000 new cases of sexually transmitted infections (other than HIV) in England.

To try to reduce STIs, American and European governments have insisted on safe sex education in state schools. An alternative offered by Christians – *The Silver Ring Movement* – tries to persuade the young to abstain from sex until marriage. Recent research has shown that increased sexual activity of people in their 50s, 60s and 70s in the UK, USA and Canada has resulted in a doubling of STIs amongst those age groups.

MRSA and Clostridium Difficile (CD)

These "superbugs" have caused illness and deaths in recent years, mainly in hospitals. They can spread quickly if strict hygiene measures are not adhered to. Apart from cleanliness problems, many older people who enter hospital have weakened immune systems because of poor nutrition, lack of exercise and the use of pharmaceutical drugs.

- A world expert in infectious diseases believes that as many as 52 million people worldwide might be carrying the superbug MRSA.

In England and Wales more rigorous hospital cleanliness led to a reduction of superbug problems after 2007. From an estimated 20,000 deaths linked to MRSA and CD in 2004, the figure dropped to about 3,200 by 2010.

Migraines and Headaches

A headache can be muscular, spinal or circulatory in origin. An estimated 70% of headaches are "tension" headaches, and 20% are "migraine" headaches. The former occurs when blood vessels of the head and neck constrict. Migraine prevalence varies considerably between the sexes – it is 3 or 4 times more common in women than in men. Diet can trigger both headaches and migraines in susceptible people. Fluctuating blood sugar levels, alcohol on an empty stomach, too much caffeine or caffeine withdrawal, food and drink temperature, MSG (monosodium glutamate), artificial sweeteners, aged cheese, citrus fruits and juices, and food chemicals can cause them. Other possible causes include stress, fatigue, poor posture, eye strain and weather changes – and in women, the use of birth control pills and hormonal changes before or after a menstrual period.

- In the UK about 20% of adults suffer from headaches and 8% from migraines.

Migraines can considerably disrupt the lives of sufferers. 1 in 3 sufferers believes that the condition controls their life. Severe episodes can last as long as 3 days, during which the person is unable to carry out the usual daily activities. In the USA an estimated 157 million workdays a year are lost to migraines. Up to 70% of people in the West use painkillers regularly, primarily for headaches. But painkillers and other pharmaceutical drugs can actually *cause* headaches.

Asthma and Allergies

Asthma is fast becoming an epidemic in developed countries. It can affect all age groups but often starts in childhood. It is characterised by recurrent attacks of breathlessness and wheezing, which vary in severity from person to person. The condition is due to inflammation of the air passages in the lungs. Nerve endings become irritated, the lining of passages swell, the airways narrow, and the flow of air in and out of the lungs is reduced. An allergy involves a substance triggering an immune response that may be uncomfortable, painful, or even life-threatening. The things that trigger allergies can also trigger asthma.

- Globally there are about 300 million asthmatics. Every year about 250,000 people die from this disease.

- Over 5 million people in the UK are currently receiving treatment for asthma, including about a million children.

- More than 21 million adults in the UK suffer from some sort of allergy.

Studies have revealed that asthmatic children are more likely to be diagnosed with anxiety, depression, as well as learning and behavioural disabilities, that air pollution triggers asthma symptoms in most sufferers, and that children born by the Caesarian procedure are 79% more likely to be asthmatic by the age of 8. Perhaps the bacteria the babies are exposed to during vaginal birth could have the effect of kick-starting their immune system. In the 1970s Caesarian births were 5% worldwide and now the figure has increased to 30%, with a parallel rise in asthma.

Infection in early childhood may help to prevent allergies and allergy-based asthma – children on farms who help with the cows and the pigs seem to have fewer allergies than urban children. This could also explain why later children in families tend to be less allergic – the older siblings bring germs home from school. A recent Welsh study found that when pregnant women and infants were given a probiotic, the children were 57% less likely to suffer from allergies.

- 25% 0f British people can expect to contract at least one allergy in their lifetime, a huge increase from the figure of 1 in 30 half a century ago.

- A UK government report in 2006 showed that the number of people admitted to hospital suffering from severe allergic reactions to food or insect stings had more than tripled in the previous decade.

The report showed that asthma, rhinitis and eczema rates had increased by between two- and three-fold. The rise in the number of allergy sufferers has been linked to oversensitive immune systems caused by people living in increasingly hygienic environments. Eczema has been found to be triggered by some foods and drinks, including dairy products and coffee, soybean products, eggs, nuts, wheat and maize (sweet corn), though food allergies vary from person to person. Immunotherapy is widely used in Europe. Patients are injected with minute doses of allergens such as pollen or bee venom to build up a tolerance in their immune system.

From the late 1980s Barbados experienced an exponential rise in the incidence of asthma, with 20% of the population now affected. The rapid transition to modern buildings, vehicles and diet have been suggested as possible causes – there are more dust mites in the buildings, more particles from traffic, and more additives in the food. In developed countries so many more people now have food intolerances and allergies. Some experience "multiple chemical sensitivity", and a small number seem to be allergic to modern life in general. Perhaps our biology has become "out of step" with the modern world, but the processes that create intolerances and ways of treating them successfully are still far from clear.

Other Health Problems

As well as more serious conditions, our modern lifestyle has also led to a whole array of relatively minor, but widespread health problems. Back pain affects 80% of the population at some point and is the cause of 1 in every 6 days taken off work. It is probably due to our sedentary lifestyle and lack of exercise. A visit to the osteopath might be useful to eliminate a problem more quickly, though prevention would be the best solution – a change of occupation, or regular exercise and stretching, at home, at work, in the gym or at yoga classes. Other common problems are too little (or disrupted) sleep, digestive disorders, and skin complaints. The first can be remedied by planning and doing less, and the other two will normally be resolved through dietary changes.

How to Avoid Disease and Illness

Disease and illness can result from hereditary, environmental, or lifestyle factors. The material in this section shows clearly that our burgeoning ill-health is largely the result of how we lead our lives. With regards to cancer this was confirmed by a ground-breaking paper from researchers at the MD Anderson Cancer Centre in Houston, published in 2008. They found that *only 5% to 10% of all cancer cases could be attributed to genetic defects*, and that environment and lifestyle factors were by far the main causes. These included smoking, diet, alcohol, sun exposure, environmental pollutants, infections, stress, obesity, and physical inactivity. Other research has shown that not only cancer but most of the systemic and widespread health problems in the developed world can be considerably reduced or avoided not only by changing the way we conduct our lives, but also – according to the relatively new science of "Epigenetics" – by changing our thoughts and beliefs.

Few people today act or consume in a truly moderate way, so don't assume that how you live is sensible just because you're not quite as indulgent, overweight or stressed as those around you. If you follow the suggestions given at the end of previous segments, you'll maintain good daily health as well as significantly decrease your risk of suffering serious illnesses. In summary, the advice is: reduce stress whenever possible, don't eat too much, consume a high proportion of natural food, give up smoking, avoid illegal drugs, drink little alcohol and few caffeine drinks, get enough rest and sleep, and exercise regularly.

- Try to eat a greater proportion of natural, healthy food. Avoid foods with too much salt, sugar or fat, and those with possibly dangerous additives such as colourings. Buy organic produce if you can afford it. Skin cancer might result from too much sun or from using sunbeds. Stay in the sun for brief periods at a time, or use sunblock. A healthy diet and regular exercise will make you look good as well as feel good, so don't endanger your health in an effort to improve your appearance.

- A review of 60 studies found that regular exercise significantly promotes good health, and conversely a lack of exercise can be detrimental. Breast cancer sufferers, for example, have a 40% reduced risk of recurrence and of dying from the disease if they do moderate exercise for 150 minutes a week. A Taiwanese study found that even a short 15-minute burst of physical activity a day adds an average of 3 years to life expectancy. And an American study showed that regular exercise for 90 minutes a week reduced the risk of vascular-related dementia by 40% and impairment in brain skills by 60%.

- Check the ingredients of personal care products, and be aware that make-up and deodorants might clog your pores, and that perfume could also be harmful.

- Avoid or minimise the use of home products that may be toxic, such as air fresheners, moth balls, and powerful cleaning products.

- Avoid risky sex. Young women should not be put off carrying condoms for fear of appearing "loose", while young men should not always succumb to the social pressure to have sexual intercourse.

- It has been shown that being poor or lonely means you are far more likely to have a lower level of health. Take steps during your life to acquire sufficient skills to be able to earn at least a moderate income, to maintain good communications with family members, and to treasure and hold on to a few good friends.

- Unless there is a genuine emergency, drugs and surgery should be avoided because they don't deal with the underlying causes and can be dangerous, or at least involve negative side-effects.

- If you have a particular health problem listed above, follow the suggestions given regarding choice of foods and exercise. Try to view your illness positively i.e. as an opportunity to re-balance your body. If you have a lot of stress in your life, first read through the awareness section and then try changing your view of life or take steps to change your situation or relationship. If that seems impossible for you to do, seek professional help.

MENTAL OVERLOADS

Self-Appraisal

"...happiness is a state that depends on inner conditions, and each of us must recognise those conditions with awareness and then bring them together."

(Matthieu Ricard)

How is your mental disposition? Do you continually feel under pressure? Is your concentration deteriorating? Do you have a sense of real motivation or purpose? Do you get anxious and fearful? How often do you feel inadequate and envious of others? How many close and fulfilling relationships do you have? How often do you experience real joy and deep contentment?

Perhaps you feel that life is not really worth living or can't wait to get a few drinks down you – or maybe indulge in some strong tasting food – to take your mind off your problems and lack of inspiration. You might well feel you're on a treadmill but have no idea how to get off. This is the reality for so many people in the developed world.

Are you always in a rush? Most people are, particularly those of us living in large urban centres. A few years after my change of diet and a little contemplation about how I viewed myself and the world, a friend and I were helping someone to move their belongings to another flat. When the job was done, instead of moving briskly on to another "engagement", I enjoyed a leisurely chat about this and that over a cup of tea. I realised then that my attitude and approach to life had begun to change for the better.

You Are Not Alone

This section of the book looks at the various ways our minds are being "overloaded". It begins with an analysis of social pressure, because that is the underlying cause of most of the stress we feel today. The final segment details the worrying results of the various mental overloads we experience – generated not only by the efforts we make to keep up with our peers, but also by our incredibly fast pace of life, the huge amount of information we have to process, the ever-increasing choice of products and services we face, and the range of technology we have to deal with. You'll see that the number and level of psychological malfunctions have greatly increased in recent decades and are set to rise still further.

You're unique, but share much with other members of the human race. You're not the only one who questions their sanity and wonders what life is all about. Everybody has difficulties, whether rich or poor, famous or not. Many people often feel stress or lack impetus – and grab some instant gratification to ease their pain or discomfort. When they struggle with their work, have problems in relationships, find their partner's or children's behaviour inexplicable and maddening, they may hit out at those around them or retreat into their shell – many are quite frequently baffled by their own behaviour, which can sometimes be self-destructive.

I have included statistics – as before, largely concerning the population of the UK – to show how people are suffering from a whole variety of mental overloads, and *you* will be in them somewhere. Once again, I realise that numbers and averages can never show the full picture, the exact situation, the whole truth, but they strongly indicate what is happening and where things are heading.

Here are some figures taken from the following pages, and you'll see that most of us are in this together. You are not alone:

- Britons spend over £2 billion a year on cosmetic treatments, and in 2009 loans of around £5 million were used to pay for some of them.

- Each day we are assailed with the equivalent of 174 newspapers' worth of data – 5 times more than in 1986.

- 68% of British teenagers and 46% of adults are "addicted" to their mobile phone.

- 1 in 5 English children regularly plays outside, 1 in 3 has never climbed a tree, and 1 in 10 has never ridden a bike.

- In the UK 29% of the 26 million British households consist of just one person. By 2031 the number of people living alone in the UK is expected to rise by 60%.

- A poll of 3,000 British parents and children found that just 1 in 10 saw themselves as part of a "caring family".

- Prescriptions for anti-depressants in England rose by 450% from 1991 to over 50 million in 2012.

- A 2010 survey found that around 40 million British adults admitted to suffering some sort of regular anxiety.

- About 1 million Britons, mostly children, have ADHD.

- 1 in 6 Britons (about 8 million) are experiencing mental problems at any one time.

SOCIAL PRESSURE

*"Even when fifty million people say a
foolish thing, it is still a
foolish thing."*

(Anatole France)

The wish to fit in with others is a basic and powerful instinct, and vital for the survival of many species including our own. Our emotional state is strongly influenced by that of others. The herd instinct is incredibly strong. We imitate each other in many areas of our lives because of this deep-seated yearning to be part of a group and aversion to being thought of as "different". We can't bear the thought of social rejection. But this trait can also cause many problems for both individuals and society as a whole. The latest fashions are slavishly followed, we stretch our resources to breaking point in order to keep up with the Joneses, and the mob mentality sometimes results in packs of feral kids or football crowds indulging in cruel or senseless activities.

Even in extreme situations we will still avoid being the odd one out, a fact dramatically demonstrated by experiments in New York during the 1960s. Unwitting subjects were put in a waiting room with actors, and the room was gradually filled with smoke. When the actors did nothing, only 10% of the subjects left the room. Though it should be obvious to take the right, common-sense action, people will follow others even when they are not acting sensibly. Studies have also shown that many people will obey the instructions of the "man in the white coat", even if he asks them to do something outrageous, immoral or painful to their fellow human beings.

It seems that there's comfort in numbers – when people are told there's an obesity epidemic, they'll feel they're not alone and put on weight. After the chef Jamie Oliver lamented that *Twizzlers* were a children's favourite in the UK, sales rose by 32%. And in 2008 it was reported that teenage girls who watched TV shows containing sexual behaviour – such as *Sex and the City* – were more likely to become pregnant. If a group of people or a famous person does something, even suicide, others may well follow. There was a 12% rise in American suicides, mostly young blonde women, soon after Marilyn Monroe died.

It's hard to resist the majority, whether misguided or not. Even the minority of relatively aware people who deliberately live simpler lives and refuse to get sucked into the usual ego, status, and money games have to be courageous to stick to their guns. The prevailing view may well be right for one occasion or for a period, but a way of thinking or course of action that may have been sensible once is not necessarily so forever. However persuasive and comforting it may be to follow the herd, it is worth remembering that conventional wisdom is often wrong – the stock and property markets with their booms and busts, for example, the "Credit Crunch" of 2008 being the most notable.

The Scale and Problems of Social Pressure

The marketing and advertising industries manipulate us into buying products by taking advantage of our basic desire to follow the crowd. Political, industrial and media leaders also understand the power of peer pressure and the human inclination to conform. The psychological pressures on people today are stronger and more numerous than before. Children are known to be heavily influenced by their peers, but adults are as well. Though emotional impulses can often have detrimental results, few people have the awareness and strength to override them – especially those created by social pressure.

I believe the problems resulting from our tendency to conform have increased significantly over the last 50 years. Because too large a proportion of time and funds available is centred on what is popular, on what the majority naturally gravitate towards and is excited by, glitter and frippery dominate our modern world – a situation that is not healthy for us all. Money, fame, good looks, gizmos, clothes, games and other light-weight entertainment are all given much greater attention than they deserve. Most things become fleeting successes, to be quickly replaced by the next fad. Gossip and brazen razzmatazz aimed at the younger members of society take centre stage almost all the time. The emphasis on the young causes many who are older to attempt – sometimes desperately – to stay young-looking, and cling to what they believe to be a necessary youthful attitude. This doesn't make people happy, it makes them anxious.

Marketing

Most of us would confidently claim that we exert free will and are not unduly influenced by marketing and advertising. This assertion clearly demonstrates our lack of self-awareness and irrationality. We think we are independent and free-thinking, but the facts show otherwise – as Vince Packard argued in his book *The Hidden Persuaders*, published in the 1950s. In fact the capitalist system, with advertisements playing a key role, has now brought us to the point where too many people are obsessed with external factors – including the views of others – rather than looking inwards to develop wisdom and peace of mind.

- British TV and print advertising expenditure was just over £16 billion in 2011. Online expenditure was almost £5 billion.

Advertising becomes ever more ubiquitous and sophisticated. We are subjected to its influence in the media, on TV, the internet, radio, and on city streets and country roads. America leads the way with the expansion of marketing techniques and boundaries – even schoolchildren are confronted by advertisements on their buses, in their hallways and in their textbooks. "Infomercials" and "advertorials" are more recent ploys used by advertisers. The former is a program-long TV product promotion and the latter is the printed equivalent – an advertisement disguised as an article. Now smells are used to seduce us to make a purchase. The scent of vanilla helps to sell women's clothing, and rose maroc for men's. Most companies won't admit what techniques they're using because they don't want to be accused of using subliminal marketing, but this is precisely what they're doing – affecting us subconsciously.

"Product placement" is another recent and growing form of marketing. A website has even been set up for designers and stylists to sell the fashions and accessories used by stars of films and TV. In the future people may well be able to point to a product on the screen and click to purchase it. In 2011 the first product placement deal in the UK was agreed between a coffee machine manufacturer and *ITV*, soon after the government allowed the practice on commercial television.

The Media

News is now just another way of making money. According to Nick Davies in his book *Flat Earth News*, recent generations are encouraged by the media to be brazenly materialistic, selfish, depoliticised and non-socially minded. He believes that in place of informed debate or political parties organising across the full spectrum of opinion, there is vacuous journalism and elections dominated by public relations, big money, political advertising and limited debate on tangible issues. Commercial values overwhelm notions of democracy and civic culture, and the wealthy few face fewer and fewer threats of political challenge. "Spin" now dominates the media, indicated by the growth of PR (public relations) agencies.

- From 1990 to 2000 the global revenue of the PR industry grew by 250%.

- The PR industry in the UK was valued at about £3 billion in 2013-14, and forecast to keep rising strongly.

Much of what is made available to the public serves a particular agenda, and money is invariably the driving force behind it. But the average person is unlikely to consider, for example, that information detailing the advantages of GM foods, exaggerating the scale and effects of climate change, or minimising the role of refined sugar in health problems, might well have come from those who are protecting or trying to further their own interests rather than from unbiased sources. We all need to maintain a high level of scepticism about the material the media presents to us as facts.

Self-Improvement

Our natural inclination to compare ourselves with others has been fostered by the burgeoning self-help industry – how to be positive, how to become fit, flexible and healthy, how to speak effectively in public, how to find that fulfilling career, how to attract and satisfy the perfect partner, how to cook the tastiest meal and run the ideal home, how to meditate properly and achieve enlightenment, and of course – how to get rich. In 2006 the US self-improvement industry has been estimated to be worth more than $9 billion, and expected to reach $13 billion by 2013.

- In 2011 British publishers earned about £60 million from self-help books over the previous 5 years.

To help us improve ourselves we can access advice and encouragement from infomercials, mail-order catalogues, holistic institutes, books, audio packages, motivation-speaker seminars, personal coaching, and programs for weight-loss and stress-management. In this area, like the health industry, solutions to life's problems are often presented as simpler than they are – the "quick fix" syndrome. After making efforts to master public speaking and business skills, diets, sex and relationships, meditation, yoga, self-actualisation, positivity and so on, people may well not be any richer, slimmer, healthier, sexier, more confident or happier than before. They may well instead feel worse because they tried but failed.

The Obsession with Image

One clear indication of the strength of our desire to impress others is the way we prioritise our looks and image rather than concentrating on maintaining and improving the condition of our bodies on the inside. When a study revealed that a "beauty" product reduced wrinkles, hundreds of British women queued to buy it. At the peak of buying frenzy, a jar was sold every 10 seconds. While anti-aging creams may have *some* effect on reducing wrinkles and softening the skin, many experts advise people to eat more healthily instead. Surveys have found that half of British girls aged 5 to 8 wished they were thinner, that 40% of young girls in Britain had considered plastic surgery, and 52% worried about their weight or shape every day. Though some of them probably do need to lose weight, others may be influenced by airbrushed images and inordinately thin models.

- The number of young girls under 18 years-old treated for anorexia in English hospitals rose by around 80% from 1997 to 2007.

It's no longer just girls and young women who are now overly concerned with how they look. An increasing number of the middle-aged are desperate to remain attractive and young-looking. We don't embrace or accept the fact that we are getting older any more, instead we wish to be like Peter Pan and stay perpetually young. Not only have older women become obsessed with being youthful looking, like girls they would also love to be thin. In 2008 it was reported that anorexia among older women was becoming more common. Men today are also desperate to maintain their youthful looks, as indicated by the huge hair transplant market – even though they cost £10,000 and patients can be left with strange, regimented tufts of hair.

Increased wealth and the advance in cosmetic procedures have led to more and more people of both sexes choosing to alter their appearance in an attempt to bolster their confidence. Correcting a disfigurement or fixing a functional problem can be vital for someone's self-esteem and quality of life, but many now turn to unnecessary procedures for minor conditions that could be improved with a changed lifestyle. Instead of using these supposed instant solutions that new technology offers, it would be better to build self-respect by eating healthily and exercising. And cosmetic surgery – like any operation – carries risks. There have been problems with breast implants, and even a non-surgical procedure like *Botox* can cause permanent damage to the face as well as health.

- In 2011, 15 million plastic surgical and non-surgical cosmetic procedures were performed globally.

- In 2011, there were 211,000 procedures performed in the UK. Britons now spend over £2 billion a year on cosmetic treatments, and in 2009 loans of around £5 million were used to pay for some of them.

The most common non-surgical procedures are *Botox* injections and dermal filler. The surgical procedures for British women most in demand are breast augmentation, eyelid surgery, face/neck lift, breast reduction, rhinoplasty (nose reshaping), abdominoplasty (tummy tuck), and liposuction – where fat is sucked out of the body.

The Obsession with Status

The media, advertising, and instant widespread communication, have now ensured that keeping up with – or looking down on – the Joneses is firmly entrenched in our culture. Instead of prioritising social responsibility, governments are happy to see the human instincts of desire and competitiveness dominate our activities because they drive economic growth. Advertisers exploit people's tendency to be greedy and envious as well as encouraging them to be overly sensitive about their image and looks. Today many children just want to be wealthy, attractive and famous rather than working hard to "earn" greater status. Being rich and looking young have been elevated to the level of obsession, resulting in the exclusion of things of real worth and achievement.

Nobody is immune from comparing himself or herself to others. At the least we are driven to maintain our status relative to our peers. Sport is so competitive that players find it hard to tone down exuberance when victorious or accept defeat gracefully – winning at all costs is now the name of the game. Trades union leaders are acutely aware of the income levels of workers who are roughly at the same level as their members, and constantly try to maintain the same pay "differentials". Top musicians and other artists compare their performances and earning power to that of their peers, the captains of industry force their income upwards by comparing their financial rewards with top company executives round the world, and even politicians are extremely sensitive to the pecking order of world leaders – one significant reason why they firmly resist secession of part of their country and are overly concerned with economic growth.

The Obsession with Money

We've all heard the adage that "wealth doesn't bring happiness", though the majority still believes it does. In developed countries money has become the number one priority because people have been persuaded that more of it will provide greater security, comfort, status and freedom – and therefore happiness. This belief is so widespread that it has been conventional wisdom for decades. Yet Clive Hamilton, the author of *Growth Fetish*, has shown that no matter how wealthy people become, they say they need still more money to be happy.

- A study found that 56% of Australians believed that they needed yet more money to be happy, with almost half of the richest households saying their incomes were inadequate.

And because people automatically adjust to a continually rising standard of living, they always believe they're spending their income on "basics" in order to live a "moderately comfortable" life. But compared to previous generations rather than their peers, they are in fact living in luxury.

- A study found that 53% of Americans believed they spent most of their money on "basic necessities". 69% said that nearly all their income was used to buy things that "allowed them to live comfortably".

People aspire to the level of the richer people in society – if not to the level of the most successful business people, artists and sportsmen, then at least to the level of those they meet who earn more or have more. Peer pressure has increased so much that competition and greed are replacing collaboration with and caring for others. In America (and most other developed nations) there was a marked shift away from civic and social engagement during the 1990s towards the pursuit of self-interest. Our obsession with money has resulted in us chasing rainbows to find that pot of gold – to overtake the Joneses and buy nirvana. And inevitably this leads us to overloading ourselves with too many working hours, too many commitments, too much food, too much drink, too many drugs, too many activities, and too many possessions – producing a cycle of greater consumption and greater stress rather than contentment.

The Gap between Rich and Poor

The financial gap between rich and poor has a significant effect on the health of the whole population. Inequality is now known to be a constant trigger to the "fight or flight" response in human beings, and over time, this perpetual stress can lead to permanently raised levels of stress hormones such as cortisol – causing depression, higher blood pressure and other biological changes. These reactions seemingly occur because of the highly social nature of human beings and their acute sensitivity to social position and status. The income and wealth gap between rich and poor in most developed countries is now far wider than decades ago.

- The gap between the top 10% and the bottom 10% of British workers widened from 8 to 1 in 1985 to 12 to 1 in 2008.

- In the UK the income of the top 0.1% (one-tenth of 1%) is about 95 times as much as the bottom 90%.

- The better-off half of Britain's households has 90% of the total wealth, while the least wealthy half has just 10%.

Today a fortunate few get far more than what most would consider as a "fair" share of the financial pot. People would not begrudge some receiving an above average recompense for their popularity, skill, hard work and risk-taking, but it is divisive – and it could be argued, unfair morally – that some get so much when others get so little. Those in the highest echelon of the business and financial arenas – the cosy "club" of movers and shakers – make sure that all members are handsomely rewarded with titles, positions of power and influence, and of course golden hellos, golden goodbyes, huge salaries and bonuses, as well as stupendous pensions. What argument can justify directors of companies and banks earning more in one week than the ordinary hard-working man can earn in a year – or in some cases 5 years? And though elite athletes and performers are rewarded through the operations of free market capitalism, are they in relative terms worthy of the sometimes obscene amounts of money they earn?

Spirit Level, a book by Richard Wilkinson and Kate Pickett, shows that wealth and income inequality correlates closely with social problems. In more equal countries, groups with similar income levels have better mental and physical health than in more unequal ones, and this holds true for both high and low income groups. Poor mental health is a significant cause of lower educational achievement and work productivity, and higher levels of physical disease and mortality, violence, relationship breakdown, and poor community cohesion. Good mental health, on the other hand, leads to healthier lifestyles, improved productivity and educational attainment, and lower levels of crime and violence.

Few, if any, would now argue that some kind of communist system is likely to work better than capitalism. In the end, fairness and reasonableness comes down to respect and love for our fellow human beings – which is in all of us, but is compromised, diminished or even crushed by the machinations of those with opportunity to manipulate the system, aided and abetted by the way our so-called democracies actually function. The baser instincts of a minority have been "allowed" to cause extreme disparity, resulting in widespread envy and greed. Because of frequent elections and the close ties between politicians and many who are well-off, democratic governments are extremely unlikely to pass legislation that would spread wealth and earnings more evenly.

Increasing Debt

We are in an age of financial decadence. Debt used to be a dirty word, and several generations ago people would only consider borrowing to buy a home. In time, taking out a loan to buy a new car was also considered reasonable. Today it is considered normal to fund almost any purchase with borrowed money. Society's view of debt has changed considerably over the last century, with so many people – encouraged by free-spending, debt-ridden governments – putting pressure on themselves by spending their future income. Once considered as an occasional, necessary evil, borrowing and debt came to be considered pragmatic, then normal, then inevitable, and finally vital. The national debts of most developed countries have burgeoned in recent decades.

- The UK national debt is now over £1 trillion – about £18,000 for every man, woman and child, and about £39,000 for every working person. On average, each household pays about £2,000 each year just to cover the interest.

The recent housing bubble persuaded many homeowners to refinance their homes at lower interest rates or take out second mortgages secured by the price appreciation. While house prices were increasing, we were saving less and both borrowing and spending more. Even after the financial "crunch" of 2008, when our leaders bailed out the banks and saddled future generations with mountains of debt, they remained obsessed with economic growth and encouraged us to consume more. Few people discuss the concept of delayed gratification these days, let alone consider practising it. The last 30 years have seen the culture of thrift in most developed countries almost disappear.

- In 2008 UK credit card debt was £50 billion. Average British household debt was £8,956, and together with mortgages totalled £56,234.

- In 2007 Britons saved the smallest slice of their incomes since 1960 – the household savings ratio (the proportion of disposable income not spent) fell to 2.1% in the first quarter of 2007. In 2008 a third of Britons in their 20s had no savings at all.

The levels of borrowing and debt, and the consequent stress on many poor people, have grown even more in recent years. The controversy over short-term "payday loans" and their exorbitant interest rates (equivalent to an annual percentage rate of well over 1,000%) occurred during the final stages of editing the book. The growth of this industry has been rapid.

- In 2011/12, the value of the payday loan industry in the UK was £2.2 billion, up from £900 million in 2008/9. An estimated 2 million people now use payday loans, up from 300,000 in 2006.

The Ever-Rising Bar

Extraordinary as it seems, most people in developed countries feel more materially deprived than previous generations, despite being so much richer. We take our affluence for granted and show little appreciation for what we have and the interesting and comfortable lives we lead. The media reinforces feelings of deprivation and discontent that the marketing industry is keen to foster.

- Consumption per head in the UK has risen almost fivefold – in real terms – since just after World War 1. At constant 2003 prices, consumption for each Briton in 1921 was £2,700, rising to £12,784 in 2006.

Consumption per capita has risen roughly threefold since the 1960s, along with that of most other developed countries. This is hardly surprising – we now have bigger houses with higher quality finish and furnishings, more possessions, more comfort, and we get involved in more activities. We have a lot more of everything – which means more to insure, more to go wrong, more to become accustomed to and have to replace, more for others to envy, more to squeeze into our lives, and therefore more to manage and worry about overall. More money will often lead to more temptation, more consumption and more ill-health – and less time for those things that lead to true contentment.

The more we have, the more we want, and unless perspectives change, we will forever hanker after yet more. Standards and expectations continually increase, so there is always pressure to consume at yet higher levels. Each generation comes into the world and – as is human nature – views the existing standard of living as "normal". The bar rises, or in other words, the number of what people consider as "basic necessities" goes up, along with comfort, finish and luxury. The following generation then takes that new, higher standard of living for granted, and so on it goes. Because the "scaling up of needs" outpaces income growth, many people who are wealthy by any historical or international standard actually feel poor.

Strawberries can serve as a typical example of ever-rising consumption caused by our indulgent, "progressive" and experimental inclinations. First we ate strawberries in season, then we added sugar, then we also ate them out of season and began adding cream. Then some decided a scoop or two of ice-cream would be nice to go with them, and finally (maybe) a sweet sauce or a Flake chocolate bar was added. Spurred on by social pressure ("everybody's doing it"), this escalation occurs in all areas of our lives. Everything has to be bigger, stronger, louder, smoother, tastier, glitzier, sexier, more powerful, more expensive, more comfortable, more exciting, more thrilling or more dynamic than before, yet we are never satisfied. Instead we become "overloaded".

Too Many Possessions

Most material goods are now purchased largely for the consumer's self-image or lifestyle, not because they are actually needed. The marketing industry employs devious methods to make people spend money, even against their best interests. Advertisements imply that a product has some special property or quality that is in fact entirely unrelated to the product itself – and the latest wheeze is to claim the product is "environmentally friendly". Modern marketing builds symbolic relationships between the product and the psychological states of potential customers – often targeting feelings of fear, inadequacy, aspiration or expectation.

Instead of searching for and accepting our real selves, we assume concocted images and identities. This is never really satisfying, and so we try harder and harder to create the desired image through buying more products. Brands create the conditions for serial disappointment, yet sustain hope that more of what has so far failed will ultimately succeed. Just as more and more junk food will never satisfy bodies, creating false images will never lead to true contentment for minds. The advertising industry employs a huge amount of talent on this "cultural brainwashing" to sustain a consumption excess that actually makes people suffer in the long term. And now we have so many possessions that they won't all fit into our homes – so we need to earn more money to pay for the overflow to sit in self-storage facilities. 1 in 10 American households now use self-storage facilities, and Britain has begun to move in the same direction.

- In 2011 the gross revenue of the British self-storage industry was about £355 million, up from about £225 million in 2006.

We waste millions of pounds buying gadgets that rarely, if ever, get used – such as sandwich toasters, coffee machines, foot spas and a host of kitchen gadgets. People don't have the time, inclination or nous to make full use of their purchases, and perhaps as many as 1 in 20 people have now become mired in debt because of their "compulsive acquisition disorder". Our houses are full of clutter because, unlike those of several generations ago, we have lost the habit of self-restraint. *The Week* magazine has featured items for sale that illustrate overblown consumption. These include *The Eclipse Lounger* that has a sunshield hood and detachable cushions on a wicker frame, with a footstool and side table, priced at £4,913, *The RainSky Shower* that produces mists, coloured lights, outdoor scents and integrated sound, for £11,000, a £200 robotic pet dinosaur which expresses a range of emotions, Newfoundland iceberg water for £13 a bottle, and the leather *Game Cube* with 20 games for a mere £20,065.

Hectic Leisure

Even leisure has become competitive and stressful. Because people have so many and very similar possessions, keeping up with the Joneses has switched to some degree from "having" into "doing". We now view frequent outings to restaurants, the cinema, clubs and pubs as not only normal, but a necessity. And on holiday people try to cram in more places and more activities in as short a time as possible. The old anecdote about American travellers ticking off names of countries they've visited applies to most nationalities today. More people feel the need to impress others with tales of expensive and exotic trips – and weddings are increasingly taking place abroad, putting relatives and friends under time, organisational and financial pressure.

Lack of Appreciation

People lead such busy, acquisitive and debt-ridden lives that they are never really aware of their affluence. They continually yearn for yet more money and stuff (and the associated status) because they are always comparing their situation with others who have more. When you focus on what you *don't* have, it stops you appreciating all the things you *do* have – whether furniture, gadgets or food. A government study revealed that in 2007 Britons threw away 18% of all food purchased, amounting to £10 billion worth of food that could have been eaten.

- In 2011 the average British household wasted £660's worth of food.

We don't really appreciate our food because we eat too much and too often, meaning we rarely feel real hunger, and when we eat we multi-task i.e. watch TV, drive or work at the same time as eating. We are also largely disconnected from our food and where it comes from – we prepare food less frequently because of the proliferation of processed, packaged food in supermarkets. We take both the abundance of food and choice for granted.

- During 2005, £38 billion was spent on clothes in the UK – and the following year over 800,000 metric tonnes of clothing and shoes were thrown away.

Even goods in perfect condition, like flatpack furniture, are thrown out. *George Foreman Griddles*, sandwich and ordinary toasters are discarded, as well as bicycles with minor problems that owners couldn't be bothered to fix. In 2008 Britons threw away £48 million in unwanted gifts over the Christmas period, and 60% of us gave gift vouchers worth £1 billion, a quarter of which would not be redeemed. Charity shop workers, overwhelmed with discarded possessions, now get annoyed with people using them as dumping centres. Without a new way of looking at life, the continual hankering for possessions and lack of appreciation will undoubtedly continue.

Loss of Communal Feeling

In his book *The Loss of Happiness in Market Democracies*, Robert E. Lane wrote that the American community was in a state of "psychic malnutrition". He believed that the "growing deficiency of the cultural immune system" was evidenced by the lack of warm inter-personal relationships, little community cohesion, fewer concerned neighbours, and a diffuse family life. Until the last 50 years, family members and those in the wider community were generally better role models and more supportive, providing children with a set of ethics that would include honesty and self-responsibility. Parental mentoring and wider family influence have decreased considerably in recent decades, along with a corresponding increase in negative influences from entertainment, advertising and the media.

Rather than a home, the family house is now a portal to the "virtual" world – TV, radio, emails, skype, video and online games, porn and gambling. Running the household is seen as a chore instead of an opportunity for social interaction and co-operation. Social activities like cooking, meal times, friends and family play, are now seen as mundane, yet these are vital factors in human contentment. Relationships are less likely to develop and conflict is more likely when individual family members are separately occupied with their particular activities. Integrating personal need and social responsibility, i.e. growing up, has almost disappeared.

As in ancient times when people lived in small groups, community spirit is still vital for human wellbeing. Whilst recognising the complexities of measuring contentment, it is hardly surprising that populations ranked higher in *The Happy Planet Index* are far less individualistic. Pacific islanders, Central American and Asian countries top the list. The Netherlands, ranked 43rd, was the only Western country in the top 50. France at 71st was just above the UK at 74^{th,} with the USA at 114th. So-called "primitive" societies were not ranked, but I strongly suspect they are the most content.

How to Deal with Social Pressure

Greater awareness will lead to a greater appreciation of all the things we have, including the natural world. We are so fortunate to have the freedom to make so many choices, which most people in the world don't have. Our approach to buying goods and services would be tempered if we understood that the priority of most businessmen is to make money – not to make consumers happy. And the modern message to work hard and make a lot of money omits the negative side – the resultant lack of time and energy required to achieve intimacy and fulfilment. Americans and Western Europeans do not seem to have become happier with yet higher affluence. Though an average income is necessary to avoid continual financial pressure, more money in itself will not bring peace of mind. Robust health, self-respect, good friends, a supportive and caring family and community, along with self-development, are the factors that create real, lasting contentment.

- Our leaders are part of the vested interests group who are not motivated to change the status quo, so it's important that each of us faces life squarely, takes responsibility for ourselves and deals with "problems" directly. We are far more likely to achieve a balance in our lives if we pay less attention to outside forces and make up our own mind about what we want to do or have.

- We all gain from improving our skills and working hard at what we do, but trying to live up to an illusory image of ourselves can make life difficult. Just being yourself is much easier and will get you what you really need in the end. Lasting and true self-esteem comes from within, not from what possessions we have, where we go on holiday, from comparing ourselves to others, or from their praise or criticism.

- Once we become aware of the often manipulative and superficial nature of much of the media, marketing and many of those around us, the power of these outside agencies over us will naturally begin to diminish. No purchase matters as much as we often think it does at the time.

- Many people overextend themselves and hope that the "rainy day" won't come. You only need to live well within your means for a while, put some reserves in the bank by "delaying your gratification" for 6 months or so, and then you'll probably be able to avoid the pressures of debt for the rest of your life. And having funds put by for unexpected expenses brings peace of mind. Those who earn a good income can use their money to create a balanced lifestyle, and where possible to help others.

- Be aware that everybody has their own agenda. Your friends want you to be like them, and they might well want to be like you. Everybody wants to experience the comfort of being part of a group. We all need friends, but you're more likely to have strong and real relationships if you are true to yourself. Just being yourself and trying to do what you feel is right will mean you'll acquire good friends and peace of mind.

- If you take responsibility for your thoughts and actions and view life positively, you're far more likely to achieve long-term contentment. This process will involve awareness, willpower and courage – particularly at the start.

WORK

"Western society is built on overwork during the week and over-consumption at the weekends."
(Dan Kieran)

Society largely looks on work as a cost or burden which allows people to achieve certain benefits and pleasures − a necessary evil to put money into consumers' pockets. Little consideration is made about the nature of the work done because it's merely a means to an end. Yet people are still evaluated by what they do (and by how much money they have) rather than by what they are, and our self-esteem is often determined by our job. Politicians seem to think that any work, however boring or dissatisfying, is better than no work − and any product that creates jobs, even arms, tobacco, or fast food, is better than none. The quality of work and the worth of the product, however, are extremely important factors that reflect human values and have a large effect on our wellbeing.

Today work certainly plays an extremely important part in our lives. As Clive Hamilton in his book *Growth Fetish* writes: "It provides time structure, social contact, collective effort or purpose, social identity or status, and regular activity. Mostly it continues to provide a sense of personal identity." Certainly we all need to *work at* something because lazing about doing nothing for any length of time would certainly drive most of us mad. But the standard 40-hour, 5-day working schedule − plus commuting time − means everything else has to be squeezed into relatively few hours. Even workers who enjoy their jobs often find that working hours use up most of their time and energy, leaving little of both available for other, arguably more important things. And though a sizeable minority might find work satisfying and rewarding, for many it is often not fulfilling or enjoyable, for others it can be boring and undemanding, and for some it can be stressful or even degrading. Sadly, the overriding or even sole reason that many people work is to earn their pay cheque.

A visitor from another planet would look at our pace of life and long working hours and surely think we are suffering from some kind of obsessive compulsive disorder. When tribal visitors from Tanna island in the South Pacific first experienced our "civilised" way of life on a visit to Britain in 2007, they were amazed that we spend most of our lives working. They were sad to see that family life had deteriorated because we have been far more concerned with increasing our material standard of living. They believe the most important things in life are love, happiness, peace and respect. Travelling faster, living longer, and making more money are prioritised in our culture, but they wisely ask the question "Why?" rather than "How much"?

Job security, empathic management, a small workplace, a relatively high income, flexible hours, part-time work, self-employment, and less commuting time, are all factors that can reduce work stress. People would feel better if they had more control over their time and activities instead of being institution-led, advertising-led, or work-led. If we became fully aware that creativity, self-development, and fulfilling our potential were far more important for our wellbeing than money and status, then the overtime culture would simply fade away. Though important, work should be taken down from its pedestal and assume its proportional place in our lives. It should be viewed as just one of several factors in a fulfilling and content life.

The Scale and Problems of Work Overload

Britain has a workplace culture that seems to value stamina and long hours too much, and flexibility and productivity too little – perhaps originating from the Protestant work ethic.

- Full-time British employees work 42.7 hours a week on average.

More enlightened cultures, though less technologically advance-ed, understand the importance of family and other activities and accord work a lower "proportionality" in their lives. The

Kapauku people of Papua think it is bad luck to work 2 consecutive days, and the !Kung Bushmen work just 2-and-a-half days per week. The working week in Samoa is approximately 30 hours, and though their average annual income is relatively low by some measures, the Samoans enjoy a good standard of living and quality of life.

Commuting

Commuting eats into the time available for other activities, as well as involving a lot more stress because of unreliable and overcrowded trains and buses – or traffic jams for those who travel by car.

- British employees' average one-way commute is about 27 minutes, adding 4-and-a-half hours to the working week.

10% of workers have a journey in excess of 60 minutes in each direction, and just over 3% (740,000 people) are "extreme commuters", travelling at least an hour-and-a-half to and from work.

Job Satisfaction

The drive of developed countries to continually expand their economies is matched by the expectation of individuals to keep rising up the hierarchy to earn more money and gain more status. Neither of these goals is necessary for contentment – in fact the opposite may well be true.

- A survey in 2011 found that only 34% of British workers were happy in their job, and 24% were "distinctly unhappy".

Some entrepreneurs prefer to stay small and do what they think is right for themselves, the community and the world. They are happy with the amount of profits they make and don't feel they have to keep expanding to be or feel successful. They have enough money and status and don't compare themselves unfavourably with Richard Branson or Warren Buffet. And there are employees who turn down promotion because they want to maintain a healthy family life by not burdening themselves with too many working hours and too much responsibility and stress.

Stress

It seems that hard-pressed businesses pass on the strain to workers.

- A 2011 survey of 2,000 British workers found that 41% were stressed or very stressed in their jobs – making work more stressful than money worries, relationships or health issues.

In his book *In Praise of Slow*, Carl Honoré states his belief that everybody now exists to serve the economy, rather than the other way round. Long hours on the job make us unproductive, error-prone, unhappy and ill, and burnout is now happening to people in their 30s and even 20s. He calls global companies "profit-driven workaholic cults" – they make little effort to nurture their employees, leading to longer workdays, less sleep, continuous learning, an extreme energy requirement, as well as a high tolerance for financial insecurity. Deadlines mount, so last minute planning, mobile phones, pagers, laptops, reduced rest, and fast food become the essential strategies for survival. Studies show that long working hours are very likely to cause health problems and burnout.

- Job stress in the UK was estimated to result in 12.8 million working days lost during 2004/5.

- In 2010, 75% of young British office workers ate lunch at their desks and were doing 10-hour days without taking a break – and increasing the risk of blood clots.

A long-hours work culture can lead to stress, anxiety and depression, high blood pressure, cardiovascular disease, diabetes and insomnia. In Europe, those who work 41 hours or more a week are significantly more likely to have high blood pressure, and middle-aged workers doing more than 55 hours a week can suffer short-term memory loss. The stress levels experienced by British workers have risen sharply – 7 out of 10 motorists in London get angry when driving to work, and stress has overtaken backache as the leading cause of absenteeism.

Many people get used to more status and money and feel they can't give them up, even though they know deep down they would probably feel better if they did. Some stay in stressful jobs because of inertia, some are afraid of the unknown, while others worry that leaving might damage their career, disappoint others, or that they might not get another job quickly or easily. Some wake up and "smell the roses" when something drastic happens to them, such as a serious accident, a death in the family, or being diagnosed with a life-threatening illness. Work "overload" tends to be acknowledged only when workers become so stressed that burnout occurs – they have a heart attack or are diagnosed with depression. Only then do they recognise that money and status are not what really matters in life.

Productivity

In his book *Enough*, John Naish claims productivity would be far greater – especially if people view their jobs as tedious – if they did fewer hours. When the hotel chain Marriott allowed workers to go home when the job was done, employees worked 5 hours fewer a week, yet productivity went up. People can get too tired, too stressed, under-stimulated, distracted or depressed and thereby under-productive. Belgian, French and Norwegian workers do fewer hours but have higher productivity than the Americans and English.

Escapism

Workaholics Anonymous was launched in 1983 in New York, and the first branch in England opened in 2000. Like consuming, work can be another form of escapism. If we had a lot of free time we would then have to ponder the big questions of life about meaning and purpose, or face up to domestic duties and relationships. Working and consuming to get wealth, power and celebrity is often used as a substitute, an escape, or a displacement activity, because – for men particularly – it can be easier to control activities and relationships at work than personal ones in the home. When some workers retire they are at a loss as to how to fill their time, and their health deteriorates along with their self-image. Retirees who have values that give direction to life, including political, spiritual and personal development interests, obtain the psychological benefits of employment by other means. They have "transcending" goals and purposes and many derive self-worth, status and identity from new activities such as voluntary work.

Safety

Machinery operators and those workers who drive or maintain vehicles require strict regulations of working practices and number of hours, otherwise there would be a danger to employees' health. The risk to office job workers is more subtle – overwork can lead to stress between employees as well as for the individual.

Children

Because of their obsession with economic growth, successive governments have encouraged mothers to work more, without considering the negative effects on children and subsequent generations. Women's work in the home was respected up to the 1950s, but the feminist movement together with the focus on material advancement led to its devaluation. Mothers and fathers are persuaded by peer pressure to work more to achieve a progressively higher standard of living, though this leads to feelings of guilt about leaving their children with minders who can't really love and care for them in the same way. And as research has shown, both parents being in the rat race is not conducive to children's development. Housework – cooking, cleaning, washing, child care, gardening, shopping and home maintenance – contributes enormously to the whole family's physical comfort and emotional contentment. Whether done by mothers or fathers, it provides a living environment that is healthy, comfortable, supportive, nurturing and loving.

It seems that Anglo-Saxons don't have a family-friendly culture, so flexibility of working hours – that could increase the wellbeing of families – is not prioritised. I believe that if society recognised fully the importance of parenting, and governments encouraged both mothers and fathers to work less and spend more time with their children, not only would their quality of life increase, but the same level of production could be maintained despite fewer working hours – people would look upon work more favourably and have more energy and enthusiasm for it.

Life Balance

Because there is usually some quotient of drudgery in many people's jobs, they would undoubtedly find work more enjoyable if they worked far fewer hours. But an overall and significant reduction of time spent at work would entail societal changes in many other areas of life. As the Australian economist Clive Hamilton wrote: "Reducing working hours will have a liberating effect only if there is a politics of time which embraces the reshaping of the urban and natural environment, cultural politics, education and training, and reshapes the social services and public amenities in such a way as to create more scope for self-managed activities, mutual aid, voluntary co-operation and production for one's own use."

Work is given priority in our lives and it uses up the bulk of our waking hours. All the other things in life – family, friends, community and voluntary activities, contemplation, sex and sleep, housework, hobbies and holidays – are forced to fit in with the work schedule. When work leaves us too little time and energy for those things, we are more likely to hit the bottle or reach for convenience foods. Everyone has to earn a living, but the endless hunger for consumer goods means that we need more and more money. Our marketing-driven consumption has led us to opt for higher incomes instead of taking productivity gains in the form of extra time off. Carl Honoré writes that being "married to a job" takes a toll on our intimate relationships, and the harm also flows the other way – research has shown that American employees with marital problems lose an average of 15 workdays per year.

- A survey of a firm's employees in 18 countries found that 71% of those born between 1980 and 1995 (as well as 63% of "non-millennials") believed the demands of work significantly interfered with their personal lives.

- A study found that 64% of Britons are too tired to play with their children, 73% are often too tired for sex, and 53% of dog owners find it hard to muster enough energy to take their pet for walks.

Inspired by the technological breakthroughs of the late 1700s, Benjamin Franklin envisioned a world devoted to rest and relaxation, with people working just 4 hours a week. Then in 1956 Nixon told Americans to prepare for a 4-day workweek in the "not too distant future". In 1966 a US Senate subcommittee was assured that by the year 2000 Americans would be working as little as 14 hours per week. Even in the 1980s, some predicted that robotics and computers would create far more free time. Instead, our insatiable desire for greater consumption and our leaders' obsession with economic growth, supported by recent technological advances, has prevented a fall in working hours. And companies today, forever trying to cut costs, reduce the workforce so that those left have more to do, and fear of unemployment pressurises everybody to work longer. This is bad for productivity, bad for home life, and bad for physical and mental health.

The particular work/life balance chosen depends on the type of job, the personality of the worker, and what else is in his or her life, but average working hours won't decrease unless people change their view about the relative importance of possessions – and money, the means to acquire them. Most people would like more control of their time and to be able to make decisions about when and how much they want to work, but they aren't prepared to relinquish their high living standard. Those who *are* prepared to work fewer hours, simplify their life and scale back their consumption, will be more relaxed, creative and productive. Spending less time on the job will not only mean less stress and more time for other things, but will also mean spending less money on the things associated with work – travel, parking, eating out, coffee, convenience food, childcare, laundry, and "retail therapy" – and a smaller income involves a smaller tax bill too. Today many people have been able to adjust their work/life balance through job-sharing, freelancing and flexible working.

Unemployment

If people who have jobs worked fewer hours and more employees worked part-time, more people could work and unemployment would drop.

How to Avoid Work Overload

After the near collapse of the banking system in 2008, our leaders encouraged us all to be patriotic, to go out and spend in order to keep the system afloat. In other words, to carry on doing the same things which were at the root of the problem in the first place. You should be bold and ignore this advice because keeping up with the Joneses is a never-ending and ultimately fruitless task. Try to resist peer pressure, put aside your basic instinct to go along with the majority, and set your own agenda. Ask yourself what will give you the most satisfaction. Owning new things will only provide a temporary fillip, but personal development will increase self-esteem and provide long-term satisfaction. If we didn't hanker after so much, we wouldn't have to spend so much, and therefore not have to earn so much money and work so much.

- Cutting down on possessions and activities can actually be liberating. A simpler life is easier to handle. Those around you, what you do, the things you own, can all be appreciated and absorbed fully. True moderation is the key. Quiet, long-term contentment is more likely to be achieved by enjoying just a few of our society's creature comforts and conveniences. A shorter working week will not only mean less pressure, it will also allow more time to recharge your batteries and develop relationships.

- Think hard before deciding to take on a job with greater responsibility and more hours, and resist the temptation to do regular overtime. If you choose to climb the corporate ladder, fix a time limit and leave the rat race after a particular number of years. After 5 years I knew that working in an office would drive me mad eventually, so I turned to music and "sacrificed" the large salary I could probably have commanded after 20 years. You don't *have* to keep rising up the hierarchy and perhaps end up with too much responsibility and stress. John Naish suggests "sideshifting" – in other words to stay quietly at the level of responsibility and workload that suits your competence best. Assess your limits and don't become paranoid about "underachieving".

- A possible alternative to "working for the man" is to start a business. Meeting the challenge of creating work and being flexible enough to handle problems that arise can bring great satisfaction. The self-employed have the freedom to decide what and how much work is worth doing, if it's moral, and if it isn't too inconvenient. Here too, though, income doesn't have to be maximised. Working for yourself can create more choice regarding workload, but there is a danger of increased stress from not delegating or trying to expand too quickly. Work should be about learning, enjoyment and purpose, as well as income. The devil as usual is in the detail, however. Each of us has to assess what is "moderate" when assessing levels of consumption, expenditure and work.

- If starting a business is not possible, then working for a small company would be a reasonable alternative. There is likely to be greater variety and fulfilment in a job where the product is seen from creation through to client. Accepting a lower salary in a smaller company that has a supportive atmosphere and where you can actually make a difference, might be a better choice for peace of mind. In today's fast-moving society, most workers are small cogs in a big wheel, and because mobility is now almost essential, qualities like loyalty and service are increasingly ignored by larger companies.

- Whatever your work, enough rest and "idle" time is vital. Resist keeping up with stressed-out, workaholic colleagues and optimise your chances of getting more done in less time by learning what habits suit your body and mind best. Where possible work at those times of the day that suit you. Some people are raring to go at the crack of dawn while others are night owls. Like me, you might prefer working in spurts and enjoy variety. Working part-time could be better for the soul – work might well be appreciated more, and others will be able to do those hours relinquished.

- In most families today both parents do full-time work in order to fund what would be considered by previous generations to be an extravagant and indulgent lifestyle. This is not conducive to raising well-adjusted children. Talented women are now beginning to opt out of the traditional rat race in increasing numbers because there is insufficient time and energy to raise children *and* hold down a demanding job. Parental leave and flexible hours are insufficient concessions to allow mothers to manage both children and work, so their options are working from home, perhaps starting their own business, or going part-time. Certainly those women (and men) who choose to work part-time or can work at home are likely to appreciate their job more, as well as be able to raise their children more effectively and enjoyably. And most will probably be glad to be off the career treadmill.

- Though making do with a lower income can mean less stress and allow you to stay sane and healthy, working long hours when younger *could* be viewed as a pragmatic compromise. It might be feasible to consider a short period of "deferred happiness" for a while, especially when in your "dynamic and thrusting" 20s and 30s and wanting to establish yourself – a temporary sacrifice of family time, of maintaining optimum health, of personal fulfilment and of a more balanced lifestyle. Then you would need to assess the right time to exercise the option to leave the rate race before getting burnt out. If you're a parent, however, it must be recognised that even a short period of a heavy workload may affect your children, partly because in a sense you'll be setting a bad example.

- You're unique. You need your own particular balance that doesn't create too much stress, but generates sufficient income and a feeling of achievement that provides self-esteem and leads to long-term contentment. A minority of people earn an adequate income from doing their "hobby", but for most this is unlikely to happen. A reduction of working hours for the majority, particularly for those engaged in stressful jobs, would mean a higher overall quality of life.

SPEED

*"I am Scrooge with a stopwatch, obsessed
with saving every last scrap of time...
and I am not alone.
Everyone around me – colleagues, friends, family –
is caught in the same vortex."*

(Carl Honoré)

Today time is viewed as a resource that we must utilise to maximum "efficiency". Consequently most of us are suffering from an overload of stress, unable to turn off the drive and stimulation. We desperately need time to "chill out", do nothing, and recharge our batteries, yet we seem to view contemplation time as somehow reprehensible because it's not "productive". We don't understand that an always-on-the-go lifestyle causes our mental and physical health to deteriorate and prevents us from achieving long-term contentment.

In his book *In Praise of Slow*, Carl Honoré describes our impossible aims: "As well as glittering careers, we want to take art courses, work out at the gym, read the newspaper and every book on the bestseller list, eat out with friends, go clubbing, play sports, watch hours of television, listen to music, spend time with the family, buy all the newest fashions and gadgets, go to the cinema, enjoy intimacy and great sex with our partners, holiday in far-flung locations and maybe even do some meaningful volunteer work. The result is a yawning disconnect between what we want from life and what we can realistically have, which feeds the sense that there is never enough time."

People used to do things when it felt right. They would "go with the flow", as many Pacific Islanders and those in so-called primitive societies still do today. In his book *How to Be Free*, Tom Hodgkinson contends that centuries ago we used to be largely carefree, but now we are governed by the clock instead of our natural instincts. For 200 years we have been on an ever-quickening treadmill of efficiency – in the erroneous belief that an increase in productivity would automatically improve our quality of life. And the speed at which we operate rises along with the self-perpetuating cycle of greater growth and greater consumption. We've become obsessed with efficiency and saving time, but the question needs to be asked: "Saving time for what?" In previous centuries there were particular seasons and days to do certain things. Now we do anything and everything at any time. Competition, peer pressure, fear and greed encourage us to apply the principle of "time is money" to every moment. The burgeoning use of time management consultants is indicative of our paranoia about wasting time.

We need to slow down, but cogitation, idling, staring out of windows, is frowned on – you're not being productive or you're missing out on the enjoyment of life. In fact the pendulum has swung so much that when the constant stimulation is removed, people feel lost, get bored, or even panic to find something to do. Reducing the pace and complexity of life is not a new idea, but we need to examine it again. Henry Thoreau opted out of the treadmill in 1845 and wrote the popular book *Walden*, which extolled a simpler way of living, there was the "counterculture" of the hippies in the 1960s, and in the late 1980s, the *Slow* movement emerged.

In response to *McDonald's* opening a branch beside the Spanish Steps in Rome, Carlo Petrini started the *Slow Food* movement in 1986, which expanded to over 83,000 members in 122 countries. Here is part of its manifesto: "We are enslaved by speed and have all succumbed to the same insidious virus. Fast Life disrupts our habits, pervades the privacy of our homes and forces us to eat Fast Foods. To be worthy of the name, Homo Sapiens should rid himself of speed before it reduces him to a species in danger of extinction." The Slow approach has since been applied in other areas of life, including travel, medicine, education – and sex.

Perhaps, like the Slow movement, the phenomenon of "downshifting" emerged as a reaction against the glorification of individual wealth creation during the 1980s. Since that decade a growing minority of people have recognised what is of real value to them and swapped their high-pressure, high-earning, high-tempo lifestyle for a more relaxed, less consumerist existence. There are probably around 16 million "downshifters" in Europe now. "Transition towns" and "eco-villages" are two other recent attempts to eschew growth, expansion and speed, and to concentrate instead on improving quality of life.

The Scale and Problems of Speed

Are you always checking the time on your watch? When someone takes too long to get to the point, do you want to hurry them along? Are you often first to finish at mealtimes? When walking along a street, do you feel frustrated because you are stuck behind others? Do you avoid neighbours because chatting to them means valuable time would be lost? Do you walk out of banks, restaurants or shops if you encounter a short queue? If you are caught in slow-moving traffic, do you get agitated? Would you become irritable if you sat for an hour with nothing to do? If you answer "yes" to most of these questions, you need to slow down, otherwise your health – and that of your family members – will probably suffer. Speed prevents us from losing ourselves in the present moment, being fully absorbed in a task, and from treating every activity or person with full respect and attention. We race around at an ever-increasing speed, doing an ever-increasing number of things, worried that we will miss out if we don't cram as much into our lives as possible.

In virtually all areas of life, the pace of activity has speeded up. We believe quantity is important. We want to earn a lot of money, buy a lot of goods, have a lot of possessions, and do a lot. Because we continually try to squeeze more into each day, we have to do everything faster, and recent "speedy" technology – like the internet and smart phones – has helped to fuel our impatience and hectic activity. The majority of us live in an urban environment, with the herd mentality and the constant traffic, noise, media and marketing bombardment. The daily hustle and bustle urges us to speed up. The continuous stimulation of the city keeps us moving, and we rarely switch off, but the advantages of anonymity, excitement and opportunity can be more than offset by stress and alienation. When there is no let-up in the hectic pace, people's lives will be out of balance, and sooner or later their wellbeing will diminish.

Urban Living

Living in large population centres has increased our pace of life – literally, when walking speeds are analysed. In 1976 a study showed that pedestrian walking speeds match the size of the city. It seems that people walk faster in larger places as a psychological response to greater stimulation. A mid-1990s study found that walking speeds were linked to a lack of empathy and health problems. As people move faster they become less likely to help others and tend to have higher rates of coronary heart disease. In 2006 another study of walking speeds in 32 cities round the world showed that average walking speeds had risen by about 10% since 1994. The largest increase was found in the fast-developing Asian countries like China and Singapore, with pedestrians walking 20% to 30% faster than they did in the early 1990s. Singapore had the quickest walkers in the world, with London the fastest-paced British city, at 12th in the overall ranking. Professor Wiseman, the study leader, believes that as we get more stressed and hurried we spend less time with our friends, don't have time to exercise, eat poorly, and are likely to drink and smoke more.

Perpetual Work

Mobile phones and the internet mean people can be contacted 24 hours of the day and every day of the week. Managers like to be able to contact workers whenever they wish, and workers feel obliged to be available, but this can be intrusive and inconvenient, and lead to unpaid overtime and resentment. The existing imbalance between work and other important activities in life has been exacerbated by the new, ultra-fast technology.

Addiction

Humans are prone to excess and addiction, and our desire to do more and more in less and less time continues to grow. We constantly worry about the next item on our list of things to do rather than enjoying what we are doing in the moment. Indicative of the desire to cram as much as possible into our lives is the "bucket list" (from "kick the bucket") – people making a list of things they "must" do before they die.

Greater Pressure on Friendships

A survey found that Britons struggle to maintain friendships because of their busy schedules. Social networking internet sites enable people to keep abreast of what their friends and relatives are up to, but this is a poor substitute for personal contact.

Greater Superficiality

Carl Honoré writes: "Inevitably, a life of hurry can become superficial. When we rush, we skim the surface, and fail to make any real connections with the world or other people… All the things that bind us together and make life worth living, community, family, friendship, thrive on the one thing we never have enough of – time." How can we possibly do anything effectively and enjoyably when we race around? We need to make time to absorb what we do, ponder on life, to understand things, ourselves and others more fully. Carl Honoré again: "Slow is calm, careful, receptive, still, intuitive, unhurried, patient, reflective, quality-over-quantity." The spirit by its nature is slow, so spiritual leaders will preach slowness. No matter how hard you try, enlightenment will not come quickly.

Lack of Appreciation

A natural corollary of consuming and taking on too much, and doing everything at a high pace, is that we find it much harder to appreciate things. Children as well as adults have now lost the frisson of anticipation, the excitement of what is to come. We have forgotten how to look forward to things, and how to enjoy the moment fully when it arrives.

Lack of Rest

People are sleeping and resting too little. The average American gets 90 minutes less sleep each night than a century ago. Apart from having to gee up our speeding bodies and minds with caffeine and maybe other drugs, too little sleep can lead to people grabbing snacks more often to boost their energy to get through each busy day. In their book *Dynamic Living*, Hans Diehl and Eileen Ludington emphasise the importance of rest. They believe that life today is fast-paced and exhausting, and insomnia is epidemic. People are gulping down millions of sedatives and tranquilisers, desperate for rest.

Rest allows the body to renew itself. Waste products are removed, repairs are effected, enzymes are replenished, energy is restored. Rest aids in the healing of injuries, infections and other assaults on the body, including stress and emotional traumas. Rest strengthens the body's immune system. Rest adds length to lifespan. A study found that people who regularly slept 7 to 8 hours a night had lower death rates than those who averaged either less than 7 hours or more than 8. As well as experiencing sufficient restful sleep each night, we also need to find moments each day to "turn off" our brains. Many people find some kind of formal meditation useful to calm their insistent thoughts.

More Stress, Irritation, Frustration and Anger

People in cities move faster, work faster and play faster, leading to more stress and burnout. People feel a pressure to use their mobile phones and the internet excessively because they fear they might not keep up with the current fads or gossip. They don't want to miss something "important" or "exciting". A study published in 2011 showed that those living in large urban areas – and that's most of us now – were more likely to suffer stress and anxiety. Unfortunately our obsession with speed has also caused more anger and frustration – demonstrated by an increase in road rage, shopping rage, relationship rage, office rage, gym rage, and even vacation rage. For the sake of our health, it's imperative that we slow down and "lighten up".

Greater Alienation

Speed helps to distract some of us from the horrors and superficiality of the modern world, or for others, to avoid confronting questions concerning why we are here and life's purpose. Racing around might even serve as an "escape from death" – a strategy to avoid thinking about our mortality. But speed weakens relationships and human bonding. Like rich food and sex, it gives us a "hit" of sensory input – and once we're used to one level we want more. After a while at a certain speed, we want to go faster, as with jet travel and the internet. Instead of being in a constant rush, we need to find time to re-connect to family, community, spirituality – and ourselves.

Quality Deterioration

Multi-tasking has become more normal. It is even admired, but it can lead to inefficiency and lack of satisfaction. People who squeeze too many things into their life and consequently do everything too fast can mean they become controlling, impatient, aggressive, hurried and stressed. The tasks they do might well then be done superficially, with the emphasis on completion rather than quality. People who adopt a Slow approach are much more likely to make real connections with people, culture, work, food – in fact with everything. *Slow* doesn't necessarily mean doing things slowly – it involves proportionality and balance.

The quality of everything we do is likely to suffer when we're trying to do too much too fast – including our work, our relationships, and our diet. Instant pre-prepared meals and the use of the microwave mean a reduction in healthy nutrients. And even before food gets to our plates, its quality has been diminished due to all the short cuts deployed on the farm to cut costs and boost yields by making livestock and crops grow more quickly – British taxpayers spend over a billion pounds a year repairing the damage that industrial farming does to the environment and human health. New computer products are rushed out before getting rid of their glitches, and as mentioned earlier, "wonder" drugs are often put into the marketplace without proper testing, which sometimes leads to products harming patients' health or even causing death. And the drafting of new laws also seems to be done in haste these days, without being properly thought through, and then they have to be repealed or modified. In the end, the obsession with speed and productivity is a false economy.

Hurried Children

Though some children are neglected because their parents are working so many hours, many are kept *too* busy. Organised sports and other activities are of course largely beneficial. They foster social skills, are opportunities for play and exercise, teach sportsmanship, self-discipline, and conflict resolution, and they're fun. But over-scheduling means children have too little free time for playing, exploring, and learning on their own. Though most parents want what's best for their children, they shouldn't try too hard and make them rush around doing too much – just as they're probably doing in their own lives. The pressure to participate in a multitude of activities and to match their peers can be physically and emotionally exhausting for both parents and children.

Children need time to slow down, ponder and just idle, but like most adults, many are now showing signs of stress. Psychologists report that children as young as 5 have upset stomachs, headaches, insomnia, depression, and eating disorders, and one reason is that they often get too little sleep – deep sleep is particularly important for children. In his book *The Hurried Child*, David Elkind, an American psychologist, points out that children are not born obsessed with speed and productivity – we make them that way. Carl Honoré believes evidence shows a "slower" environment makes children less anxious, more eager to learn and better able to think independently, and that an unhurried approach is more effective for the development of young children's social and language skills, their creative powers and their ability to learn. They need to be trained to concentrate on one thing fully from an early age, and they need unstructured time.

How to Avoid Speed Overload

It will take some time to get used to putting on the brakes. Resisting the pressure to live by the clock requires a different perspective, a new way of looking at things. Though it would inevitably mean you couldn't do or have so much, your appreciation of life and general wellbeing will certainly increase when you apply the Slow approach.

- Rather than doing too much in a half-hearted way or less effectively, try simplifying your life – buy less, own less, do fewer things, and have fewer contacts. Hundreds of acquaintances you hardly ever see and just stay in touch with on social networking websites are no substitute for strong, long-lasting and worthwhile relationships with just a few friends. Assess how much you can deal with, which will vary according to the energy available (determined largely by your mental and physical health), your personality, and the skills you've developed. This calculation requires awareness and self-reflection. Many people have unrealistic expectations, take on too much, and then become discouraged because things don't work out. To be persistent and consistent, yet flexible when necessary, takes practice – but in time, achieving a balance in your life becomes easier.

- We are creatures of habit, and if we work out our priorities and organise a routine that suits us, we can achieve what we want. Doing less enables us to do things better – to live in the moment and appreciate our work, leisure activities and those around us. Avoid multi-tasking because it will cause stress and inefficiency. The self-respect and sense of achievement from doing our best will lead to long-term contentment. By taking time to do things properly, we can enjoy and absorb the activity and maximise the satisfaction from whatever we're using, doing or creating. The main advice of M. Scott Peck's best-selling book from the late 1970s, *A Road Less Travelled*, is that we should strive to do everything as well as we can – because we'll feel better about ourselves, and make others feel better too.

- If you can't grow and cultivate some of your food, at least try obtaining, preparing and eating your food at a more relaxed pace. Food, like anything else in life, should be given time and respect. Eating should be Slow – methodical and considered, and thus healthier. And because it takes about 15 minutes for the brain to register the signal that we've eaten enough, avoid wolfing down food – because the signal will come after you've eaten too much.

- Your mental state can affect your physical wellbeing, and the Slow approach can help. The average GP visit in the UK lasts 6 minutes, with doctors and patients all wanting quick diagnoses and quick fixes. For a less hurried approach, you could try some "alternative" therapies, like herbalism, aromatherapy, acupuncture, massage and energy healing. *The Hale Clinic* in London provides "integrative" medicine, where time and physical contact are recognised as essential factors in the healing process.

- Maurice Holt, a professor of education, lectures widely on a Slow approach to learning. He published a manifesto calling for a worldwide movement for Slow schooling, which would help to broaden and invigorate young minds, giving scope for invention and response to cultural change.

- The Dutch historian Dylan van Rijsbergen believes that a Slow approach to sex would result in a more considered, rounded view of sexuality. Then people would reject pornography, which causes sex to degenerate into erotic boredom and eventually to smother genuine desire. Sex should instead be "elusive, exciting, intense, playful, authentic, dynamic and sublime, stretched beyond the single moment of the male orgasm". The 5,000 year-old *Tantric Sex* discipline also involves a slower approach to sex, where awareness is increased and partners united on a spiritual as well as physical level.

- Frequent breaks from work are important, both during the normal working day and away from the job. Where possible, try to get away for an occasional 3-day mini-break. And when holidaying, avoid scheduling every waking hour with sightseeing or museum visits.

- Try to sleep between 7 and 8 hours a night. If necessary and feasible, take a short nap during the day – it will renew your vigour and focus, and sharpen your memory. Avoid mobile phone calls in the hour before going to bed because it might prevent you from getting a good night's sleep. It seems to affect the brain so people take longer to get into the first stage of deep sleep, and spend less time in deep sleep.

- One way of slowing down and easing the stress engendered by our hectic lives is to take up a Slow hobby or activity, like walking, yoga, chess, painting, creating music, gardening, knitting and reading. Walking can serve two purposes – gentle exercise and reflection. It's inherently slow, and as long you avoid multi-tasking by listening to music at the same time, you can acquaint yourself with the subtleties of the world around. A study analysed the effectiveness of different activities in reducing stress. Stress levels and heart rate were increased with a range of exercises before being tested with different activities to slow things down. Reading worked best, reducing stress levels by 68%. Subjects only needed to read silently for 6 minutes to slow down the heart rate and ease tension in the muscles. In fact their stress levels were lower than before they started. Listening to music reduced levels by 61%, having a cup of tea or coffee lowered them by 54%, and taking a walk by 42%. Playing video games brought them down by 21% from their highest level, but still left the volunteers with heart rates above their starting point.

- Eastern meditation methods were brought to the attention of Westerners in the 1970s and are now used by a large number of people to help them slow down and look inwards. Meditation can help because it stimulates an area of the brain associated with resilience, contentment and optimism, and damps down the area of the brain associated with negative emotions like fear and anxiety. Scans of Western meditators show increased development in regions of the brain associated with memory and attention.

- Try to avoid using the car where possible. Walking short distances or cycling for slightly longer journeys will allow you to take in more of the surroundings. You'll become fitter, avoid the stress of driving on overcrowded roads, it will be better for the environment, and may well take less time than the car.

- Try pausing several times a day – take a few deep breaths and realise what an amazing and fortunate life you lead. Have a lukewarm bath before sleeping. Do little at weekends, just potter in the garden and take stock of the beautiful smells and plants. Stretch out on the grass and stare up at the clouds. Find time each day to be alone with your thoughts (or indeed without any thoughts).

INFORMATION

*"In your thirst for knowledge, be sure
not to drown in all the information."*
(Anthony J. D'Angelo)

In 1984 Jonathan Porritt, the ecological campaigner, observed that despite the arrival of the so-called "Information Age", people were not well-informed. He believed this was largely because their tolerance levels had been surpassed. Even if his conclusion about that period might be questioned, few would deny it now. The amount of information available to us today is extraordinary when compared to 100 years ago, and so much greater than even 15 years ago – and a lot of it is largely unnecessary, irrelevant, or distracting nonsense.

- We are now assailed with the equivalent of 174 newspapers' worth of data each day – 5 times more than in 1986.

As well as a multitude of TV channels, radio stations, newspapers and magazines, we have the internet with its millions of websites and the more recent addition of blogs and twitter. Even when on the go, a huge amount of information can be accessed with personal electronic gizmos, including details of products and services. Price, specifications and availability of items for the home, books and music, holidays, flights and trains, medical and other self-help advice, or news and weather from around the world, are at our fingertips. And through *Skype* and social websites like *Facebook* we can also keep abreast of what's happening in the lives of family members and friends wherever they are.

Surely the availability of all that information has to be positive by increasing our freedom and empowering us as individuals? Well, maybe, but the downside is that it entices us to have, do and follow so much that it can become stressful. We can easily find ourselves overstretched and buried under tons of data. Just having to sift through all of it to make choices and determine what is of use to us can be overwhelming. The old adage certainly applies in this area of life – sometimes we can have too much of a good thing. As with food, we have gone beyond saturation point. We are now experiencing an information "overload".

The Scale and Problems of Information

The amount and range of information for us to process in our daily lives would have scarcely seemed credible even 50 years ago – jobs, educational courses, holidays, places to live, homes to buy, electronic personal devices, gadgets, labour-saving machines and design possibilities for the home, food, clothes, entertainment to enjoy, and media to read, watch and listen to. We are assailed by a growing and relentless barrage of marketing and advertising that supposedly assists us in making decisions as to what to buy or do. We also have to discover, work our way through, and remember a large and increasing quantity of manuals, rules and regulations, codes, passwords and phone numbers. In 2006 the economist David M. Levy said many people were expressing greater concern about the difficulty of sorting through and managing vast amounts of information and overly full schedules. Since the Industrial Revolution began, the goal has been to maximise speed, output and efficiency, and now the inexorable drive to provide and consume more products and services has spread across the planet via globalisation.

What can be processed successfully, i.e. be absorbed fully and without stress, is limited. We are bombarded daily with advertisements, news bites, messages and gossip from colleagues, friends and family, with greater frequency, intensity, and urgency. Separating the valuable from the trivial is difficult and time-consuming. The trend is forever upwards and things have gone way beyond our limit already. Information is not only almost limitless, its veracity is uncertain – and finding out whether it is true or not can also be difficult as well as time consuming. The more information we have to deal with, the greater the probable stress, especially because we are also trying to fit too many other things into our lives. One of the functions of our education system must be to teach children how to assess information – and how to ignore most of it so as not to become stressed. But even assuming we can somehow process the incessant stream of data, how much use is it? Do we really need to know what's going on all round the world, what all our friends or celebrities are getting up to minute by minute, the results of every sports game, or the weather in other parts of the country?

Work

A study found that an overload is caused by too many interruptions and distractions as well as the greater amount of work expected of employees today. The resultant multi-tasking produces stress hormones and decreases creativity because people are unable to focus on the same task for long enough – and this makes them less productive. Though better filtering and management devices might help, workers should turn off their internet and phone from time to time, focus their concentration more narrowly, and ask themselves whether what they are doing is constructive or just a mere "activity".

Choice

Part of our discomfort from information overload comes from something that we would expect to be positive – choice. At no time have humans experienced so much choice in virtually every area of their lives. Professor Barry Schwartz, a psychologist and author of *The Paradox of Choice*, does not believe that maximising freedom and choice increases welfare. Increased choice has made decision-making more complex, adding to life's daily pressure. Just deciding what food and drink we might buy, for example, can be stressful.

- The average supermarket today sells about 50,000 products, 5 times as many as the number available in 1975.

In your local supermarket there might well be 30 choices of milk, including organic, skimmed, soya, omega-3 enriched or filtered for purity, 120 flavours of jam, 80 varieties of pasta, and 50 types of fruit cordial. Carefully considering every relevant factor before deciding what to purchase – flavour, price, ingredients, and maybe ethics and food miles – would take considerable time. And the same bewildering array of product choice is found in all other areas of life, including over-the-counter drugs and personal care items, mobile phones, computers, software, games consoles and other electronic gadgets, clothes, furniture, house fixtures and fittings and interior designs, cars, restaurants, or holidays at home and abroad. Having too much choice is probably as bad for our mental health as having no choice. Many become anxious about their purchasing decisions because of the level of choice – it is pressurising and confusing, consumes so much time and energy, and contributes to our general "overload".

Excess choice can lead to paralysis rather than liberation, and as consumer choice continues to rise, shop employees are becoming less capable of providing information to customers. Either we can't make a decision, or do so and then worry we've missed out on other opportunities, or feel inadequate or dissatisfied with our choice. A study found that consumers who tested 6 jams went on to buy more and feel happier than those offered 24 jams to taste. Another showed that giving students a choice of fewer essay topics made them produce better work. More people subconsciously realise that always making a "correct", rational decision based on the factors for and against would be impractical. This means they often stick to the tried and tested – which the marketing men understand and why they try to instil brand loyalty in their customers.

Marketing

The purveyors of the ubiquitous and often irritating marketing material like to say that they are helping consumers make informed choices about how best to spend their money. We are constantly assailed by advertisements and manipulated with marketing ploys. To generate sufficient consumption to maintain the economies of developed countries today is possible only by making people constantly dissatisfied with what they have. And just as the pharmaceutical companies tell us to pop a pill to put things right, manufacturers tell us that their product is just the thing to guarantee our happiness.

Because we have everything we really need, advertisements are now more numerous, more expensive and more persuasive – and target basic human instincts of greed, envy, inadequacy, and indulgence. They entice us to get a bargain, improve our image, keep up with (or ahead of) the Joneses, and to lead an easier or more exciting life. Marketing is invariably aimed at the younger demographic, and the young go for stimulating things – so everything is louder, faster, and more visually arresting than before. Loud music with heavy beats accompanies repetitive TV and radio program trails, adverts and programs. Music and advertisements seem to accompany our every activity – in lifts, shops, malls, streets and at home. Many adults find all of this daily "in your face" barrage at best annoying. At worst it can have a negative effect on our health. This constant stimulation imbalances our lives and makes it almost impossible for us to consider or absorb information fully.

Apart from BBC TV channels and radio programs in the UK, virtually all entertainment and information comes with advertising. In the USA there are a multitude of "infotainment" programs, i.e. very long adverts, as well as product promotion in soaps and other top shows. Advertising also assails us in our homes via the internet and front door. We receive metaphorical mountains of electronic junk mail as well as real mountains of junk mail, along with the miniscule amount from those businesses about which we would actually want and need information. Who doesn't get pizza restaurant leaflets or taxi cab cards landing on the hall mat every other day? Just in case all that isn't enough for us to look at, ponder over, discard or recycle, there is the burgeoning practice of unsolicited phone calls trying to persuade us to change energy suppliers or follow the advice of some financial adviser or other.

Media

Conventional wisdom says the public needs to know what's going on in the world immediately, so news outlets of all kinds gather, assemble and deliver their "facts", stories and analysis as fast as possible. And though we believe we are receiving the news as it actually is, and hearing about the current events and people that really matter, the "news" is regularly manipulated and managed for sensationalism and greater sales, or to promote some business agenda, including that of the proprietor. But the public is also to blame for sloppy, inaccurate and sometimes downright dishonest journalism, because people can be titillated and convinced too easily. As well as being overloaded by the daily torrent of data from the variety of media outlets, much of it is irrelevant, biased or just untrue, and its largely negative tone also makes us feel helpless, anxious and depressed.

Rules, Codes, Numbers and Manuals

New laws are being passed all the time. Parking regulations constantly change and are often different in different areas. The central government frequently tinkers with tax rules. Passwords are required for so many activities we do today, like banking, purchasing goods, and getting into buildings. A plethora of phone and card numbers are now in our lives that weren't necessary several generations ago. Having to change codes and numbers when cards are lost or stolen means new ones to log and remember. Gadgets and machinery are continually being replaced and updated in our world of "built-in obsolescence", forcing us to read more manuals or instruction leaflets to master more and more kinds of operations.

How to Avoid Information Overload

We can avoid stress by ascribing far less importance to the trivia of life, including most of the huge volume of information that assails us daily. Each of us is different when it comes to managing different levels of information and activity – and indeed, stress. Some can deal with more of everything, at least for a while, and actually be inspired by what our hectic modern life has to offer, but most of us try to handle too much for our own good. If you're feeling stressed, try slowing your pace of life by cutting down on things and activities, including the amount of information you're trying to process.

- If you get to understand yourself better, know what drives you, what satisfies you, what you need for fulfilment and long-term contentment, your decisions and direction in life will be less affected by outside factors. Your instincts should determine what you do, how you do it, and what you need to buy – without anxiety or using up an undue amount of time processing information.

- Re-learn to appreciate the so-called "simpler" things in life and avoid getting caught up in the vortex of over-activity and over-consumption with the concomitant overload of information to process. Constantly remind yourself that good health, a roof over your head, food on your plate, basic comfort, a supportive family and a few good friends, as well as the freedom to be creative and develop yourself, are the things that *really* matter.

- The daily barrage of news and entertainment is not important. When you're away on holiday you get along fine without it. In fact simplifying your life will almost certainly increase your wellbeing. Just like an employee is not indispensable, nothing is indispensable. Having the latest information, gadget, three exotic holidays a year, or a multitude of TV channels, is not essential. And it really doesn't matter if someone else has done something, seen someone, knows something, or watched something that we haven't. Each of us can be different. Understanding what you want and appreciating what you have will mean you won't spend too much time and psychic energy worrying about other people and greener grasses.

- Paradoxically, the same technology that overwhelms us with so much information can help control whether, where and when we receive any of it. Make full use of software that blocks and separates potentially useful information and marketing. Look at emails occasionally, perhaps just once a day, and answer them – or text messages and phone calls for that matter – only when you're ready. And display a "No Junk Mail and Cold Callers" sign beneath your letter box if you'd prefer to avoid pizza fliers and the like.

- Make mundane, less important choices more quickly, leaving analysis and concern for the bigger decisions in life. Barry Schwartz advises that contentment is more likely to be achieved by being a "satisficer" who accepts a good-enough choice, than a "maximiser" who always wants to make the best possible decision.

TECHNOLOGY

*"Technology is the knack of so arranging
the world that we don't have to experience it."*

(Max Frisch)

While acknowledging the many benefits that technological advances have brought, perhaps the time is ripe to examine its negative effects. Apart from ecological damage, it can be argued that technology has led to a significant reduction in exercise and physical effort that used to be an inherent part of our daily activities, a loss of control in our machine-dominated lives, and an increasing alienation between human beings and the natural world – and even worse, between each of us. It is ironic that the inventions which connect us to one another and to the world faster and more effectively are now starting to have the opposite effect. This disconnection causes health problems and a general decline in wellbeing, as well as a reduction in our ethical, social, and political faculties. Incessant technological intrusions leave us with too little opportunity to analyse, reflect, appreciate and absorb things fully, or to cultivate our humanity.

The Scale and Problems of Technology

The ubiquity and sophistication of technology has been increasing for 150 years, and particularly over the last 50 years, so has the pace of expansion. Today almost everything we in the developed countries have in our homes, workplaces and public spaces has been created by technology, and in every area of our lives machines have become indispensable. In recent decades digital electronics have added to the daily load we have to deal with by bringing us computers and the internet, mobile phones and all kinds of personal gadgets. Exposure to technology now begins at a young age and continues throughout our lives. 40% of 3-month-old American babies and 90% of infants aged 24 months and under regularly watch TV, DVDs and videos. TV and computer use by British and other European children is also extensive.

- In the UK children aged 4 to 9 watch TV for an average of 17 hours and 34 minutes per week.

- In 12 European countries, 81% of children under the age of 2 have a digital dossier and 58% aged 2 to 5 know how to play a basic computer game.

Stress

If we weren't already suffering from technology overload, the plethora of electronic personal gadgets that emerged in the last 20 years has certainly ensured that we are now. The multitude of machines and gadgets we own have to be chosen, bought, mastered, and frequently updated. And we have to deal with inevitable and frequent malfunctions. Cars are convenient and comfortable but can break down, and travel stress, sometimes causing "road rage", is far more frequent because of street repairs, gridlocks, and the sheer volume of traffic. We travel far and wide by plane but often struggle to get to the airport and then endure queues for passports and security. We rely on professionals to keep products functioning, and often don't know what's gone wrong, why it should cost so much to put right, and whether the expert is honest. Bound in servitude to electricians, plumbers, mechanics, computer experts, telephone engineers and a variety of scientists, we feel to varying degrees inadequate, ignorant, incapable – and not in control.

Technology has allowed us to do more and more things at an ever-increasing pace, but this has led to more stress. The internet, laptop computers and mobile phones have made "quiet time" almost impossible. Email is extremely convenient but can pressurise people – a study found that 50% of interviewees checked their inbox every hour for new messages, and 33% every 15 minutes. Some even logged on to email as often as 40 times an hour. We have taken efficiency to the limit – clients and bosses can disturb workers while on holiday or having breakfast. Even networking sites cause stress – the more time students spend on them, the more anxious they become. They can feel guilty about turning down a request to be an online friend or about not managing the ones they already have. And because others might be having a better, more popular time on the site, they feel they have to be "entertaining". Online bullying has become another problem, causing stress for the victims and sometimes even leading to suicide.

On top of the numerous daily activities, tasks, choices, obligations and roles we already have to juggle with, technology tempts us to cram yet more into our lives, putting us under even more stress. The ever-increasing speed of innovation and our inability to cope with it was discussed as far back as the 1970s by Alvin Toffler in his book *Future Shock*. As in the constantly re-inventing worlds of fashion and music, the cycle of change in the technological sphere has shortened since then from decades, to years, and now often to just months. We're enticed to replace old products with new ones because they are "vital" for efficiency, for our personal pleasure, and for maintaining or elevating our social position. After each new wave of technological advance raises the bar we somehow muddle through and a new norm is established, but the stress level keeps rising and we are less able to cope.

Lack of Exercise

So much technological advance has made things "easier" for us. In the past, the necessary tasks at home or work involved much physical graft, for both men and women. Today the supermarket provides all we need for our sustenance, so we don't have to use energy to tend gardens and grow our own food. Machines have eliminated the need for us to expend energy automatically as we go about our daily business, incidentally resulting in a lowering of our "pain threshold". Few would argue against labour-saving devices like washing machines, or cars to travel some distance, but our health suffers because most of what we do now is sedentary. As well as trains and buses, there are lifts, escalators and moving walkways. In the home there are dishwashers, vacuum cleaners, blenders, crushers and choppers. We have electric car windows, electric mowers, electric screwdrivers, electric razors, electric toothbrushes, and remote controls for TVs and garage doors.

Dangers to Health

Computers are everywhere, in most homes and in virtually all business premises. They are extremely useful for information gathering and communication, and are now considered essential, but they can result in health problems (other than from EMFs, discussed previously). Many regular computer users suffer from RSI (repetitive strain injury). People's neck, upper back, shoulder and lower arm, elbow, wrist or hand – or a combination – can be affected.

- 15% to 25% of computer users worldwide have RSI.

- In 2006 half a million Britons suffered from some form of RSI.

RSI affects 7% of adult Americans. An Indian study found that 75% of computer professionals reported musculoskeletal RSI symptoms. In 2009 a health warning was issued to British "twitterers" that they should take a break every hour from typing to lessen the risk of RSI. There could also be a danger to people's eyesight from the use of computers – "computer vision syndrome" is used to describe eye fatigue or strain from computer work. And a study found that spending hours staring at a computer screen may raise the risk of glaucoma, a progressive eye disease that can lead to blindness.

Scientists and health authorities use the concept of "acceptable risk" when new products or processes are developed, but technological innovation tends to outpace scientific understanding. "Nanotechnology" is a recent example. This involves the control of matter on an atomic and molecular scale. There has been very little research into the potential health dangers of nanoparticles, which are already used in 600 products like socks, sunscreens, car tyres and various foods. Studies suggest they could pose a serious risk because their size allows them to easily penetrate organs and cells. There should at least be clear labelling so consumers can choose whether they want to be part of this experiment.

There are regular health scares about various new products. A study found that a third of laser printers commonly used in offices and homes emit high levels of particles fine enough to infiltrate the lungs and cause a range of health problems, from respiratory irritation to cancer. Very loud music from personal listening devices may produce tinnitus and inner ear drum damage and cause the brain to hear "phantom" music. One problem of mobile phones and other gizmos was perhaps harder to anticipate – people texting or calling someone while driving, or being distracted by ipods and phones while crossing the road. And social networking has been blamed for various health problems such as narrow arteries, heart disease, cancer and dementia. When we are face-to-face with people we release the chemical oxytocin, which promotes bonding, but this and other important chemical changes do not occur when contact happens with others in the virtual world. Real-life conversation develops our sensitivity to voice tone, body language and body scent, which screen-to-screen contact doesn't.

Lack of Appreciation

Previous generations had far more appreciation of the (far fewer) things they owned and used, and certainly new purchases gave them more pleasure and excitement because they were far less frequent. The lack of credit meant that both children and adults had to wait until products could be bought with savings, which increased the pleasure of anticipation and subsequent satisfaction following the purchase. Today we can have things immediately through the use of credit, and our high standard of living means we continually reward ourselves. The frisson of getting new gadgets, eating out, holidaying abroad, or receiving presents, has been considerably diminished because we have and do so much.

Receiving another gift is no longer special for our children because they are given treats throughout the year and get so many things on their birthday. Our material affluence means we are all continually thinking about what we still want to acquire, rather than appreciating what we already have. And who doesn't find it extremely difficult these days to buy others something that might actually be welcomed, appreciated, and made full use of?

Greater Alienation

Though counter-intuitive and therefore largely unexpected, one significant negative side-effect of newer technology has been its tendency to alienate family and friends from one another. This is examined later in "alienation".

Obsession

Another largely unexpected negative side-effect of technology has been the level of obsession with gizmos and internet activities. Our ability to focus seems to be undermined by bursts of information that appeal to a primitive impulse to respond to immediate opportunities and threats, and the stimulation provokes excitement that can be addictive – and in its absence, people can feel bored. The tendency to become slaves to *Cyburbia* – the virtual village identified in a book of the same name by social analyst James Harkin – has become endemic. "Internet addiction" has now been recognised by *The American Journal of Psychiatry*. People have become enslaved by technology, according it a status and importance that it doesn't really deserve.

As well as calling and receiving texts and phone messages, many are forever fiddling with their mobile phones and feel bereft without them. We have become mesmerised by the virtual world, sending material across the ether, playing chess and poker with strangers we'll never meet, updating Facebook profiles, and inventing new names, images and personalities for ourselves. Adults as well as children can get hooked on the plethora of games online as well as those on their own games consoles, computers and phones. And keeping up with electronic gadgetry has become an obsession for many people. Products like the latest smart phones and high definition flat-screen TVs were recent status symbols, but now, like other developments, they are becoming completely standard and "indispensable".

- A 2012 study revealed that 68% of British teenagers and 46% of adults were "addicted" to their mobile phone.

The fear of not being able to make contact by mobile phone has even been given a name: "nomophobia". Research has found that those who play violent video games are more prone to have aggressive thoughts, feelings and actions, that the widespread availability of online pornography has caused more addiction, that in Britain an estimated 233 million hours a month are spent on social networking sites, that the average British teenager spent 100 minutes a week browsing for pornography and more than an hour looking at weight loss sites, and that the value of "virtual worlds" on the internet – massive multiplayer online games – is more than $1 billion.

Fraud and Privacy

Criminal gangs and rogue states can now cause major disruption and even threaten national security by targeting networks that run utilities, air traffic control, financial markets and government affairs. It seems there have already been cases of national security services disrupting another country's computer systems. In America a new unit has been specifically set up to deal with these dangers. On the personal level, if people buy products and services online and use social network sites, they will find it extremely difficult to prevent their online activities being tracked and "leaked" – and find themselves bombarded with personalised advertising. And huge amounts of money are siphoned fraudulently from bank accounts via the internet.

- Over £21 million was fraudulently taken from British bank accounts in just 6 months during 2012.

Children's Development

Too much TV and internet activity may well have an adverse affect on adults, but the negative effects on children can be much more significant and long-lasting. Excessive use of entertainment devices can stunt children's emotional and academic growth. TV watching has been linked to sleeping difficulties, behavioural problems and obesity in children. It seems that children are far more likely to be overweight the more electronic devices they have in their bedroom, and those who watch more than 2 hours a day when between 5 and 15 years old will often suffer from poor health years later. One study found that adults who had been avid TV watchers as children were more likely be overweight, smoke and have high cholesterol – whereas children who watched an hour or less a day were the healthiest when older.

In 2006 a third of British children's bedrooms were filled with £2,000 worth of technological devices. A third of children under the age of 4 now have a TV set in their bedrooms, and pre-school children typically watch it for 2 hours of a day. Dr. Aric Sigman, a leading London psychologist, advises that children under 3 shouldn't be allowed to watch TV at all and that TV sets should be removed from their bedrooms. He believes that screen media must be considered a major public health issue.

An American study found that 14-year-olds who watched TV 3 hours a day were twice as likely not to go to university as those who watched just 1 hour. Learning abilities and socio-economic background were taken into account. It seems that watching TV can make children "intellectually lazy", so they then find less passive tasks such as reading difficult and boring. Adolescence is known to be a critical period for acquiring many important cognitive skills. Children's development may well suffer if they spend too much time watching TV instead of reading, doing homework and having other valuable learning experiences. And social websites may make it less likely that teenagers form lasting relationships. The generation born in the 1990s that grew up online might have a distorted view of the real world. Used to the quick pace of online social networking, they may not find life stimulating enough without it, potentially leading to more extreme behaviour to create sufficient excitement.

Moral Degradation

The internet has been extolled for having empowered creativity, democratised media, and levelled the playing field between experts and amateurs. Some argue, however, that it has infantilised a generation and encouraged the "embrace of the self" by encouraging everybody to express and realise themselves – even the most poorly educated and inarticulate. Some have argued that it has led to a fall in moral and academic standards, has severely damaged the music and movie industries, has turned a whole generation into potential gambling and pornography addicts, has increased the risks of criminals acquiring personal health or financial details, and has pushed us further along the road of control by businesses and government. Even worse, there are many who say it has created an amoral generation in thrall to sensationalism, spending much of their time in a virtual world.

The internet did indeed play a part in American, German, and Finnish massacres of the young by the young. The "depersonalisation" of cyberspace seems to foster abnormal behaviour, like just watching or even willing someone to commit suicide, and advising anorexics how to eat less. The anonymity and remoteness offered by the internet has led to some people encouraging violence against others with little fear of retaliation – the victim is effectively depersonalised when a "cyberstalker" can harm another person at a distance. Perhaps in time the worst features of the internet will be eliminated by search engine designers and government laws working in tandem.

Waste

Time and social pressure – and higher incomes – mean we buy many things we don't really need. We get short-term gratification from purchases and a little excitement from the novelty, but often acquire things we don't use fully, or don't even use at all. Many of us don't make the effort to examine the specifications or functions of products. We can't or don't bother to work out how to make full use of gadgets and home machines, and just stick to a few functions. Some get into a habit of impulse buying, whether food, clothes or gadgets. This consumption addiction is fed by manufacturers who frequently bring out new products – and if anything goes wrong, it's virtually always cheaper to buy a new one rather than get the old model fixed.

- A study found that Britons were harbouring £23 billion of unused gadgets, with an average of £375 worth of technology gathering dust in each house.

A survey estimated that Britons would collectively spend over £9 billion on gadgets during their lifetime, including £4 billion on gizmo gifts for friends and family which remained unused. 24% admitted they might never use them. At the top of the list of unused products were sandwich toasters, followed by bathroom scales, coffee machines, foot-spas, face saunas, electric knives, tin openers, bread-makers, soda streams, and vegetable preparation devices like potato peelers. The dawn of digital TV means 41% of the population own a video or DVD player they no longer use, and 32% have an old mobile phone handset around. Young people are the biggest culprits as they try to keep up with the latest fashion, with men twice as likely to upgrade their gadgets – 21% compared with 11% of women.

How to Avoid Technology Overload

Technology excites us, attracts us and distracts us. It both helps us and hinders us. We have become mesmerised with form rather than substance, with spin rather than dealing with issues effectively, with good intentions rather than action, and this inclination is encouraged by a continuous stream of novel but unneeded machinery and gadgets that advertisers convince us to buy. We need to lose this childlike obsession with machines and reduce the time, energy and hard-earned money we sacrifice on the altar of technology.

- If you become aware that man-made products will not create long-term contentment, you'll change your priorities and re-balance your life.

- Try not to let machines dominate your life. Consider carefully what is positive and what is negative, and don't meekly accept any "advance" that occurs. Working, consuming, gadgets and gizmos can take up so many hours that there are too few left to spend on those things that really matter for your wellbeing.

- Try switching off your phone for parts of the day, particularly during mealtimes, and maybe check your emails just once a day. Take steps to remove your name from non-essential mailing lists.

- Find a hobby that doesn't involve machinery – perhaps one that takes you out into the fresh air and away from computers and the internet.

- Limit the time you watch TV, go online or use your mobile phone. When you go out, try leaving the phone behind. With practice and in time you'll eventually understand that it's not vital for you to be in constant contact with others or them with you. In fact, you'll get to appreciate some "quiet time".

- To help your fitness, walk up escalators and use stairs instead of lifts. Organise your time to include regular exercise. This doesn't have to be sport. It could be just brisk walks. Unless the membership cost is hard to afford, join a gym and use the weight and aerobic apparatus, even though they are pieces of machinery…

- If you have children, carefully monitor and control their use of electronic gadgetry and the hours they watch TV or spend online. It is vital for their current life balance and their future health and wellbeing that they do regular exercise and have time for face-to-face activities with friends.

ENTERTAINMENT

*"We aren't in an information age;
we are in an entertainment age."*

(Tony Robbins)

Availability and choice have been increasing exponentially in every area of modern life. We all accept this unquestionably as "progress". The notion that more is better pervades our culture, and it certainly applies to the field of entertainment. The huge increase of films, music, DVDs, books, magazines, TV channels, radio stations, toys and games has been embraced as positive, but the sheer quantity is overwhelming us and has led to a surfeit of repetitively similar and substandard material – though often technically brilliant and wonderfully produced.

Of course there are times when we need to sit back, relax and be transported away from the stresses of every day life, to turn off our brains and have some instant enjoyment when we've been working hard – but there is too much uninspired and uninspiring material pumped across the airwaves. The veteran broadcaster Michael Parkinson memorably said that television programs were no longer made "for an audience reckoned to have an IQ larger than the numbers you would find in a bingo bag", while in the cinema, films like Lord of the Rings, Star Wars and Harry Potter, all from original books intended for teenage or younger children, became mainstream for adults.

Many critics have used the phrase "dumbing down" to describe the trend of modern broadcasting, citing as examples the plethora of soaps and reality shows. An ever-growing number of cookery shows, "shockumentaries", police-in-action, Big Brother, stars competing in the jungle or on the dance floor, human oddities, soft porn and a myriad of talent shows are just some of the recent crop of low-brow entertainment. The proliferation of channels and the drive to provide entertainment and news 24 hours a day, every day of the year, has inevitably resulted in lower quality. But often it's deliberate. Over the last 50 years broadcasters have increasingly simplified content for those who don't have the time or inclination to exercise their brains much, or jazzed things up to appeal to the younger demographic. Even the news has largely been reduced to repetitive bite-size chunks, along with much unnecessarily aggressive yet ineffective interviewing.

Most of us like some sport, some gossip and trivia, but do they have to fill most of the time on and in the media? Unfortunately the answer to that question is yes, because in the capitalist system, entertainment that is more middle-of-the-road and undemanding will maximise audiences and therefore profits. Sadly the BBC is increasingly obliged to measure the success of its output by audience numbers. Even if the balance between "dumbed-down" material and that which is thought-provoking or intellectually challenging was to be evened up, should we spend so much time being passive, soaking up other people's output and efforts? Perhaps we might consider producing our own entertainment like they did "in the old days" – to be actively involved in the creative process or in just doing things.

The Scale of Entertainment

Apart from the unavoidable box in the corner of every lounge – and many bedrooms – there is now another box in most homes via which we can access the internet and thereby a whole range of entertainment. And we have a smaller gadget that allows us to continue to communicate with others and connect to the internet while on the move. We can also be entertained by radio programmes, at the cinema and theatre, in pubs, and in music and comedy clubs. In case that's not enough, there are a myriad of books, magazines and newspapers. Should we be so inclined, we can also gamble at betting shops or online, and play games on or offline. Much of all this "entertainment" is now available 24 hours a day, every day.

TV, Radio, Cinema and Theatre

Radio exercises the brain more than most TV programs. It encourages us to use our imagination. Cinema is a communal activity and can be appreciated as an infrequent pleasure, and theatre involves an interaction between audience and actors. But even these forms of entertainment have not been immune from the commercial pressure to "dumb down". TV has dominated most people's leisure time for decades, and still does. 104 channels are beamed into the average American home, and the number of channels has substantially increased in the UK since the advent of cable and satellite TV.

- On average, the British watch 28 hours of TV per week.

- 63% of British children aged 5 to 16 have a TV in their room and spend an average of 4 hours and 30 minutes a day looking at a TV or computer screen.

The Centre for Screen Time Awareness is a national non-profit organisation founded in 1994 to raise awareness about the harmful effects of excessive television-watching. It encourages Americans to reduce their TV hours and replace them with activities that lead to more literate, productive lives and engaged citizenship. An American lobby group called *TV-Turnoff Network* encouraged people to turn off their sets for a whole week each year. The name *TV Turnoff Week* was changed to *Mental Detox Week* to reflect the growing predominance of computers and other digital devices.

The Internet

Over the last two decades the internet has become an integral part of people's activities both inside and outside their homes, and is gradually becoming indispensable in many areas of life, including entertainment. A variety of games and puzzles are now automatically included in the software of new computers. Online entertainment is huge and still growing, involving games, social sites, music, radio and TV programmes, as well as blog sites, twitters, gambling and pornography. In recent years there has been a blurring of the line between the computer and TV, with the computer gradually taking over the functions of other technologies. Before too long the melding of TV and computer will be complete.

Books, Magazines and Newspapers

There is a multitude of newspapers and magazines and hundreds of thousands of books in libraries or for sale in bookshops and online available to entertain us. About 230,000 new books are now published in the UK each year, and over 300,000 in the USA. Because we have to use our imagination with the written word, whether books, magazines and newspapers, it could be argued that they exercise the brain more than TV. Like all forms of entertainment, however, the capitalist system puts pressure on publishers to look for greater sales, often at the expense of quality. In recent years, so-called celebrities have dominated the bookshelves with their "reveal-all" biographies. Many famous people have managed to generate even more publicity and profits for themselves and undiscerning publishers by churning out novels or children's stories – often ghost-written. And the latest fad has been so-called "female porn" books.

The Problems of Entertainment Overload

Society tells us to aim for "the easy life", and entertainment in particular encourages us to be passive. To remain physically and mentally healthy, we should rather be active – as we have been during most of our evolution. We should be participating in sport, not just watching it, and much more of our leisure time should involve us creating our own amusement, instead of always relying on professionals. We have so much choice of entertainment that decisions become difficult, we are inclined not to appreciate it, and are almost always assailed and manipulated by advertising when we do make our choice.

Apart from the fact that children watch TV and attend to their personal online profiles so much they have to squeeze other activities into less time, program content, whether produced for children or adult material that many younger viewers get to see, can accelerate their move into adulthood without the concomitant emotional maturity. They are turned into consumers at a young age – the average British child will see thousands of commercials every week – and are exposed to grown-up issues.

Studies suggest children viewing violence on TV or in computer games are more likely to be aggressive, restless and unable to sit still and concentrate. And it seems that extreme visual speed can affect young brains. A junk food diet combined with TV exposure and electronic games may well have contributed to the huge increase in ADHD.

Advertising

Apart from public service broadcasting, advertisements are necessary to fund programs. This means that those who are more passive, watch a lot of TV, and are not aware of their unconscious desires, will be influenced by advertisers. Many of these people will get drawn into consumption for instant gratification and for supposed instant status, quite likely becoming fat and in debt in the process.

Choice

The previous segment on information discussed the problems of an excess of choice. This is certainly so in entertainment. The number of TV and radio channels and programs, films, DVDs, music CDs, electronic games, plays, books, newspapers and magazines has risen considerably in the last 50 years. Many studies have shown that the surfeit of choice makes our daily decision-making difficult, time-consuming and stressful.

Appreciation and Absorption

The huge volume of entertainment makes us less appreciative. A myriad of channels constantly beam news, chat shows, soaps, reality shows, cop chases, whodunits, nature programs, music and films into our homes. We can record them and if we happen to miss their initial broadcasting, we can even listen to or see them again through the wonders of modern technology. It is a natural human trait to take things for granted when so much material is on tap, instantly available and cheap – as with food, so with entertainment. Even if we do appreciate what newspapers, magazines, the radio and TV have to offer, we read, listen to, and watch so much that we are unlikely to absorb it all fully.

"Dumbing Down"

Purveyors of entertainment focus on greater sales and making profits for shareholders, just like other business people. They're not primarily motivated to create intelligent, different and inspiring material. They'll usually produce films, newspapers, magazines, radio and TV programs to maximise the number of consumers – often by targeting younger people with instantly accessible and controversial material. And then marketing is used to hype up the interest and increase peer pressure. It seems that older British viewers have become disillusioned with what is on TV and are turning to radio: *BBC Radio 3* now has a weekly audience of over 2 million a week, and *Radio 4* almost 11 million.

Most radio and television programming has to be financed by advertising, and the larger the audience the greater the advertising revenue. Thus there is pressure on producers to focus on audience numbers rather than quality – yet there are many Britons who believe the market knows best and resent paying their licence fee. We should in fact be grateful for the countervailing force of the public service broadcasting in the USA and the BBC in the UK, which provide an alternative to commercial outlets and which – to some extent at least – serve to hold back the general "dumbing down" trend.

Passivity

Because TV is easily available in the home, it entices us to be passive for too much of our time. Like food manufacturers, programme producers know how to turn us into addicts. Over the decades they have learnt all the things that will grab our attention and keep us watching – like soaps, quizzes and reality shows. Once we start watching them we become intrigued by the characters and feel we have to follow them to see what happens. If only we would spend more time in the real world instead, getting to know our family, friends and neighbours better and being interested in what happens to them. A major problem with our penchant for passive entertainment, particularly TV, is that it prevents us from taking sufficient physical exercise. And ironically, though so many are interested in sport, we're not actually sporty – we do very little ourselves. Radio at least allows us to do things while listening to programmes – like housework or gardening for example.

- A study found that on average, every hour sat watching TV reduced a viewer's life by about 22 minutes.

Though we often work too many hours and try to do too much in a hurry, in our leisure time we can be extremely passive. Though we've reached saturation point with the various forms of entertainment available, almost all of it involves little participation or brain-power. Both physical and mental passivity when being entertained is a danger to people's development, particularly children's. As usual a balance has to be struck, and studies suggest that children watch far too much TV for their own good. Guidelines recommend a total of at least 60 minutes of at least "moderately intense" exercise for children each day, including activities to improve bone health, muscle strength and flexibility at least twice a week. But 45% of English families watch TV or play non-active video games before school, and only 22% do something active after their tea.

In 2009, following official predictions that 90% of English children would be overweight or obese by 2050, the *Change4Life* initiative was launched as an attempt to wrest them away from electronic games – and guess which companies were part of the campaign? Yes, as with the Olympics, it was the global brands like *Coca-Cola* and *Mars* – whose products contribute to obesity!

Loud, Violent, and Explicit

To compete for our attention, and following the usual convention of aiming for the younger demographic, everything emanating from the different forms of media is becoming excessive. Extremes are de rigueur today, including violence, sex and uncouth language. Sports commentaries have increased their volume and stridency, newspapers and news programs ridiculously exaggerate the negative (and occasionally the positive), magazines seek out and magnify people's flaws, while the decibels and intensity of program trails and advertisements continually rise, often involving loud, repetitive, driving music. Everything's got to be up-beat, dynamic, loud and "in-your-face". This criticism has nothing to do with prudery or sensitivity, but proportionality and balance.

Multi-Tasking

We often try to do two things at once and do both badly. Or at least we don't really "absorb" or appreciate either of the activities. A huge percentage of American homes have the TV on most of the day, yet don't give it or visitors and family their complete attention, and drivers will always have the radio on in their vehicles. The British are following suit, using noise and images as a "comfort", to make them feel something's going on and they're part of it. It may sound harsh, but constant distractions may well help some people avoid facing the fact that they're living such empty lives, having lost the art of communication, socialising, and entertaining themselves.

How to Avoid Entertainment Overload

"The bottom line" is what matters these days. Money-making now drives almost everything, including entertainment. The movers and shakers in all developed countries are rich and live exciting, high-status lives. They are content to see a largely passive population – comatose, anaesthetised by indulgence and soporific entertainment, citizens who are unlikely to question the situation or rock the boat. This means we cannot rely on the powers that be to improve or control the media and the various forms of entertainment. Each of us can take steps, however, to re-balance our life by relying less on "professional" entertainment and more on that which is home-grown.

- Long-term fulfilment, self-respect and contentment will not come about by being passive. Life should largely be about action because our satisfaction would be greater if we were more dynamic more of the time. We could create some of our own entertainment rather than always rely on the TV and radio. Children should certainly be encouraged to find their own amusement and maybe make their own toys, rather than be given expensive, manufactured ones that they use for 5 minutes and then get bored with. My brother and I spent huge amounts of time constructing "marble machines" out of cardboard boxes with flour paste, and playing with self-hewn bows, arrows and spears. Children should also be exhorted to be more physical – to get out and play with friends.

- Many adults and children alike are obsessed with technology, which can contribute towards an imbalanced life. If you're a parent you need first to assess whether you spend too many hours watching TV or using the computer, because you're the main role model for your children. You need to set an example if you are to control your children's choice and amount of entertainment. Parents and teachers need to encourage children to express themselves and be creative – to participate in and experience all kinds of art, literature and other entertainment.

- We should make it a priority to increase our children's awareness, so as adults they can think for themselves and make considered decisions in all areas of their lives, including entertainment. Choices based on their own real preferences will be more satisfying in the long term. If they are made aware of the power of peer, societal and advertising pressure to conform – and encouraged to resist it at least some of the time – they will be far more likely to create a balance in their lives.

EDUCATION

"Data is not information, information is not knowledge, knowledge is not understanding, understanding is not wisdom."

(Clifford Stoll)

The effects on children of our current lifestyle choices are discussed frequently in this book, even though most of the emphasis is on adults. In this particular section, however, they are inevitably the main focus. Teachers and parents share the responsibility of educating and mentoring children, but stressed parents now have little time and energy to fulfil their obligations effectively. And though many things are taught in school, children are *not* taught how to live fulfilling and content lives. I believe an alternative approach to education is needed – one that expands pupils' awareness so they become wise rather than merely knowledgeable.

According to *Wikipedia*, education involves: "The teaching and learning of knowledge, proper conduct, and technical competency, focusing on the cultivation of skills, trades or professions, as well as mental, moral and aesthetic development." Unfortunately current economic preoccupations mean too little attention is paid to the last part of that definition. A headmistress of a London school recently expressed the view that a curriculum geared towards the job market meant schooldays were becoming a daily grind, and lessons structured to enhance the competitiveness of the nation were causing cultural and intellectual impoverishment for pupils. She was frustrated that her teachers were struggling to demonstrate the richness of their subjects and impart to their pupils the "sheer enjoyment" of studying them.

It is to be expected that those who finance and create educational establishments will always have an agenda of some kind. In ancient Greece, philosophy, politics and abstract mathematics were prioritised. In the Middle Ages importance was accorded to religious doctrine and philosophy. From the 19th century and the Industrial Revolution onwards, the economy took centre stage, becoming the new philosophy *and* religion in most other areas of life as well as education. And today virtually all governments are still concerned primarily with children becoming trained to take their place in the workforce. Though important, having a job is just one factor in wellbeing.

"Awareness" is the word I use to encompass the wisdom and inner sensibility that are vital for us to conduct our lives calmly and contentedly. This is what parents and teachers need to cultivate in children. The emphasis should be on social skills, self-awareness, and philosophical reflection about life and learning. Some of these "life skills" – including morals – are listed in the official "aims" of English education, but PSHE (personal, social and health education) is labelled as "non-statutory", meaning schools are not required to follow it. And one lesson a week over just a few years is nowhere near sufficient for them to acquire these varied and vital skills.

Rather than making all children fit the same mould, imagination and individuality should be favoured rather than frowned upon. Sadly most parents, educational establishments, and society as a whole, are happy for pupils to learn merely how to regurgitate facts, join the rat race, and kowtow to current conventional wisdom. This is a recipe for closed, uninquisitive minds, and an unquestioning acceptance of the status quo. I believe the overarching aim of education should instead be to produce dynamic, enthusiastic, confident, open minded, self-reliant, self-responsible adults with well-rounded, balanced personalities – with a variety of perspectives and opinions on society, the world, and life.

Sadly, those in the cosy club of privilege are more inclined to foster a docile population. They would not welcome an educational system that nurtured and encouraged the worthwhile aspects of human life and allowed them to flourish, because this might well create problems for the establishment and shake the status quo. Noam Chomsky, the acclaimed academic, believes students with wider horizons would be more likely to challenge the authority and domination of powerful people and institutions. Integrity, creativity, and individuality might clash with the hierarchic, authoritarian structure of the institutional framework: "Schools filter out independence of thought, creativity, imagination, and in their place foster obedience and subordination."

The Problems of Education

Specialisation and division of labour enabled the great technological leap from the 19th century onwards, but it encouraged the natural human inclination to categorise and label to such a degree that it also had an extremely detrimental effect on the way we conduct our lives. In order to cram young heads with what they need to know to earn a living in our specialised world, we divide knowledge into different subjects. We then provide far too much detail in these discrete segments but far too little information on how everything is interconnected. The result is that few people can see the wood for the trees. Focusing almost exclusively on jobs and the economy has also led to prioritising what is measurable and quantifiable rather than what is creative, philosophical, psychological, spiritual, and difficult to measure – yet the latter is actually far more important for human wellbeing.

Too Much Material

The amount of material that children are expected to learn in school is excessive, matching the overload of ever-expanding information that is now swamping the average adult. A minority of quicker and motivated children can "get up to speed", but most are unable to process fully all the information they're given, resulting in very little "absorption". It would be better if each pupil dealt with the amount of information that he or she could absorb, appreciate and master. Even if they pass exams, many children sense that their grasp of subjects is inadequate. That means they move into adulthood either lacking confidence and self-respect, or believing that a level of incompetence is normal and acceptable. Learning fewer things well rather than many things badly would be much more preferable.

Instead of trying to cram too much into young minds, it would be far better for pupils to learn fundamental skills more fully. These include computer operations, spelling and grammar, simple arithmetic and accountancy, and basic practical competence. Do all children really need to learn quadratic equations? Do they need to know every king and queen in Tudor times? They are taught to memorise facts rather than how to find information, coached to pass tests rather than how to present an analysis, an argument, or viewpoint. Pupils need time, opportunity and encouragement to discuss, argue, and reflect upon knowledge and ideas, and so become more aware. They need to learn how to find information as and when they might need it, and be inspired to use their imagination, think for themselves, and take some responsibility for their own learning.

The Curriculum

Parents today are failing to mentor their children in the skills that will enable them to live a more aware, peaceful, fulfilling and content life. These include self-awareness, self-control, will-power, application and delayed gratification; social and psychological skills for relating to others; the maintenance of good health through regular exercise and diet; ecology and the natural world; ethics and a moral code; and philosophy – about purpose, truth and spirituality. These "life skills" will provide a well-rounded and secure foundation to enable children to see the bigger picture when they grow up, act more rationally, and be happy and successful both in work and at home – and be far more likely to change the world for the better. The expansion of awareness in children is so important that if parents don't instruct their children in these matters, then schools must.

Philosophical analysis, meditation, and music have all been shown to have a positive influence on children. When 5 to 11-year-olds were taught philosophy in a pilot scheme, their IQ increased by 6.5 points, a lead maintained at secondary school, even when the pupils had no further philosophy lessons. Meditation instruction in some of the worst schools in the USA led to a drop in stabbings, suicides and drugs. And after free music lessons for 6 months, a group of children performed better in IQ tests.

Because we are social beings, the ability to relate to each other is vital for our wellbeing and happiness. This means we should encourage the expansion of children's empathy by exploring other cultures and discussing the differences between their own and others' lifestyles and beliefs. A thorough analysis of relationships – including in particular the psychological similarities and differences between men and women – would enable pupils to relate more easily to the opposite sex. And their lives would be less stressful if they were taught about their own basic instincts, the influence of their subconscious mind and the importance of exerting control over their emotions. Vital topics hardly addressed at present include ethics and the concepts of delayed gratification and long-term contentment.

Most parents today have neither the time nor ability to teach their children practical skills, so the school curriculum also needs to find space for fostering manual dexterity. The increasing time spent in the virtual world of computers and the ludicrous snobbery about manual work have served to displace hands-on play and hands-on learning, but using the hands when young is necessary as part of the brain's healthy development of intelligence. Research has shown that experiencing how the world works in practice – materials and processes – enables pupils to make informed judgements about abstract concepts. And if vocational, practical, and artistic subjects, more central to the lives of many children, were given greater prominence, pupils would gain in confidence and be more likely to deal with social stress and negative emotions.

Last but definitely not least, the school curriculum should include *daily* exercise, whatever form it may take. Whether individual or team, competitive or not, regular exercise is necessary to maintain a healthy body as well as help to keep lives in balance. If parents don't make their children understand how important and beneficial exercise is, and don't give them the opportunity and encouragement to exercise, then schools must.

Testing Stress

English children are thought to be the most tested in the world, sitting an average of 60 tests before they're 16. Whereas other countries like Japan and Switzerland emphasise the disciplined acquisition of knowledge and the enhancement of the imagination, UK politicians are obsessed with score charts and point averages. Children are getting tested more often and at a younger age in more subjects, which not only increases the stress on children and their parents, but also means the children merely get better at passing tests rather than become more aware and better educated.

Starting Too Young

The *Montessori* teaching method advises that small hands must explore the world: "They learn by grasping, touching, throwing. These tiny hands must not be imprisoned with a pencil and forced to write before the age of 5 or they will be stunted in their personality development. Some as young as 2 or 3 are confined in shoes, shirt with ties, books and four walls – no wonder modern man is growing up feeling he has missed something." Scandinavian children start primary school as late as 7 years old and in the end surpass British children. Many British politicians seem to believe, however, that the longer children are at school, the better – indicated by the misguided desire to expand the economy by freeing women from child-care duties so they can join the workforce, the raising of the age for compulsory schooling, and the arbitrary target of 50% of people attending university.

The Type of School

There are about 25,000 schools in England, of which around 7,000 are faith schools. Because faith schools are to some extent selective, and because religious people tend to have the work ethic and perhaps on average a stronger moral foundation, there is a greater parental impetus on children to work hard and achieve more. The very existence of these schools, however, is divisive, and they create more division to the extent that they indoctrinate pupils in a particular belief system. Today there are even a number of schools, some part-funded by the state, that teach creationism rather than evolution.

Religious parents will argue that they have the right to indoctrinate their children in a particular belief system, but schools – especially when funded by the state – should only be allowed to provide information *about* various religions and their mutually exclusive beliefs. It is of fundamental importance that each of us should be able to decide our own philosophy of life. For their sake and to engender a more tolerant and aware society, children should have the freedom to pursue their own truth as they mature.

School and Class Size

Reflecting a society that prioritises economic matters, schools have been growing to take advantage of economies of scale, but this tendency to "gigantism" has unfortunately proved – as in other areas of life – to have many negative ramifications. Private schools are normally moderate in size and have smaller classes because control and discipline are easier to maintain. And equally important, there can be more instructional and emotional support for every pupil. Smaller schools are much more likely to produce cohesiveness and positivity when teachers – including head teachers – know each child by name. Pupils will achieve far more and become well-rounded adults when at school they feel they are more than just a number.

Indiscipline

However large schools or classes may be, whatever the material being presented, and however it is put across, a lack of discipline means a waste of time and effort for everybody concerned. The pupils who disrupt classes with their bad behaviour lose out, as do the other pupils who are better behaved and want to concentrate. And as for the unfortunate teachers – we should not expect them to make up for bad parenting and an overly liberal society by being police officers, social workers or warriors trying to maintain control. They should be able to do what they've been trained to do – teach.

Bullying and Truancy

Smaller schools and classes would certainly help to lower the incidence of bullying. The current lack of respect in society means that teacher authority and control must be rigidly maintained, with clear-cut rules and firm and consistent sanctions for all errant behaviour. We should at the same time reassess our insistence on children having to be in school. Some children just don't want to be there – 5% of English pupils are not in school on an average day. For some teenagers, leaving school before the compulsory leaving age of 16 would be far more productive than being forced to be at an institution which at best bores them or at worst they loathe, leading to bad behaviour, disruption or truancy.

How to Improve Education

The psychotherapist Professor Sidney Jourard wrote: "We begin life with the world presenting itself to us as it is. Someone – our parents, teachers, analysts – hypnotises us to 'see' the world and construe it in the 'right' way. These others label the world, attach names and give voices to the beings and events in it, so that thereafter, we cannot read the world in any other language or hear it saying other things to us. The task is to break the hypnotic spell, so that we become undeaf, unblind and multilingual, thereby letting the world speak to us in new voices and write all its possible meanings in the new book of our existence. Be careful in your choice of hypnotists."

When a child is born, he or she has an open and receptive mind which is not yet imprinted with the prevailing culture. For him or her, everything is possible. As children grow, their freedom of thought and action fade, sometimes along with their natural energy and optimism, as they slowly incorporate the current belief system and restrictive practices. Their instincts to explore and enjoy new experiences are almost always damped down by the conservatism and anxiety shown by those around them.

- Parents play the initial and vital role in how their children view and deal with the world – except when nannies and other helpers are involved much of the time. The behaviour and values of mothers and fathers, and expectations for their children, are hugely important in their progeny's achievements and future wellbeing. Today many fail to monitor and mentor their children effectively because they are under too much pressure, unaware, unable – or unwilling. A headmaster of an English comprehensive school believed that about 40% of his pupils had parents who put their own desires ahead of their children's development.

- Parents need to find a work/life balance that frees up enough time for them to give their children guidance, boundaries, approval and love. The young need to be listened to and encouraged to think about anything and everything, and to voice their opinions. Given responsibility and being excited by an activity will mean children develop a larger attention span. Learning self-responsibility and moral values will take a long time and require consistent encouragement and input from adults, particularly parents.

- Whatever is taught in schools, discipline has to be maintained for learning to be effective. The rights of individual pupils seem to take precedence today, with a disruptive minority having little respect for authority, little self-control and a low level of concentration – and parents often try to justify their children's bad behaviour.

- It is vital for children to be made aware that self-discipline, self-respect, application, and concentration are essential in life. Self-discipline has indeed been shown to be twice as important a predictor of good exam grades as IQ. The effectiveness of our education system would be greatly enhanced if it focused less on facts and more on encouraging children to take responsibility for themselves and what they do. It needs to make them understand that overcoming challenges and developing themselves will increase their self-esteem, choices, fulfilment and contentment.

- As adults most of us have the opportunity to widen our knowledge and skills, and can at least make up to some extent for any lack of learning or inspiration during our school years, but things shouldn't have to be fixed later. Parents and teachers should foster awareness, passion, compassion, willpower, dynamism, spontaneity, creativeity, and spirituality in children.

ALIENATION

"How long can men thrive between walls of brick, walking on asphalt pavements, breathing the fumes of coal and of oil, growing, working, dying, with hardly a thought of wind, and sky, and fields of grain, seeing only machine-made beauty, the mineral-like quality of life?"

(Charles A. Lindbergh)

How many people are truly content in our "brave new world"? How many people feel at home in their own bodies, feel comfortable at work, with their families or with strangers? Millions are unable to find meaning, purpose and peace of mind in a materialistic society. The Industrial Revolution advanced our material wellbeing but at the same time separated us from the real world – from natural landscapes, from the natural daily and seasonal cycles of daylight and weather, from our sustenance, from other people, and from our own bodies and minds.

The Scale, Causes and Problems of Alienation

We are living in an era of alienation, demonstrated clearly when wars or disasters occur – it is only during these calamitous events that people show their humanity by pulling together. Though it would be reasonable for us to welcome some increase in comforts and opportunities we have for an interesting and fulfilling life, the sheer scale of our "progress" has served to distance us from nature and each other – and we have yet to work out a way of dealing with this alienation and the concomitant personal and social problems.

Surrounded by tarmac, concrete and steel, we feel alienated from the sights, sounds and flow of nature. Urban areas have a paucity of fresh air, grass, trees, landscapes, birds and animals that used to be a major part of our daily lives. We are alienated from the food we eat because it is grown, packaged and delivered to stores by others from a distance – and much of it synthesised and addictive, foreign to our bodies. We are alienated from the multitude of machines, gadgets, and other products in our homes and workplaces because they are designed and manufactured by unknown others in unknown places – and our attachment to them has become fleeting due to "built-in obsolescence".

Family and community bonds have been broken or reduced. Alienation within immediate families has occurred because new technology and convenience food have helped to reduce family group activities, or parents are too busy working to keep up with the Joneses – or have separated. We are alienated from extended family members and friends because of travel opportunities and required worker mobility. Urban anonymity has meant we are alienated from our neighbours and the wider community, and increased income and wealth differentials have exacerbated the alienation between those at lower levels of society from our leaders and others of privilege, influence and wealth. Most tragically of all, the erosion of our essential moral and spiritual dimension by the obsession with money, possessions, image, status and trivia, has meant that we've even become alienated from ourselves.

Urbanisation

It's a paradox. As more and more people choose to live in closer proximity with others and as the speed and efficiency of communication has increased, the connection between us has diminished. The huge increase in the world's population and its concentration into more and larger urban conglomerates has been a major cause of alienation. It seems that the closer we live together physically, the more remote our relationships to each other become.

In his book *American Mania*, Peter C. Whybrow contends that the family is no longer the core of economic, social or recreational activity, so the distinction between personal need and social responsibility has been blurred. When communities become too large, the experience of living, working and learning in close proximity with others is weakened or lost altogether, along with a moral framework and accepted standards of conduct. Because so many of us live in urban centres there has been an erosion of traditional community and family responsibility. The last century witnessed the rapid urbanisation of the world's population, as the global proportion of urban population rose from 13% (220 million) in 1900, to 29% (732 million) in 1950, and to 49% (3.2 billion) in 2005. By 2050 over 6 billion people, then probably about two-thirds of humanity, will be living in towns and cities.

- May 23rd, 2007 was estimated to be the day that a major milestone in human history had been reached – when Earth's population became more urban (3,303,992,253) than rural (3,303,866,404).

Our fundamental needs were "programmed" by our evolution, and they haven't changed or lessened over hundreds of thousands of years. We need to feel part of nature, at one with our surroundings and the natural world, and we need to give and receive love, warmth and support to and from the members of our family and community. For virtually all the history of the species, homo sapiens lived in relatively small groups consisting of maybe up to 50 or so adults and children, yet now we live in high-density population centres of millions – which works against these needs being satisfied. Modern urban life has disconnected us from natural things and from each other by prioritising individualisation, consumption and a high standard of material wealth, with riches, status and power viewed as the loftiest of aspirations. The opportunity to live anonymously and like kings and queens, indulging in whatever takes our fancy, has come at a huge price – the sacrifice of fulfilment and peace of mind.

The Natural World

Since 1686, when Newton's *Mathematical Principles of Natural Philosophy* was published, people have distanced themselves from the natural world. Nature came to be seen as a commodity, a utility to be exploited – and something to be fought against. Largely removed from nature, governed by technology, timetables, money and everything quantifiable, we feel alienated from the things we instinctively value. Urban dwellers see tarmac, concrete, brick, signs, satellite dishes, adverts and traffic, which are hardly food for the soul. Deep down we crave for landscapes, trees, lakes, rivers, and wildlife – though arguably not for a while between puberty and the mid-twenties, when distracted by other more compelling urges.

The unfulfilled yearning for nature is illustrated by the success of the Seattle radio programme that broadcast birdsong. This is one listener's comment: "Each morning I drive into a depressing and run-down city and work out of a crumbling, dilapidated office building. Listening to *BirdNote* cheers me up and reminds me of the beautiful world that exists outside of the wasted remains of human brokenness." A Scottish study found that living near parks, woodlands or even playing fields can boost people's health and counteract the negative effects of poverty and inner-city deprivation. A study of English death certificates between 2001 and 2005 showed that the gulf in health between rich and poor in the greenest areas was half that in the least green parts of the country. Undeveloped open areas of grass and trees encourage people to take more exercise, reduce blood pressure and stress levels, and may even promote faster healing after surgery.

Food

Today we have become far removed from the food most of us eat – which is largely processed and increasingly synthesised and unnatural. The average person knows little about what they are eating and drinking, unaware of where their food comes from and no clear understanding of its possible effects on their bodies. When the chef Jamie Oliver attempted to teach Americans how to eat more healthily, young children didn't know the names of vegetables or even that French fries came from potatoes. Before the advent of large industrial scale farming – agribusiness – people lived close to those who grew the food they ate, or they grew vegetables and owned animals themselves. They and their children would have had experience of dealing with animals and preparing natural ingredients for their meals.

- In a British survey, 17% of interviewees thought that *pig wings* existed as a cut of meat and *tofu ribs* came from an animal. 23% believed *chicken chops* or *lamb drumsticks* could be bought at the supermarket.

The multinational corporations that produce and sell food wish to exploit the opportunities of the vast global market – they are not concerned with people's health and wellbeing. Their priority is to produce as much food as possible, as cheaply as possible, in order to maximise profits for their shareholders. With the support of governments they control increasing areas of farmland and seeds, and grow food in monocultures and huge fields of depleted or poisoned soil. As well as the production of meat and the main ingredients of processed food, they also control much of the retail market. If we understood more about the source of our food and its nutritional value, we would be more likely to make choices that are healthier for us.

Work

Division of labour supplanted craftwork in which the individual was responsible for the whole production process and not just a part of it. The vital role it played in economic progress cannot be denied, but division of labour and its corollary, specialisation, caused much of the alienation of modern life. People were deskilled, and creativity, responsibility and inventiveness were removed from the work process. This trend continues today with computers and digitisation – development specifically designed to replace labour, as always to create higher productivity, greater efficiency, and bigger profits. Technology has the potential to liberate us, but has instead increased the degree of servitude. The drive for labour-saving developments comes from a powerful minority who are able, through the selective funding of scientific research and the even more selective use of technology, to benefit them rather than society as a whole.

Most people work for medium and large companies, or in large institutions run by the state. A sense of alienation is felt by these workers because of rigid hierarchal structures and lack of opportunities for genuine participation. They are just small, unimportant cogs in a huge machine, have little influence on and find it hard to relate to the whole process. For much of the 20th century, jobs – even in larger firms – did at least involve demonstrations of loyalty from employee to employer and vice versa. Workers often stayed at the same company for all their working life, and in return the management would be more considerate of their welfare and provide them with decent pensions on retirement.

Required worker mobility and the short-term culture for cost-cutting today have largely eroded any empathy and goodwill of managers and owners towards their employees. In order to keep costs low and profits as high as possible, medium and large firms in particular lay people off as soon as markets deteriorate, and most have stopped providing "final salary" pension schemes. More and more firms – as well as local and state organisations – are increasingly employing workers on a "zero-hours contract", where the amount of work is not guaranteed.

Businesses are forever merging and growing to take advantage of economies of scale. Today the shareholder-driven urge for expansion together with globalisation has resulted in soulless "gigantism". The smaller the better is not necessarily and always true, but as Jonathan Porritt warned in his book *Seeing Green*, large institutions can erode our individuality or dignity, make us passive recipients rather than active participants, make us become dependent rather than self-reliant, and alienate us from the work we do and the people we live with. The larger an organisation becomes, the more likely it is that standardised, depersonalised methods of operation will increase the amount of alienation people feel.

Technical Ignorance

In pre-industrial times, people would greatly value and fully understand their tools and other equipment and have a detailed knowledge of how things worked. Many were jacks-of-all-trades, but specialised in one or two to make a living. Everybody would have to help with animal husbandry, planting, harvesting, and household chores. Today, however, we are all, to a greater or lesser degree, ignorant of how most things in our life actually work. We must rely on "experts", the specialists, to sort out problems when they occur. The number of technically complicated items in our daily lives makes it impossible for us to feel we are in control. This is a form of alienation that has decreased our self-esteem and increased our anxiety level.

In the 1970s, British schools began to switch emphasis from practical skills like metalwork and woodwork to the more "intellectual" skills of design and technology. In the 1980s, the advent of the computer in schools put paid to any meaningful amount of time being spent on manual skills. The main teachers of practical skills have traditionally been parents – it wasn't that long ago when mothers would pass on cooking and sewing skills while fathers taught their children how to wield a hammer and clean a paint brush.

- A survey of 3,000 British men up to the age of 50 found that 15% couldn't change a light bulb, and that 26% would struggle to rewire a plug.

25% found it difficult to put up shelves or bleed a radiator. Even hanging a picture on a wall was difficult for many. More than 37% said they weren't at all handy round the home, 58% had messed up a DIY job in their home because they didn't really know what they were doing, 22% claimed they were too busy to do the jobs themselves, and almost half said they were not interested in trying their hand at DIY jobs.

Technological Obsession

Though most of us have to rely on specialists to solve the technical and mechanical problems that regularly occur, we have become more and more infatuated with gizmos. For two centuries people have had a fervent belief in the power of technological advancement to bring us long-term contentment, and the recent proliferation of gadgets has taken this belief to the level of obsession. Technology's success at increasing "efficiency" and providing addictive internet activities has led to a reduction in human interaction.

On public transport we use swipe cards and have little contact with drivers and station staff. Computerised answering systems provide a fair queuing system for callers, but speaking and reacting to machines is unsatisfying for social beings. As substantial and satisfying personal relationships were diminishing, "social networking" websites emerged. These are convenient for more remote social interaction, but they can never provide the same value as people actually spending time together. Just as using wi-fi and a screen to "play" sport at home is an incredibly poor substitute for getting out in the fresh air and participating in real sport, so communication through machines is never going to be a satisfactory replacement for face-to-face contact.

- In 2012 there were almost a billion *Facebook* subscribers, about 33 million users of *myspace.com*, 30 million users of *bebo*, and 800 million users of *YouTube*.

- British *Facebook* users spend an average of 150 minutes on the site every day, with 25% spending between 3 and 4 hours a day.

As discussed in the entertainment and technology segments, TV, mobile phones and the internet are increasingly capturing our attention and time – with the result that we are becoming estranged from each other. Electronic communication is tending to substitute for relating face-to-face. Few people spend more than an hour a day talking to family members or people they love partly because they are captivated by the growing number of gizmos. The emphasis on self-fulfilment, self-gain and self-expression means little attention is paid to self-awareness, self-responsibility and empathy. Motivation is largely concerned with short-term personal reward rather than social responsibility – and many relationship problems are associated with computers.

The operation of technological devices now seems to take precedence over everything else. Phones ring and we feel an urgency to answer them, email is checked over and over, and TV or radio programmes cannot be missed, even when friends or relatives are enjoying just being together and chatting. Texting often interrupts face-to-face socialising or absorbing and enjoyable activities. The almost non-stop use of mobile phones demonstrates the "life is elsewhere" attitude, where you can always be with a "better" friend, lover or companion at the end of the line, rather than enjoying what you're doing and where you are. It indicates people's greater insecurity today, their inability and unwillingness to be alone with their thoughts, and their belief that there's always something more satisfying somewhere else – the "grass is greener" syndrome.

Research has found that mobile phones make people less socially reliable. 20% admitted to being purposely late because then they might "reschedule" if necessary. 75% said mobiles have made them "more flexible when meeting friends" – meaning they can wait till the last minute so nothing potentially more exciting is missed. Dr. Sigman warned that emails and the internet were causing workers to become "desocialised" – they were losing the ability to take time away from their desks and communicate directly. He said people risked isolation and ill-health if they relied too much on "virtual" socialising because we need the "cuddle" chemical oxytocin. The incredible success of virtual life activities on the internet clearly demonstrates our increasing alienation from real life.

- In 2007 the value of virtual worlds on the internet (massive multiplayer online games) topped $1 billion.

Second Life, created by *Linden Labs* in 2003 and boasting 4 million users, had the most advanced virtual economy based on its own currency, the *Linden dollar*, which can be bought and sold on the *LindeX* exchange for hard cash. Like cities, the internet is unlikely to knit people together in any meaningful and lasting way as a giant community because it's too big and too remote – it will never duplicate the intimacy of personal attachment. Direct communication between friends and family members, involving empathy and support, enables us to discuss and resolve our problems and uncertainties – to reduce stress. It is vital for our psychological wellbeing.

A newspaper article detailed a woman's experience when she and her children took a 6-month sabbatical from technology. She was concerned that they had ceased to function as a family: "We were just a collection of individuals who were very connected outwards – to friends, business, school and sources of entertainment and information. But we simply weren't connecting to one another in real space and time in any sort of authentic way." Her 18-year-old daughter was obsessed with social-networking sites, her 14-year-old daughter seemed to be logged on to the internet for much of the night, while her 15-year-old son was forever playing on his games console.

Their technological deprivation meant they ate together more, talked to each other more, played board games, and went on outings to the cinema and restaurants. Though her youngest child struggled with the restrictions, she did cut down her late-night online sessions and eradicated her erratic sleep patterns. Her eldest daughter took to studying in the university library and found time to cook, and her son rediscovered his saxophone and read more. Potential boredom made them become more creative and resourceful.

The Growing Gulf between Rich and Poor

Modern capitalism has cultivated base human drives like greed and envy, which serve to destroy our wellbeing. The farming land of the Third World is used to provide the populations of the First World with all-year-round produce, while First World companies export arms, pesticides, refined foods, drugs and cigarettes to the Third World. Multinationals exploit cheap labour and tax havens, helping undeveloped or developing countries as little as possible. Along with the continuing disparity of wealth and income between rich and poor countries, the rise in individualism has meant that the gap between rich and poor within developed countries has widened.

A growing feeling of alienation has resulted from what the poorer sections of society consider to be one law for the rich and another for them. Wealthy and powerful people are members of the "vested interests club", supporting each other with status, power and substantial rewards – for failure as well as success. The richest no longer fear criticism, while the poorest are faced with such an unbridgeable gap that they decide there's no point in playing the social game. The result is a severe weakening of moral sensibility and hence an increase in rudeness, anti-social behaviour, and a "grab what you can when you can" attitude. In the end, both rich and poor are adversely affected. A democracy cannot function smoothly when there are extremes of income and wealth.

For decades those in the higher echelons of society have refused to acknowledge or take responsibility for their mistakes, yet at the same time take huge financial advantage of their privileged position whenever possible – justifying their greed with the excuse that their peers are also being rewarded with obscene levels of pay, expenses or bonuses. Most prosecutions by far are against the "small fry" rather than the rich, who are rarely brought to book for "aggressive tax avoidance" or financial fraud like insider trading and tax evasion. It is scarcely surprising that most of those at the lower levels of society believe life is unfair, feel dispirited and alienated, and don't view themselves as part of the community. They don't see themselves as "stakeholders" in public services and spaces, some being disenchanted enough to litter and vandalise them.

The number of gated communities in countries round the world is an indication of the growing alienation between rich and poor. These date back to the earliest civilisations, where the very wealthy favoured high walls and closed gates. In addition to providing increased security, the purposes of these communities were to foster segregation, and increase the sense of exclusion – the rich desired to separate themselves from what they considered to be their less socially advanced neighbours. Driven largely by the fear of crime, well-off city dwellers are increasingly shutting themselves away in high-security compounds, with surveillance cameras, electronic gates and even private security guards. Fuelled by a media that almost constantly bombards the public with images of violence and crime, people have become more fearful. Walls and controlled access gates reduces this fear. Inside the walls people feel safer, surrounded by neighbours who share their values.

- The USA leads the way with about 11% of residential communities that are classified as gated or secured communities.

Many see gated communities as another divisive trend in America and believe the major reason they exist is to isolate the residents from segments of society they consider inferior. These communities are becoming less the exclusive haven of the very rich, but more the choice of the upper middle-class and even middle-class homeowner. And newer communities are isolating themselves further by including more parks, recreational fields, shopping centres, and even schools within the walls and behind the gates. A UK report warned that the growth of US-style gated communities would divide British towns and cities into rich and poor ghettos, breeding hostility and threatening the social cohesion.

Family Estrangement

In her book *The Anxiety Toolbox*, Gloria Thomas writes that our pressurised existence, where we are all continually and almost exclusively striving for individual goals, has meant that we talk to each other much less – though this is vital for day-to-day functioning as well as for long-term contentment. The resultant selfishness and intolerance in relationships has lowered the level and clarity of communication between the sexes. A survey found that 10% of couples in Britain sleep in different beds every night, 25% sleep on their own regularly, and 40% go to bed at a different time than their partner. The addiction to electronic gadgets may be one cause, with a third of people admitting to making phone calls and sending text messages in bed. The distractions and pace of the modern world entice us away from experiencing human closeness.

- A poll of 3,000 British parents and children found that just 1 in 10 saw themselves as part of a "caring family", where the priority was to look after each other's wellbeing.

- The poll found that the average family spent just 49 minutes a day together, with almost half of the parents admitting they didn't spend enough "quality time" together as a family.

Apart from working long hours, 35% of mothers blamed household chores for cutting into family time, with 23% of fathers saying time with friends got in the way. Family time for 1 in 3 households involved eating. For 1 in 6 it was watching TV or playing computer games. Shopping and holidays were popular, but only 5% did sports together, 3% read stories and just 2% helped with homework. British family life is often under stress from time pressures and money worries. More than 1 in 5 children complained that neither of their parents spent enough time with them. 1 in 8 families spent no more than 2 hours together each week, while 3 out of 10 parents and children estimated 2 to 4 hours. 1 in 5 claimed that family members don't want to spend time together. The plethora of home technology today has significantly reduced the communication between children and parents.

The emphasis on individual fulfilment and decrease in self-responsibility and self-control has been a major factor in the rise in relationship problems and breakdown of the traditional family unit. Scattered families alienate children from parents, siblings from each other, and grandparents from the whole family. There were over 66,000 children under 11 years-old in English and Welsh families that went through divorce in 2010. The children involved can suffer not only emotional problems, but also physical and sexual abuse. Research has suggested that children are at much greater risk of abuse from stepfathers, stepmothers or other non-blood relatives than from their natural parents. The NSPCC calculated that children are up to 33 times safer if they live only with their natural parents.

Research has also shown a strong link between involvement of grandparents and the wellbeing of children, teenagers in particular, yet almost half of British grandparents lose all contact with their grandchildren after the parents separate or divorce. There is no legal right for grandparents to see their grandchildren – they have to resort to the courts and apply for some sort of contact, a lengthy and expensive process.

Weakened Friendships

Because TV, the internet and other technology serve to distract us from "real" life, it is much harder to maintain close relationships with friends. More and more people are replacing true companionship and support with artificial stimuli and illusionary friends supplied by the very same technology. Gospel channels (in the USA), reality programmes, soaps and sitcoms serve as a substitute for friends. Viewers form strong attachments to contestants and fictional characters. The more recent twittering service on the internet quickly resulted in hundreds of thousands of American and British sycophants following every move, thought and comment of individual celebrities.

Fractured Communities

Large population centres tend to alienate people from their community. An individual is just a number, one of a multitude, so neighbours seldom know, communicate with, or help each other. The elimination of small communities and the breakdown of the traditional family unit have contributed to a significant increase in one-person households. In the USA 1 in 7 adults live alone – over 30 million people.

In an increasingly fragmented America, intimate social ties – once seen as an integral part of daily life and associated with many psychological and civic benefits – have shrunk or are non-existent. The safety net of close friends and confidants had greatly diminished in size – 25% of Americans have no one with whom they can discuss personal troubles, more than double the number in 1985. Those who could count on a neighbour as a confidant had dropped from 19% to 8%. Overall, the number of people that Americans have in their closest circle of confidants has fallen from around 3 to 2. The same trend is undoubtedly happening in the UK and other developed countries.

- In the UK 29% of the 26 million British households consist of just one person. By 2031 the number of people living alone in the UK is expected to rise by 60% – and then single occupancies would outnumber any other kind of household.

Research has found that being lonely is as unhealthy as smoking. Being cut off from the family can raise blood pressure and weaken the immune system. The number of single, British women has doubled over 30 years, with more and more opting for an independent life. 1 in 3 women live alone by retirement age and 1 in 5 will never have children. More than 2.5 million female pensioners live alone – sometimes referred to as the "Eleanor

Rigby" generation, after the Beatles song about an elderly woman whose funeral no one attended. And the number of men over the age of 65 living on their own is over a million. About 500,000 pensioners leave their house less than once a week, and more than 300,000 feel like prisoners in their own homes because they can't get out without assistance.

- In 2011 *Friends of the Elderly* estimated that up to 850,000 of the old would be alone during the Christmas period. Sadly, the only person that many see is the postman.

An American 7-year study concluded that over such a period a gregarious person has a 50% better chance of surviving than a lonely one – taking into account factors such as age and pre-existing illness. Research has found that chronically isolated people have patterns of behaviour which weaken their immune systems, and are more likely to die prematurely or suffer from infections, high blood pressure, insomnia and cancer. Feelings of loneliness and isolation can cause stress, low self-esteem, and contribute towards depression, all of which can affect people's health either by leading them into unhealthy habits or by directly affecting the body. In the book *Loneliness: Human Nature and the Need for Social Connection,* the authors argue that our brains are hard-wired to have regular contact with others to aid survival, so isolation will affect our wellbeing. Loneliness impairs the ability to feel trust and affection, and those who lack emotional intimacy are more vulnerable to bullying as children and exploitation by the unscrupulous in old age. So intense is the need to connect, that isolated individuals sometimes form "parasocial relations" with pets or TV characters.

The health of older men who live alone can suffer more than previously recognised. Many risk their health because they view a visit to the doctor as a sign of weakness, and often wait till they are very sick, with potential long-term adverse health consequences. Divorced men are less likely to join formal organisations or have contact with family, friends and neighbours, and many indulge in heavy drinking and smoking. Those who are older prefer not to frequent day centres and lunch clubs because they see them as largely geared to the needs of older women. And groups aimed specifically at older people are viewed by men as places for people who have "given up".

Segregation of the Old

As the populations of developed countries have grown older proportionally, so has the alienation of the elderly, which is not healthy for society as a whole. As well as in the USA and the UK, the separation of the old from the rest of society has been increasing over the last 50 years in many other countries – due to families breaking up, reduced respect for those in the latter stage of their lives, and the efforts to keep people alive at all cost with drugs and machinery. Dementia and various kinds of bodily deterioration have led to a large number of elderly moving into sheltered housing, old people's homes, or nursing homes.

- About 500,000 Britons are in care homes. 80% have dementia.

In America there is an ever-increasing number of gated communities designed for retired people, where at least one household member must be over 55 years old and children under the age of 18 are banned. The first town exclusively for retirees was created in Arizona 50 years ago. In 2008 about 12 million Americans were living in age-restricted communities. The biggest is *The Villages*, in Florida. It is nearly twice the size of Manhattan, with 100,000 people and 30 golf courses. This particular kind of community segregation of older people is not yet on a large scale in Britain. In 2009 approximately 25,000 across the UK were living within a retirement village model.

Pressure on Children

Though much more consideration is now given to children's physical and psychological welfare than in Victorian times, the structure of society today has produced a new set of pressures on children. Because they are the future, the importance of how we treat the next generation cannot be overstated, and the omens are not good.

- In 2012 there were nearly 2 million single parents with dependent children in the UK.

- In 2011 over 100,000 British children under 16 experienced their parents' divorce. They were 75% more likely to have drug, alcohol and debt problems.

Child protection services are often failing to recognise abuse partly because doctors, schools and community health workers under-report it. Dealing with this problem is critical, as there is clear evidence that effects from abuse are carried into adulthood, with abused children more likely to grow up to be violent or misfits. The definitions of abuse are wide-ranging, including violence and rape, neglect and emotional abuse – such as making a child feel worthless or unwanted. Parents account for most maltreatment except sexual abuse, which is usually committed by other family members or an acquaintance.

- In the UK about 15% of girls and 5% of boys are estimated to have been exposed to sexual abuse of some kind by the age of 18.

British society appears to have a schizophrenic relationship with children. Middle-class parents often over-indulge and over-praise their children, while a sizeable minority of parents of all classes are at best indifferent to their children's progress. In public places many adults have little patience with children who behave in a lively and noisy manner – pubs and restaurants generally don't welcome families with younger children. One survey found that for 62% of fathers, going to work provided a "welcome break" from their children, and 40% said it was stressful going straight from work to a house full of "rowdy" children. Another survey found that 53% of British adults thought the nation's children were beginning to behave like animals, 49% believed they were a danger to themselves and others, and 43% said something had to be done to protect them from children. In reality under-16s were responsible for just 12% of crime.

Fear

Fear has helped to increase alienation in society. We've all become afraid of each other. The older generation used to be looked up to and respected, and they in turn provided unconditional love and support to grandchildren and guidance to younger people in general. Now the old have become more afraid of teenagers – or even younger children. The trust and goodwill that pervaded much of society and benefited everybody has largely disappeared. In recent decades there has been a huge decline in hitch-hiking because drivers think the person they pick up could be dangerous or difficult to relate to, with drivers on the other hand not stopping to offer someone a lift in a town or city because they themselves might be thought of as unusual in some way. Discipline of any kind can be labelled "abuse", and teachers now can't get too close to pupils – and are very unlikely to touch them – because they might be sued. And men hesitate to get close to or touch young children because they might well be treated with suspicion or even be accused of being a paedophile. An English council actually banned adults from two play areas unless they had been cleared by *The Criminal Records Bureau*.

Distrust of Politicians

Voters are disconnected from politics partly because issues are complex and almost impossible to understand fully. We are also alienated from our leaders because our so-called democratic governments are over-centralised and hamstrung by short-term goals, party politics and lobbyists. The political system does not encourage the appointment of or support for visionary leaders. In the USA and Britain and many other so-called democracies, voters have a choice between marginally different parties which pursue the same goals of economic growth – and are content to sit on the sidelines for a while before taking the reins once again. Politicians, like top businessmen, are part of a cosy, Masonic-like club, where the members look after each other – and voters have become more aware of and frustrated by their self-serving activities. In the UK and elsewhere, the number of those in positions of influence who have not even been elected has been steadily growing – members of quangos, for example, earn large salaries and are almost always members of the "club". They interview and appoint each other to positions of high status, power and financial reward.

The alienation of ordinary Americans from their leaders and each other is similar to that in the UK. In his book *Bowling Alone*, Robert D. Putnam discussed the steady reduction since the 1970s of social capital – the connections among individuals' social networks and the norms of reciprocity and trustworthiness that arise from them. He believes there has been a collapse of trust in public authorities. In the 1950s and 1960s, 75% of Americans said that they trusted their government most of the time. By 2009 it was just 19%.

- In 1974 38% of Britons trusted the government most of the time, falling to 20% in 2012.

Diminished Spirituality

The most damaging form of alienation to have occurred in this period of skewed priorities and excess is the alienation from our inner selves. There has been a gradual deterioration in our natural, instinctive ethics and spirituality – which should be at the heart of human society because it is extremely important for our wellbeing. The dominant philosophy throughout Europe for over 200 years has been that of "scientific materialism". All explanations of life are reduced to the material – what cannot be scientifically proved cannot exist, and what cannot be measured cannot matter. But a life without a non-material, spiritual dimension is unlikely to be a full or fulfilling one. Our culture has almost completely lost that vital element required to create a balance in our lives.

The emphasis on individual rights and personal advancement has happened at the same time as the decline in organised religion, and both have certainly contributed to the current moral and spiritual vacuum – which we have attempted in vain to fill with materialism. This has resulted in an increase of negative human traits like fear, suspicion and mistrust of others, whether because of wealth, class, race, age, accent, colour or education. We need to re-learn our empathic and communication skills to interact with others, to understand, trust and help our fellow human beings. Blind faith in a particular religion is certainly not a prerequisite for us to explore the value and purpose of our lives and how we should live in relation to each other, but we are unlikely to be truly content without an ethical and spiritual underpinning. We need to look inwards to find awareness and peace of mind. An advance in prosperity can never substitute for a moral code, character development and spirituality.

How to Avoid Alienation

We think that the human being is special, the central character in the story of life on Earth. We believe that only what we do really matters. Christianity, Judaism and Islam encourage us to consider ourselves separate from other living things because we have souls, with each religion teaching that (only) its followers are "God's chosen ones". The capitalist system also isolates us with its support of individualism, encouraging us to be mainly concerned with our own welfare and progress. This causes alienation between people, as well as between people and the natural world. But each person is part of the global human community and the human species is just one part of nature, and it would be to everybody's advantage if we reconnect with the other parts quickly. The sooner we accept this and start feeling and acting with some humility, the better for the Earth and everything on it, including us.

- Solving the problem of alienation requires greater awareness to make us less self-focused and more concerned with the welfare of others and alert to our environment. It can be difficult in towns and cities, but make time to get to know your neighbours. And look up at the sky, admire the architecture of buildings, listen to and watch the birds. When you're out and about shopping and travelling to and from work, take a look around and notice who and what is around you. Take an interest in something other than your newspaper, ipod or mobile phone.

- Everybody has to earn money to pay for life's necessities, but if you choose work that gives you little satisfaction, it may well become stressful over time, whether or not the monetary rewards are high. It would be far better for your health if you chose a job where you can connect with like-minded people and have an enthusiasm for the product or service involved. Even if you enjoy your job and get on with colleagues, working too many hours will mean a lack of time for rest and exercise, communication with family and friends, spiritual and other personal development – activities that are at least as important as work.

- If you're fortunate enough to have a garden, the effort to grow some fruit or vegetables would be rewarding. When shopping, try to be aware of where the products you buy come from, how they are grown or manufactured, or in the case of meat, how the animals are raised and treated. And look at the ingredients used in processed food so you can make informed choices.

- We need to satisfy our innate yearning for open spaces and natural scenery. While young we might appreciate the excitement, opportunities and even the fast pace of urban life, but bringing up children in rural areas or smaller conurbations would mean a greater connection to nature. If you stay in cities most of your life – as I have done –

take regular trips away from the hustle and bustle to remind yourself of the "real" world beyond the concrete.

- Is your life dominated by machines and technology? If you watch a disproportionate amount of TV, play online games on a daily basis and almost constantly listen to music, perhaps you should consider re-balancing your life because you're probably not devoting enough time to build fulfilling relationships with family and friends. Do members of your family usually eat on their own and enjoy separate modes of entertainment? Do they watch TV and go online in their bedrooms and spend too little time together? Are you always fiddling with your smart phone when you're out and about, instead of taking in your surroundings and relating to others? Try taking regular time out from technology and reconnect with things that matter more.

- In the "old days" several generations would often live under the same roof, in the same street or at least the same town. This meant a continuity of heritage, the passing on of wisdom and a variety of people to provide automatic support. Today families are scattered far and wide, contributing to the huge increase in one-person households and a commensurate increase in alienation, loneliness and ill-health. Try to make time to visit and communicate with your family members. Develop your empathy and enjoy "quality time" with them, particularly children, and that may involve altering your work/life balance. Good friends need to be cherished too, then you and they will have someone to confide in and use for support when necessary. These connections may also help to reduce the chance of you being lonely in old age…

- Is the frantic pace of your life distracting you from contemplating the amazing things you have and the extraordinary things you can do? Your wellbeing is sure to increase if you find enough time to fully absorb and appreciate the things in your life. Try to take nothing for granted, whether those around you, your health, your lifestyle, or the machinery you use. Slow down and simplify your life so you can find space for "just being". For your peace of mind, every now and again, pause and reflect on how incredibly fortunate you are, and remind yourself of those things that *really* matter to you.

POLLUTION (visual and aural)

> *"Everyone has the right to walk from one end
> of the city to the other in secure and beautiful spaces.
> Everybody has the right to go by public transport.
> Everybody has the right to an unhampered view
> down their street, not full of railings, signs and rubbish."*
>
> (Richard Rogers)

The effects of visual and aural pollution are perhaps more subtle than those of other problems we confront today, but they can also have a significant impact on our health and contentment. Our surroundings can affect how we feel, and the views and sounds in built-up areas – where most of us now live – are inherently not as relaxing or pleasing to us as the countryside, mountains, lakes and seas. With so many people in the world it would of course be naïve to believe that we could all have water and open spaces nearby and hear just the sounds of nature, but at the very least our environment should not be unpleasant to look at or irritating on the ear.

Visual Pollution

We may not always be fully aware of the details of our surroundings, but the first impression of a community, whether rural, suburban or urban, is generally visual. Every day we are at least subliminally affected by what's around us. Within our own homes most of us take great care to create a mood-enhancing environment, but what is beyond our garden boundary is not under our direct control and can often be far less positive. In parts of the countryside, in many villages, and in every town and city, our wellbeing is reduced by a variety of visual pollution. As well as individual things being unattractive to the eye, a general "visual clutter" can have a negative effect on our mood. This might include buildings that are either badly-designed or out of character, spaghetti junctions, business signs and advertising, street signs, telephone and utility poles, graffiti, weeds and litter.

The homogenisation of towns and cities can also be justly labelled as visual pollution. People like variety, and want to feel part of a distinctive community. Europe has followed America and its culture of mass buying and marketing, resulting in identikit chain stores on almost identical high streets. Commercial buildings of all kinds are mass-designed and mass-produced and used in a multitude of both urban and rural locations. Roads, signs, recreational facilities, schools, building materials, utility poles and mobile phone towers also look similar. It is now extremely difficult for a community's appearance to express uniqueness and reflect its history, present vitality, and future potential. We would appreciate our local environment far more if it was different, coherent and vibrant, and not cluttered with visual pollution.

Litter

One particularly annoying and unnecessary form of visual pollution is litter. Our welfare is severely diminished when public places are defaced with discarded wrappers, chewing gum, cigarette butts, cartons or plastic bottles. Though there are natural causes of litter – like rubbish bins spilling their contents by high winds or wild animals looking for food – most unsightly mess is of course caused by people. Ignorance, apathy and lack of environmental awareness are some reasons for littering. Many Americans admit to littering yet also say they appreciate a clean environment. A study in the state of Texas discovered that those most likely to litter are males, youths under 25, smokers, and frequenters to bars, parties and fast food restaurants. Research has shown that areas which are allowed to remain dirty are prone to becoming dirtier, i.e. areas near fast food restaurants and bus stops, and wherever cigarette smokers congregate. It seems that litter "gives permission" to litter.

Graffiti

Some perceive graffiti as a method of reclaiming public space or to display their particular art form, while most regard it as an unwanted nuisance, or as expensive vandalism – requiring repair of the targeted property. In most countries, defacing property with graffiti without the property owner's consent is considered vandalism, which is punishable by law. Graffiti might be elaborate wall paintings, but often involves names or monikers, scribbles, images, lettering, scratched, scrawled, painted or marked in any manner on property. Sometimes it might be used to communicate social and political messages. Spray paint and markers are the materials commonly used. Graffiti contributes to a general sense of squalor and a heightened fear of crime, and can trigger anti-social behaviour and petty crime. Dutch researchers left an envelope with a 5-euro note protruding out of a post-box, and found that it would more likely be taken if litter and graffiti were nearby.

In 1995 the mayor of New York initiated the largest anti-graffiti campaign in US history which started as a crackdown on "quality of life crimes" throughout the city. The sale of aerosol spray-paint cans to children under 18 was banned, and sellers of spray-paint had to lock it in a case or display cans behind a counter, out of reach of potential shoplifters. Fines of $350 were imposed for violations of the city's anti-graffiti law. Another approach to reduce the problem of graffiti has been taken by many Australian cities. They have designated walls or areas exclusively for budding artists to produce better art without the worry of being arrested for vandalism or trespassing.

Vandalism

Like litter and graffiti, vandalism is anti-social and illegal, and creates a negative impression of an area, contributing to people's fear of crime. Vandalism includes breaking the windows of houses or commercial premises, the destruction of phone boxes and bus shelters, damaging street lights or street furniture, dumping refuse, abandoning vehicles, fouling pavements and green spaces, interfering with road signs, and damaging vehicle bodywork, wing mirrors and tyres.

- The British Crime Survey for 2009/10 showed that 25% of all crime was vandalism.

40% of vandalism was against vehicles and 25% against homes – with damage to walls, fences and other garden items the most common. It seems that offenders are predominantly aged 21 and under and commit crimes because they are bored, have consumed too much alcohol, or want revenge. Over 80% of offences are committed on the spur of the moment. CCTV, wardens, and improved street lighting are used to prevent vandalism.

Signs and Billboards

If a traveller's view of the rolling hills or the rustic village is obstructed by advertisements or billboards, it is visual pollution. In the USA billboards proliferated in the 1940s and 1950s, spurred by the growth of automobile traffic and construction of the interstate highway system. In the 1960s some states banned billboards totally, though there were some loopholes. To a lesser extent than in the USA, advertisements of all sizes, shapes and colours fight for attention in towns and cities of all countries. There are signs on and in front of buildings, and billboards tower above them. There are billboard controls in various countries. The Norwegian city of Bergen has imposed a ban on them, the mayor of Moscow introduced regulations to reduce their number and size, and many other towns and cities in Europe impose severe restrictions on their use. In the UK there are regulations about the size of "for sale" signs and how long they can be used. São Paulo in Brazil has banned advertisements on taxis and buses, and imposed strict limits on shop-front signs.

Air Pollution

Once the Industrial Revolution began, virtually all air pollution has been man-made. Because of its negative effect on people's health, laws were passed many decades ago in all developed countries, including the UK. The improvement in visual pollution was a side effect of this clean air legislation. The visual pollution of haze occurs when light is absorbed or scattered by pollution particles such as sulfates, nitrates, organic carbon compounds, soot, and soil dust. Nitrogen dioxide and other pollution gases also contribute to haze, which increases with summer humidity because sulfate and other particles absorb moisture and increase in size. The larger the particles, the more light they scatter.

Haze is most dramatically seen as a brownish-grey cloud hovering over cities, but it also obscures beautiful countryside vistas. At Acadia National Park in Maine, for example, visual range on a clear day can be 199 miles, but on a hazy day that can be reduced to 30 miles. Utility boilers and vehicle emissions are both major sources of haze-causing pollution. Interstate co-operation through *The Environmental Protection Agency* helped to improve visibility in 156 national parks and wilderness areas. *The Clean Air Act* of 1956 initiated the prevention of haze and smog in British towns and cities. The lack of effective controls and co-operation between countries over industry and traffic pollution means that people in many eastern countries are still suffering from poor air quality. In 2013 illegal fires started by farmers to clear trees caused smog to rise to dangerously hazardous levels in Indonesia and Singapore.

Other Visual Pollution

Power lines, phone masts, and even ugly buildings, are visual pollution. Utility companies have sometimes been persuaded to bury power and telephone lines. To preserve scenic beauty, masts that are needed to provide mobile telephone service have been disguised as trees or cacti, encased in an existing structure (such as a bell tower) or placed on top of one (such as a barn silo or water tower). Parking lots, expansive areas of asphalt, and franchise architecture involving the usual fast food restaurants and stores can all be considered "visual clutter". In America these visually-cluttered areas are often the gateways to communities – the roads leading into the commercial, tourist or economic centres. The visual impact of these sprawling strip commercial zones creates a lasting image of the community and can overshadow its individuality. Visual pollution can be slightly different in the context of the countryside. Bright colours and jarring colour combinations will stand out boldly against the greens, browns and whites of the summer and winter wilderness.

Another form of visual pollution is "light pollution". Various forms of this type of pollution were examined in a report published in 2009: glare, light trespass, light clutter, light profligacy, absence of darkness and sky glow. When there were no clouds, our ancestors enjoyed crystal clear views of the moon and stars, but most of us rarely enjoy the experience. Darkness of the sky is measured on a scale of 1 (the darkest) to 9. The sky in Galileo's time was a 1, whereas New York City today is a 9. The typical American suburb is 5, 6, or 7. Similar levels apply to most cities of the world.

- There are only a few places on earth where the sky can be seen as our ancestors viewed it – the Australian outback is one of them.

Noise Pollution

As well as missing views of landscapes, mountains, lakes, rivers and the sea, we also miss the sounds of nature that we appreciate at the depth of our being. We want to hear the lapping of waves, the breeze through the trees, the buzzing of bees and the songs of the birds. Though we are born into an unnatural environment of noisy over-activity which we learn to accept as normal, deep down our instincts tell us different. Our evolution "programmed" us with a need to hear the sounds of nature, not man-made artificial noises.

- In 2008 a radio station in England began broadcasting birdsong from a country garden, and it attracted 500,000 listeners.

At our psychic cost, most natural sounds are not only absent, but have been replaced by a huge range and levels of unnatural and unwelcome noise that early man did not have to endure. In our urban and suburban environments our ears are accosted with unwanted noise that for many has become something of a menace. Our "soundscape" is now heavily polluted by the cacophony of traffic, rattling and whistling trains, helicopters, planes, car and house alarms, ambulance and police sirens, construction work, power tools, lighting and generator hum, neighbour noises, loud music, and mobile phone rings, often followed by loud conversations.

- A 2008 survey revealed that only 57% of UK respondents could enjoy a quiet time in their gardens, a drop of 2% on the previous year.

Health problems can occur from unwanted noise. Research has shown that even when asleep, our ears, brain and body continue to react to sounds, raising levels of stress hormones. And if these stress hormones are in constant circulation, they can cause long-term physiological changes that could be life-threatening. The end result might be anything from heart failure and strokes to high blood pressure and immune system problems. Noise may be the root cause of around 3 deaths in every 100 traditionally blamed on heart disease. In 2006 a study by *The World Health Organisation* estimated that 44% of Europeans (more than 210 million people) were regularly exposed to noise levels considered potentially dangerous to health. The study found that each year 245,000 people in the EU suffered cardiovascular diseases "provoked" by traffic noise, 2% suffered severely disturbed sleep because of noise pollution, 15% suffered severe annoyance, and chronic exposure to loud traffic noise caused about 3% of all cases of tinnitus, where sufferers hear constant noise.

The Effect on Animals

Man-made noises sometimes have a detrimental effect on other creatures. They can cause stress, increase the risk of mortality by changing the delicate balance of predator/prey detection and avoidance, and interfere with the use of sounds in communication, especially in relation to reproduction and navigation. Sonar, wind and oil rig turbines all have a negative impact on animal life, perhaps causing a reduction of usable habitat, which in the case of endangered species may be one factor leading to extinction. One of the best known cases of damage caused by noise pollution is the death of whales whose beaching was brought on by military sonar. Noise also makes species communicate louder: the "Lombard vocal response". Studies have shown that Zebra finches become less faithful to their partners when exposed to traffic noise, which suggests that aural pollution might even alter a population's evolutionary direction by selecting particular traits that battle against the noise we create.

Noisy Neighbours

For a significant minority of the population, neighbourhood noise is an issue that reduces quality of life – and in some cases almost destroys it. In the home, loud music, shouting, arguments, banging and noisy children are the most common causes of disturbance. Annoying noises made by neighbours outside the home include barking dogs, cars, motorbikes, and vehicle or house alarms. Problem noises vary according to local and personal circumstances. For example, noise from fireworks can have a greater negative effect on older people, children and animals, and problems with loud music are more common for people living in flats as opposed to detached houses, whose residents are more concerned with noises from pets, cars or motorbikes.

- A 2009 survey found that the lives of more than a third of Britons were being made a misery by noisy neighbours.

For some people the problem becomes so severe that it leads to violence. Domestic noise pollution is not just an urban nuisance; the problem of noisy neighbours is rapidly becoming the scourge of suburbia. Living with persistent noise can be very debilitating, increasing stress levels and leaving people feeling like prisoners in their own homes. This problem has been reduced because new buildings have to be constructed in accordance with strict regulations with regard to noise penetration, and rigorous testing is conducted to ensure compliance.

Traffic Noise

The source of most noise worldwide involves transport of one sort or another. In towns and cities there are ambulance and police car sirens blaring frequently, motor vehicle engines revving or tyres screeching, aircraft drones and trains rattling on the rails or blowing their whistles. A Swedish study found that even reasonably low levels of noise had a damaging impact on men's health – anything greater than 55 decibels is a danger, and heavy traffic produces sound levels of around 80 decibels. The researchers found that a man's chance of having dangerously high blood pressure is 3 times greater after 10 years of living with constant noise.

Music

Music is usually positive. It brings great pleasure to many people throughout their lives. Like every good thing, however, there is a time and place for it. Apart from music played too loud or at the wrong time by neighbours, it's hard to escape from it in all kinds of public places. And it has also become louder. We hear recorded music in lifts, shops and restaurants, amplified live music is played inside and outside tube stations, people often play loud music in their cars or on a radio, wherever they are, and "spilt" music from personal music gizmos has become an irritation for commuters on public transport.

Other Noise Pollution

In airports and in train, bus and tube stations, loud, regular, repetitive messages provide passengers with information about security and services. Adverts and trails on TV and radio have become louder and more frenetic. On public transport and in public buildings and spaces, the ring tones of mobile phones – usually irritating and at high volume – frequently interrupt any peace and quiet there may be. There is a brief respite when the call is answered, but the relief gives way to tedium or irritation for other travellers who have to hear people's (uninteresting) conversations when they talk too loudly. Some countries have now designated certain train carriages as "quiet".

How to Avoid Visual and Aural Pollution

If you understood the important contribution that public spaces and services make to how we feel, you wouldn't resent paying taxes to pay for the maintenance of our streets, playgrounds, sports grounds, parks, and public transport. They are all vital for our wellbeing. We must learn to appreciate them and not to pollute them with litter and graffiti, and also educate our children to respect them. And because most of us have to share our crowded world in urban and suburban settings, we need to treat others as we would want to be treated ourselves – and not to diminish the neighbours' enjoyment of life by our unreasonable behaviour.

- With most of the world's population now in towns and cities, the close proximity of people and homes makes the potential for noise nuisance much greater. Public spaces and facilities are an important part of our "social capital", and we all suffer when they are polluted or function poorly. We must as individuals do what we can to look after them, i.e. not to litter and not to make too much noise. Local pride in an area's appearance would perhaps increase if every householder kept the frontage of his or her home clean and free of litter or graffiti.

- You could increase the mass of the dividing wall or floor with an extra layer of plasterboard to reduce the effect of noisy neighbours. You could block some traffic noise with double glazing or by installing a fence and lobby the local council to install speed bumps or cover local roads with low-noise surfaces. You could also reduce your own noise-making by lowering your vehicle speed in residential areas (31mph to 19mph reduces noise by 2.5dB), swapping the car for a bike, or at least by using "quiet" tyres. Hypnotherapy or cognitive behavioural therapy could help you cope with low-frequency noise, such as the hum of an air-conditioning unit.

- Young people often litter and make graffiti because parents don't educate them to understand the vital importance of public places and facilities to social wellbeing. They need to be trained to treat public spaces as they would their own home. Your children might grow up to be vandals if they aren't mentored to respect others and understand the full effects of the damage they cause. If they were taught social responsibility as well as self-responsibility as young as possible, they would understand that their rights do not extend to doing what they want when they want, particularly if their activities diminish the satisfaction of others.

- There are laws to deal with the problems of visual and aural pollution, but they are not always enforced rigorously enough. Local officials are more likely to act if people provide them with information about any pollution they become aware of. Authorities should assess more carefully the pros and cons of new businesses, stores or structures in order not to change the unique character or cohesion of communities. But individuals can do the most to eliminate visual and noise pollution by not littering and being sufficiently aware to keep noise levels down – in other words, to be considerate. If we become more empathic and use self-discipline to control our emotions and what we do, we would all benefit. Life can be tough enough without people being insensitive to others.

FEAR and ANXIETY

"It has been said that our anxiety does not empty tomorrow of its sorrow, but only empties today of its strength."

(Charles Haddon Spurgeon)

Evolution has ensured that basic, survival instincts are built into us, with fear playing an important role – fear of going hungry, fear of abandonment, fear of being rejected, fear of accident and pain, and fear of death. A certain amount of fear and anxiety is unavoidable and useful. When crossing the road or tending fires we need to pay attention to what we're doing because it may be dangerous, and some anxiety is important to increase concentration and make us ready to do as well as we can for interviews, exams, playing competitive sport or performing. Compared to the regular life and death situations that early humans had to face, however, civilised 21st century men and women have little to fear. Our material comforts, governmental laws, institutional and overarching societal support mean we should have much less to worry about – yet somehow a substantial and growing number of us are plagued by anxiety, much of it irrational.

Risk and uncertainty are in fact essential factors for our appreciation of life. They make our days exciting, interesting and varied – so they should be embraced instead of feared. It sounds ridiculous, but many of us are actually afraid of life itself. A 2011 *BBC TV* programme about Papua New Guineans building a home at the top of an extremely tall tree illustrated the difference between our stultified way of life and the way things used to be. Children climbing 80 feet up on their own and wandering unsupervised round the tree-house would horrify our health and safety officials. Yet in stark contrast with our uptight urbanity, the sheer joy of living emanated from these jungle dwellers – who most of us sophisticated Westerners would consider "primitives".

In his book *How to Be Free*, Tom Hodgkinson says that we have to rely on other people doing things for us, so our built-in stupidity keeps us fearful; that people have been institutionalised, fear experiment, and have developed a fear of freedom. He believes that people view life as something to be put up with, to get through, rather than having a zest for existence that was so intense in earlier civilisations: "Fear keeps us observing life rather than living it. We are spectators rather than participators. Little children are fearless and they have that drummed out of them. They are trained in docility so they'll put up with some boring job or other." He exhorts us to create our own lives and enjoy them.

Of course some people may be perfectly justified in feeling a little afraid or anxious – about crime or anti-social behaviour for example – but in most cases the perceived danger or pressure is often much greater than it actually is. The media and our politicians like to ratchet up the fear factor for their own agendas. By instilling fear in their populations, governments can justify new legislative controls that suit their aims, while most of the media portray situations as black or white (usually black), because they know readers or viewers are attracted by extremes, and will be more likely to buy the "information" they're selling.

Much of the stress and anxiety we feel is the result of chasing impossible goals, to "have it all". Despite the comfort and style, the mechanical and technological aids, and the opportunity to travel far and wide, we have not been very successful at making ourselves happy. Many people in less developed countries, and most Buddhists, Muslims and Pacific Islanders, believe we are on the wrong path. The prioritisation of possessions, money, image and status has meant most of us face a continuous struggle to keep up with what is expected – by society, employers, our peers and ourselves. The goals we have set for ourselves make us anxious, though we are largely unaware that our anxiety levels are directly affected by our lifestyle choices. Intense worry that is repetitive can have a detrimental effect on both body and mind. When feelings of worry escalate and everything in life is seen as a potential catastrophe, an individual's wellbeing will be affected enough to sabotage his or her performance in many areas of life.

The Scale and Problems of Fear and Anxiety

Though few of us feel outright fear very often, the general level of anxiety has certainly increased, with most of us fretting about something or other most days. Some worry during all the stages of their life. Anxiety can be rooted in childhood, due to abuse, emotional deprivation, or trying to live up to parents' high expectations. Teenagers might fret about their self-image, exams or early relationships, while in our 20s and 30s we might well worry about our career, how our friends see us, about our professional status, about marriage and parenthood. Our 40s and 50s bring anxieties about getting older, about losing our hair, looks or our job, about our level of debt, and about our retirement or health, security and mortality. We can get overly concerned about our children, how they view us and whether we're good parents. We worry about our partners, spouses, sex life, and our health. Information beamed in from around the world also means we worry about terrorism, wars, famine, global warming, and other potential disasters. We often fret about what we've done wrong or what we haven't achieved in the past – and few of us at any age are immune from general worry about the future.

Our privileged lifestyle is actually the cause of much of today's anxiety – the more comfort, freedom, security, and possessions we have gained, the more we have to lose and the more we become concerned about any potential loss. The increasing skill of marketing and the media to create artificial needs, then persuade us to consume more in the vain attempt to satisfy them, has made each successive generation yet more dissatisfied and anxious. The relatively new science of "epigenetics" has shown that our thoughts and attitudes have a significant influence on our physical as well as mental condition – together with diet and exercise they can make our genes "express" or not. This means our "genetic blueprint" is not an inevitable predictor of our health – what we do and think during our lives are by far the most important factors. Understanding ourselves and the world better would allow us to view life differently, change our priorities, resist the pressure and worry less. It is simple to say but not so simple to achieve, but we need function only as we were evolved to function and we would make ourselves physically and mentally healthy again.

- A 2007 survey found that 37% of the British felt more frightened than they used to, and 77% believed the world had become more frightening over the previous 10 years.

- A 2010 survey found that around 40 million British adults admitted to suffering some sort of regular anxiety. 40% worried about finances, 24% about health, 22% about work problems, and 21% about losing their job.

The pressures of modern life have caused anxiety to grow steadily across all classes and age groups, indicated by rising numbers with sleep and energy problems. We have largely lost touch with our own real, inner feelings – we often don't appreciate what we have, can't absorb what we do, live in the future instead of the present, and are obsessed with what other people think of us. Though it may not be acute enough to become diagnosed as mental illness, daily anxiety can significantly decrease our wellbeing.

The Media

The media likes to portray the world as a dangerous place. Because much of its time or space is filled with crime and potential calamities of whatever nature, rare or common, our fearfulness remains at a high level. Editors and producers love to highlight crimes, financial stresses and potential calamities, sometimes to the level of hysteria, because they want to capture the public's attention. In 2008 a newspaper reporter broke ranks and questioned the purpose of publishing ever more sensational warnings when such gloom-mongering promotes irrational anxiety and disproportional responses.

A prime example was the "millennium bug" scare – reaching the year 2000 was *sure* to bring disasters because computer systems would go haywire and planes would fall out of the sky. In the 1960s we worried about nuclear war and today we worry about terrorist attacks. In 2009 the fear of swine 'flu was brought to the level of hysteria by media-hungry health officials together with newspapers and drug companies who would benefit financially. Even the Mayan "prediction" of the ending of the world in December 2012 was ubiquitously reported and discussed.

"The Nanny State"

Central governments claim they want to reduce fear of crime, but in practice they actually like to build up people's fear in general – of accidents, disease, terrorism and other crime, because that bolsters the power of politicians and justifies the provision of "strong" government. Local authorities in the UK also encourage people to worry much more by finding potential danger in activities that have been taken for granted and no one has been overly concerned with for generations. Our leaders increasingly want to "protect people from themselves". After the Labour government came to power in 1997, an average of 2,685 health and safety regulations a year were introduced. It has now reached epidemic proportions, and we're all at the mercy of the health and safety zealots.

Health and Safety

The Irish-American comedian George Carlin pointed out that an essential part of the enjoyment of life is the fact that some things are dangerous. And we can't eliminate all risk anyway, though this is what we seem to be trying to do. Preventing unnecessary and excessive risk is sensible, but society as a whole has now become obsessive about avoiding risk. A friend who had been on holiday to Iceland remarked how liberating it was to see no warning signs or railings near the hot, steaming geysers.

Like the UK central government, local authorities are keen to show that they are taking their responsibility of protecting the public seriously. One council decided that park benches were 3 inches too low for old people and had to be replaced, another told an amateur drama group to keep two plastic swords and a popgun under lock and key, while another ordered allotment holders to take out £5 million public liability insurance because of danger from thorns, stones and metal tools (each of the 12 gardeners would have had to pay £375 per year for land they rented for an annual fee of £10), and villagers in East Anglia had to watch a film of a bonfire on a giant screen because they couldn't get insurance for a real one on Guy Fawkes Night. Christmas lights on Britain's high streets are also under threat because of crippling insurance costs and absurd safety requirements.

Others have expanded the health and safety epidemic – an engineering company advising local authorities on sustainable transport projects banned its employees from cycling to work because it was considered too dangerous, *The Royal Society for the Prevention of Accidents* decided there should be no glassware in pubs, in 2008 a pancake race held almost every year since the 15th century was cancelled because the risk assessment cost £250 and medical staff had to be present, police and local authorities forced the cancellation of a 200-year-old cheese rolling competition, and students were asked not to throw their mortar boards in the air at their graduation ceremony in case they fell on someone's head and hurt them. The university's website asserted that "the health and safety of our students is paramount". In fairness to many authorities, however, health and safety laws are often introduced to protect against probable and expensive litigation.

Crime

Studies in the USA and Australia point to high rates of anxiety about crime, and the fear of crime is now widely recognised in Europe as one of the most pressing concerns affecting people's mental wellbeing and general quality of life. It also has an impact on their physical health, albeit less pronounced. Fear can stop people taking part in the physical and social activities that are good for their health and wellbeing. Fearful people – and not just those who are vulnerable due to their health or age – exercise less, see friends less often, and participate in fewer social activities compared with those who are less fearful.

Certain sections of society have been identified as being more fearful: those who live near to a fast or dangerous road or in an area that has become rundown or derelict, those who have witnessed crime or have been a victim of a crime (including victims of domestic violence), those who live alone or have a low income and cannot afford travel or leisure pursuits, those who have no access to transport or live in an isolated rural area, those who have a disability or illness, those who have no access to community facilities or local information, those who are a member of a minority group, and the old and infirm. And some people do indeed have greater reason to feel fear: those who live in neighbourhoods where crime rates are higher than the average for the area, those whose home is not well secured, those who are intimidated by anti-social behaviour, those whose home or neighbourhood is poorly designed, those whose area is inadequately lit, and those whose area has no visible policing.

Though the number of recorded crimes has risen in the UK from 1,000 per 100,000 people in 1950 to over 10,000 today, much fear of crime is in fact irrational. Of the offences uncovered by a British survey, only a very small proportion of crimes involved serious violence. And very few were higher-level property crimes such as burglary or car theft – the actual risk was well below 10%. *The Home Office* has tended to blame the media for stoking up fear, and has perhaps tried to "massage" crime figures. The authorities should instead concentrate on methods of reducing crime, particularly that involving violence, and rehabilitating prisoners – which means tackling the drug problems that drive much crime.

Anti-social Behaviour

Anti-social behaviour like vandalism and sexual or racial harassment can make people feel anxious and fearful, even to the point where their lives are made a misery. A study found that in a London borough 61% of white women and 72% of black women under 24 years-old had been upset by harassment in the previous 12 months. Those kinds of incidents usually go unreported because victims judge them too trivial to justify calling in the police.

Older People

A British survey of older people found that 50% of those aged over 75 were too afraid to leave their homes after dark because they believed they would be subject to verbal abuse or mugging, 67% believed they would inevitably become victims of crime as they got older, while 20% said this fear had contributed to a sense of loneliness and isolation. An *Age Concern* survey found that old people were becoming prisoners in their own homes because of an unrealistic fear of street crime. While 90% of elderly people told the survey they enjoyed living in their neighbourhood, 25% said street crime was a big problem where they lived. 67% of those who had been mugged or assaulted had reported the crime, but only 50% of them were prepared to tell the police about anti-social behaviour such as verbal abuse. 40% of over-50s said they no longer attended social events after dark because of fear of crime, a figure which rose with the age group. 75% of respondents thought their risk of being affected by crime was increasing year-on-year.

Fear of Ageing

A study showed that we have the new (and maybe justified) fear of what will happen to us when we get old. 40% of Britons fear being lonely in old age, and 66% are frightened by the idea of having to move into a care home. More than 90% worry that they couldn't survive on a state pension. On top of the anxiety about actually growing old, more and more people worry about *looking* old. The media and the general cultural bias towards youth have fuelled an unhealthy obsession with trying to look younger.

"Cotton Wool Kids"

A British survey found that parental anxiety about their children's present and future is now widespread. They worry about the excessive pressure to do well at school and conform to commercial values, about family life breaking down, about the culture of respect disappearing, about children being forced to grow up too soon, about policy-driven demands on schools, about climate change, and the increasingly insecure life outside school. As the number of women in positions of authority has risen, a greater focus on personal danger and protection issues has occurred. Perhaps because women are more "attuned" than men to caring and nurturing, they worry more about paedophiles lurking on corners or near playgrounds. They worry that children might be attacked, get run over or catch cold, so they are driven to school. They worry about children getting lost or scared, so they are supervised, watched and monitored. And their worry about the indiscipline, knife crime, drugs, and bullying in schools has led to more home education.

- A 2011 English poll found that just 1 in 5 children regularly played outside, 1 in 3 had never climbed a tree, and 1 in 10 had never ridden a bike.

- A study found that 43% of adults thought children should not be out with their friends until they were 14 or over.

An English council considered removing trees because children were climbing them to get conkers and could get hurt, a Welsh council was going to chop down a 150-year-old monkey puzzle tree because its needle-like leaves could present "a pricking risk to children", and a 10ft-high slide in Birmingham was replaced because a health and safety audit raised concerns about its height – though in 50 years of use no child had been hurt on it, and no parent had complained about it. A young child was encouraged by his parents to ride his bicycle to school, but the headmaster considered this to be dangerous and threatened to report them to the social services. In America, a journalist mother wrote about letting her 9-year-old son make his way home from a shopping trip on the New York subway. People called it child abuse, but the boy was "ecstatic with independence".

Our children are being over protected. They need to face risks and enjoy more freedom – playing outdoors will not only strengthen their immune system, but also allow them to develop some independence and learn lessons about life by getting muddy, wet, scraped, and stung by nettles or wasps. They need to confront some dangers, find out what hurts, what's slippery and what can be tripped over. When children *are* allowed out, playing ball games in the street like cricket and soccer is either frowned on or banned. Psychologists warn that this "cotton wool kids" attitude will cripple children socially – we might be producing a generation which is incredibly skilled at playing computer games but has little real life experience and common sense.

Many institutions have contributed to the anxiety of both parents and children with regards to sexual abuse – a survey found that most schools and nurseries either had an explicit rule banning teachers from touching children, or an "implicit understanding" that contact was to be avoided wherever possible. A nursery in Kent introduced a fingerprint scanner which parents had to use when dropping off and picking up their kids, and – as mentioned earlier – a council banned parents from watching their children in local recreation areas because they hadn't been CRB checked.

Children's Worries

At the same time as being mollycoddled, our children are exposed to greater anxiety and stress – partly because of their parents' fears. A study found that Britain's 7 to 11-year-olds worried daily about global warming, terrorism and violent crime, that school tests made them perpetually anxious, and that primary schools were being engulfed by a wave of anti-social behaviour, materialism and the cult of celebrity. This followed a *United Nations* report saying that British children were the unhappiest in the developed world. Educationalists are clear that our values and habits are to blame – parents working long hours, children locked into technology for 4 to 5 hours a day, the decline of the family meal, and parents not talking to their offspring. The expanding media has caused gaps to occur in the "traditional information barriers" between children and adults, especially with regards to sexuality and violence, leaving children both worldly and confused, inducted prematurely into the adult world of stress.

Increased Risk

Paradoxically a safety culture may make us less safe. Norway rejected compulsory cycle helmets because in New Zealand and Australia compulsory helmet-wearing had led to an increase in accidents and deterred people from using bicycles. The Netherlands has just 1% helmet use, but the best safety record. Studies suggest motorists are more careful with cyclists who have no helmet, and if wearing seat belts or helmets make us feel safer, we might take more risks. When many road signs were removed in Kensington, West London, drivers, cyclists and pedestrians took greater care, resulting in fewer accidents. Airports in the UK have signs telling us that "these doors might open", and signs near luggage carousels warn that "trolleys might operate in this area". On buses we are advised to "stand clear of the doors". Other countries seem to manage perfectly well without people walking into doors and trolleys, whereas British people for some reason are treated like imbeciles. If anything, too many rules and signs will discourage people from taking responsibility for themselves and their behaviour and from using common sense.

How to Avoid Fear and Anxiety

Fear and anxiety cause stress. Even when anxiety doesn't become chronic i.e. turn into depression, phobias or other chronic mental illness, it can seriously reduce your quality of life. Accept that risk and uncertainty is inevitable and indeed plays a vital part in life, then assess the level you can manage – and reduce the number of things you do to lower your stress. When you make your lifestyle decisions, consider how they will affect the level of risk and uncertainty you'll face in the future. If you can develop a realistic attitude to the inevitable pressures and challenges that do come along, they won't cause you as much stress. Dealing with situations or "problems" and successfully handling them is a necessary part of life. Though fear and anxiety hold many people back, we are all more capable than we often believe.

- Over-praising, over-criticising, unwarranted worry, debilitating fearfulness and caution are all rife today. Once aware of the hyperbole of the media and politicians, we can read between the lines and seek our own truth. And then with a more relaxed frame of mind get on with things we want to do and do them in our own way – nothing *really* matters that much, certainly not enough to stop us making the most of and enjoying the one and only life we have.

- Improving "outside" factors is of course necessary from time to time, but whatever our circumstances, changing what is in our head can make a huge difference to our wellbeing – thought processes largely create the level of anxiety we feel. Every thought is energy, and it activates a physiological response. When you feel anxious, your body's in a constant state of arousal. Negative thoughts do physical damage, whereas positive thoughts aid the immune system. Thoughts create our attitude and state of mind, and the more you hold on to particular thought patterns the more "expert" you become at them – anxiety can become a habit. What we think today influences what we think tomorrow. Our thoughts become us and affect our circumstances. It is wise, therefore, to regularly challenge your beliefs and assess their efficacy.

- Greater awareness will change your thoughts, beliefs and behaviour. Ways to expand awareness include contemplation, meditation, self-hypnosis, setting goals, positive affirmations of positive beliefs, watching the language we use, and visualisation. A clear direction and peace of mind can emerge from regular meditation, which induces the relaxation response in the body. Studies have shown that those who meditate regularly are less likely to suffer from high blood pressure or depression, and more likely to have stronger immune systems and live longer.

- Even when your lifestyle is moderate and your general approach is positive, there are still bound to be "good" and "bad" days, ups and downs, happiness and sorrow – sadness is a natural part of life. Opposites are the two halves of a circle. Without one we wouldn't have or appreciate the other, it's the natural yin and yang of life. And not feeling perfectly content encourages us to change things.

- Not only will we all experience ups and downs in life, facing risk and uncertainty is also inevitable. One major factor why we appreciate what we have, what we do and who we associate with, is because the outcome is uncertain. That is not to say you should disregard the likelihood of negative results. An unhealthy diet, too little exercise, too much work, insufficient rest and sleep, and getting into debt, for example, are factors likely to reduce your physical health and increase stress and worry. Each individual must assess what level of risk he or she is prepared to accept, and the devil, as always, is in the detail – some people need more risk or danger to feel "alive".

- Diet can have a significant effect not only on our bodily health, but also on our state of mind. In their book *Dynamic Living*, Hans Diehl and Eileen Ludington advise eating fresh, natural foods at regular intervals to decrease physical stress, and to have only fresh fruit for a day or two to clear the mind and banish fatigue. They believe that the brain uses a great deal of energy so it is vital that it gets the food it requires, which includes complex carbohydrates that supply it with slow-release energy. Otherwise concentration, attention span and memory may suffer – and anxiety increase. Should a change of diet have little effect on your anxiety levels, a qualified nutritionist might help to determine any vitamin or mineral imbalance. We're all different to some degree, and a professional could help set up a diet regime to match your particular psychological and physiological requirements.

- You may think of exercise as a "slog", but using our bodies dynamically is vital for our wellbeing. Regular, daily exercise will elevate your mood, improve sleep, relieve stress, promote health and help to prevent disease. It doesn't have to be jogging or sport, it could be a brisk 30-minute walk each day. Studies have shown that moderate but consistent exercise releases endorphins and reduces stress hormones to make us feel better. It can also increase social interaction, create a sense of confidence and self-achievement, as well as improve concentration, memory and alertness. Enlightened doctors recommend it as therapy because it lowers anxiety levels.

- Sleep will counteract anxiety, and experts recommend 7 to 8 hours. Insomnia and lack of sleep contribute to tension and make people irritable and anxious. Problems and any existing anxiety might then expand out of all proportion, thereby creating a vicious circle of mental, emotional and physical fatigue. Avoid sleeping pills because they don't provide reparative sleep. Regular exercise tires the body and makes it easier to sleep, and meditation can calm the mind. Things near to bedtime that can induce sleep are gentle music, reading, herbal tea or a relaxed bath. If you feel drowsy during the day and the time and opportunity can be found, have a short nap.

- A good support network is an important part of managing anxiety. Keep the channels of communication open to family members, friends and the wider community. Listening to other people's concerns and trying to help them would not only attract people to you but would also be satisfying and stop you focusing on yourself. Any kind of pet can be therapeutic and take your mind off your own perceived difficulties. Taking a dog for a walk involves exercise, and a pet provides companionship, affection and loyalty. Apart from using friends to steer you through hard times, a meditation or other support group might help. Research has found that books, poetry and music can "banish vexations of soul and body". It seems that art of all kinds is therapeutic.

- Conventional wisdom says our lives should be perpetually comfortable, easy and untroubled. Whatever it takes, we've somehow and always got to stop people feeling down – and the quicker the better. The first approach to anxiety is often drug treatment because doctors' training emphasises the use of drugs – and patients want quick fixes. Mainstream medicine does not focus on prevention, even though bad lifestyle choices create most mental as well as physical problems. Except for short-term emergencies, sleeping pills, anti-depressants and other drugs should be avoided because they have side effects and merely mask symptoms – and might even make things worse. Whether legal or illegal, over-the-counter or prescription, drugs will never be a long-term solution, and are unnecessary for anxiety or mild depression.

- If lifestyle changes don't reduce your anxiety sufficiently, then you might try "complementary medicine". Unlike orthodox medicine, it presupposes that mind, body, and spirit are connected. Possibilities include psychotherapy, thought field therapy, hypnotherapy, acupuncture, homeopathy, neuro-linguistic programming, acupressure, Reiki healing, meditation, applied Kinesiology, cognitive behavioural therapy, reflexology, Ayurvedic medicine and massage. There are also natural substances that might help to reduce depression or induce relaxation, like St. John's wort, Bach flower remedies, Valerian, Kava, lavender, chamomile, passionflower and skullcap.

- Challenges in life are perfectly normal. We can use them as opportunities for acquiring wisdom and growing. The feeling of achievement will grow, along with self-respect, when "problems" or difficult situations have been successfully endured or dealt with. If we can raise our children to be more aware and to worry less, future generations may then modify society's priorities and change the prevailing over-competitive culture. This would reduce negativity, greed, envy, aggression, anti-social behaviour and crime – and then there would be even less for people to be anxious about.

- We are creatures of habit. Structure in our lives provides stability and security – and helps us to achieve more. Set realistic goals for yourself and try to do something useful each day to make you feel productive. A sense of accomplishment will keep anxiety and depression at bay. If you're a worrier, take time to build your confidence and reduce your anxiety by taking on small challenges to begin with, then add to them gradually. If you are unable to reduce persistent anxiety in this way, or if you have already developed extreme behaviour like obsessive compulsive disorder or overpowering phobias, you should seek professional help.

MENTAL ILLNESS

*"If I had not already been meditating,
I would certainly have had to start.
I've treated my own depression for many years
with exercise and meditation, and I've found
that to be a tremendous help."*

(Judy Collins)

In the segment on disease and illness I stated that we are all ill to some extent. Not only are most people's bodies working below the optimum level, but many people's minds are also functioning poorly. Mental health statistics show clearly that the overall mental condition of people in developed countries has been deteriorating, and there is a particularly worrying upward trend of mental problems amongst the young. Of course everybody experiences psychic disturbances, but for most these are episodic and brought on by particular circumstances or events. Daily stress and worry, however, can prevent people enjoying their lives to the full, and anxiety will be more likely to worsen if physical health falls below par – through obesity, diabetes, or other problems. And when pressures, negative experiences and indulgences are frequent and continual rather than occasional, they might well result in personality aberrations significant enough to be labelled as mental illness.

A diagnosis of mental illness means an "overload" has occurred, and our modern lifestyle is the reason why more and more people are becoming mentally overloaded. Just like the widespread physical problems experienced today are caused by people choosing to eat a poor diet and do insufficient exercise, our increasing psychological problems are the result of prioritising goals that create daily pressures – pressures that have been examined in this section. For an increasing minority, our current mode of living – hectic, indulgent, competitive, challenging, demanding – has caused an inability to cope, abnormal behaviour or depression. For some, both young and old, the vicissitudes of modern life can lead to self-harm and even suicide. Anxiety becomes a disorder when people have ongoing sleeping problems, are continually tired, worry about things on a daily basis, find it hard to concentrate, become more forgetful, experience regular tearful or panicky episodes, and have feelings of intense anxiety that won't go away no matter how hard they try. As anxiety escalates to depression or phobia, sufferers might suffer from headaches, breathlessness, rapid heartbeat, or skin and digestive disorders.

Once our needs for food, water and shelter are met, we look for social communication and support. If these fundamental emotional needs are not met, people can become anxious or depressed. In traditional communities like the Amish society in the USA, some Pacific islands, or the Kaluli tribe of New Guinea, major depression is almost unknown – because individual concerns are group concerns and vice-versa. People in developed countries also instinctively understand the necessity for altruism, but urban life and the emphasis on individuality tend to smother their inclinations to put these feelings into practice. We are so self-focused today, the concept of the wider community being more important than the self is almost impossible for most of us to accept, or even consider. When relatives, friends or the local community are unable to relieve the anxiety that many people feel today, it all too often becomes depression or other mental illness.

The Scale and Types of Mental Illness

Mental illness means a person is unable to function normally. There are a range of mental difficulties, and the seriousness of the condition is determined by how much it affects the sufferer and their ability to cope with life. *The World Health Organisation* believes mental and neurological disorders are the leading cause of ill-health and disability in the world, and that by 2030 depression will be the leading cause of the global disease burden.

- An estimated 450 million people worldwide have a mental health problem, with over a third of those in most countries reporting a problem at some time in their life that could be classified as a mental illness.

- 27% of Europeans (83 million people) suffer mental health problems.

Clinical (major) depression is now the fourth most disabling condition in the world, and the second in the developed world – and it's growing. 10 times more people suffer from the condition now than in 1945. Up to 20% of people experience symptoms, with the average age of the first onset between 25 and 29. At the current rate of increase, depression will be the second most disabling condition in the world by 2020, behind heart disease. A 2010 report found that mental illness was the leading cause of suffering, economic loss, and social problems in developed countries, representing 15% of the disease burden – more than that caused by cancer. The research found that depression was related to a number of chronic physical diseases like coronary heart disease and cancer, and has more damaging long-term effects on health and wellbeing than angina, arthritis and diabetes.

- 25% of Britons experience some kind of mental health problem at some point in their life.

- At any one time, 1 in 6 Britons will be experiencing a mental health problem.

- Over 1.25 million people used NHS mental services in 2009/10, a 4% increase on the previous year in a continuing upward trend.

Childhood was once viewed as an idyllic time, when youthful exuberance could be expressed and enjoyed, unadulterated by responsibilities, cares or worries. If there ever were such halcyon days, they have almost completely disappeared now, indicated clearly by an upward trend in stress, anxiety and depression amongst the young. Anxiety often begins in late childhood, mood disorders in late adolescence, and substance abuse in the early 20s.

- In 2004, 1 in 8 British adolescents suffered from depression, an increase of 70% from 1979.

Today 1 in 10 children under 16 in the UK have some kind of mental disorder, ranging from sleep disorder to depression and self-harming. Self-harm and eating disorders among under-10s have been rising. In a poll of young people by the Prince's Trust, 47% said they were regularly stressed, 37% of those not in paid employment or education said they were frequently down or depressed, and 27% said their lives had no purpose.

Other than dementia, which was examined in the section on physical overloads, these are the main categories of mental illnesses recognised today, with statistics based on adult populations:

Depression

Anxiety and depression often go together. With depression, dark moods don't pass. 9% of the British (4 million) suffer from mixed anxiety and depression.

General Anxiety Disorder

GAD is characterised by consistent, chronic worry about all kinds of things in life. *The American Psychiatric Association* uses a time of 6 months as the criterion for diagnosis. It is estimated that between 2% and 5% of the British (1 million to just over 2 million) suffer from GAD.

Social Anxiety

This means feeling particularly insecure in social situations. An estimated 7% of the British (3 million) suffer from social anxiety.

Panic Disorder

This affects 0.7% of Britons (over 300,000). An episode can last from 5 to 30 minutes, and can come on at any time.

Obsessive Compulsive Disorder

An OCD is produced by a perceived threat. and involves repetition of time-consuming rituals. Over-cleaning is a common one. About 1.2% of Britons (500,000) suffer from OCD at any one time – though some research has estimated 3%.

Body Dysmorphic Disorder

Given the increasing obsession with appearance, this disorder is also rising. There are perceived flaws in physical appearance that are thought by the sufferer to be repulsive. Any part of the body can be involved. Men as well as women suffer from BDD – regarding penis size, lack of muscle and hair loss. Perhaps 1% to 5% of Britons (500,000 to 2.5 million) suffer from the condition.

Phobias

A phobia is an intense and persistent fear or aversion for a specific object or situation that poses little or no danger. Women suffer from phobias more than men. Symptoms are fear, panic and nausea. About 5% of the British (2.5 million) have phobias.

Post-Traumatic Stress Disorder

PTSD is caused by exposure to a real-life event that has a traumatic effect on the psyche. It can last for years. About 1% of Britons (500,000) have the condition.

Hypochondria

Anxiety about health is prevalent in Western society because when people's basic needs are taken care of, they are more likely to be anxious about their health. It is estimated that up to 14% of patients examined for health problems may suffer from hypochondria, and up to 20% of healthy people and 45% of people without major psychiatric disorders have intermittent, unfounded worry about illness.

In addition to the above, a growing number – mainly the young – have eating and behavioural disorders.

Eating Disorders

Abnormal eating habits are an indicator of mental dysfunction. As well the growing numbers of the obese – who obviously have an eating disorder, but one that's not normally diagnosed – there is also an upward trend in anorexia (eating too little) and bulimia (gorging then self-induced vomiting) in most developed countries. These are usually the result of a perceived or actual lack of control over their lives – and weight is something they can control. BDD may also be a factor – they feel they are too fat.

- An estimated 1.6 million Britons are severely affected by anorexia and bulimia, but far more have issues regarding eating, diet and weight.

- From 2000 to 2010 there was a 69% increase in young girls being admitted to English hospitals for anorexia.

Behavioural Problems

ADHD is a condition that becomes apparent in some children in the pre-school and early school years. It is difficult for these children to control their behaviour and/or pay attention. Though to some extent it may be an "invented" modern condition, there is little doubt that behavioural problems have been growing amongst children. 3% to 5% of children globally are estimated to have ADHD.

- In the UK an estimated 5% to 10% of those up to the age of 19 (from 650,000 to over a million) have ADHD.

There has been considerable research into ADHD in America, and the findings are probably applicable to the UK as well. 50% of American children with ADHD also have learning problems. Boys are 3 times more likely to have the condition than girls, and emotional development is 30% slower for those with ADHD. 25% of children with ADHD have serious learning disabilities with oral expression, listening skills, reading comprehension and/or maths, and 65% exhibit defiance problems with authority figures, like verbal hostility and temper tantrums. 75% of boys and 60% of girls diagnosed with ADHD are hyperactive.

The Causes and Problems of Mental Illness

Daily anxiety can affect people's health and put them in danger of losing control of their life. They might experience high levels of overall stress, low self-esteem, nervousness in many social situations, difficulty in managing pressure, and expect too much of themselves and others. They might become a workaholic, move from job to job, have unclear boundaries, and unhealthy or short relationships. They could be sick more often, frequently visit the doctor, and have to take regular medication. They might often feel unhappy, unsettled and experience erratic emotional behaviour, like being quick to get angry. Their anxiety could make them feel overwhelmed or disconnected from reality and life, be inwardly focused and unreliable, dwelling on their health condition and personal problems. They might also live a restricted lifestyle within self-imposed "safe zones" – and have the feeling that life is passing them by.

Because house size and splendour, fashionable possessions and expensive activities have been prioritised, people have to try too hard to maintain or increase their income and wealth. The resultant rise in anxiety disorders has caused family and community relationship problems. For many, the striving for more money and status is habit-forming. High-powered parents demand high-energy offspring, with achievement prioritised above warmth, caring and intimacy. Extra-curricular activities often involve financial extravagance, with money replacing parental involvement. The phrase "quality time" indicates what is wrong with society – snatched moments are now a substitute for general togetherness. And free, idling, contemplative periods have almost disappeared.

Drug Use

Those who experience anxiety and stress have a very high propensity for drug use, abuse, and addictions. The high and increasing consumption of drugs, prescribed and otherwise, is arguably an accurate indicator of the mental state of the population.

- In 2012 the prescriptions for anti-depressants in England rose by 7.5% from 2011 to over 50 million. There has been a startling 450% increase since 1991.

Stress

Life has become more stressful. Stress is sometimes caused by a single factor, such as an accident or losing a loved one, but usually occurs from an aggregate of various overloads in different areas and periods of life – peer pressure, relationships, finances, acquiring skills, work, mastering technology, looking after children, setting up and running a home, and caring for elderly parents. For some, stress is actually increased in the longer term through misguided short-term attempts to lower it – by overeating and using legal and illegal drugs. Society still functions moderately well because most of us can still control our emotions enough despite rising pressures, but the current level of stress is causing the more vulnerable to become mentally ill – those with particularly difficult circumstances, those with little family or community support, and those with an inherited disposition to mental problems.

Our thoughts and emotions can affect our physical health. If they are positive they can improve it, and if negative they can worsen it. And our physical condition will affect our mind. A healthy body will help us to feel more upbeat, while obesity or other physical problem can adversely affect our mental outlook. The autonomic nervous system tries to keep the body in balance. The sympathetic system mobilises the body for handling danger and the parasympathetic system works to counteract this after the perceived problem has passed. In today's hectic world the sympathetic system tends to be dominant, so healing processes and relaxation may not take place – resulting in the body's breakdown. If stress is ongoing and there is a prolonged release of cortisol, sleep patterns will be disrupted and stop the body's natural repair operations. This can lead to depression, make the immune system weaker, cause muscle loss, excess fat, fatigue, lack of energy and a reduced sex drive.

Poor Diet

A report found that dietary changes over the last 50 years had contributed to the increase in conditions such as depression, schizophrenia, dementia, and ADHD, and suggested that mental problems could be prevented or treated by diet and exercise. Those who exercise regularly, drink little alcohol and don't smoke, stay slim by eating well and moderately, are far more likely to avoid dementia and other forms of ill-health when older. The overweight, and in particular obese, are not only more likely to suffer physical ill-health, but also stress from poor self-image and low self-respect – quite apart from the effort required to drag round the equivalent of a sack or two of potatoes just going about their daily activities. And scientists believe a diet high in processed foods stops a child's brain from working properly, leading to under-achievement, bad behaviour and learning difficulties.

"Junk" foods don't have the vitamins, minerals and essential fatty acids that boost brain power. They might also reduce the body's uptake of nutrients that improve concentration. On the other hand, a better diet can improve children's mental function. Bill Sears MD, a children's development expert, believes that about 50% of the children diagnosed with ADHD actually have "nutritional deficit disorder" – and simply by changing their diet most could take less medicine or even none. Studies show that giving children essential fats found in fish and nuts can increase their ability to learn and dramatically improve their behaviour, and nutritional supplements of omega-3, vitamins and minerals can reduce the violence and aggression of prisoners. Research also shows that the IQ of young children who largely eat sugars, fats and processed foods may later be much lower than the IQ of those who ate home-cooked foods, fruit and vegetables.

The negative effects of poor diet will be more obvious nearer the beginning and end of life, but how much the average person is affected during the decades between childhood and old age is more difficult to assess. It is extremely likely, however, that the level of physical and mental health of those in the prime of their life or the middle-aged will be affected by lifestyle choices as well – particularly diet and exercise – even though they might not be fully aware of it or want to acknowledge it.

Family Pressures

Studies have shown that childhood stress from deprivation or abuse increases the likelihood of anxiety and depression in adulthood. Children of lone parents have been shown to be at greater risk of mental illness, alcoholism and suicide.

Lack of Sleep

Our requirement for sleep is an ancient biological necessity. Today more people are feeling tired and stressed. Stress and insomnia can feed on each other. A survey found that the average American "borrowed" up to 2 hours each night from sleep during the working week. The demand for coffee indicates the need to make up for sleep deprivation. Sleep problems in the USA were estimated to cost $150 billion each year in higher stress and reduced worker productivity. In one survey 43% of participants said sleepiness interfered with their normal daytime activities, including work.

- An estimated 25% of the UK population suffers some form of sleep disorder that results in excessive daytime sleepiness, and stress is a major cause.

Cost

In 2010, mental illness in the UK was estimated to cost £105 billion per year, including production output losses and an estimated value attributed to the disability and distress suffered. A report recommended family-based solutions to counter the continuing increase in mental illness.

How to Avoid Mental Illness

The difference between elevated levels of worry or depression and a diagnosis of mental illness is just a question of degree.

- Strategies listed at the end of the fear and anxiety section can prevent anxiety reaching a level that significantly diminishes your wellbeing, or help to stop it continuing for a long time. If you were unaware of these preventative possibilities and didn't put any of them into practice, you may have developed full-blown depression or other debilitating mental problem of some kind, i.e. your fear and anxiety levels have remained high for some time, making you unable to rest and sleep or function normally, or causing you to act strangely or irrationally. In this case you should seek professional help.

- If drugs have been prescribed for you, use them for only as long as they are necessary – be bold enough to ask the doctor questions about your condition and what alternative therapies there may be.

- If you suffer from depression, follow the advice given at the end of the previous section when you are able to (during or after treatment).

AWARENESS

THE MASTER KEY

"Before you can break out of prison, you must first realise you're locked up."

(Anonymous)

Awareness is the master key you need to live a balanced, fulfilled and content life. Knowing the underlying reasons behind the things we do and what happens in the world is vital for us to act rationally, decrease stress, and increase our wellbeing. Yet almost the whole emphasis of education today is on passing exams to enable children to join the workforce when they are adults – to earn enough money to satisfy their basic needs and help drive the economy. You may think there's nothing wrong with that. Why bother to look at sociological, psychological and philosophical matters when just some practical and rudimentary knowledge is enough for us to get through life? Surely those highfaluting ideas could mess with our heads and make things more difficult?

Why not just live a life that meets our basic needs of air, water, food, shelter and sex and not think too deeply? You might argue that a simple, repetitive and indulgent life is enjoyable enough, but sadly that approach has resulted in far more physical and mental illness in recent years. In any case a materialistic way of life can't give us real peace of mind and long-term contentment. It could never be as fulfilling as one that is moral, inquisitive, questioning, and spiritually expansive.

Without awareness people's lives often proceed in a random or even chaotic manner, resulting not only in less contentment, but probably greater difficulty, anxiety, anguish, and ill-health as well. Lack of awareness and its effect on those in today's world is expressed by the modern philosopher Eckhart Tolle in his book *A New Earth*: "Many people are alienated from themselves, as well as from others and the world around them. You see tension in their face, the furrowed brow, the absent, staring expression in their eyes... They don't really see you and are not really listening to you. They are not present in any situation, their attention being either in the past or future... or they relate to you through some kind of role they play and so are not themselves."

Quality Not Quantity

Greater awareness shifts our focus towards the *quality* of life and away from the *quantity* in life. We learn to live much more in the present instead of romanticising about the past or dreaming of a better future. And rather than just playing a role or living up to an image we have created in our mind, we function instead as a multifaceted, adaptive human being.

As our awareness expands we get to know what makes us content, become grateful for what we have, and are able to lead a more balanced life. Our constant hankering after more "stuff" diminishes as we begin to understand that our wellbeing will not rise much, if at all, from greater consumption – because our material needs have been more than satiated. We realise that it amounts to little more than indulgence, and is in fact likely to reduce our wellbeing in the long run. Greater awareness will lead us to appreciate our privileged situation, how fortunate we are to have the opportunity to satisfy our "higher" needs – to develop ourselves creatively, intellectually and spiritually – unlike most people in the world.

An Open Mind

Awareness can expand, however, only with an open mind attitude, and this might prove difficult because of the cultural and educational brainwashing we all experience – or because we might be afraid to face facts which at first may be discomfiting. Meekly accepting the views of parents and society, or those of religious and political leaders, might in the short term be easier and "safe", but in the long run far less fulfilling. Being courageous enough to question everything and everybody – including oneself – is the best and only truly honest way to live.

Meeting challenges is the primary source of real satisfaction, and expanding awareness is our most important challenge. A spark is often necessary to start the fire in us to seek out the "truth" and become more aware – the initial realisation that our awareness *needs* to expand for us to achieve fulfilment and long-term contentment. For many people an open and inquisitive attitude does not come naturally, but that vital spark could be engendered by a teacher or a book – or by life itself if it becomes difficult enough.

- Different people will be aware of different facts about the world and to different degrees – we all see things from different angles. Some will be aware of more than others, but we are all capable of expanding our awareness.

- Like everything worthwhile, expanding awareness will take time.

- Abraham Maslow – the psychologist renowned for his "hierarchy of needs" – believed that once a person begins the process of expanding his or her awareness, it will continue for life.

SELF-AWARENESS

> *"Awareness requires a rupture with the world we take for granted; then old categories of experience are called into question and revised."*
>
> (Shoshana Zuboff)

The first step in expanding your awareness is to look inwards. Greater self-awareness will provide a platform for further awareness. Some people are naturally more aware of their emotions, desires and motivations, and open to seeking and facing the truth, but most of us need mentoring and encouragement for these traits to flourish.

If you're prepared to question everything you've taken for granted, you'll be able to see things in a fresh way and discover what drives you – why you think or do particular things, and what you really need to feel content with your lot. Knowing your thought processes better and what lies behind them will produce significant and positive changes in you and your behaviour – changes that will lead you to do the right things with the best motivation. That in turn will increase your understanding of the outside world and help you to lead a more harmonious and fulfilling life.

Subconscious Drives

Much of what we do is reflexive, i.e. done without conscious awareness. We have evolved with animal instincts, emotions and drives – and most people are oblivious of their power. In addition to – and intermingled with – those evolutionary drives, our subconscious mind contains all our past experiences and the effects they had on us. These lead us to react in a particular way to a particular situation or stimulus, though again we are usually unaware of this "conditioning". Psychiatrists believe that the events in our early life strongly influence our behaviour as an adult, but what happens in later years determines our subsequent reactions too.

You need to become aware of what is in your subconscious, because what lies there creates many of your negative thoughts and responses. Destructive behaviour can be driven partly by instinct, but emotions like greed, jealousy, despair, anger or hatred are often caused by deeply buried, painful memories. Constructive and supportive reactions can also occur instinctively, but again are likely to be the result of your previous experiences – in this case, positive ones – as well as through "conscious" self-knowledge and willpower. Though it may be uncomfortable or even distressing initially, to achieve a greater level of awareness, each of us needs to delve into our subconscious to discover our underlying feelings and their sources. Once we become aware of how human evolution, our upbringing, and our current environment can affect our thinking and behaviour, they begin to lose their power – and then we can take control over ourselves and our life.

Contemplation

It is vital to stand back and reflect on your inner drives and the way you live in an open and non-judgemental way. The hyper activity of modern life is not conducive to contemplation, so make the effort to find time, perhaps 15 minutes each day, to sit quietly with no distractions and become aware of your thoughts. Meditation techniques are one way to release tensions and subconscious influences, thereby allowing for more creativity in dealing with life as well as producing enhanced clarity of perception. Observing one's breathing is often used to still the mind and create a "space" between incessant thoughts.

As Eckhart Tolle says, when you listen to the voice in your head you are not only aware of your thoughts, but also of yourself as their observer. Most thoughts will probably be the result of conditioning by the collective, cultural mind-set you inherited. Many will be repetitive, useless, dysfunctional, negative and often harmful. They might involve judgements, speculations, comparisons, complaints, likes and dislikes, terrors from the past and fears for what is to come. They are unlikely to be relevant or helpful to perform the particular task you're undertaking. Those incessant thoughts can deprive you of vital energy, but monitoring them and seeing them for what they are will mean they will lose their negative effect on you.

- It doesn't matter when it happens, how it's done, or exactly how long it lasts, as long as our incessant flow of thoughts is at times stilled, and worldly matters set aside.

- Some people prefer to allocate a period of quiet time at a particular hour each day, and many prefer a "formal" meditation method. Others – like me – have random and frequent moments of contemplation during the day.

- Knowing yourself is vital for you to function effectively. Each of us alone can truly know ourselves.

- Be patient and brave. It takes courage, effort and time to become self-aware.

BREAKING OUT OF PRISON

*"Do not believe in anything simply because
you have heard it. Do not believe in anything
simply because it is spoken and rumoured by many.
Do not believe in anything simply because it is
found written in your religious books. Do not believe in
anything merely on the authority of your teachers and elders.
Do not believe in traditions because they have been
handed down for many generations. But after observation
and analysis, when you find that anything agrees
with reason and is conducive to the good and
benefit of one and all, then accept it and live up to it."*
(Gautama Siddharta)

From the moment you took your first breath, a particular view of the world and "right" way of living began to be imprinted on your innocent, impressionable and trusting mind. If you examine your own views, behaviour and goals – with as open a mind as you can muster – you'll see that your parents, your teachers, your local community and your country created them.

Cultural Conditioning

Very few people bother to question and modify the vision of the world and life with which they were raised – our cultural conditioning. The multitudes that don't question the life view they were given fall into three groups: those who have never felt any reason to question it, those who sense that it may prove inconvenient, uncomfortable or painful, and those who don't have the analytical ability to determine its veracity. I believe that almost all of those who don't escape their cultural "prison" are in the first two groups.

It can be difficult and scary to abandon our childhood inculcation, but we need to extricate ourselves from our cultural baggage and examine our thought processes afresh. Only then will we become more aware of the factors that motivate our actions and the reasons for what happens in the world – and truly think for ourselves.

Religion

Religion still plays a strong part in cultural conditioning in America and many other countries in the world, though its role has diminished in England and elsewhere in Europe. Questioning the religious dogma presented to us when young as the unassailable truth requires strength and courage, particularly when we are threatened with "eternal damnation" if we don't accept it.

To be aware, however, everything *must* be challenged. We need to ask, for example, "Why is it that those born in particular places in the world believe in the doctrine of a particular religion to the exclusion of all others?" The odds are that those born in Europe will follow Christianity, and those born in the Middle East will be Muslim, yet both religions claim what they believe is the only truth and their followers are "God's chosen ones". Awareness will not be expanded if the whole package of an organised religion is meekly accepted – especially when most religions have murky pasts and some highly contentious beliefs when the small print is examined.

Social Pressure

We are social animals. Human evolution "programmed" us that way. We used to live in small groups, with every person playing a vital role in supporting each other and ensuring the survival of the group. We learnt to read each other's moods and intentions through facial expressions and gestures. We had to rely on one another, practically and emotionally.

Unfortunately these human traits that were vital for survival have now been subverted by marketing experts to make us act irrationally. They encourage us to compare ourselves constantly with the Joneses, and our desperate efforts to keep up with them mean we buy things we don't really need, and do things we don't need to do. Inequalities in our modern society together with the media's tendency to spread information about them have exacerbated our tendency to categorise and compare, creating a climate of greed and envy – as well as a fragility of self-esteem in most of us.

We are largely unaware that our desires and self-assessment are affected by expectations, comparisons, and our peers. This considerable influence of culture and community, however, often prevents us from acting in our best interests. The social context and setting can have a significant effect on the level of our enjoyment, or encourage us to lose our inhibitions and do things that may be bad for us and for others too.

Most people don't understand the incredible power that the opinions, actions and lifestyles of colleagues, friends and family members have on them. When someone joins a group of fat people, they are likely to become fatter – because being overweight and indulgent eating habits are accepted as "normal". If those around us smoke, drink, or watch too much TV, we are also more likely to do so. If we experience violence during our upbringing, as adults we may well be violent. The only sure way we can act more rationally is to become aware of the motivations that lead us to think and act as we do – which will help to diminish the influence of our upbringing and other people on our self-esteem and behaviour.

Awareness and Intelligence

Awareness is much more about feeling and less about intellectual prowess. You might assume that being clever and being aware go together. Surely bright people must also be aware? But in fact many "well-educated" or clever people are not very aware. Someone may be extremely knowledgeable, extremely quick-witted or extremely talented at something or other, yet still unaware. In a sense, they can be described as "one-trick ponies" because they are wearing blinkers, unable to see further than their particular expertise or comfort zone.

Truly aware people are imaginative, creative, humble – and in particular, open-minded. Having an open mind means you are willing to keep searching, experimenting, questioning and analysing – and are able to listen to different points of view, consider both sides of the story, see the bigger picture, admit you might be wrong, and be willing to change your opinion or behaviour.

Countless so-called intelligent people are actually narrow-minded, act stupidly and lead immoral and unhappy lives. They may well be politicians, priests, scientists or artists – or even philosophers. You will undoubtedly have heard about some of them and maybe come across similar people who are not in the public eye. But those who are aware will *act* intelligently, even though they may not necessarily have an intellect or skill that impresses others.

The limited, focused approach of clever people who are motivated, ambitious and determined, will invariably bring them the success they seek. They might well achieve notoriety, power and status, or amass a fortune, but they don't have the awareness to understand that these things will not bring them long-term contentment. If on the other hand they were to use their power and money to help people and improve the world, they would then be showing that they had become more aware and were exercising true intelligence, because these actions would increase their own wellbeing as well as that of others.

Emotional Intelligence

The concept of awareness that I discuss in this book encompasses what has recently been defined as an "intelligence", but not the kind measured by IQ tests. "Emotional intelligence", a term first coined in the 1980s to encompass social and psychological skills, was used as a book title by Daniel Goleman in 1996. In the book he argues that scientific research has produced enough evidence for us to understand and control our emotions. Emotional intelligence includes self-awareness, impulse control, inspiration, persistence, motivation, empathy and social aptitude, and is far more likely to lead to a fulfilling and content life than just a high IQ.

- Most of us are unaware of our conditioning. When I began to question my beliefs and aims in life, I discovered more and more ways I had been "programmed". It was certainly a startling revelation.

- The multitude of "intelligences" that are in all of us, though to differing degrees, can be expanded through having an open mind and being prepared to ask questions about ourselves and the world.

- To the extent that we are unable to remove the shackles of our early conditioning, we will also be unable to expand our awareness, fulfil our potential and achieve long-term contentment.

SELF-RESPONSIBILITY

> *"The willingness to accept responsibility for one's own life is the source from which self-respect springs."*
>
> (Joan Didion)

Accepting responsibility for yourself is necessary for your self-esteem, which determines how you react to others and life in general. You can build respect for yourself by assuming responsibility for every emotion you feel, every thought in your mind, every action you take, whether positive or negative. This will lead to greater awareness, a richness of experience, and the acquisition of skills and knowledge. Don't just blame others or the world for the problems you face. Pause to consider whether you may have contributed to the situation. Confront and resolve your past conflicts and forgive those who have hurt you – because holding grudges will only harm you more and anchor you in the past. You may have suffered from bad childhood experiences and may not have been responsible for them, but as an adult you are responsible for overcoming the effects they had on you.

With greater awareness you can take control of your thoughts and emotions. Don't expect anything from the world and don't feel you owe anything to the world. The main thrust of this book is indeed about self-reliance. The developed world has reached the stage of over-indulgence and moral vacuum because people have relinquished too much power and control to outside forces.

Institutionalisation

Even when you have freed yourself from your cultural indoctrination and other shackles from the past, in order to take full responsibility for yourself you need also recognise and resist institutional pressures. Comfort, convenience, conformity, coercion and control are the main traits of the modern world. We all kowtow to the "experts"; we've all been institutionalised.

While we live in luxury with facilities available at the turn of a tap, flick of a switch or press of a button (and voice-activation has begun), while global companies are keen to supply us with anything we want as quickly as possible and from anywhere in the world, while advertising continually persuades us that we desperately need yet more products, while the entertainment industry controls what we do in our leisure time, while schools, the media and organised religion tell us what we "should" know and believe, while parents have no time or ability to mentor children to think for themselves – and while we are greatly influenced by peer pressure – then self-responsibility is very unlikely to flourish, and most of us will remain childish to a greater or lesser degree.

Maturity

We need to show some maturity. We need to grow up. We've become soft, take things for granted, and accept the status quo. Over several generations the gradual increase in material comforts and their ready supply has had such a soporific effect on us that we have largely abrogated responsibility for ourselves. We need to wrest back control and take responsibility for our wellbeing. Only the individual is capable of knowing precisely his or her needs, what he or she is going through, and the potential solutions.

You must decide what kinds and levels of consumption and activities will make you content – whether food, clothes, travelling, work, exercise, technology, information or entertainment. *You* must take far more responsibility for your health, security, work, and your spirituality. Greater awareness will enable you to find the strength – that is inside everyone – to act more maturely, be braver, more confident and much more dynamic. Don't rely on society's leaders when they are largely concerned with maintaining their status and power. Pay less attention to marketing ploys, the views of your peers, and conventional wisdom. Think your own thoughts, make your own decisions, do your own thing, and work out what you really need for your long-term contentment. Don't leave it to other people and institutions. Resist all those outside pressures and start taking responsibility for your life.

- Nathaniel Branden: "The more a person grows in self-awareness, the more he is prepared to acknowledge responsibility for his actions, responses and psychological state."

- Though at first it can feel daunting, the realisation that your life is in your own hands is in fact exhilarating.

- Like most people, I used to think the individual could have little influence. I now understand that each of us – especially in societies with more freedom – is perfectly capable of changing the conduct, content, and direction of our life, and thereby of society as a whole.

NEEDS

*"Contentment comes from wanting
what we need, not needing what we want."*
(Wayne Gerard Trotman)

We all have needs and we are continually trying to satisfy them. Though seemingly obvious, most people live their lives without reflecting on this simple fact and the potential ramifications.

The Basic Requirements

Abraham Maslow divided human needs into five categories. The first four are basic needs, which he called "survival needs". The fifth is the need for self-development. Our fundamental needs are physiological and include air to breathe, food to eat and water to drink. We also need to be active, to rest, sleep, avoid pain, and have sex. As well as the physiological requirements there are safety and security needs, which include employment, health, and property. Then we have to satisfy our social needs – the need for friends, a partner, children, and the need to be part of a community. Maslow believed that those who experience significant problems as they grow up, such as a period of extreme insecurity or hunger as a child, the loss of a family member through death or divorce, or significant neglect or abuse, may well "fixate" on that set of needs for the rest of their life.

Self-Esteem

A hugely influential factor in human behaviour is self-esteem. Everybody needs to feel they are making a worthwhile contribution and gain some recognition for it. We need to feel accepted and valued in our profession, family, and circle of friends. Deep down what we are all really looking for is love – in the widest sense of the word. We want others to acknowledge us, to observe, take notice of and know us, to be around us, to sympathise with us and help us, to respect, admire and trust us, and in particular, to like us.

Lack of self-esteem can lead to an inferiority complex and compensatory behaviour. Those with low self-esteem look for and need constant signs of respect from others, or attention and praise in other ways – which can irritate or even annoy the people they associate with. A high level of insecurity can make someone act in irrational, emotional and often destructive ways, harmful to the person as well as those around him or her.

Many people's view of themselves is largely influenced by what others think. What others think, however, will vary considerably from one person to another and from one moment to another, and their views might well be biased by a lack of awareness or feelings about their own status. Why is it so hard for many to celebrate a friend's success? Because we are forever assessing our own achievements against those we know – and we feel that somehow our status diminishes when that of our friends rises. Those with very low self-esteem might even feel secretly pleased when associates or friends experience setbacks. Aware people understand that long-lasting self-respect actually comes from within – which will be generated automatically if you take responsibility for living your life, use willpower to acquire skills, and do what you can to develop yourself.

Self-Image

Lewis Wolpert, a developmental biologist and author of *Six Impossible Things Before Breakfast*, believes that the average person's self-perception is "peculiarly unreliable". People's view of themselves is generally flattering, with a large majority thinking they have above average intelligence and are less prejudiced than the average. And it's certainly interesting how most of can remember our good deeds more clearly and often than our bad, and our successes more than our failures. A rosy view of ourselves might involve a lack of awareness or a deliberate intention to impress others. Either way, it's not a good idea to build an image of yourself in your mind because you'll then feel pressure to protect or bolster this largely illusory identity you've created – and that can be far more stressful than being honest, straightforward and natural.

A person's self image may well be formed partly from or boosted by the role that he or she plays – the doctor, musician, engineer, parent, and so on. If people get "taken over" by the position they hold, they are acting out a part they have concocted in their minds instead of just being themselves.

Wants and Needs

There is a big difference between wants and needs, and many people don't understand the difference. Wants are merely what we would like to have, and are often short-term desires – as opposed to needs which we must satisfy for our survival and to maintain optimum physical and mental health. We satisfy a kind of need when we choose to eat strong-tasting unhealthy food or drink too much alcohol, but the impetus is psychological rather physiological – our body doesn't actually need it. And in the long term such self-indulgence can be harmful. The media, the marketing industry, along with many of our peers, attempt to convince us that our wants are actually needs. We are persuaded that we can't do without this and that product, when in fact we would be better off not having so many things that the miracles of technology provide today – especially if we put ourselves under financial pressure to acquire them.

The Obsession with "Lower" Needs

In contrast with the "deficit motivation" of our basic needs, Abraham Maslow described our "higher" needs as being "growth motivated". These are largely neglected in the developed world because we remain obsessed with our already satiated material needs. Our higher needs – which involve various facets of self-development – are discussed later.

- Nathaniel Branden: "Self-esteem is the psychological result of a sustained policy of commitment to awareness."

- Liking ourselves is a fundamental need we must satisfy for us to function well. If we take steps to build our self-esteem by doing the best we can with the right motivation, we will like ourselves.

- Life is simpler if you can just be yourself.

MOTIVATION

*"Your talent determines what you can do.
Your motivation determines how much you're
willing to do. Your attitude determines how well you do it."*

(Lou Holtz)

If we can expand our awareness we will get to understand what motivates us to think and act in the way that we do. Of course any action we take is driven by some form of motivation, but in order to deal with our life more competently we have to examine exactly what factors inspire us to make decisions and take a particular path. We know we have an in-built instinct to satisfy our basic needs, but why do we seek short-term comfort through indulgence? Why are we often motivated to achieve goals that are shallow and inevitably fail to produce long-term contentment? Our anticipation and imagination allow us to plan ahead and to accomplish complex goals, but why do we live *so much* in the future?

Selfishness

Though it may seem a radical statement, everybody is selfish, even an aware person. We always try to increase our contentment, though sometimes what we believe will benefit us may well not – and this could be due to lack of awareness. Whether we recognise it or not, whether we want to admit it or not, we are by nature selfish. If we acknowledge that fact, the conduct of our lives becomes clearer and simpler. Our strong, natural instinct of survival – of protecting ourselves and furthering our own aims – means we all primarily strive to satisfy our own needs and to increase our wellbeing.

Our evolution in small groups meant that a vital factor in surviving and satisfying our needs was co-operation with others. When we give time, money, or things to others, and care for others in whatever way, we normally do so because it makes us feel good. Even when protecting and helping our children, parents or friends, we are fundamentally still acting for ourselves. We either want something from them in return – and that could be nothing more than their friendship, support or company – or our self-respect would suffer if we didn't help them.

Because our own wellbeing is intricately bound up with and affected by the wellbeing of others – the wider community as well as those close to us – trying to maximise our long-term contentment at their expense would be self-defeating. When we accord others the same attention, understanding and respect we would like to receive, we will be far more likely to achieve our "selfish" goals.

Looking for Comfort

The default human inclination is towards "comfort" – in the widest sense of the word. When stressed, people will often look for short-term comfort, and life today certainly creates a great deal of stress. In the developed world particularly, huge profits are made satisfying the resulting demand for comfort – with rich food, sex, alcohol or illegal drugs for the body, and TV or online games for the mind, for example. We are also inclined to look for longer-term comfort without necessarily being aware of our motivations and the possible ramifications. Social pressures lead many to seek what they think will bring a lasting comfort, including more possessions, money, success, power, recognition, or a "special" relationship. But none of these will actually provide *real* comfort, i.e. fulfilment and peace of mind, for very long, if at all.

Those who follow a particular faith may well do so not because they actually believe everything they're told, but because their beliefs give them comfort, support and a feeling of security by being part of a community, in this case a religious one. To help us survive, our evolution programmed us to find order in the universe, to impute causality – which we often do even if there is no obvious cause for an event. Human beings instinctively look for explanations not only because we are curious, but also because uncertainty makes us feel uncomfortable. There just *has* to be a reason for everything that happens, including our existence – so people invent a "god" or other force that is in everything or guiding events. And who can say categorically that there is or isn't some driving force in the universe, and that we have a part to play in it? We will never know for certain one way or the other. The aware person will recognise and accept that uncertainty, yet still find a purpose in life. That is one strand of taking responsibility for ourselves.

Our emotions, including the powerful need we have to belong, are instrumental in many irrational things we think and do. Some might argue that whatever comforts us, whatever distracts us, whatever reduces anxiety and pain, should be welcomed and even encouraged. But this approach – like drugs – can stop us facing up to disturbing truths and mask the symptoms of a deeper problem. And it will almost invariably make things worse. Knowing the reasons why we look for comfort is extremely important in the conduct of our lives.

Primary and Secondary Motivations

The well-known authors James Allen, M. Scott-Peck, and more recently Eckhart Tolle, have written about the motivation that lies behind our actions and how it can significantly affect our long-term contentment. If we are doing something for the "wrong" reasons, our peace of mind and wellbeing may be negatively affected. On the other hand, the "right" motivation will increase our satisfaction. Whatever you do, whoever you're dealing with, in any situation, your state of consciousness is what *really* matters – why you're doing what you're doing, what you feel about it, and how you approach it.

You will of course have a plan in mind for the end result of any task you undertake, but what you want to accomplish should always be secondary in importance. The primary motivation for every task should be to do it as well as possible. Try to come to everything with understanding, respect, care and attention. Don't be overly concerned about the possible result of what you're doing, but concentrate instead on the "doing" itself. If you are more concerned with arriving at your goal than wanting to do what is necessary to achieve it, you're sure to feel stress. And should your aims be largely concerned with enhancing your own comfort, status or power, your actions won't bring you peace of mind. Striving for excellence is worthwhile, but "success" should not be its purpose. Fame and status, just like your self-image, are merely illusory mental constructs that are in any case fleeting – and for you to amass more wealth or achieve more so-called success will generally mean others have to achieve less or fail.

Valuing Small Tasks

All large and impressive accomplishments arise out of a series of small steps that are valued and honoured. In fact everybody's life consists of small things. If you recognise the importance of rote learning, playing scales, or fitness training, for example, and give your full attention to them, you can learn not to view them as boring, irritating or stressful. With practice you can learn to value even common daily tasks and household chores like cleaning your teeth, shaving, vacuuming, washing clothes or putting out the rubbish. Once you acknowledge that these are tasks that have to be done, you can at least accept them with equanimity, if not actually enjoy them.

Eckhart Tolle advises that at least one of three factors is vital for any activity: acceptance, enjoyment and enthusiasm. He believes that if one of these "modalities" is not operating in whatever people are doing, whatever size or type the task may be, they'll create suffering for themselves and possibly others. Enthusiasm occurs when enjoyment of what you are doing is combined with a goal or vision that you are working towards. If you can neither enjoy nor bring acceptance to what you do, then you need to stop and do something else that actually inspires you. Otherwise you are not taking responsibility for your life and won't achieve contentment.

- When facing any physically demanding task or activity, learn to view it as an opportunity for exercise rather than a chore.

- Because we cram so many things into our daily lives, it's difficult to accept, enjoy, or be enthusiastic about many of them. Simplifying your life will help you to approach everything you do with the "right" attitude.

- I now concentrate on doing just a few things as well as I can – whether work or leisure. I pace myself, work in bursts, and give myself ample time to recharge my batteries.

- With practice I have learned that less can often be more.

MORALITY

*"The most important human endeavour
is the striving for morality in our actions.
Our inner balance and even our very existence
depend on it. Only morality in our actions can give
beauty and dignity to life."*

(Albert Einstein)

Morality is one facet of motivation important enough to be dealt with separately. Our self-esteem, our peace of mind, and the quality of our relationships are considerably affected by the integrity of our thoughts and actions, so a vital element for achieving fulfilment and contentment is "right" conduct – living a life based on a moral code. Religions claim to have provided mankind with God-given rules for moral behaviour, but humans have a "built-in" sense of fairness – an intrinsic moral code, the origin of which probably lies early in our evolution when co-operation in small communities was essential for survival.

Most people, religious or not, would probably agree with the humanistic values of tolerance, non-violence, charity, courage, compassion, honesty, and respect for the value and autonomy of all human beings. How you feel about and act towards others impinges directly on your own long-term wellbeing as well as theirs. If you are true to yourself by doing what you feel is right, life becomes easier. If you go against your gut instincts, on the other hand, you will suffer stress. Understand what's in your subconscious and listen to your conscience – pay attention to your inner guide.

Integrity

Integrity involves speaking your truth even though it might create conflict or tension. It means behaving in ways that are in harmony with your personal values, and making choices based on what you, not others, believe. Acting without integrity and being dishonest with yourself and others can be harmful to your health. If you knowingly act with the "wrong" motivation, i.e. from greed, envy or anger, or don't take responsibility for what you think, say and do, you will suffer physically from the resulting stress hormones that will course through your body. And you can be affected psychologically if your lack of integrity prevents you having open, real and satisfying relationships. First be honest with yourself, and then you're much more likely to be honest with others. If on the spur of the moment you say or do something that harms someone else, acknowledge it to yourself – and to the aggrieved person where feasible.

Many in authority today behave badly or dishonestly and routinely avoid accepting blame for their actions. A recent report suggested that the level of integrity in the UK had decreased significantly. The author believed that one reason why young people were likely to be more dishonest than older people was because of poor role models. It seems that those in the public eye have become more corrupt – politicians are "economical" with the truth, bankers have unfairly manipulated the financial market, and many sportsmen find it perfectly normal and acceptable to cheat. The negative effect on ordinary members of the public has been inevitable – the trust they have in those in authority is extremely low and their own behaviour has become more dishonest.

Honesty and Stress

Do you bend the rules on occasions or try to impress others by exaggerating your attributes or qualifications? Do you avoid a little tax by not declaring all your income, tell "white lies" to avoid upsetting people, or use excuses because you don't have the time or energy to deal with some situations? If so, acknowledge it to yourself and resolve to do better. Do you over-react if an unresolved issue or painful past event is triggered, or avoid dealing with an issue or person you need to confront? You might convince yourself you're being kind and don't want to hurt someone's feelings, when actually you're being weak, afraid or insecure – and in fact dishonest.

Telling yourself that others are probably behaving badly and therefore it's okay if you do too won't convince your "inner guide" – harmful hormones will still be released. The crucial questions to ask yourself are: "What was my motive?", and "Can I live with it?" Or in other words, "Am I disturbed, deep down, by what I do and would I be more content if I acted differently?"

It can be a slippery slope if you build yourself up, don't admit to gaps in your knowledge or lack of skills, or if you make excuses, obfuscate, procrastinate, bend the truth and slide out of your obligations. Your stress levels will rise if you know you should do or say the "right" thing but choose not to, if you stubbornly refuse to change your mind and direction even when it is necessary, or avoid dealing with problems. If instead you are fundamentally true to yourself, stress will be minimised and self-respect maximised. Honesty is indeed the best policy.

- Making that extra effort to deal with things quickly and with integrity will avoid stress and bring dividends in due course.

- Now I always try to follow my "inner guide", I rarely feel any tension. Though I certainly never deal with everything and everyone perfectly, I remind myself to treat all tasks and people with respect.

- Doing your best and acting with the right motivation will help to bring you peace of mind.

WILLPOWER

> *"It's not that some people have willpower and some don't. It's that some people are ready to change and others are not."*
>
> (James Gordon M.D.)

Awareness of our good fortune to have the opportunity to explore the world in all its wonder and complexity should provide the impetus to do things. And the greater our inspiration to achieve goals, the greater our willpower is likely to be. In the book *Willpower: Rediscovering Our Greatest Strength*, the authors assert that willpower is what separates us from other animals. It is the capacity to restrain our impulses, resist temptation – to do what's right and good for us in the long run, not what we want to do right now. Willpower is described as a kind of "moral muscle", which can be trained. But like a muscle, it can also get tired if it's overused. Exercising willpower, making decisions and choices, taking initiatives, as well as the operation of the immune system, all seem to draw on the same well of energy. So avoid trying to do too many things involving mental effort at the same time, and if you're ill, reserve your energy for getting better.

You can strengthen your willpower with small, daily acts of control – such as maintaining good posture, speaking in complete sentences, or using a computer mouse with the other hand. This will reinforce longer-term self-control in completely unrelated activities. The strain on your willpower can be reduced if you establish sensible and regular habits. Avoid putting yourself in temptation's way, or at least make it much harder for you to succumb. Use your willpower to make plans and to commit yourself to action – and stating your aims to those you know will bolster your perseverance. Less aware people use what willpower they can muster to get themselves out of crises, whereas those who are more aware use their greater willpower to avoid crises in the first place.

Delayed Gratification

Making effort in the short term, perhaps putting up with some boredom and discomfort, can result in greater satisfaction in the medium and long term – a vital lesson for everybody to learn, and the younger the better. It would be better still if we learnt to *enjoy the process* of acquiring strength, knowledge, good health or skills – not view it as tedious or a slog. This would be much easier if we understood fully that "delaying gratification" will lead to more accomplishments, more self-development, and more self-esteem. It is vital that parents and teachers devote sufficient time to teach children the importance of application – to help them understand that they will feel good about themselves after using their willpower to meet challenges and to become more skilful or knowledgeable; that if they can resist the temptation to take what might seem at the time the "easy" route – giving up or not concentrating – it will bring them rewards in the long run.

One of the attributes of "emotional intelligence" is willpower – the ability to motivate oneself and persist in the face of setbacks and frustrations, to control impulse and delay gratification, to regulate one's moods, to empathise and to hope. It seems that even when very young, people have a varying ability to exert control over their impulses. The "marshmallow test" in the 1960s demonstrated a marked difference in the ability of preschoolers to control their emotions and delay gratification. They were brought individually into a room with just a chair and table. They sat on the chair next to the table, which had a plate and a marshmallow on it. The researcher told them that they would be left alone in the room for a short period, and that they could eat the marshmallow whenever they liked, but if they could resist eating it until the researcher returned, they could have two marshmallows. Of course 10 or 15 minutes proved too long for some of the 4-year-olds to resist the temptation.

Follow-up analysis showed a significant difference between those who had been impulsive and those who had been able to delay their gratification for an extra reward. At graduation age, those who had resisted temptation were more socially competent – personally effective, self-assertive, and better able to cope with the frustrations of life. They were less likely to go to pieces, freeze or regress under stress, or become rattled and disorganised when pressured; they embraced challenges and pursued them instead of giving up even in the face of difficulties; they were self-reliant and confident, trustworthy and dependable; and they also took the initiative and plunged into projects. If children – or adults – who are less able to control their impulses can practise delaying gratification, in time it will become habitual and lead to a more satisfying life.

Habits

Once we understand what drives us to act the way we do, we can take control over our lives and act more rationally. One indication of rationality is habitual, beneficial behaviour. In his book *The Seven Habits of Highly Effective People*, Stephen Covey argues that habits must be the foundation of achievement: "All you are is what you do on a regular basis." He believes that good habits are shied away from by many because they require exercising discipline: "Self-discipline is, however, freedom. The strength of your ability to exercise and control your thoughts is the distance between your freedom and your lifetime bondage to blame, other people's agendas and opinions."

By using willpower to set up good habits, we can avoid pitfalls and problems. We could, for example, resolve to eat only at set times, do some sort of exercise five times a week, watch TV for a limited number of hours a day, restrict alcohol consumption just to the weekend, regularly ask how friends are doing, talk daily to our children, siblings or other family members, and make space for some quiet contemplation once a day. If you also get into the habit of dealing with things quickly and with good grace, make sure you complete tasks competently, and always be honest in your relationships, you'll achieve more, develop more, and increase your long-term contentment. Though it takes more willpower to get into good habits initially, in time little or no willpower is needed – things become routine, natural and normal.

Slow Suicide

On the other hand we can get into bad habits – what I describe as a kind of "slow suicide". Each of us has free will. We can all choose to use the power of our will or not, to try hard or give up, to over-indulge or control our impulses, to respect or use others, and to look at the world positively or negatively. The more aware you become, the more enthusiastic and dynamic you will become. A positive, upward spiral will be generated. Those who are unaware are unlikely to acknowledge the interesting, exciting and awe-inspiring aspects of nature, wildlife, and other human beings with their huge diversity of personality types and activities. Taking the "easy" way by succumbing to whims, indulgence and passivity can mean getting caught in a downward spiral from which it's hard to escape.

Willpower will come mainly from looking at things in a positive way and finding one or many inspirational "purposes" or goals. The old adage of "you only get out of life what you put into it" is absolutely true. Exercising our willpower is an essential factor in achieving self-respect and fulfilment. Anything of real and lasting value does not come easily, without effort. If it did, it wouldn't mean much to us. Striving towards goals and dealing with the challenges we face are the very essence of life.

Controlling the Mind

The British philosopher James Allen, in his book "As a Man Thinketh", advises us to take control of our mind, because indulging at the beck and call of appetite and inclination is to be a "mere animal and not a man with will and reason". He tells us to avoid procrastination and to concentrate on any task fully; that perfection should be aimed at in doing any task, small or large: "The large task is but a series of small tasks. A task successfully accomplished brings joy. A task half-finished or done by a shirker brings him misery." He tells us to live by rules, by one's own principles, the deep down gut feelings about what we feel we "ought" to do; that we should think before acting or speaking and not to have evil intent: "Every man is a mind builder. Debilitating thoughts about one's health, enervating thoughts of unlawful pleasures, weakening thoughts of failure and sickly thoughts of self-pity or self-praise, are useless bricks with which no substantial mind temple can be raised." He believed we should work towards achieving a life of justice, rectitude, sincerity and kindness, and that by meditation we can reach the perfect peace of a Buddha.

- Humans have evolved to be dynamic, both physically and mentally.

- Why some feel a stronger sense of purpose and are able to exercise more willpower than others is difficult to explain. One reason is that people are held back by fear – fear of change, fear of the unknown, or fear of failure.

- You and everybody else will surely experience "failure" on some occasions in your life. So when your efforts don't bring an immediate, "favourable" result, learn to view it as a mere setback and don't be disheartened. Remind yourself that whatever you strive to do will always expand your awareness, skills and knowledge. Perseverance and a positive attitude will in time lead to "success".

- I believe that just ticking over is unsatisfying for the individual and a waste of human potential in general. We are all capable of much more than we think – or are told.

RISK, PROBABILITY and PREVENTION

*"It's easier to prevent illness than to reverse it.
You don't have to be sick to notice the improvements
when you change your diet and lifestyle.
People lose weight, they feel lighter, happier,
freer, more full of joy."*

(Dr. Dean Ornish)

Particularly since the start of the Industrial Revolution, the aim of the economically advanced countries has been to achieve control over as much as possible. Today scientists are still trying to subdue nature by increasing crop yields, modifying food products, eliminating illness, and extending lifespan, while individuals in their private lives attempt to make things as comfortable, predictable and safe as possible. And indeed crop yields have risen, there's been a burgeoning of laboratory-created foods, a huge rise in the material standard of living, and an extension of lifespan. Instead of the level of illness going down, however, there's been a large increase in physical and mental ill-health, especially at the end of people's lives – and it's set to carry on increasing.

Underlying our desire to control the vagaries of nature is the belief that life would be so much better if risk and uncertainty were eliminated. Conventional wisdom has for some time held out the possibility of a permanently comfortable, pain-free world as humanity's ultimate goal. This is ludicrous, because try as we might there will always be risk, uncertainty and difficulties in life. We should in fact *welcome* the inevitable unpredictability because otherwise life wouldn't be exciting and interesting – it would be tedious. In fact life wouldn't be life without risk and uncertainty, without ups and downs. This is not to suggest everything should be left to chance and we shouldn't take steps to limit or even stop negative occurrences, but rather that we should be cautious and selective in what we try to control as a society or individuals.

Yin and Yang

Though our actions can modify what happens, there are bound to be fluctuations. For life to have any meaning there must be two sides of a coin, i.e. opposites. In eastern philosophy this is encapsulated in the concept of "yin and yang", which concerns opposites and impermanence. Opposites are like two halves of a circle and one couldn't exist or occur without the other – and we couldn't appreciate one without the other. Without feeling cold we wouldn't enjoy warmth, without sickness we would be unaware of health, without pain we wouldn't know pleasure.

There is also a natural cycle of yin from yang and yang from yin that occurs constantly, with neither continually dominating. There is a natural limit to both principles – wealth, for example, contains the seeds of poverty, and failure lies concealed in every success. As something reaches an extreme, sooner or later it will become its opposite – a storm is preceded and followed by stillness, cold replaces hot in the constant cycle of the seasons, a balloon will burst if over-inflated, an organisation that is too demanding of its employees will result in strikes, and too little parental discipline will result in disruptive behaviour.

Every thing and everybody will in a sense "fail" sooner or later. There is a limit to everything. While we should enjoy "good" times, we need to be realistic about how long they might last. If we are aware that change is natural and always happens, we will be less disturbed or anxious when obstacles or "hard" times come along. Nothing "good" or "bad" lasts forever. In fact, the less we label things as "good" and "bad" or as "success" or "failure", the more we will maintain peace of mind. With greater awareness we won't treat everything that happens like a life and death situation, and with practice we can accept whatever happens with greater equanimity.

Lady Luck

In his book *The Drunkard's Walk*, Leonard Mlodinow suggests that much of our life is actually in the hands of Lady Luck, and most of us are unaware that random influences are often as important as our skills, qualities and actions. Though much in life is governed by chance, we impute logical reasons for most events and situations – like viewing wealthy people as heroes and the poor as failures. We also tend to assess our own worth in a similar way. We are inclined to believe our peers if they over-praise us, and feel dispirited when they criticise us. And in our minds we generally exaggerate our effort and skill and minimise the part that timing and good fortune have played in our success. Mlodinow suggests that we can improve our skill at decision-making and eliminate some of the bias that leads to poor judgments and choices – and that we can learn to be less surprised or downhearted when plans go awry, and not react with negative emotions that can harm our health.

Probability

Though some level of risk and unpredictability should be expected and welcomed rather than feared, we would be wise not to leave things to Lady Luck when our wellbeing might well be significantly reduced. Assessing the probability of outcomes is a key skill in life and part of our awareness. Of course we take care when something immediate and drastic may happen – when stepping off a curb or when we're driving, for example – but not always when the results of our actions are longer-term. Because our physical and mental health is vital for us to function fully and effectively and thus central to our enjoyment of life, it's important for us to be aware of the probable outcome of what we do and don't do with regards to stress, diet and exercise. It has been shown that we can significantly reduce the risk of health problems through our own actions, yet many people still remain confused or unconvinced.

As I have argued in the overload sections, most bodily "disharmonies" that undermine the health of virtually every individual are the result of dietary, environmental or social factors. Heart disease, high cholesterol, hypertension, diabetes, and cancer account for most ill-health in developed countries – and lifestyle is the cause in almost all cases. Most cancers, for example, have no genetic cause. It's very rare for somebody to inherit particular genes that make them more susceptible to cancer. And even a cancer-susceptibility gene does not cause cancer directly – it makes a person carrying such a gene more vulnerable to environmental factors that contribute to the risk of developing cancer. When identical twins are reared in separate environments, the rate at which each twin develops cancer is comparable to the cancer rate in the adoptive family, not the biological family.

The relatively new science of epigenetics suggests that our beliefs as well as our behaviour can prevent the activation of "bad" genes and cause the activation of "good" genes that are in our "genetic blueprint". There may always be a small minority, however, who have weaknesses that are extremely difficult to counteract. Some might be born physically disabled or mentally challenged, while others might have such a strong genetic disposition to disease that lifestyle changes may not prevent them becoming ill. In certain Icelandic families, for example, breast cancer is endemic, and some women choose to have a double mastectomy as a preventative measure. At the other extreme there are the few very indulgent people who live to a ripe old age despite abusing their bodies – with cigarettes and alcohol perhaps. *But these are exceptional cases.* Though the result of what we do can never be guaranteed on an individual basis (scientific knowledge is far less advanced than we imagine, so there are too many unknown factors), it is irrefutable that our chance of living a long, healthy and fulfilled life will rise – on average – in proportion with the effort we make to adopt a sensible lifestyle.

As well as good health, adequate funds and fulfilling relationships are key factors in our lives, and there is a high probability that our wellbeing will suffer without them. Because a certain level of income is necessary to avoid financial stress and provide us with a large degree of freedom and choice, we should take steps to cultivate skills of one kind or another to achieve it. And because we are social animals, we need to control our communication and behaviour in our dealings with friends, relatives and colleagues in order to maintain close, harmonious and fulfilling relationships.

Prevention of Ill-Health

The probability of illness occurring is largely determined by lifestyle choices, yet mainstream medicine is almost entirely concerned with people's health from the point of diagnosis. The conventional theory is that a person becomes sick because he or she contracts a disease. Each disease is seen as an independent entity which can be fully understood without regard to the person it afflicts or the environment in which it occurs. Standard treatments therefore focus on diseases rather than people, and are more concerned with eliminating symptoms and keeping people alive longer – rather than dealing with the causes of ill-health and improving quality of life. Prevention is of much greater importance than creating therapies for illnesses post-diagnosis, however, because it's far harder to heal the body when it's malfunctioning than to take the necessary steps that will keep it healthy.

Mainstream medicine does have its concept of "prevention" (vaccinations, screening and gene therapy, for example), but they represent today's "quick fix" approach to problem solving. The conventional emphasis on germs and other "outside agencies" has resulted in an extremely narrow view of prevention and contributed to the lack of personal responsibility. In contrast, the holistic approach to good health emphasises that lifestyle choices are key to the prevention of illness. The diagnostic and therapeutic focus is always on the person who is ill and the context in which the illness occurs, rather than on the disease itself. Sickness is viewed as a dynamic event in the life of an individual, as a problem of balance and relationship, the result of disharmony between the person and his or her environment – which includes thoughts and emotions. The healer's job is to assess the disharmony so it can be corrected.

For there to be any likelihood of a reversal in the trend of ever-rising ill-health, I believe the medical profession should be split into two groups, one specialising in surgery and drug treatments for emergencies, and the other specialising in prevention and keeping people as healthy as possible. The current practitioners of Western conventional medicine, who are extremely skilled in life and death situations – and in correcting mechanical malfunctions – would make up the former group, while doctors trained in holistic therapies would make up the latter. Following therapy or surgery, they would guide patients in how to strengthen their immune system and regain their body's equilibrium. And if GPs were holistically-trained, they could provide regular advice and encouragement to their patients regarding lifestyle choices – and help them to prevent the deterioration of their bones, organs, and blood flow, so disease or illness is very unlikely to develop to the stage of being diagnosed.

Prevention of Relationship Problems

With relationships too, prevention is easier than cure. The probability for relationships of all kinds to flourish will increase when both parties communicate with each other, appreciate each other, are honest with each other, and compromise with each other – and don't automatically expect anything from each other. As Eckhart Tolle states in his book *A New Earth*: "In a genuine relationship, there is an outward flow of open, alert attention to the other person in which there is no wanting whatsoever." With regards to "falling in love" in particular, we are still encouraged to have extremely unrealistic ideas, desires and expectations of the relationship that are very unlikely to be fulfilled.

Parent-child relationships are particularly important because they set the pattern for the future. If parents have their children's best interests at heart and don't just play a role or try to boost their own image, treat them with respect and show they love them unconditionally, major difficulties will probably be prevented. And if they can find the strength to set down guidelines and stick to them, be consistent and fair, children are less likely to have problems in their own relationships when they grow up – and more likely to maintain strong and lasting relationships with their parents.

- Research shows that consuming mainly natural, unprocessed food and drink – similar to that our ancestors consumed – significantly increases the probability that we will stay healthy.

- Research shows that being physically active on a daily basis – as our ancestors had to be – significantly increases the probability that we will stay healthy.

- Research shows that supportive relationships – like those our ancestors needed – will significantly increase the probability of good mental health.

BALANCE

"Next to love, balance is the most important thing."
(John Wooden)

The right balance for you will differ from someone else's, so the first step in achieving an optimum life balance is to become aware of your own needs and priorities. Then you can try to arrange the things in your life in the proportions that will minimise stress and maximise your fulfilment and wellbeing. You'll know you've achieved a balanced life when you fully appreciate each of its components and are not "hankering" after anything else. Many people don't actually realise their lives are out of balance until something drastic occurs.

Avoiding Extremes

Moving too far to one extreme or the other will necessarily involve a radical adjustment to rebalance things. Creating a balance somewhere in the middle by steering a more moderate course means that just fine tuning will be necessary from time to time. There are people who prefer to work steadily, while some like to work in bursts. Some like to be around others more of the time, others prefer more time and space to themselves. We need to know ourselves and reflect on the best way for us to conduct our lives. Avoiding extremes – not being too yin or too yang – will normally make for a smoother and less stressful life. Those who are highly "driven" and always working and rushing about, for example, are too yang and their stress levels will rise, with the result that they sooner or later burn themselves out. On the other hand, "couch potatoes" who can't tear themselves away from the TV and don't have any goals or ambitions are too yin – and their stress levels will rise through inactivity, probably resulting in bad physical health or depression.

People often get so used to a stressful situation, job or relationship, or so locked into a type of behaviour, that they don't view it as extreme. They take no steps to adjust things. Their life may be causing them grief, but they aren't aware enough to do something about it – or they may know something's wrong, but aren't brave or dynamic enough to make changes. The issues we face are complex and their analysis can never be put in simple, black and white terms, but we would be wise to keep an open mind and assess our situation from time to time. Some stress may well be normal and even useful, but as with everything, the level that is harmful needs to be determined.

Moderation

Though it's a term that's often used, moderation is a nebulous concept. It doesn't actually involve any fixed measure. Most people believe they are being moderate by comparing what they do to the activities of those around them, and different people's interpretation of it varies considerably depending on their education, the society they're part of, and how they were brought up. The concept of moderation is so important in these times of over-indulgence that we need to find a better definition – one that is based on the degree to which our activities affect our bodily and mental health.

To determine what is truly "moderate" is to work out what level of consumption will prove to be advantageous – or at least not detrimental – to our long-term wellbeing, whether it's regards to fast food, sweets, alcohol, gambling, clubbing, TV gazing, or getting ensnared by the "virtual world". Those recommending behavioural limits may well be viewed as killjoys, and guidelines of any kind will always be objected to by some. Yet we all accept that parameters must be set for children – despite their inevitable objections and resentment. Many people either don't understand, or don't want to recognise, that we adults need limits too, constraints that will benefit us in the long term.

Cultural Norms

Humans have a tendency to become bored, indulgent and inquisitive. Aided and abetted by increasing wealth and a surfeit of temptation, these traits have now brought us to an era of extremes and excesses. We use a huge variety of toppings for sweet or savoury meals, combine more and more foods and drinks together, and multi-tasking has become normal. We can't walk down the road without talking on the phone. We can't just watch a film, we have to slurp on a soft drink and chomp on a huge tub of popcorn. We can't just exercise in the gym, we need to listen to music or watch TV at the same time. We can't just go dancing and have a few drinks, we have to get blind drunk or take illegal drugs. The rising level of indulgence makes what used to be viewed as satisfying and normal to be considered boring or banal. Those who are wise enough to eat simple food or concentrate on just one thing at a time are considered ascetic or peculiar today – yet this is *true* moderation.

It seems that humans, and other creatures too, have a need to go to excess every now and again – to experience change, to relieve boredom or stress that may have built up, or perhaps to celebrate the wonders of life. Up to a hundred years ago people would let their hair down just once in a while – they were "moderate" in their excess, so to speak. Though many of us think we are moderate today, in comparison to previous centuries and elsewhere in the world, we certainly aren't. Those in developed countries exhibit excessive behaviour on a daily basis.

The Ever-Rising Bar

Our natural inclination is to accept as normal – or "moderate" – what people are doing at the particular time we join the human race. Over the last 50 years or so the bar has been continually rising, so what is considered moderate today would have seemed extremely indulgent several generations ago. In so-called primitive societies "heavy" food – like a roasted pig for example – would be eaten on special, festive occasions. This might be once in a season, around four times a year. Similarly, a mind-altering drug, whether alcohol or something else, would only be used every now and again, if at all. The bar has risen so far in rich countries that we don't understand how indulgent we are – and how harmful it can be. Many decades ago it was decided to define poverty in relative rather than absolute terms – with the result that a family today might have a place to live, food on their plates, more than one TV in the house, a computer, several mobile phones and a play-station, plus a steady supply of cigarettes and alcohol, yet still be defined as living in poverty!

Industrialisation and technology has largely eliminated drudgery and back-breaking work. It has allowed us to lead more comfortable, "civilised" lives but has also caused our "pain threshold" – the level at which we feel discomfort or loss – to decrease as much as our level of indulgence has been rising. We have all become much more sensitive to problems and discomfort. We look for magic pills or other quick fixes whenever we feel slight discomfort. Encouraged by political and business leaders, we desire, expect, and take for granted an ever-increasing quantity and quality of services, and whenever there is a diminution in any of these we react as if it's a major calamity.

Proportionality

Proportionality is inextricably linked with moderation and balance, and greater awareness will mean we make better choices about the proportions in our life – what types and quantity of food and drink we consume, what time we apportion for sleep, work, exercise, hobbies, rest, education, meals, holidays, entertainment, family and friends, and what proportion of our income we save. Work is important to earn money, to have a structure in life, to exercise the brain, and for camaraderie, but our time must be split in such a way that our other needs are also met. Socialising is important, but we also need to be alone sometimes to gather our thoughts, to contemplate. Sufficient rest and sleep are vital for our physical health, but we need to be aware of how much we need – too much or too little might affect our health and how we deal with life.

Eating should be enjoyable, but many people are obsessed with food, grazing all day, every day, and spend an inordinate amount of time thinking about it. Regular exercise is vital for energising body and mind, as well as an important counter-balance to our largely sedentary lives, but most people don't do enough. Neatness, style, personal cleanliness and home comforts are important, but some people can be unduly concerned with them. Distraction – resting our brains – is necessary because we can't spend all our time being productive or ruminating on the grander questions of life and the universe, but watching TV for 5 hours every day is too much. We can't be perfect and keep everything moderate and in proportion all the time, but even letting our hair down has to be moderate and in proportion!

Material and Spiritual Balance

Decisions about our material and social environment can affect our enjoyment of life, but the time and effort to improve the "outside" should not be out of proportion with that spent on developing the "inside" – our awareness. Possessions, relationships and our activities are important, but we are prone to lose ourselves in the external world. The way we view life should be accorded at least equal status to making changes to our circumstances. When our basic, material needs have been satisfied, and we have supportive, stable relationships, inner self-development is important for our wellbeing. We are no longer continually fighting famine, drought, pestilence, heat, cold, damp, war and plague any more, and have a rare and golden opportunity to turn our attention to satisfying our more subtle needs – and thereby become more fulfilled and content.

If we balance the time and energy we expend on technological and other "material" activities with that on meeting our higher needs, we can develop our spiritual side and recapture the awe, dreams and excitement of our childhood. Organised religions have traditionally been the focus of ethics and philosophy, but following a particular faith is not a prerequisite to explore non-material matters – aware people understand that there is a difference between spirituality and religion. And just as the benefit of gym visits is cumulative and your body becomes increasingly toned, so the time and effort you spend on contemplation or meditation will serve to increase your peace of mind.

Short- and Long-Term Balance

Like it or not, we go through different phases in life, and it's normal for us to have different viewpoints according to which one we find ourselves in. Our experiences will modify our needs and desires, so our priorities and "proportional situation" must therefore be frequently reassessed. Just as a person's perspective on their own culture changes when they live abroad, his or her perspective on themselves – their activities and views – will change as they get older. Our lives are also complicated by the fact that partners, other family members and friends will all be at different stages in their lives, with different priorities and different levels of awareness.

In our teens and early twenties we learn to be self-reliant and independent, and then our late 20s, 30s and early 40s is the period for honing our skills and making our mark – and usually for creating a family. If not understood earlier, the late 40s should be a time to realise there is more to life than status, work, and wealth. The natural phase which follows the achievement of financial security and bringing up children involves putting something back into society by concentrating on helping others, whether family, friends or community.

Many people get locked into a way of thinking and acting and don't "grow up" i.e. don't pass through the normal phases of life. Some children remain childish when they're older and avoid taking responsibility for themselves. They may avoid hard work or over-indulge in alcohol or other drugs. Some adults don't relinquish their role as a parent and continue to treat their adult offspring as children, refusing to let them lead their own lives. Many carry on the "thrusting" phase by continuing to chase money, status and possessions, being unaware that these in themselves will never result in peace of mind. If people resist the natural phases of ageing, they are more likely to increase the stress they feel – and it demonstrates that they haven't matured, acquired wisdom, or developed personally.

- An open mind and frequent reassessments can act like stabilisers on a ship – they can calm choppy waters.

- Nobody will be able to maintain a perfect balance throughout their life, but through greater awareness you will avoid extreme imbalance by making frequent, small adjustments.

APPRECIATION

"Those who are wise – and those who are happy – embrace and appreciate life. Those who are unhappy and unwise do not."

(Rasheed Ogunlaru)

You probably have a full-time, 5-days-a-week job that involves commuting. You watch TV for several hours most weekday evenings, and go out with friends on weekends. Each week you prepare and eat meals, read the paper, do some exercise, update your Facebook site, answer emails, text and call friends and relatives, and you somehow take care of some household chores. These and many other things you normally squeeze into your busy life mean you get little opportunity for contemplation, except perhaps to talk about the past or worry about the future.

When merely keeping up with modern life takes all your time and energy, it's hardly surprising if you have little opportunity or inclination to go into the depth of things – you're unlikely to fully understand what you watch, read, and listen to, or be able to interact and empathise enough with your family and friends. You may consume a lot and do so much over the years, yet fail to experience the real satisfaction of digging deeper, absorbing things, and really appreciating what you have, what you do, and those who share your life.

Superficiality

Most of us are impressed by our super-busy, acquisitive lives, believing that all this "quantity" will satisfy our needs and make us feel fulfilled and content. But the constant hustle and bustle actually prevents us from properly using, understanding, and appreciating the things in our life. Moving frequently and quickly from one activity or acquisition to another leaves little opportunity to absorb or appreciate each of them fully – and in recent decades we have been spending far less "quality time" with family members and friends necessary to develop close and full relationships. The pressure of our busy lives has inevitably encouraged a shallow approach to life, indicated by the obsession with looks, image, possessions and wealth.

Most things in life today mirror the sound-bite approach of media news and advertisements. We want quick information and instant answers, and the result is that we understand much less and only know what is going on in the world in an extremely superficial and simplistic way. Our minds shift speedily from one sound-bite to the next. And convinced that what is to come will be somehow bigger and better and more satisfying than what we are experiencing now, we don't live fully in the present moment. Workers "can't wait" for the weekend to come, those in social gatherings look over the shoulder of the person they are talking to, and young people text and phone others instead of relating to the friends they are actually with.

Living in the Present

Eckhart Tolle advises us of the importance of being "in the now" instead of being trapped in the past or distracted by the future. This sounds obvious or common sense, but most people are unaware how much of their time, energy and thoughts are taken up by the past and future. Other animals live in the present, but we can relive past moments and anticipate future developments. Evolution gave us the capacity to think in the abstract and understand cause and effect. As to be expected, both advantages and disadvantages resulted from these developments. Though we can plan our lives and make ourselves more comfortable, we can also be distracted by our imagination and roaming thoughts – and become obsessed with where we're heading rather than concentrating on what we're doing right now.

Most of us would gain from doing less. We would then be better able to reflect on, absorb, and appreciate all the things and people in our lives. Absorption takes time. Appreciation takes time. Real enjoyment takes time. We need to find time to give our full attention to and concentrate on an activity to the exclusion of all else. To be preoccupied, captivated and energised by any task increases our wellbeing, whereas rushing through something while thinking of what else we have to do will not. To absorb anything well, we must be engrossed and immersed in it, fascinated by it, centred and focused on it – resulting in a fuller and more satisfying, emotional and intellectual understanding.

Gratitude

Gratitude is the expression of appreciation, and those who are grateful for everything in their lives have been shown to have higher levels of alertness, enthusiasm, optimism, determination and energy. They feel motivated to exercise more often and are less inclined to be materialistic. We are incredibly fortunate to be living on this fascinating, beautiful, wonderful planet – and we are capable of experiencing great joy much of the time, provided we look at things in a positive way.

Because we are social animals, we need fulfilling relationships – which are fostered when we appreciate and show gratitude to those who share our lives. Aware people understand that much satisfaction comes from giving – whether in the form of love, care, sympathy, advice, money or time. If you express your gratitude to others you will also value yourself more. If you respect others and make efforts for them your life will be more fulfilling and enjoyable, and so will theirs.

- With practice, we can avoid incessant thoughts about the future and learn to be in the "now" – and appreciate everything in our lives far more.

- I remind myself frequently – every day – how fortunate I am to have the freedom to do so many interesting things, and how important friends and relations are to me.

- I have learned to appreciate the wholesome meals that are available to me, and remind myself how fortunate I am to remain healthy.

DETACHMENT

*"Events may create physical pain,
but they do not in themselves create suffering.
Resistance creates suffering."*

(Dan Millman)

Having a more detached view on life can reduce the stress we experience. Greater awareness means we don't take ourselves and what we do *too* seriously. If we imbue the world and human affairs with a heaviness and absolute importance, take ourselves too seriously and perceive life as a struggle for survival, then that's what it will become.

Instincts, spontaneity and feeling are vital components of human life, but blind, misleading or destructive emotions need to be understood and their role in what we do minimised. If children are encouraged to observe their thoughts and emotions from an early age, they will be able to recognise potentially destructive arguments or approaches that become self-perpetuating. Suffering and stress will be lessened if we can stand back and reflect on what happens in our lives in an open, detached, and non-judgemental way.

Acceptance

When things happen that haven't been anticipated, conditioned mind-patterns can lead to the stirring of negative emotions. Greater awareness allows us to accept what happens in our life more readily, whether "good" or "bad". Acceptance means an acknowledgement of the situation as it is – not complaining, questioning, or resisting. If we don't resist things, if we yield to whatever happens, if we go with the flow, if we have an inner acceptance of what is, then we will be open to life and suffer little stress. Thus at worst we can remain undisturbed by events, and at best embrace them.

An accurate but what seems a more emotive term for acceptance is "surrender". Being in alignment with what happens and not resisting the "now" will make life easier and more enjoyable. Surrendering to events and situations doesn't mean you smile and do nothing to bring about changes – though that may sometimes be the sensible option. It sounds paradoxical, but accepting what is and taking steps to change things are not mutually exclusive.

Surrendering to the moment will in fact mean that if you take action it will be more astute – because you won't be acting under the influence of resentment or other emotion. If you mentally resist what happens, negative stress hormones will harm you physically, and how you view things will determine the level of resistance. Most people are unable to surrender to situations and events, in other words just "to be", until they are confronted with a life-changing experience. When a close friend or family member dies, or someone is close to death, then awareness of "just being" is more likely to occur.

You can learn to increase your level of acceptance or "surrender" to unexpected "negative" events, thereby lessening the degree of irritation or sadness you feel. With awareness, willpower and practice you'll be able to gradually reduce both the length and level of your negative emotions when unexpected things occur – like receiving a parking ticket, a gizmo malfunctioning, or a friend letting you down. With practice it will become more natural to avoid categorising and to view life's events of all kinds in a dispassionate, neutral manner. Though it is highly unlikely you will reach perfection, i.e. feel no disappointment, anger, or jealousy at all, you should keep trying because you'll suffer less stress.

Defensiveness

An aware person will listen to other opinions and consider them more dispassionately – and then be prepared to adjust his or her view and act differently if it seems logical to do so. Those who are not aware, on the other hand, will probably "resist" by immediately becoming defensive. If their plans go awry or others criticise them, unaware people with conditioned mind-patterns will react negatively. Instead of assessing the merit of other people's views or working out a way to put their plans back on track, they take things personally – their hackles rise, creating a surge of negative emotions and accompanying stress hormones. Their resistance makes them suffer. Though it is commonplace for people to take things personally in today's world, it is actually irrational because it has a negative effect on them and those around them.

Relationships

Practising acceptance is particularly important in relationships. An aware person will accept his or her partner – or family member, friend or other person for that matter – completely, with all their quirks and personality traits. An aware person does not rely on a partner or others to provide emotional comfort, or anything else for that matter. It is wise not to *expect* anything from anybody else, because we are sure to be surprised by people's irrational behaviour on occasions. But we can of course appreciate it when people do act kindly, sensibly, warmly and supportively towards us.

Aware people won't morally judge others or want to change them, though that doesn't mean they won't recognise dysfunction when they see it. Instead of criticising others, aware people will show respect and feel sympathy; they will be glad to provide support and advice where possible and asked for.

Assessing events or other people's behaviour and taking steps to alter a difficult situation or environment is perfectly natural and necessary, but it is far better that our actions and thoughts are not driven by emotion. Sometimes it may well be wise to remove ourselves from a particular relationship, but greater awareness will mean we avoid demeaning, criticising, or looking down on the other person. A detached approach means not trying to boost our own status or image by attacking others. It means acting humbly and not thinking we know it all. It means listening to other people's opinions attentively without getting defensive. An aware person keeps an open mind, stays calm and works at seeking the "truth", or at least ways of improving things. Name-calling, swearing, shouting, or violence – unless someone is being physically attacked and there is no option of escaping from the situation – are all unnecessary and self-destructive.

Humility

Though we are such a small part of the universe, and may in fact have just a limited existence as a species, we human beings are not humble; we are full of self-importance. We value ourselves above other creatures – many of us set ourselves apart by pompously ascribing "souls" to us but not to them. Instead of trying to live by the rules of nature, we arrogantly try to subdue or outdo her. We take ourselves, our activities, our achievements and our history far too seriously, either to bolster our egos or provide ourselves with a meaning and purpose in life – or probably both.

Humility was one of the virtues encouraged and admired in bygone days. More recently, however, the demonstration and display of one's wealth, status, skills and looks has come to be applauded and encouraged. Today nobody wants to accept their place in the pecking order or take any responsibility for failure, but everyone is quick to trumpet their achievements and claim credit for success.

Aware people know that we are all born with different strengths and weaknesses and are reared in more or less favourable circumstances. Though there is nothing wrong with feeling a "quiet pride" because of our efforts and achievements, we also need to be humble enough to acknowledge that luck has played a part in our "success", and that everybody has something to contribute to society.

- Whenever something unplanned or unexpected happens, I remind myself how trivial and short-term most "problems" actually are in the grand scheme of things.

- I was caught speeding in Australia a few years ago. It was the first time I had been in a police car, and the police station was short-staffed (it was "Australia Day") so for a while I was locked in a cell. I managed to avoid feeling much stress because I knew after accepting my punishment, normal life would resume – and I actually managed to view it as an interesting experience. I wrote a song about the event a few months later.

- Near to the completion of this book I lost my landline and internet connection due to a technical mix-up. Though I needed to be online to update references and statistics, there was nothing I could do but wait for my provider to sort out the paperwork and send an engineer – so instead of getting irritated and feeling frustrated for several weeks, I simply turned to other projects.

- If you've invested time and effort to do or create things, it's virtually impossible to remain entirely detached when someone criticises what you've done. I may still feel an initial negative emotion, but the level is now much lower and the time much shorter.

SELF-DEVELOPMENT

*"Unless you try to do something beyond
what you have mastered, you will never grow."*

(C.R. Lawton)

We are the lucky ones. We had the good fortune to be born into the small percentage of the world's population whose basic needs of sustenance, comfort and security are met from cradle to grave. Only we in the wealthy countries are privileged enough – apart from a small number in developing countries – to have the freedom and opportunity to attend to our higher needs. Yet incredibly, most of us continue to obsess about our basic needs instead of using some of our time and energy to develop ourselves, fulfil our potential, help others and contribute something to the world – and thereby achieve far greater personal satisfaction.

People in the developed nations can be divided roughly into three groups – a majority and two growing minorities. One minority is unaware and dysfunctional, whose poor physical and mental health affects their ability to cope with life, let alone meet their self-development and spiritual needs. The other minority is sufficiently aware to be able to lead a fulfilled life and achieve peace of mind.

The majority is the largest group by far, and lies somewhere between the two minority groups. It consists of those who are just partially aware of the negative effects of their hectic and indulgent lifestyles. They don't know why, but they feel to a greater or lesser extent dissatisfied, unhealthy and anxious – and aren't quite sure what to do to improve their wellbeing. Though not affected so much by peer, marketing and other pressures of life as to become dysfunctional, they could achieve a much higher level of fulfilment and long-term contentment if they increased their awareness, developed a new mindset, and then made different decisions about the way they live.

Not all people are overweight and over-stressed, chasing fame and fortune and failing to absorb or appreciate what they have. There are indeed many people who have sufficient awareness and willpower to maintain good physical and mental health at the same time as taking advantage of the undoubted benefits of the industrial and technological advances that have accrued over the last two centuries. This is the minority with far greater awareness – the self-actualisers that Abraham Maslow discusses in his "hierarchy of needs".

Self-Actualisers

"Self-actualisation" was Maslow's term for the instinctual human need for self-development, to make the most of our abilities and to strive to be the best we can, to reach our fullest potential. He believed that humans have a need to acquire a better understanding of themselves and the world around them; a need to learn, explore, discover, and create. His description of self-actualisers echoes most of the themes in this section.

Maslow believed that self-actualisers are self-aware and accept themselves. They understand facts and situations and face reality. They are empathic, with a non-hostile sense of humour, preferring to joke at their own expense or at the human condition. They appreciate life, embrace spontaneity and simplicity, and are not pretentious or artificial. They may be unorthodox, but are often conventional on the surface. They have an appreciation of the variety of people and things in the world, as well as a feeling of awe for its splendours. They operate their own system of morality that is independent of external authority, and are spiritual but seldom conventionally religious in nature. They tend to enjoy deeper personal relations with a few close friends and family members rather than maintain shallower associations with many people. They accept others as they are, yet work to change negative qualities in themselves. If some trait of theirs isn't harmful, they let it be, even enjoying it as a personal quirk.

Self-actualisers are philosophical, creative, and independent. They are relaxed and content with their own company, and indeed have a need for solitude. They enjoy autonomy, are relatively independent from physical and social needs. They are not susceptible to social pressure to be "well adjusted" or to fit in, but are non-conformists in the best sense. They are interested in solving problems – including those of others. Solving problems is often a key focus in their lives. They treat life's "difficulties" as situations demanding solutions rather than personal troubles to be complained about. They feel that the ends don't necessarily justify the means, that the means could be ends themselves, and that the means – the journey – is arguably more important than the ends.

- Being more aware of what really matters in my life – and the myriad of things that are merely short-term and inconsequential – helps me to focus my time and effort to be sufficiently productive and to enjoy what I do.

- Greater awareness leads to greater self-development, which then increases the feeling of fulfilment.

CONTENTMENT

"I have learned that everyone wants to live on the peak of the mountain, without knowing that the real happiness is in how it is scaled."

(Gabriel Garcia Marquez)

A variety of words are used to describe a positive feeling about life. Many could be considered more intense and represent shorter-term feelings. I have chosen the word "contentment" to represent what we'd all like to achieve. Rather more than a passing experience of pleasure or joy, contentment is a long-term feeling of wellbeing in both body and mind. It is an absence of "wanting". It is peace of mind at a person's core that involves a sense of fulfilment and being at ease in one's current situation, not dwelling on past events or feeling anxious about the future.

It sounds paradoxical, but contentment is not something that we can actively seek, but a "condition" that will naturally increase as our awareness grows – because greater awareness helps us to view and approach life more positively. That in turn effects beneficial changes in our situation, which will further increase our appreciation of it.

As awareness expands, the concepts in this section – summarised below – will be understood and absorbed more fully. And practical exploration will in time cause them to become habitual, allowing for positive lifestyle changes and the reduction or elimination of "overloads". I hope that the material in this book has inspired you to join me on the road to contentment.

- Awareness is necessary for avoiding stress and for self-development, self-fulfilment and long-term contentment.

- Self-awareness will remove the often negative influence of conditioning and bias in your view of life and the way you react to people, events and situations.

- Self-responsibility is vital for your self-esteem and self-development.

- Understanding your needs will mean you will behave rationally to satisfy them.

- Approaching tasks with the right motivation will avoid stress and increase your satisfaction.

- Your self-respect and wellbeing will increase the more you respect and help others.

- Being honest with yourself and with others will reduce stress for you and for them.

- Don't choose "easy", short-term options which will cause you future stress.

- Habitual, destructive behaviour will lead to a downward, negative cycle.

- Use willpower to set up constructive habits for an upward, positive cycle.

- To avoid stress, acknowledge there are limits to what you can be and do, and steer a course between extremes.

- Assess the level of risk and uncertainty that you can manage, then do your best to fulfil your potential.

- Carefully consider your lifestyle choices and the potential impact they might have – on your health and relationships in particular.

- Make decisions about the proportionality of the constituent parts of your life and its overall balance without comparison to or the influence of others.

- Simplify your life to the level at which you absorb things fully and can appreciate what you do, what you have, and the people around you.

- Learn to accept what happens and avoid the stress caused by "resisting".

- To avoid stress, don't take things personally and don't expect too much from others.

- Contentment is a condition that will increase as your awareness grows.

THE WAY AHEAD

*"We can change our own life and
ultimately change the world."*

(Kristi Bowman)

The focus in this book has been on the "micro" – how the individual is affected and what each of us can do personally. There are three reasons for this. Firstly, I believe that for our sanity, self-esteem and fulfilment, we need to take charge of our own lives. Secondly, many books have already been published that deal with macro matters such as the world's diminishing resources, the ecological damage caused by industrial activities, over-population, and geopolitical stresses. And thirdly I believe that given the current institutional framework and our so-called "democratic" governments, those in charge are extremely unlikely to manage society in such a way as to improve the health of the general population.

Even on those rare occasions when politicians devise sensible initiatives or enact regulations that might promote better health, they are inevitably very late in the day and so weak that they effect only marginal changes.

- A report by *The Overseas Development Institute* was published just before this book. It revealed that globally, between 1980 and 2008, the percentage of adults who were overweight or obese grew from 23% to 34% – with a startling 400% increase in developing countries.

The reasons given for this by the report authors were precisely those that I have discussed at length. As incomes rise, people exercise less and eat far more animal produce and processed foods that are high in fat, salt and sugar. Steve Wiggins, one of the authors, stated that these lifestyle choices will result in yet more heart disease, diabetes and cancer, and expressed his belief that it was high time that politicians in all countries acknowledged the enormity of the problem and started taking more effective steps to influence what food ends up on our plates.

Indeed many experts and a growing number of the public now advocate much tighter controls over business services and products that harm us physically or mentally. But even if a majority could agree on exactly what adversely affects our health and what methods should be employed – taxes on processed food and statutory limits on salt, fat, and sugar, or tighter regulations over the internet and entertainment for example – this is extremely unlikely to happen. While conventional wisdom equates economic expansion with increased wellbeing and quality of life, and while there are strong ties between most politicians and business leaders, governments are extremely unlikely to curb their activities effectively.

And of course there is the question of personal freedom – perhaps an even more important consideration. Do we really want to live in a "nanny state" that decides what is good for us and what is not and severely limits our choice? On the one hand almost everybody in the developed world would approve of people having the freedom to make their own decisions about what they have and do, provided they don't impinge on the wellbeing of others; on the other hand, with ill-health increasing exponentially, and the pressure on our resources and finances fast becoming unmanageable, we surely have to do something.

I believe the way out of this increasingly dire situation requires more *education* rather than more *legislation* – then the solution would lie within each person. If the general level of awareness could be raised sufficiently for enough of us to instigate beneficial lifestyle changes at our individual, micro level, a significantly positive effect will then occur at the societal, macro level.

As well as showing how the way we live is harming us physically and mentally, the material in this book also provides suggestions as to how we might avoid the cycle of stress and excess. If people become aware enough to voluntarily alter their habits and live more simply and wisely, they will enjoy the improvements in their own lives from that point on and others will subsequently benefit from the inevitable societal changes that will be generated. The adjustment in lifestyle choices will not only lead to better health and lower care costs, but also influence businesses to develop and sell less harmful products – and in time, produce a new mindset in the political arena.

Are you ready to change the world?

References

Food

http://www.nejm.org/doi/full/10.1056/NEJMsr043743
New England Journal of Medicine – potential decline in life expectancy in USA because of obesity.

http://www.dailymail.co.uk/news/article-1045104/Obesity-poses-big-threat-nation-terrorism-Government-adviser-warns.html
UK government adviser – life expectancy could fall because of obesity effects.

news.bbc.co.uk/1/hi/health/3752597.stm
UK Commons Health committee – obese children might die before their parents.

http://www.diabetes.org.uk/About_us/News_Landing_Page/Lost-generation--Todays-children-face-obesity-alcohol-abuse-and-tooth-decay-crisis/
Liverpool's Alder Hey Hospital – children could die before their parents.

http://www.telegraph.co.uk/health/children_shealth/8570733/Obese-child-stroke-victim-aged-just-six.html
UK 44 hospital trusts – childhood obesity and chronic health problems.

http://www.dailymail.co.uk/health/article-1081450/Boy-aged-seven-obese-children-taken-care.html?ITO=1490
UK Local Councils – morbidly obese young kids taken into care.

www.bbc.co.uk/health/tools/bmi_calculator/bmi.shtml
Calculate your BMI.

www.msnbc.msn.com/id/14407969/
University of North Carolina – a greater number of overweight people globally than undernourished.

http://www.watoday.com.au/lifestyle/the-weight-of-the-world-20120416-1x2ev.html
In 2012, 1.6 billion of planet's population overweight.

http://epp.eurostat.ec.europa.eu/statistics_explained/index.php/Overweight_and_obesity_-_BMI_statistics
19 European countries' obesity data.

http://www.hivehealthmedia.com/world-obesity-stats-2010/
Countries' obesity and overweight statistics.

www.telegraph.co.uk/health/healthnews/7251478/Eight-in-10-men-will-be-overweight-or-obese-by-2020.html
UK overweight and obesity predictions.

http://www.aso.org.uk/wp-content/uploads/downloads/2011/04/StatisticsonObesityPhysicalActivityandDietEngland2011.pdf
2009 – UK overweight and obesity statistics, adults and children.

http://www.bbc.co.uk/news/health-11999521
20% of English children end primary school obese.

http://www.aso.org.uk/useful-resources/statistics-england-2012/2010
English overweight and obesity statistics, adults and children.

http://www.sixwise.com/newsletters/05/10/19/all-the-health-risks-of-processed-foods----in-just-a-few-quick-convenient-bites.htm
90% of food Americans buy is processed.

http://www.manicore.com/anglais/documentation_a/greenhouse/plate.html
80% of food bought in France is processed.

en.wikipedia.org/wiki/Western_pattern_diet
The Western meat-sweet diet.

www.fao.org/docrep/005/AC911E/ac911e05.htm
Global and regional food consumption – patterns and trends.

http://www.annecollins.com/weight_health/diet-fat-intake-uk.htm
British Food Standards – UK fat intake.

http://www.ncbi.nlm.nih.gov/pubmed/8054331
UK increase in fat proportion of diet.

www.who.int/nutrition/topics/3_foodconsumption/en/index4.html
Increased global meat consumption.

http://www.eblex.org.uk/documents/content/markets/m_uk_yearbook12_cattle240812.pdf
Per capita British meat consumption.

http://www.academia.edu/2486553/Meat_consumption_in_Europe_Issues_trends_and_debates
Meat consumption in Europe from 1961 to 2007.

http://www.guardian.co.uk/environment/datablog/2009/sep/02/meat-consumption-per-capita-climate-change
Meat consumption increase in China and other countries.

http://www.bbc.co.uk/news/health-17345967
Harvard Medical School – health risks from fresh and processed meat.

http://www.guardian.co.uk/g2/story/0,3604,682864,00.htm
British sugar consumption.

http://www.guardian.co.uk/uk/2007/oct/13/lifeandhealth.britishidentity
More on British sugar consumption.

http://www.macrobiotics.co.uk/sugar.htm
http://rheumatic.org/sugar.htm
http://www.healthylifestyleart.com/sugar-is-a-poison-the-toxic-truth-about
http://www.bhf.org.uk/default.aspx?page=15828
Health dangers of sugar.

http://forum.lowcarber.org/showthread.php?t=100479
Sugar industry's denials of health problems like those of the tobacco industry.

http://www.sciencedaily.com/releases/2010/01/100121092008.htm
USA salt consumption.

www.eatwell.gov.uk/healthydiet/fss/salt/
NHS – daily salt limit recommended.

www.food.gov.uk/news/pressreleases/2008/jul/sodiumrep08
UK – fall in salt consumption.

http://yougov.co.uk/news/2012/05/15/do-you-get-your-five-day/
Proportion of British adults eating 5 portions of fruit and vegetables a day.

http://www.bhf.org.uk/plugins/PublicationsSearchResults/DownloadFile.aspx?docid=e9994c21-ec6c-4fad-b741-ad96bacd69ed&version=-1&title=Physical+Activity+Statistics+2012&resource=M130
UK levels of physical activity.

http://www.obesitymyths.com/myth5.1.htm
Obesity may be due more to lack of exercise than over-eating.

http://www.ic.nhs.uk/pubs/opad12
Obesity, physical activity and diet statistics for England.

www.sciencedaily.com/releases/2009/03/090319224823.htm
How obesity and exercise can reduce and increase life span respectively.

www.reuters.com/article/idUSTRE49J7T420081021
McMaster University – diets heavy in fried foods, salty snacks and meat account for 35% of heart attacks globally.

en.wikipedia.org/wiki/Red_meat#Health_risks)
European study – red meat increases risk of death, cancer and cardiovascular disease.

well.blogs.nytimes.com/2010/01/06/phys-ed-can-you-be-overweight-and-still-be-healthy/
Uppsala University – overweight men with healthy blood pressure, cholesterol, blood glucose etc. still had significantly higher risk of developing heart disease.

http://www.telegraph.co.uk/health/healthnews/5088741/Failing-to-brush-teeth-properly-linked-with-increase-risk-of-heart-attack.html
University of Buffalo – not brushing teeth properly increases the risk of a heart attack by 50%

http://www.ncbi.nlm.nih.gov/pmc/articles/PMC3045642/
American study – increased meat consumption related to higher cardiovascular disease and cancer.

http://www.cbn.com/cbnnews/healthscience/2012/October/Cholesterol-Myth-What-Really-Causes-Heart-Disease/
The causes of heart disease.

http://www.bbc.co.uk/news/uk-scotland-north-east-orkney-shetland-11968364
University of Aberdeen – whole grain foods reduce blood pressure.

http://www.heartattackproof.com/
http://www.whfoods.com/genpage.php?tname=diet&dbid=5
http://www.diseaseproof.com/archives/cardiovascular-disease-reversing-heart-disease-with-a-nutrient-dense-diet.html
Switching to a plant-based diet with little or no processed food can prevent and reverse heart disease.

http://en.wikipedia.org/wiki/The_China_Study_(book)
Animal-based diet increases the risk of many cancers as well as heart disease, while plant-based diet can reverse Type 2 diabetes.

www.politics.co.uk/opinion-formers/press-releases/health/diabetes-uk-diabetes-explosion---more-than-4-million-in-the-uk-to-have-the-condition-by-2025-$1226501$1226186.htm
UK diabetes statistics and prediction for 2025.

http://www.dailymail.co.uk/health/article-1323448/One-adults-danger-obesity-diabetes-toll-soars.html
UK's accelerating increase in obesity and diabetes.

en.wikipedia.org/wiki/Cancer
Global deaths from cancer, 90% to 95% of which is caused by lack of exercise, diet and obesity, as well as tobacco, infections, radiation.

http://www.cancer.gov/cancertopics/factsheet/Risk/obesity
Obesity link to certain cancers.

http://www.guardian.co.uk/science/2009/feb/22/cancer-obesity-link
University College – obesity is leading cause of cancer deaths, which will double in next 40 years.

www.guardian.co.uk/uk/2003/jul/18/research.sciencenews
Lancet article – high fat diet and breast cancer link.

en.wikipedia.org/wiki/Estrogen
Mushrooms and green tea suppress the oestrogen level, which is linked to breast cancer.

http://www.thedailybeast.com/newsweek/2007/12/01/fat-carbs-and-the-science-of-conception.html
The Harvard nurses' health study – fertility linked to diet and exercise.

http://heartburn.about.com/cs/causes/a/heartburncauses.htm
Possible causes of heartburn.

http://www.diabetes.co.uk/news/2008/Oct/Cost-of-diabetes-hits-GBP1-million-per-hour.html
UK cost of diabetes.

http://www.nhs.uk/news/2012/03march/Pages/ice-cream-food-addiction-like-drugs.aspx
Oregon Research Institute – ice-cream may be addictive.

http://articles.mercola.com/sites/articles/archive/2013/03/21/addictive-junk-food.aspx
The addictive nature of processed food.

http://www.fas.org/sgp/crs/misc/R40545.pdf
Food prices still low despite recent increase.

http://www.newscientist.com/article/dn12431-fast-food-branding-makes-children-prefer-happy-meals.html
Johns Hopkins Bloomberg School of Health – children significantly affected by branding.

http://theconversation.com/branding-drives-children-to-make-healthy-choices-too-study-8952
Cornell University – branding can persuade children to make healthier choices of food.

http://www.marketingweek.co.uk/news/european-snacks-association-pledges-to-reduce-tv-ads-to-children/3012686.article
Snack food companies pledge not to advertise to children.

bps-research-digest.blogspot.com/2006/06/power-of-one-why-larger-portions-cause.html
University of Pennsylvania – larger portions make us eat more.

dailymail.co.uk/health/article-1225176/Stressful-modern-life-fuels-obesity-rushing-meals-stops-feeling-full.html
Laiko Hospital Athens – rushed meals mean we eat more.

http://www.wltx.com/news/article/141335/291/Weight-Gain-Linked-to-12-Foods-What-Made-the-List
New England Journal of Medicine – list of the most fattening foods.

http://news.bbc.co.uk/1/hi/health/7909865.stm
UK – obesity surgery rises.

http://www.bbc.co.uk/news/health-20495676
UK – male breast surgery rises.

http://www.dailymail.co.uk/news/article-2147071/Boys-young-10-having-breast-surgery-NHS-remove-moobs.html
UK – breast surgery for boys rises.

http://www.businessgreen.com/search?query=food+waste+revolution&per_page=25
UN calls for less food waste in the whole food chain.

http://en.wikipedia.org/wiki/Food_waste
Global food waste.

http://news.bbc.co.uk/1/hi/uk/7389351.stm
WRAP – British households throw away food needlessly.

http://news.bbc.co.uk/1/hi/7939630.stm
UK – fire crews needed to move obese patients.

http://www.wired.com/autopia/2009/01/australians-so/
Obese Australians and Canadians need bigger planes and stretchers for patients.

http://arbroath.blogspot.co.uk/2009/04/obese-gowns-for-hospital-patients-are.html
UK – the NHS needs extra large gowns for obese patients.

http://info.cancerresearchuk.org/healthyliving/dietandhealthyeating/foodnutrientsandcancer/
Cancer Research UK – dietary advice.

http://www.physorg.com/news94906931.html
UCLA – diets don't work.

http://www.metabolic-syndrome-handbook.com/content/why-processed-food-is-bad
The problems with processed foods and why diets don't work.

http://www.quitsmoking.com/books/nonag/weightgain.htm
Strategies for not putting on weight when quitting smoking.

http://ipod.about.com/od/bestiphoneapps/tp/Best-Weight-Loss-And-Diet-Apps-For-The-Iphone.htm
Diet apps may help to assess your calorie intake.

news.bbc.co.uk/2/hi/health/2814253.stm
WHO – eating less processed food can reduce obesity.

http://en.wikipedia.org/wiki/Dean_Ornish
Comprehensive lifestyle changes affect gene expression in only three months.

http://www.peta2.com/TAKECHARGE/t_factsheet_vegdiet.asp
PETA – vegetarian diet reduces the risk of many chronic degenerative diseases and conditions.

www.vernoncoleman.com/downloads/poc.htm
Vernon Coleman – 80% of cancers can be avoided through diet.

info.cancerresearchuk.org/healthyliving/
Cancer Research UK – advice on avoiding cancer.

news.bbc.co.uk/1/hi/health/2991629.stm
European study – doubling fibre halves the risk of bowel cancer.

http://www.raysahelian.com/flavonols.html
A diet high in flavanols might reduce vascular disease risk.

http://www.independent.co.uk/news/science/smearing-skin-with-broccoli-can-help-reduce-risk-of-cancer-513467.html
University of New Mexico – some vegetables may reduce risk of breast and skin cancer.

http://www.psychologytoday.com/blog/shrink/201209/how-get-over-your-sugar-addiction
Advice on beating a sugar addiction.

http://www.heart.org/HEARTORG/GettingHealthy/Overweight-in-Children_UCM_304054_Article.jsp
American Heart Association – how to manage childhood obesity.

http://www.sleepcouncil.org.uk/2013/03/first-ever-great-british-bedtime-report-launched/
2012 – 33% of Britons get by on 5 to 6 hours a night, and 70% sleep 7 hours or less.

Caffeine

http://www.culturalsurvival.org/publications/cultural-survival-quarterly/botswana/hallucinogenic-plants-and-their-use-traditional-so
Use of hallucinogenic plants by traditional societies.

en.wikipedia.org/wiki/Prohibition_of_drugs
History of legal and illegal drugs.

http://www.professorshouse.com/food-beverage/beverages/caffeine-in-food.aspx
Caffeine in foods and beverages.

http://www.fas.usda.gov/psdonline/circulars/coffee.pdf
Global coffee consumption 2012/13.

http://www.statisticbrain.com/coffee-drinking-statistics/
USA – average coffee consumption per person per day.

http://en.wikipedia.org/wiki/List_of_countries_by_coffee_consumption_per_capita
Annual average consumption of coffee by country.

http://www.indianexpress.com/news/india-china-propel-global-tea-consumption-fao/919967
Consumption of tea is rising in China and India.

http://www.independent.co.uk/life-style/health-and-families/health-news/what-you-need-is-a-nice-cup-of-tea-698600.html
UK – the average Briton drinks 3.5 cups of tea a day.

http://www.independent.co.uk/life-style/health-and-families/features/energy-drinks-do-they-work-1805598.html
UK – quantity of sports and "energy" drinks consumed and their health dangers.

www.news-medical.net/health/Caffeine-Pharmacology.aspx
Caffeine pharmacology and effects.

caffeine-content.com/
Caffeine sources and content in food and drink.

www.e-teas.co.uk/page.php?xPage=news.html
Potential benefits of drinking various teas.

http://www.vanderbilt.edu/AnS/psychology/health_psychology/caffeine_sports.htm
How caffeine can help in endurance sports.

en.wikipedia.org/wiki/Caffeine
The stimulant effects and dangers of caffeine.

http://aje.oxfordjournals.org/content/138/12/1082.abstract
Caffeine consumption can reduce fertility.

news.bbc.co.uk/2/hi/7494249.stm
Radboud University – coffee can reduce chances of woman with fertility problems getting pregnant.

http://www.newscientist.com/article/mg19726405.200-coffee-increases-miscarriage-risk.html
Just one cup of coffee a day can increase the chance of miscarriage.

http://en.wikipedia.org/wiki/Fecal_incontinence
Caffeine can contribute towards incontinence.

www.healthy.net/scr/article.aspx?Id=1378
Health dangers of caffeine.

http://www.dorchesterhealth.org/caffeine.htm#effects
Possible side effects and recommended limits of caffeine consumption.

www.cbc.ca/health/story/2010/07/26/f-caffeine-daily-intake.html
The dangers of high caffeine consumption, particularly for children.

http://kidshealth.org/teen/drug_alcohol/drugs/caffeine.html#
Caffeine content in foods and drinks, its effects, and how to cut down.

Alcohol

http://en.wikipedia.org/wiki/Alcohol
The history and chemistry of alcohol.

www.adanz.org.nz/Helpline/faq
The level of alcohol in standard drinks and safety levels.

http://www.patient.co.uk/health/Recommended-Safe-Limits-of-Alcohol.htm
UK – recommended alcohol consumption limits.

http://www.drinkaware.co.uk/check-the-facts?gclid=CL26guaQqbYCFXDKtAodfWYArg
Drink Aware – various facts about alcohol

http://www.who.int/substance_abuse/facts/alcohol/en/
WHO – global annual deaths from alcohol.

http://www.nhs.uk/news/2012/02February/Pages/uk-alcohol-deaths-predicted.aspx
NHS Information Centre – average weekly consumption and prediction of deaths from alcohol over 20 years.

http://www.nhs.uk/news/2009/01January/Pages/BingedrinkingBritain.aspx
NHS – British adults who are drinking more than the recommended limits.

http://www.alcoholpolicy.net/2011/05/statistics-on-alcohol-england-2011-alcohol-related-admissions-pass-1-million-mark.html
Alcohol Policy UK – alcohol-related hospital admissions and other statistics.

www.talkaboutalcohol.com/uploads/parentsguide.pdf
The average age of the first alcoholic drink.

http://www.medicalnewstoday.com/articles/154104.php
Abuse of alcohol by 11 to 15-year-old Londoners.

www.addaction.org.uk/core/core_picker/download.asp?id=52
UK – children's drinking habits.

http://www.alcoholconcern.org.uk/media-centre/news/117-increase-in-alcohol-related-liver-disease-hospital-admissions-for-under-30s-in-england-since-2002
England – increase in hospital admissions for alcohol-related liver disease for under-30s and for over-60s with alcohol-related mental health problems.

http://christinegreer.com/main/wp-content/uploads/2011/05/AJADD-final-publication-Feb-2011.pdf
Effects of early onset of Alzheimer's on the children of sufferers.

http://www.channel4.com/news/alcohol-can-cause-cancer-even-in-moderate-amounts
UK – cancer of various kinds can be caused by even moderate drinking.

http://www.telegraph.co.uk/health/3273552/More-than-10-million-drinking-at-hazardous-levels.html
UK – more than 10 million British adults drink alcohol at hazardous levels.

http://www.independent.co.uk/life-style/health-and-families/health-news/middle-aged-three-times-more-likely-to-drink-every-day-than-younger-people-7545802.html
UK – many young people binge drink, and many over-45s drink alcohol every day.

http://www.bbc.co.uk/news/uk-20880957
UK – rise in liver disease and cirrhosis and "give your liver a rest" campaign by charities.

http://www.alcoholissues.co.uk/alcohol-older-person.html
UK - rise in alcohol-related hospital admissions of over-60s.

news.bbc.co.uk/2/hi/health/4381120.stm
UK – 1 in 4 adults are binge drinkers.

http://www.guardian.co.uk/society/2009/may/06/binge-drinking-women
UK – rise in women's binge drinking.

www.salagram.net/AlcoholEffects.html
Harmful effects of alcohol on different body parts.

http://www.dailymail.co.uk/health/article-85248/How-alcohol-affects-body.html
Various harmful effects that alcohol can have on the body.

www.pressandjournal.co.uk/Article.aspx/1950419
Aberdeen University – binge drinking could be fuelling a rapid rise in cancers of the mouth, throat and gullet among young people.

http://onlinelibrary.wiley.com/doi/10.1097/01.ALC.0000130812.85638.E1/abstract
27 drinks per week increased chance of breast cancer pre-menopause, and more than 6 drinks of spirits increased risk of breast cancer in post-menopausal women.

news.bbc.co.uk/2/hi/8193639.stm
UK – alcohol is blamed for rise in oral cancers.

http://www.nhs.uk/Conditions/Alcohol-misuse/Pages/Risks.aspx
Short- and long-term health problems from alcohol consumption.

www.drinkaware.co.uk/facts/factsheets/alcohol-and-diabetes
How drink can contribute to diabetes.

http://www.webmd.com/osteoporosis/features/alcohol
Alcohol can weaken the bones.

en.wikipedia.org/wiki/Wernicke-Korsakoff_syndrome
A syndrome that occurs in chronic alcoholics from thiamine deficiency.

http://www.britishsnoring.co.uk/stop_snoring/alcohol_sedatives.php
Alcohol can cause snoring problems.

www.guardian.co.uk/science/2008/dec/01/mobile-phones-alcohol
Alcohol hangovers can make driving dangerous.

http://www.nao.org.uk/publications/0708/reducing_alcohol_harm.aspx
UK – cost of alcohol-related ill-health.

http://www.alcoholconcern.org.uk/assets/files/Publications/Keeping%20it%20in%20the%20family.pdf
Effects on children who have alcoholic parents.

http://www.nhs.uk/news/2011/02February/Pages/doctors-predict-uk-alcohol-deaths.aspx
University of Southampton – prediction of alcohol deaths.

http://www.bbc.co.uk/news/health-12999000
Excessive alcohol consumption raises the risk for all cancers.

http://webarchive.nationalarchives.gov.uk/+/www.dh.gov.uk/en/Publicationsandstatistics/Publications/AnnualReports/Browsable/DH_4903444?IdcService=GET_FILE&dID=5682&Rendition=Web
UK – a large increase in deaths from cirrhosis of liver over 30 years.

http://www.patient.co.uk/health/cirrhosis
Explanation of cirrhosis of the liver, which affects 1 in 10 heavy drinkers.

http://79.170.44.126/britishlivertrust.org.uk/home-2/liver-information/liver-conditions/cirrhosis/
Information about cirrhosis of the liver and what causes it.

www.yorksj.ac.uk/docs/alcohol%20health%20advice.doc
Explanation of alcoholic units and the risks of various consumption levels.

http://www.alcoholconcern.org.uk/assets/files/Publications/Keeping%20it%20in%20the%20family.pdf
Alcohol Concern – alcohol consumption has doubled in 50 years and is 65% more affordable than in 1980.

http://en.wikipedia.org/wiki/Alcoholism
Causes of alcohol dependency and the effects of withdrawal.

www.screensafeuk.co.uk/policy.html
The need for businesses to operate a substance abuse policy at work.

http://www.alcoholpolicy.net/workplace/
UK – alcohol interventions in workplaces.

http://www.alcoholconcern.org.uk/concerned-about-alcohol/alcohol-services
Help groups for those with alcohol problems.

http://www.bbc.co.uk/news/magazine-16466646
10 radical solutions to reduce binge-drinking and other alcohol problems.

http://www.drinkaware.co.uk/check-the-facts/health-effects-of-alcohol/mental-health/alcohol-dependence
The signs of alcohol dependence and what to do about it.

Tobacco
en.wikipedia.org/wiki/Tobacco_smoking
The history of tobacco and methods of consumption.

quitsmoking.about.com/cs/antismoking/a/statistics.html
Global smoking statistics.

http://ash.org/resources/tobacco-statistics-facts/
ASH – number of tobacco users and global tobacco revenue.

http://ash.org.uk/files/documents/ASH_106.pdf
UK – smoking statistics.

http://www.wpro.who.int/mediacentre/factsheets/fs_201203_tobacco/en/index.html
WHO – various facts about tobacco consumption.

en.wikipedia.org/wiki/Health_effects_of_tobacco
The harmful effects of tobacco.

info.cancerresearchuk.org/cancerstats/types/lung/smoking/
Cancer Research UK – the scale, demographic, and effects of smoking.

www.ncbi.nlm.nih.gov › ... › BMJ › v.328(7455); Jun 26, 2004
British Medical Journal – the mortality risks of smoking at different ages.

http://news.bbc.co.uk/1/hi/health/583722.stm
University of Bristol – lifespan lost from smoking.

http://info.cancerresearchuk.org/cancerstats/types/lung/
Cancer Research UK – statistics for lung cancer and smoking, its major cause.

http://jnci.oxfordjournals.org/content/96/2/99.full
University of Torino – prediction of deaths from tobacco by 2030.

http://www.ox.ac.uk/media/news_stories/2009/090918_3.html
Oxford University – middle-aged men who smoke can lose 10 to 15 years.

http://quitsmoking.about.com/od/tobaccostatistics/a/heartdiseases.html
Harmful effects of smoking.

http://news.bbc.co.uk/1/hi/england/4561437.stm
Northumbria University – prolonged heavy nicotine use has a negative effect on memory.

http://www.bbc.co.uk/news/health-11622484
Heavy smokers are at much higher risk of Alzheimer's and vascular dementia.

http://jama.jamanetwork.com/article.aspx?articleid=1653534
China – ETS exposure can cause dementia.

www.havetoquitsmoking.com/smoking...effects/the-effects-of-smoking-on-your-skin
Smoking causes the skin to clog and thin, become discoloured, and make the smoker look older.

http://www.dailymail.co.uk/health/article-496326/Smoking-turns-men-bald-new-research-claims.html
Taiwan – smoking might cause hair loss.

http://www.fertilityexpert.co.uk/cansmokingaffectfertility.html
Smoking is bad for the fertility of both men and women.

http://www.ncbi.nlm.nih.gov/pmc/articles/PMC2116991/
NIH – women smoking while pregnant and pre-natal can cause psychological problems in their children.

en.wikipedia.org/wiki/Passive_smoking
Harmful effects of ETS.

http://news.bbc.co.uk/1/hi/health/7410876.stm
Smokers tend to give up in groups.

http://www.cdc.gov/tobacco/data_statistics/fact_sheets/fast_facts/
Global and American smoking statistics of deaths and costs.

http://www.bbc.co.uk/news/health-20463363
Alzheimer's Research UK – smoking affects memory, learning and reasoning.

http://www.aerias.org/DesktopModules/ArticleDetail.aspx?articleId=37
Aerias – the scale and effects of environmental tobacco smoke.

http://www.washingtonpost.com/wp-dyn/content/article/2006/06/27/AR2006062700710.html
ETS significantly increases the risk of heart disease and cancer in children and non-smoking adults.

http://www.independent.co.uk/life-style/health-and-families/health-news/passive-smoking-causes-1-per-cent-of-all-worlds-deaths-2144075.html
WHO – passive smoking causes 1% of global deaths.

www.quit-smoking.net/101-reasons-continued.html
Various aids for quitting.

Pharmaceutical Drugs

http://en.wikipedia.org/wiki/Pharmaceutical_industry
Estimated global pharmaceutical drug sales for 2014.

http://pharmamkting.blogspot.co.uk/2013/01/bad-pharma-cherry-picked-non-evidenced.html
Pharmaceutical industry's spending on marketing and research and development.

http://www.who.int/trade/glossary/story073/en/
WHO – profit margin of the pharmaceutical industry estimated at 30%.

http://data.gov.uk/dataset/prescriptions-dispensed-in-the-community-england-statistics-for-2001-to-2011/resource/b295dbd4-19b7-49e1-a829-b808ac2f6a29
UK – increase of average prescriptions per head in a decade.

http://www.express.co.uk/news/uk/355789/Statins-in-new-health-alert
UK – statin use.

http://www.telegraph.co.uk/health/8270156/Statins-for-all-and-billions-for-drug-firms.html
UK – does statin use mean the pharmaceutical industry's dream of selling drugs to everybody is coming true?

http://www.healthcentral.com/high-blood-pressure/treatment-000014_10-145_3.html
Lifestyle changes to reduce blood pressure.

http://psychcentral.com/news/2012/01/03/money-woes-behind-uk-jump-in-antidepressant-prescriptions/33244.html
England – rise in prescriptions for anti-depressants.

http://www.independent.co.uk/life-style/health-and-families/health-news/sleeping-pills-spending-by-nhs-reaches-50m-7736575.html
UK – sleeping pill prescriptions and their cost.

http://www.dailymail.co.uk/health/article-2111863/Almost-SIX-BILLION-painkillers-bought-year-Britain.html
UK – number of painkillers bought.

http://news.bbc.co.uk/1/hi/health/6425977.stm
UK – rise in ADHD drug prescriptions.

http://www.free-press-release.com/news-supressing-the-minds-of-a-generation-1300884106.html
UK – rise in spending on ADHD medications could be from over-diagnosing and over-prescribing.

http://www.bbc.co.uk/newsbeat/13473941
UK – NHS expenditure on anti-obesity drugs.

news.bbc.co.uk/2/hi/health/8234484.stm
UK – huge rise in weight-loss drugs.

http://www.adhdnews.com/adhd-drug-side-effects.htm
Side effects of various drugs.

http://anh-europe.org/news/polypharmacy-increases-risk-of-death-in-over-65s
http://www.tcd.ie/tilda/assets/pdf/PolypharmacyReport.pdf
http://qjmed.oxfordjournals.org/content/99/11/797.full
http://www.scie.org.uk/publications/briefings/briefing15/
http://www.dailymail.co.uk/health/article-2007544/Drug-cocktails-elderly-risk-Mixing-medication-fatal.html
Polypharmacy treatment of older people – defined as the use of 5 or more drugs – is now widespread. This may cause inappropriate prescribing, incorrect usage, or harmful synergistic effects.

http://www.bbc.co.uk/news/health-19622016
UK – many people suffer from headaches caused by taking painkillers.

http://www.rightdiagnosis.com/mistakes/common.htm
Many deaths are caused by mis-diagnosis or mis-prescribing.

www.ritalinadvisor.com/abuse
Ritalin abuse.

http://www.ncbi.nlm.nih.gov/pmc/articles/PMC2093926/
England – ADRs (adverse drug reactions) are rising and considerable.

http://www.patient.co.uk/health/Medication-for-High-Blood-Pressure.htm
Different hypertension drugs and possible side effects.

http://depression.emedtv.com/prozac/prozac-and-suicide.html
Increased risk of suicide in the young from anti-depressants.

http://www.drugwatch.com/prozac/
Dangers of Prozac and other anti-depressants.

news.bbc.co.uk/2/hi/7633400.stm
Anti-depressants may harm sperm.

http://injury-law.freeadvice.com/injury-law/drug-toxic_chemicals/seroquel-side-effects.htm
Seroquel for schizophrenia can cause diabetes.

http://www.webmd.com/cholesterol-management/side-effects-of-statin-drugs
Possible side effects of statins.

http://www.huffingtonpost.com/martha-rosenberg/statins_b_1818370.html
Are statins really necessary?

http://asthma.about.com/od/asthmabasics/a/art_MED_SE.htm
www.indoorpurifiers.com/medicine.htm
Possible side effects of asthma medication.

www.nytimes.com/2008/12/06/health/policy/06allergy.html
Warning about the risk of death from 4 asthma drugs.

http://www.rester-en-bonne-sante.com/ayurveda79.html
Causes of asthma and alternatives to drugs prescribed.

www.drugs.com/sfx/aspirin-side-effects.html
Possible side effects of aspirin.

http://en.wikipedia.org/wiki/Aspirin
Chemistry and side effects of aspirin.

www.mayoclinic.com/health/warfarin-side-effects/HB00101
Side effects of warfarin.

http://www.ehow.com/about_5420788_side-cold-flu-gel-caps.html
Side effects of Tylenol, used for colds and flu.

http://www.rxlist.com/voltaren-drug-patient.htm
Side effects of Voltaren, used for arthritis.

http://www.healingwithnutrition.com/adisease/add-adhd/adddrugs.html
Side effects of drugs for behaviour problems.

http://www.guardian.co.uk/society/2011/mar/18/behaviour-drugs-four-year-olds
UK – drugs are being prescribed for 4-year-olds with behavioural problems.

http://www.helpguide.org/life/sleep_aids_medication_insomnia_treatment.htm#side
Information about sleeping pills, including side effects.

http://www.canada.com/health/Sleeping+pills+increase+risk+death+study+suggests/3505436/story.html
Sleeping pills can increase risk of premature death.

http://www.herbal-supplements-guide.com/melatonin-side-effects.html
Side effects of Melatonin, used for sleeping problems.

news.bbc.co.uk/2/hi/8237626.stm
Codeine painkillers can be addictive.

http://en.wikipedia.org/wiki/Codeine
Chemistry of codeine, its side effects and risk of dependency.

http://www.nhs.uk/Conditions/Painkillers-ibuprofen/Pages/Side-effects.aspx
Side effects of Ibuprofen and other painkillers.

http://www.netdoctor.co.uk/medicines/100002749.html
Information on Viagra including the possibility of dangerous side effects.

http://en.wikipedia.org/wiki/The_Million_Women_Study
Study on the increased cancer risk of HRT.

http://www.premproadvisor.com/research-outted-prempro
Prempro, the suspect HRT drug.

http://www.metro.co.uk/news/860181-superbugs-could-take-world-back-to-pre-penicillin-era
WHO – the overuse of penicillin has resulted in loss of effectiveness.

http://www.who.int/mediacentre/news/statements/2011/whd_20110407/en/index.html
WHO demands action to reduce antibiotic use.

http://www.bbc.co.uk/ethics/animals/using/experiments_1.shtml
The moral considerations regarding animal experiments.

www.animalaid.org.uk/images/pdf/booklets/makingakilling.pdf
UK Animal Aid – drug companies exploit people and animals.

http://www.addictionsearch.com/treatment_articles/article/prescription-drug-addiction-abuse-and-treatment_32.html
Prescription drug addiction, abuse and treatment.

http://news.bbc.co.uk/1/hi/programmes/panorama/tranquillisers/1325909.stm
Tranquiliser drug addiction.

http://www.telegraph.co.uk/health/healthnews/3516916/Sleeping-pills-could-double-risk-of-road-accidents.html
Sleeping pills can cause driving accidents.

http://www.usatoday.com/news/health/2009-09-30-drug-overdose_N.htm
Dangers of addiction and overdose of opiates.

www.economist.com/node/4174305?story_id=4174305
Drug for Parkinson's turned people into gamblers.

en.wikipedia.org/wiki/Paracetamol_toxicity
Paracetamol toxicity.

http://www.essortment.com/lifestyle/healthweightlo_sjlq.htm
Dangers of appetite suppressants.

news.bbc.co.uk/2/hi/health/7687311.stm
Dangers of anti-obesity drug Rimonabant.

www.citizen.org/congress/article_redirect.cfm?ID=935
USA – drug companies attack the reduction of drug prices.

http://www.dailymail.co.uk/health/article-1286404/Common-blood-pressure-drug-raises-cancer-risk.html
ARBs (angiotensin-receptor blockers) cause increased risk of cancer.

http://www.painkillerabuse.us/content/prescription-drug-statistics.html
2006 USA – the level of abuse and harm from painkillers.

http://cancer.stanford.edu/information/cancerTreatment/methods/chemotherapy.html
Side effects of chemotherapy.

http://group.bmj.com/group/media/latest-news/widely-used-sedatives-sleeping-pills-linked-to-increased-fatal-pneumonia-risk)
Sedatives and sleeping pills can increase risk of fatal pneumonia.

http://www.mayoclinic.com/health/weight-loss-drugs/WT00013/NSECTIONGROUP=2
Dangers of weight-loss pills.

http://www.msnbc.msn.com/id/19587389/ns/health-diet_and_nutrition/t/diet-pills-icky-side-effects-keep-users-honest/
"Leakage" problems of diet pills.

http://www.drugs.com/sfx/alli-side-effects.html
Side effects of Orlistat for weight loss.

http://en.wikipedia.org/wiki/Placebo
The placebo effect and use in medicine.

http://www.guardian.co.uk/society/2008/feb/26/mentalhealth.medicalresearch
Prozac and similar drugs don't work better than a placebo.

http://edition.cnn.com/2007/HEALTH/07/09/antidepressants/index.html
Doctors are medicating for unhappiness.

http://news.bbc.co.uk/1/hi/health/4898488.stm
University of Australia – pharmaceutical companies are labelling conditions as disorders that need medication.

http://www.bbc.co.uk/news/health-23044579
Tamoxifen available through the NHS for prevention of breast cancer.

http://wiki.answers.com/Q/Should_you_feed_a_fever_or_starve_a_cold
Advice on treating colds and 'flu.

http://www.sciencedaily.com/releases/2007/12/071203164750.htm
Honey is better for colds than OTC medicine.

http://www.howlatthemoon.org.uk/index.php?p=1_20
Natural therapies for health problems.

Supplements

http://www.ncbi.nlm.nih.gov/pmc/articles/PMC2430660/
Little or no nutrition training for medical students.

http://howtoeliminatepain.com/inflammation/medical-doctors-have-little-or-no-knowledge-of-nutrition-because-medical-schools-offer-little-or-no-education-on-nutrition-vitamins-or-minerals/
Few graduating physicians in the USA have any training in nutrition.

http://www.naturalnews.com/036702_doctors_nutrition_fatalities.html
USA – minimum 25 hours of recommended nutritional training not fulfilled by medical schools.

http://bmjopen.bmj.com/content/2/1/e000417.full
http://www.sarahbesthealth.com/think-doctors-know-about-nutrition/
UK – improved nutrition training is necessary.

http://www.reportlinker.com/ci02037/Vitamin-and-Supplement.html
Euromonitor – the global vitamin and supplement market.

http://www.nhs.uk/news/2011/05May/Documents/BtH_supplements.pdf
Number of Britons regularly taking vitamins or supplements and market value.

http://www.euromonitor.com/vitamins-and-dietary-supplements-in-the-united-kingdom/report
Forecast of UK supplement market worth in 2017

http://www.thedoctorwithin.com/vitaminc/ascorbic-acid-is-not-vitamin-c/
A pill is not the same as nature provides.

http://en.wikipedia.org/wiki/Alternative_treatments_used_for_the_common_cold
Examination of efficacy of alternative treatments for the common cold.

http://www.arthritis-treatment-and-relief.com/how-glucosamine-help-arthritis.html
Glucosamine can help arthritis.

http://www.umm.edu/patiented/articles/health_benefits_of_vitamins_carotenoids_phytochemicals_healthy_foods_000039_5.htm
How vitamins do or don't improve health.

http://www.thisislondon.co.uk/news/article-23478646-vitamins-a-c-and-e-are-a-waste-of-time-and-may-even-shorten-your-life.do
Vitamins don't aid health and in fact may increase risk of death.

www.bmj.com/content/341/bmj.c5702.full
Vitamin E seems not to lessen the risk of stroke.

http://www.ajcn.org/cgi/content/full/85/1/308S
On balance multi-vitamins don't seem to prevent cancer or heart disease.

http://www.telegraph.co.uk/news/uknews/1565053/Herbal-medicine-risks-harmful-side-effects.html
Only 10 to 20 of several hundred herbal products sold in Britain might be effective.

http://jnci.oxfordjournals.org/content/94/16/1187.full
Some herbal medicines may interfere with pharmaceutical drug efficacy.

http://www.sciencedaily.com/releases/2011/10/111010173019.htm
Taking vitamins and other supplements appears to be associated with an increased risk of death in older women.

http://www.libraryindex.com/pages/649/Endangered-Plants-Ecosystems-PLANT-CONSERVATION.html
Herbal medicine growth combined with the use of ingredients from plants might lead to the extinction of some medicinal plants.

Illegal Drugs

http://www.guardian.co.uk/uk/2007/jan/25/drugsandalcohol.drugstrade
UK – police warn about spread of crystal methamphetamine use.

http://www.drugscope.org.uk/Resources/Drugscope/Documents/PDF/Good%20Practice/Statistics_on_Drug_Misuse_England_2011v3.pdf
England and Wales – official statistics on drug misuse 2010/11.

http://www.mirror.co.uk/news/uk-news/heroin-addiction-figures-drop-in-england-83434
England – fall in heroin and crack cocaine use.

en.wikipedia.org/wiki/Illegal_drug_trade
Retail value of global illegal drug trade.

en.wikipedia.org/wiki/Effects_of_cannabis
Information on cannabis.

en.wikipedia.org/wiki/MDMA
Information on ecstasy.

en.wikipedia.org/wiki/Cocaine
Information on cocaine.

en.wikipedia.org/wiki/Amphetamine
Information on amphetamine.

www.reference.com/browse/amphetamine
Information on the use of amphetamines and their side effects.

http://en.wikipedia.org/wiki/Methamphetamine
Information on metamphetamine.

en.wikipedia.org/wiki/Heroin
Information on heroin.

http://www.drugscope.org.uk/resources/faqs/faqpages/what-are-the-dangers-from-using-drugs
Information on illegal drugs.

http://news.bbc.co.uk/1/hi/health/7150274.stm
Cannabis has more harmful toxins than cigarettes when smoked.

www.bbc.co.uk/dna/h2g2/A2398818
Ecstasy – information, including short- and long-term side effects.

http://www.thesite.org/drinkanddrugs/drugsafety/drugsatoz/crystalmeth
Information on the effects and risks of crystal meth.

http://medicalmarijuana.procon.org/view.resource.php?resourceID=000881
USA – medicinal use of marijuana.

http://www.marijuana.com/news/2013/05/massachusetts-official-medical-marijuana-rules-and-regulations/
Information on use of cannabis medicinally.

www.doitnow.org/pages/115.html
Information and advice about LSD.

http://en.wikipedia.org/wiki/Anabolic_steroid
Information on anabolic steroids.

http://www.sportsci.org/encyc/anabstereff/anabstereff.html
Side effects of anabolic steroids.

http://www.medicinenet.com/drug_abuse/article.html
Drug abuse and addiction information.

http://neurobonkers.com/2011/12/22/the-year-in-drug-deaths-and-data-fraud/
UK – deaths from illegal drugs compared to deaths from legal drugs.

http://www.webmd.com/fitness-exercise/human-growth-hormone-hgh
Uses and dangers of human growth hormone.

http://en.wikipedia.org/wiki/Arguments_for_and_against_drug_prohibition
Both sides of the drug prohibition argument.

http://transform-drugs.blogspot.co.uk/2009/04/transform-publishes-comparative-cost.html
UK – cost and other information on drug prohibition.

http://www.netdoctor.co.uk/interactive/news/theme_news_detail.php?id=18482688&tab_id=254
UK – cost of drug prohibition

www.tdpf.org.uk/Policy_General_DrugPolicy.html
UK Government drug policy failure.

http://www.nta.nhs.uk/uploads/ndtmsannualreport2009-10finalversion.pdf
UK – drug treatment statistics.

http://lifering.org/?gclid=COiTyJDOsbcCFUfLtAodE24AnA
Lifering – help for addicts.

http://www.nhs.uk/Livewell/drugs/Pages/Drugtreatment.aspx
NHS – treatments for drug addiction.

http://www.addaction.org.uk/
Addaction – help for addicts.

http://www.urban75.com/Drugs/helpline.html
UK national drugs helpline.

http://www.ukna.org/
Narcotics Anonymous – help for addicts.

Pollution of Water, Soil and Air

http://www.naturalnews.com/019434.html
Interview with Randall Fitzgerald, author of "The 100-Year Lie". Suggestions for avoiding toxins.

www.scientificexploration.org/journal/reviews/reviews_21_1_kauffman.pdf
Critique of Fitzgerald's book.

http://www.pesticideresearch.com/site/docs/nowhereToHide.pdf
Pesticide Action Network's report on persistent toxic chemicals in US food supply.

http://colganprograms.wordpress.com/tag/alkaline-diet/
EPA report – toxins far exceed the recommended daily maximum in our daily diet.

http://news.sciencemag.org/sciencenow/2011/03/are-we-in-the-middle-of-a-sixth-.html
Conservationists warn that a mass extinction of living things might occur because of man's activities.

http://www.actionbioscience.org/environment/trautmann.html
Dose level often determines toxicity, but not always.

archive.treasury.gov.uk/pub/html/docs/soss/soss.pdf
UK Governmental guide on setting safety standards – divide by 10 for humans after animal studies, and divide by 10 again for the more vulnerable members of society.

http://www.sustainableproduction.org/precaution/back.brie.faci.html
Manufacturers should carry the burden of proof of safety, untested chemicals be kept off the market, and suspect ones should be eliminated in a timely fashion.

http://democrats.energycommerce.house.gov/documents/20100729/Cook.Testimony.07.29.2010.pdf
Ken Cook's evidence to a House subcommittee in 2010 – health risks from largely unregulated chemicals that contaminate air, water and food.

www.wwf.org.uk/filelibrary/pdf/biomonitoringresults.pdf
WWF-UK National Biomonitoring Survey – 300 chemicals found in human bodies and in foetuses.

www.ens-newswire.com/ens/jul2005/2005-07-22-02.html
Contaminants in American babies' blood.

http://www.asrm.org/detail.aspx?id=2322
American infertility.

http://rcrc.org/issues/environment.cfm
Man-made, hormone-disrupting chemicals.

linkinghub.elsevier.com/retrieve/pii/S0074775005300073
Pesticide effects on endocrine system and fertility.

http://www.greenpeace.org.uk/media/press-releases/greenpeace-report-reveals-the-impact-of-toxic-chemicals-on-reproductive-health
Fertility problems caused by man-made chemicals.

http://www.ourstolenfuture.org/newscience/reproduction/sexratio/sexratio.htm
Decline in male births due to exposure to man-made chemicals.

www.chem-tox.com/infertility/
Environmental causes of infertility.

http://www.independent.co.uk/news/science/scientists-warn-of-sperm-count-crisis-8382449.html
General decline in sperm count and quality.

http://www.medicalnewstoday.com/articles/253609.php
France – steady decline in sperm count.

http://www.telegraph.co.uk/health/healthnews/7824699/Girls-now-reaching-puberty-before-10-a-year-sooner-than-20-years-ago.html
British girls reaching puberty earlier, perhaps due to unhealthy lifestyles or exposure to chemicals in food.

generalhealthtopics.com/lifestyle-factors-affect-fertility-958.html
Lifestyle choices can affect fertility.

http://www.guardian.co.uk/lifeandstyle/2006/aug/20/foodanddrink.shopping
Possible toxic additives in British children's food.

www.foodreactions.org/allergy/additives/100.html
Dangers of food colourings.

http://www.eatwell.gov.uk/healthissues/foodintolerance/foodintolerancetypes/foodadditiv/
Food additives or germ-free childhoods perhaps to blame for food allergy increase.

http://www.relfe.com/aspartame_92.html
Dangers of Nutrasweet (aspartame).

www.naturalnews.com/011804.html
Aspartame approved for use despite tumour findings in rat study.

http://foodmatters.tv/articles-1/the-dangers-of-msg
MSG can lead to weight gain and be harmful to health.

http://www.telegraph.co.uk/news/uknews/1570442/Top-doctor-blocks-plan-for-folic-acid-in-bread.html
Folic acid in bread debate.

www.allaboutnutritionalhealing.com/foodallergies2
Reasons and solutions for food intolerance and allergies.

www.healingdaily.com/detoxification-diet/pesticides.htm
Pesticides kill living things, so are likely to be dangerous to humans. Fewer pollutants in organic food.

http://en.wikipedia.org/wiki/Attention_deficit_hyperactivity_disorder
Environmental pollutants may be a cause of behaviour disorders like ADHD.

http://www.reuters.com/article/idUSTRE65R3E420100628
USA – FDA advice against use of antibiotics to promote growth.

www.naturalnews.com/028031_antibiotics_infections.html
Increase in drug-resistant "superbugs" due to the widespread use of antibiotic drugs.

http://en.wikipedia.org/wiki/Genetically_modified_food_controversies
Controversy over genetically modified foods.

http://en.wikipedia.org/wiki/Water_pollution
Water pollution and its causes.

http://www.drinkable-air.com/waterfacts.htm
World Economic Forum – prediction of water shortages from climate change, population growth and poor water management. Chlorine could be dangerous to human health. Pollutants in American drinking water.

http://en.wikipedia.org/wiki/Drinking_water_quality_in_the_United_States
American drinking water regulations.

http://water.epa.gov/lawsregs/guidance/cwa/305b/upload/2000_07_07_305b_98report_98brochure.pdf
USA – report on the percentage of polluted waters.

http://www.ewg.org/tap-water/reportfindings
USA – tests carried out between 2004 and 2009 found 316 contaminants.

http://www.globalhealingcenter.com/water-toxins.html
USA tap water is not necessarily safe if it contains arsenic and chlorine.

https://www.gov.uk/government/policies/improving-water-quality
UK – open water bodies classified as being of "good status" set down by the EU Water Framework Directive.

https://www.gov.uk/government/uploads/system/uploads/attachment_data/file/82602/consult-udwp-doc-20121120.pdf
UK government proposal for water pollution.

http://www.telegraph.co.uk/earth/environment/4283806/New-evidence-that-river-pollution-could-be-causing-male-fertility-problems.html
UK – anti-androgens in English rivers.

http://www.minddisrupted.org/documents/MD%20Perchlorate%20Fact.pdf
Percholate in drinking water and crops.

www.fluoridealert.org/health/
Potential health problems from fluoride.

http://en.wikipedia.org/wiki/Water_fluoridation_controversy
Arguments for and against using fluoride in water supplies.

http://www.thenhf.com/article.php?id=99
Canada – painkillers and hormones found in tap water.

http://www.sciencedaily.com/releases/2010/04/100407110819.htm
Ingredients in household cleansers may lead to formation of a cancer-causing contaminant in water supplies.

http://en.wikipedia.org/wiki/Bottled_water
Bottled/tap water controversy.

http://www.alternet.org/story/142270/how_farm-raised_salmon_are_turning_our_oceans_into_dangerous_and_polluted_feedlots
Water contamination from fish farming.

http://www.ncbi.nlm.nih.gov/pmc/articles/PMC2702425/
Water and fish contaminated by pharmaceutical and personal care products.

http://www.cbsnews.com/8301-18563_162-57563739/study-finds-unsafe-mercury-levels-in-84-percent-of-all-fish/
Unsafe mercury levels in most fish.

http://water.epa.gov/scitech/swguidance/fishshellfish/outreach/advice_index.cfm
USA official advice not to eat fish types that contain high levels of mercury.

www.bluevoice.org/news_toxicarctic.php
Ocean contamination in the arctic.

http://water.epa.gov/scitech/swguidance/fishshellfish/techguidance/pcb99.cfm
PCBs in various people, particularly the Inuit.

www.ncbi.nlm.nih.gov/pmc/articles/PMC2790179/
Some musk fragrances from personal care products remain after lime treatment of water.

http://tuberose.com/Water.html
Possible fresh water shortage in the near future.

http://www.uk-water-filters.co.uk/tap_water_problems.html
UK – possible tap water contaminants.

http://en.wikipedia.org/wiki/Pesticide
Most sprayed insecticides and herbicides reach a destination other than target species and harm people.

http://en.wikipedia.org/wiki/DDT
Information on DDT and its eventual ban.

news.bbc.co.uk/2/hi/science/nature/6730713.stm
UK – fall in soil and vegetation dioxin level.

http://en.wikipedia.org/wiki/Soil_contamination
Information on soil contaminants.

www.ncbi.nlm.nih.gov/pubmed/908308
Inconclusive study on arsenic in soil.

www.bioline.org.br/pdf?ja09018
Drilling fluids can cause soil contamination and significantly affect marine life.

http://www.greenmedinfo.com/blog/pesticides-may-increase-risk-adhd-children
Possible links between pesticides and ADHD.

http://www.hiye.org.uk/climatechange/lecture08.htm
UK – suggested change to small-scale farming.

http://en.wikipedia.org/wiki/Air_pollution
Definition and dangers – including estimated deaths – from air pollution.

http://www.dailymail.co.uk/news/article-1259592/UK-air-pollution-killing-50-000-people-year-warn-MPs.html
UK – estimated numbers killed by air pollution.

http://www.publications.parliament.uk/pa/cm200910/cmselect/cmenvaud/229/22906.htm
UK – estimated health cost due to man-made air pollution.

http://news.bbc.co.uk/1/hi/health/3761012.stm
Traffic jams increase risk of heart attacks.

http://www.sciencedaily.com/releases/2008/03/080311075339.htm
Nano-particles in diesel may negatively affect the brain.

www.sciencedaily.com/releases/2009/03/090311170627.htm
Smog ozone impairs lung function, aggravates asthma symptoms, and kills people.

http://www.sciencealert.com.au/news/20100311-21527.html?utm_source=feedburner&utm_medium=feed&utm_campaign=Feed:+sciencealert-latestnews+(ScienceAlert-Latest+Stories)
Asthma attack dangers for young children from traffic-related air pollution.

http://en.wikipedia.org/wiki/Electromagnetic_radiation_and_health
EMR and EMF harm not proven.

http://www.wellsphere.com/healthy-living-article/is-your-cell-phone-a-silent-killer/885437
EMFs cause damage to cells that can make people more susceptible to cancer.

www.emrnetwork.org/pdfs/PATPHY_621.pdf
EMFs cause physiological changes that indicate allergic response and may be causing rise in allergies, asthma and other over-sensitivities.

http://www.badscience.net/2007/06/dr-george-carlo-responds-to-andrew-goldacre/
Dr Carlo's worrying hypothesis about EMFs disputed.

http://www.emwatch.com/Cellmasts.htm
Possible dangers of mobile phone masts.

www.globalresearch.ca/index.php?context=va&aid=7025
Summary of possible EMF mobile phone mast dangers.

http://www.ncbi.nlm.nih.gov/pubmed/21331446
Risk of brain tumours from mobile and cordless phones.

http://www.guardian.co.uk/technology/2011/oct/21/mobilephones-cancer
People using mobile phones for 13 years had no more tumours than others.

http://www.nhs.uk/news/2011/05May/Pages/health-impact-wifi-mobiles-electromagnetic-fields.aspx
Council of Europe call for ban on mobile phones in classrooms and dramatic reduction in exposure to other wireless devices.

emf.epri.com/EMF_Health_Risk_Evaluations_Updated_2_%207-09.pdf
Possible increased risk of childhood leukaemia and adult brain tumours from EMFs.

en.wikipedia.org/wiki/WiTricity
Wireless energy transfer claimed to be safe.

http://www.radiation.org/projects/tooth_fairy.html
Living within 100 miles of a nuclear power plant increases the risk of breast and prostate cancer.

http://ehp03.niehs.nih.gov/article/fetchArticle.action?articleURI=info:doi/10.1289/ehp.9861
German nuclear plant radiation study.

http://www.ippnw-europe.org/en/nuclear-energy-and-security.html?expand=176&cHash=abf6cd63d1
German government accepts research findings – children living near nuclear plants more likely to develop cancer and leukaemia.

http://www.ehjournal.net/content/8/1/43
Various nuclear plant radiation studies.

http://www.theecologist.org/green_green_living/health_and_beauty/555157/can_i_trust_my_natural_or_organic_body_cream.html
Unclear labelling of possibly harmful ingredients in personal care products.

water.epa.gov/drink/standardsriskmanagement.cfm
USA Environmental Agency regulations for drinking water purity.

http://en.wikipedia.org/wiki/Pharmaceuticals_and_personal_care_products_in_the_environment
Possible effects on health and environment from pharmaceutical and personal care product ingredients.

http://www.telegraph.co.uk/news/uknews/1555173/Body-absorbs-5lb-of-make-up-chemicals-a-year.html
Possible harm to women from beauty product chemical absorption.

http://www.theworldwomenwant.com/yourworld/care/
Average use of personal care products with untested chemical ingredients.

http://www.network54.com/Forum/281849/message/1164918958/Toothpaste+Ingredients+and+Hyperactivity-++The+Ecologist
Possible dangers of toothpaste ingredients, including risk of hyperactivity in children.

news.bbc.co.uk/2/hi/health/3597404.stm
Fumes from home solvent and cleaning products may cause asthma in young children.

http://en.wikipedia.org/wiki/Passive_smoking
Dangers of passive smoking, particularly for children.

www.epa.gov/iaq/pubs/insidest.html
EPA advice on home pollutants and irritants.

http://en.wikipedia.org/wiki/Air_freshener
Possible dangers from air fresheners.

www.ncbi.nlm.nih.gov/pmc/articles/PMC2772199/
Phthalates in coatings and personal care products may affect men's fertility.

www.cerebral-palsy.net/headlines/phtharticle.html
Mother's exposure to phthalates may result in demasculising problems for boys.

www.pbs.org/now/shows/412/ban-phthalates.html
Phthalates banned in Europe and being phased out in USA.

http://www.wellsphere.com/healthy-eating-article/we-are-bombarded-with-synthetic-chemicals/7352
"The 100-Year Lie" – of 25,000 chemicals in cosmetics sold in the USA, less than 4% tested for toxicity and safety.

http://www.hazards.org/cancer/preventionkit/part1.htm
1 in 10 cancers may be the result of preventable, predictable workplace exposures.

www.chem-tox.com/infertility/
Balance of hormones in body can be disrupted by exposure to various chemicals. Firemen and those who work in microelectrics, anaesthesia, painting, dentistry, are all at greater risk of exposure.

http://opac.yale.edu/news/article.aspx?id=3297
Yale University – greater risk of brain cancer for a variety of workers.

www.wecf.eu/cms/download/2007/WECF_breastcancer_07.pdf
Breast cancer risks and causes – including environmental.

http://erj.ersjournals.com/content/7/6/1048.full.pdf
Increased risk of respiratory diseases from occupational causes.

news.bbc.co.uk/2/hi/health/4579021.stm
Pesticide use may be linked to Parkinson's.

http://www3.imperial.ac.uk/newsandeventspggrp/imperialcollege/newssummary/news_21-1-2013-16-36-46
Occupations linked to asthma.

http://www.nhs.uk/conditions/Sick-building-syndrome/Pages/Introduction.aspx
Explanation and possible causes of "Sick Building Syndrome".

www.medicalnewstoday.com/articles/4757.php
Ultraviolet light in ventilation system can cure "sick-building syndrome".

http://en.wikipedia.org/wiki/Legionellosis
Information on Legionnaire's disease.

http://www.ourstolenfuture.org/newscience/oncompounds/pfos/2001-04pfosproblems.htm
Story of PFOS, now banned.

http://inspiredhealthandhappinessblog.com/2013/02/5-tips-to-reduce-your-toxic-load/#
How to reduce your toxic load.

http://ezinearticles.com/?Reducing-Harmful-Chemicals-in-Our-Everyday-Products&id=2089911
Natural alternatives to possibly harmful products.

http://www.natural-skincare-authority.com/cosmetic-chemicals.html
Information on toxic ingredients of personal care products.

http://en.wikipedia.org/wiki/Mobile_phone_radiation_and_health
Authorities advice on mobile phones use to reduce EMF exposure.

http://www.cell-phone-radiation.com/cell-phone-mast-shielding/
Phone mast shielding.

http://www.aboutclay.com/info/Articles/practical_guide.htm
How you might remove toxins from the body.

www.evenbetternow.com/hmp.asp
How you might eliminate metals from the body.

www.electrosmogsolutions.ca/
How you might lower electro-pollution in your home.

Disease and Illness

http://www.cancerquest.org/mutation-and-cancer.html
Cancer cell mutations

http://www.esmog-responders.com/research-science/from-dr-george-carlo.html
Dr Carlo – "environmental" influences on health include "external insults" from air, water and EMFs, as well as "internal insults" from ingested foods and pharmaceuticals.

http://jap.physiology.org/content/98/1/3.full.pdf
University of California study – human genome programmed for daily physical activity and a high-fibre diet. Research that includes migration and identical twin studies, shows irrefutable link of physical inactivity and inappropriate diet consumption to most chronic diseases.

http://en.wikipedia.org/wiki/The_China_Study
A book that correlates animal foods with "Western" systemic diseases and claims that those who follow a plant-based diet can avoid them.

http://www.beyondveg.com/billings-t/comp-anat/comp-anat-8b.shtml
Studies on hunter-gatherer diet – chronic degenerative diseases rare when traditional lifestyles followed, but disease incidence rises as Westernisation occurs.

http://www.staffanlindeberg.com/TheKitavaStudy.html
Papua New Guinea island population who ate what "primitive man" ate earlier in our evolution, did not get heart disease, cancer and all the usual diseases of civilisation.

http://en.wikipedia.org/wiki/List_of_countries_by_life_expectancy
Life expectancy of various countries.

http://en.wikipedia.org/wiki/Longevity
Genetic influence on lifespan.

http://www.ons.gov.uk/ons/dcp171778_277684.pdf
UK healthy life expectancy.

http://www.who.int/topics/chronic_diseases/en/
WHO – 63% of all deaths due to chronic diseases.

http://www.cdc.gov/chronicdisease/resources/publications/AAG/aging.htm
80% of Americans 65 and over have one chronic condition, and 50% have 2 or more.

http://www.bbc.co.uk/news/health-18007951
Most Britons over 65 and 23% of all patients suffer from 2 or more chronic conditions.

http://www.guardian.co.uk/society/2010/jul/02/poor-in-uk-dying-10-years-earlier-than-rich
UK – gap in lifespan between rich and poor.

http://books.google.co.uk/books/about/Rich_You_ll_live_17_years_longer_in_West.html?id=YWm_mAEACAAJ&redir_esc=y
UK London – Westminster's rich live 17 years longer than Westminster's poor.

http://www.bbc.co.uk/news/health-12819538
England and Wales – number working for the health service.

http://www.nhshistory.net/parlymoney.pdf
UK – rising cost of the NHS.

http://www.nhsconfed.org/priorities/political-engagement/Pages/NHS-statistics.aspx
England and Wales – rise in cost of NHS from 2001/02 to 2011/12.

http://en.wikipedia.org/wiki/List_of_countries_by_total_health_expenditure_(PPP)_per_capita
Per capita health expenditure for various countries.

http://www.bbc.co.uk/news/health-21667065
The leading causes of death in England.

http://image.guardian.co.uk/sys-files/Guardian/documents/2012/11/06/Factfile_deaths_2_2011.pdf
England and Wales – proportion of deaths from circulatory diseases and cancer.

http://www.cancerresearchuk.org/cancer-info/cancerstats/keyfacts/Allcancerscombined/
UK – rise in cancer incidence rates since the mid-1970s.

http://www.cdc.gov/mmwr/preview/mmwrhtml/mm4830a1.htm
Reasons for decline in heart disease since 1960s.

http://who.int/mediacentre/factsheets/fs310/en/
WHO – numbers and causes of death for low, middle and high income countries.

http://www.wcrf-uk.org/research/cancer_statistics/world_cancer_statistics.php?gclid=CJz81K6HyLQCFSbMtAodei4AUA
Global cancer cases and prediction for 2030.

http://en.wikipedia.org/wiki/Cancer
Just 5% to 10% of cancer cases are the result of hereditary factors.

http://www.cancerquest.org/mutation-and-cancer
How cells mutate and produce cancer.

http://www.cancerresearchuk.org/cancer-info/cancerstats/incidence/prevalence/prevalence-uk
There are more than 200 types of cancer. Number of Britons alive post-diagnosis.

http://cancer.about.com/od/cancerlistaz/a/commonUK.htm
The 10 most common types of cancer.

info.cancerresearchuk.org/cancerstats/keyfacts/Allcancerscombined/
UK cancer statistics.

http://www.webmd.boots.com/cancer/news/20110714/more-than-4-in-10-of-us-will-get-cancer-diagnosis-charity
UK – 64% of cancer sufferers will die from the disease. At 3% a year rise, 4 million Britons could have cancer by 2030.

http://www.beatingbowelcancer.org/facts-and-figures?gclid=CM6Swcizqq0CFSEhtAodAlFenQ
UK – over 41,000 Britons are diagnosed with bowel cancer each year. The number of cases in younger people is rising rapidly.

http://www.cancerresearchuk.org/cancer-info/cancerstats/types/testis/incidence/uk-testicular-cancer-incidence-statistics#Trends
Large rise in testicular cancer over the last 40 years in USA, Canada, Europe, Nordic countries, Australia and the UK.

http://www.cancerresearchuk.org/cancer-info/news/archive/pressrelease/2012-12-19-lifetime-cancer-risk-for-men-to-climb-to-one-in-two
UK – men's cancer risk set to reach 50% by 2027, up from 44% in 2010, and women's risk to 44% from 40%.

http://www.cancerresearchuk.org/cancer-info/cancerstats/childhoodcancer/incidence/childhood-cancer-incidence-statistics#Trends
UK – childhood cancers rose by 43% between 1966-70 and 2001-05, about 1% a year.

http://www.cancerresearchuk.org/cancer-info/cancerstats/types/breast/incidence/uk-breast-cancer-incidence-statistics
UK – breast cancer rose by 72% between 1975-77 and 2008-10. The lifetime risk for women is now about 1 in 8.

http://www.ncbi.nlm.nih.gov/pmc/articles/PMC2515569/
Lifestyle and environment account for 90 to 95% of the most chronic illnesses, as indicated by migration studies.

http://www.guardian.co.uk/society/2011/dec/07/cancers-prevented-lifestyle-changes-study
Researchers estimate that 40% of cancer in women and 45% in men could be prevented by a healthier lifestyle.

http://www.environmentalhealthnews.org/ehs/news/environmental-cancers
60% of cancers are caused by smoking and diet.

www.healthy-communications.com/5cancercausingchemicals.html
125 possible carcinogenic chemicals in personal care and beauty products.

http://www.bhf.org.uk/plugins/PublicationsSearchResults/DownloadFile.aspx?docid=2cc83960-2173-4fd4-a46c-0fb43c22baa4&version=-1&title=Trends+in+coronary+heart+disease%2C+1961-2011&resource=M129
UK – gradual decrease in heart disease deaths.

http://my.clevelandclinic.org/disorders/hypertension_high_blood_pressure/hic_high_blood_pressure_and_heart_attack.aspx
Information on hypertension, including causes.

http://www.ncbi.nlm.nih.gov/books/NBK45688/
Contributing factors to the fall in heart disease since the 1960s.

news.bbc.co.uk/2/hi/health/6949526.stm
High blood pressure sufferers expected to top 1 billion and maybe 1.5 billion worldwide by 2027.

Coronary Heart Disease Statistics 2010 Edition
UK 2008 statistics – heart and circulatory disease, hypertension, high cholesterol and stroke.

www.hypertension-bloodpressure-center.com/hypertension-statistics.html
Hypertension statistics for different countries.

http://wholehealthsource.blogspot.co.uk/2009/05/coronary-heart-disease-epidemic_19.html

Omega-6 fat in industrial vegetable oils may have caused heart disease epidemic.
http://ajcn.nutrition.org/content/97/3/597
Vegetarians have a 32% lower risk of ischemic heart disease.

http://www.jdrft1.org.uk/page.asp?section=255&sectionTitle=Type+1+Diabetes+Facts
UK – peak age of Type 1 diabetes diagnosis is 10-14, and it's getting younger.

http://www.diabetes.org.uk/Documents/Reports/Diabetes-in-the-UK-2012.pdf
2011 global and UK diabetes statistics.

http://www.diabetes.org.uk/Guide-to-diabetes/Introduction-to-diabetes/What_is_diabetes/
Information about diabetes and 2013 UK statistics.

http://www.nhs.uk/Conditions/Arthritis/Pages/Introduction.aspx
Types of arthritis and their symptoms.

http://www.nhs.uk/Conditions/Arthritis/Pages/Introduction.aspx
About 10 million Britons have arthritis, of which 8.5 million have osteoarthritis. Information on treatments and symptoms.

http://www.bbc.co.uk/news/health-17995938
UK osteoarthritis prediction for 2030.

http://www.jaoa.org/content/104/11_suppl/2S.full
Study of arthritis treatments.

http://www.nhs.uk/Conditions/Arthritis/Pages/Diet.aspx
http://www.cbsnews.com/stories/2004/12/02/health/webmd/main658797.shtml
http://www.gp-handbook.co.uk/articles/20130307_63
http://www.ukgoutsociety.org/docs/2009FinalDietsheet.pdf
Foods that may cause arthritis and those that might help sufferers.

http://news.bbc.co.uk/1/hi/health/7875192.stm
Complementary therapies for rheumatoid arthritis seem to be largely ineffective.

http://en.wikipedia.org/wiki/Parkinson's_disease
Information about Parkinson's Disease.

http://www.pdf.org/en/parkinson_statistics
An estimated 7 to 10 million people worldwide live with Parkinson's Disease.

www.nhs.uk/conditions/Parkinsons-disease
Symptoms and effects of progressive brain damage from Parkinson's Disease. 127,000 sufferers in UK.

http://www.biomedcentral.com/content/pdf/1471-2377-8-6.pdf
Contact with both herbicides and pesticides significantly increases risk of PD.

http://news.bbc.co.uk/1/hi/health/3519874.stm
Perhaps more men than women suffer from Parkinson's Disease because of greater exposure to toxic chemicals and incidence of head injuries.

http://www.ninds.nih.gov/disorders/parkinsons_disease/parkinsons_research.htm
Treatments for Parkinson's Disease, but no mention of diet.

en.wikipedia.org/wiki/Multiple_sclerosis
Information about MS including possible causes – environmental and infections.

http://www.nationalmssociety.org/about-multiple-sclerosis/what-we-know-about-ms/treatments/index.aspx
Various treatments for MS. No mention of diet.

http://en.wikipedia.org/wiki/Thyroid
Information about the thyroid gland.

www.emedicinehealth.com/thyroid_problems/article_em.htm
Thyroid information, including problems.

http://www.wrongdiagnosis.com/t/thyroid/stats.htm
Information on thyroid problems.

en.wikipedia.org/wiki/Chronic_fatigue_syndrome
Information about CFS (chronic fatigue syndrome), also referred to as ME (myalgic encephalomyelitis). Estimated numbers of Americans and British sufferers.

en.wikipedia.org/wiki/AIDS
Information about HIV and AIDS

www.avert.org/std-statistics-uk.htm
UK – types and statistics on STDs, including HIV.

http://www.digitaljournal.com/article/318945
UK – rise in STDs in older people.

news.bbc.co.uk/2/hi/health/6385323.stm
UK – statistics for MSRA and C Difficile.

http://www.guardian.co.uk/society/2009/apr/16/c-diff-superbugs-nhs
Fall in C Difficile numbers due to improved hygiene.

http://www.netdoctor.co.uk/diseases/facts/headache.htm
Types of headache and causes.

http://www.who.int/healthinfo/statistics/bod_migraine.pdf
Estimated 11% of the adult population in Western countries suffer from migraines.

http://www.headacheexpert.co.uk/facts-figures-about-headaches.html
WHO – migraines and headaches in top 20 causes of global disability. Number of sufferers in USA and UK.

http://www.bupa.co.uk/individuals/health-information/directory/m/migraine
Symptoms and treatment of migraines.

www.asthma.org.uk › News & media › Media resources
The NHS cost of asthma, working days lost due to breathing or lung problems. 1 in 11 British children have asthma – the highest worldwide.

www.bbc.co.uk/2/hi/health/7766656.stm
Tristan da Cunha and Barbados – genetic and environmental reasons for asthma.

http://en.wikipedia.org/wiki/Allergy
Information about allergies and their causes.

en.wikipedia.org/wiki/Eczema
Information about eczema. Mainstream medicine has treatments but no cure.

http://eczema-natural-healing.com/eczema-diet.html
Dietary changes can cure eczema.

http://www.wikihow.com/Treat-Eczema-Naturally
Suggested ways – including diet – to deal with eczema.

http://www.nhs.uk/Livewell/Allergies/Pages/Allaboutallergies.aspx
UK – information and statistics on allergies.

en.wikipedia.org/wiki/Hygiene_hypothesis
Children's exposure to germs may strengthen the immune system to resist allergies.

http://www.nhs.uk/Conditions/Coronary-heart-disease/Pages/Causes.aspx
Causes of CHD – smoking, high blood pressure, high cholesterol, diabetes, and too little exercise.

http://www.nhs.uk/Conditions/Blood-pressure-(high)/Pages/Causes.aspx
Causes of hypertension.

http://www.bhf.org.uk/research/statistics/morbidity/prevalence.aspx
UK 2012 statistics for heart attacks and strokes and living with CHD.

http://www.bhf.org.uk/heart-health/conditions/high-blood-pressure.aspx
UK – causes of hypertension and numbers with undiagnosed high blood pressure.

http://www.who.int/gho/ncd/risk_factors/blood_pressure_prevalence_text/en/index.html
Estimate of global deaths from hypertension.

http://www.endocrineweb.com/conditions/type-1-diabetes/type-1-diabetes
Information on Type 1 diabetes.

http://www.diabetes.org.uk/Professionals/Publications-reports-and-resources/Reports-statistics-and-case-studies/Reports/Diabetes-prevalence-2012-March-2013/
UK– 2012 diabetes statistics.

http://www.diabetes.co.uk/diabetes-prevalence.html
UK diabetes doubled from 1996 to 2011. Global estimate of sufferers.

http://www.who.int/mediacentre/factsheets/fs355/en/
Estimated global deaths from diabetes.

http://www.nhs.uk/Conditions/Diabetes-type2/Pages/Treatment.aspx
Conventional treatment for Type 2 diabetes – insulin tablets or injections.

http://www.naturalsolutionsmag.com/health-and-wellness/features/fighting-type-2-diabetes-without-drugs
http://diabetes.webmd.com/guide/natural-remedies-type-2-diabetes
http://www.guardian.co.uk/lifeandstyle/2013/may/12/type-2-diabetes-diet-cure
Regular exercise, eating healthily and losing weight can improve or even reverse Type 2 diabetes.

http://www.bbc.co.uk/news/health-17465403
England – heavy drinking, obesity and hepatitis caused large rise in liver disease deaths over 10 years, with 60% rise in alcoholic liver disease in young people over 7 years.

http://www.who.int/mediacentre/factsheets/fs164/en/
Global deaths from hepatitis C, numbers chronically infected, and causes of infection.

http://www.parliament.uk/documents/post/postpn349.pdf
Official diagnosing of dementia.

http://www.who.int/mediacentre/factsheets/fs362/en/
Global number of dementia sufferers – expected to double every 20 years.

http://www.reuters.com/article/2010/09/21/us-dementia-costs-global-idUSTRE68K0HL20100921
Cost of worldwide dementia.

http://www.ox.ac.uk/media/news_stories/2011/111028.html
UK – number of dementia sufferers.

http://www.telegraph.co.uk/health/healthnews/8853171/Alzheimers-and-dementia-cost-has-risen-to-34-billion-a-year.html
UK – estimated number of dementia sufferers and cost of care.

www.rcn.org.uk/development/practice/dementia/rcn_dementia_project
UK – number of dementia sufferers expected to rise to 2 million by 2033.

http://www.webmd.com/alzheimers/guide/preventing-dementia-brain-exercises
Staying mentally active delays cognitive decline.

http://christinegreer.com/main/wp-content/uploads/2011/05/AJADD-final-publication-Feb-2011.pdf
Effects of early onset of Alzheimer's on the children of sufferers.

http://www.name-us.org/
Information on Chronic Fatigue Syndrome (ME)

http://www.meassociation.org.uk/?page_id=1666
UK – estimated number of ME sufferers.

http://www.amfar.org/about_hiv_and_aids/facts_and_stats/statistics__worldwide/
Global numbers of those living with HIV/AIDS. New infections and deaths in 2011.

http://www.nat.org.uk/HIV-Facts/Statistics/Latest-UK-Statistics.aspx
UK – numbers living with HIV in 2011.

http://www.dailymail.co.uk/health/article-2003739/Drop-number-sexually-transmitted-diseases-time-10-years.html
UK – numbers of various STI cases in 2010.

http://www.bbc.co.uk/news/health-14636224
England and Wales – fall in "superbug" deaths.

http://articles.mercola.com/sites/articles/archive/2012/12/24/food-allergies-trigger-migraines.aspx
Suggestions of causes and how to deal with migraines.

http://www.nyrnaturalnews.com/article/headaches-healthier-ways-to-make-the-pain-go-away/
UK – 20% of adults suffer from chronic headaches, 8% of them migraines.

http://www.betterhealth.vic.gov.au/bhcv2/bhcarticles.nsf/pages/Headache_and_diet
Possible causes and suggested treatments for headaches and migraines.

http://www.headaches.org/content/headache-sufferers-diet
Possible dietary triggers of headaches.

http://www.who.int/respiratory/asthma/definition/en/
Definition of asthma.

http://www.cdc.gov/nchs/data/databriefs/db94.htm
Possible asthma triggers.

http://www.dailymail.co.uk/indiahome/indianews/article-2130628/Breathing-easy-Alarming-rise-asthma-leads-doctors-adding-lifestyle-changes-prescriptions.html
Global deaths from asthma. WHO estimates there could be 100 million more asthmatics by 2025. Possible causes and remedies.

http://www.scientificamerican.com/article.cfm?id=why-are-asthma-rates-soaring
Research supports the hygiene hypothesis with regards to allergies, but maybe not for asthma. Inhalers may make things worse.

http://en.wikipedia.org/wiki/Allergy
UK 2007 – 5.7m (5.5%) asthma, 5.8 m (9.4%) atopic eczema, 5-7% infants and 1-2% of adults food allergies, 2.3 m (3.7%) multiple allergies (asthma, eczema and allergic rhinitis together.

http://www.bbc.co.uk/radio4/science/allergicreactions.shtml
UK – 1 in 3 children were allergic in 2008. Figure expected to be 1 in 2 by 2015.

http://news.bbc.co.uk/1/hi/health/7766656.stm
Barbados study – is the increase in asthma due to industrial progress?

http://www.bbc.co.uk/news/uk-wales-18115560
UK numbers who suffer from some sort of allergic reaction. Probiotic supplement for pregnant women and babies reduced allergic risk.

fooddemocracy.wordpress.com/category/booksmoviesvideos/
Cow's milk and wheat are two most commonly reported allergens in the world – and they're in a huge number of products.

www.nhs.uk/conditions/back-pain
Information on back pain.

http://www.johnlant.co.uk/back%20facts%20(1).htm
UK – in 2009 back pain resulted in 81 million certified days of incapacity and 7 million visits to GPs at a cost of £350 million.

www.dailymail.co.uk/health/article-387363/DIY-way-beat-pain.html
Advice on ways you can treat back pain at home.

http://www.health.harvard.edu/newsletters/Harvard_Heart_Letter/2009/October/11-foods-that-lower-cholesterol
Foods that can lower cholesterol.

http://www.cbsnews.com/8301-500368_162-57349422/diet-patterns-linked-with-brain-health/
Healthy diet means less brain shrinkage as with Alzheimer's. Avoid trans fats.

http://news.bbc.co.uk/1/hi/health/4904082.stm
Mediterranean diet lowers risk of Alzheimer's.

http://www.sciencedaily.com/releases/2010/10/101013122601.htm
Luteolin – in carrots, peppers, celery, olive oil, peppermint, rosemary and chamomile – helps to reduce age-related inflammation of the brain and related memory deficits.

www.nhs.uk/Conditions/Arthritis/Pages/Diet.aspx
How diet affects arthritis.

http://www.guardian.co.uk/society/2012/feb/18/fasting-protect-brain-diseases-scientists
Fasting can reduce the risk of Alzheimer's and Parkinson's.

http://www.bbc.co.uk/health/treatments/healthy_living/fitness/motivation_why.shtml
Reasons why exercise is necessary and important for health.

http://www.dailymail.co.uk/health/article-2226446/Just-1-5-hours-exercise-week-dementia-away--preserve-memory.html
90 minutes exercise a week reduces the risk of vascular dementia by 40% and impairment in brain skills by 60%.

www.bbc.co.uk/news/uk-wales-25303707
2013 Cardiff University – large study of men showed exercise reduces risk of dementia significantly.

http://www.playengland.org.uk/news/2012/01/play-england-calls-for-community-action-to-help-children-missing-out-on-outdoor-play.aspx
England – childhood activity is low because few children regularly play outdoors.

http://www.macmillan.org.uk/Aboutus/News/Latest_News/Inactivityriskslongtermhealthof16millioncancersurvivors.aspx
Exercise helps recovery from cancer treatment and reduces risk of reoccurrence.

http://www.bbc.co.uk/news/health-14526853
Daily exercise boosts life expectancy and cuts risk of death. 6 hours of TV a day cuts lifespan by 5 years.

http://www.internalmedicinenews.com/single-view/weight-lifting-improves-physical-function-in-parkinson-8217s/a9d9c4cac9.html
Weight training programme for P D patients significantly improved their condition.

http://www.guardian.co.uk/uk/2006/jan/17/health.healthandwellbeing
People over 65 who exercise 3 times a week are 40% less likely to develop dementia.

www.sciencedaily.com/releases/2009/06/090608162428.htm
Less sleep means higher blood pressure.

http://www.washingtonpost.com/wp-dyn/content/article/2005/10/08/AR2005100801405.html
Too little sleep increases risk of cancer, heart disease, diabetes and obesity.

http://health.usnews.com/health-news/articles/2012/05/25/want-to-lose-weight-get-some-sleep
Too little sleep makes craving for unhealthy foods increase and metabolic rate decrease – causing weight gain.

http://www.nejm.org/doi/full/10.1056/NEJM200008243430802
Obesity increases risk of heart disease in women, while stopping smoking and better diet lessened the risk.

Social Pressure

http://www.uncommon-knowledge.co.uk/articles/bystander-apathy.html
Explanation of "bystander apathy".

http://psych.princeton.edu/psychology/research/darley/pdfs/Group%20Inhibition.pdf
New York University group inhibition experiment with smoke-filled room

http://en.wikipedia.org/wiki/Milgram_experiment
Milgram experiment on obedience to authority figures.

www.newsweek.com/2007/08/28/chain-of-tragedy.html
Copycat suicide.

http://en.wikipedia.org/wiki/Copycat_suicide
Increased suicides after deaths of celebrities.

http://www.nytimes.com/1987/03/18/nyregion/pattern-of-death-copycat-suicides-among-youths.html
Copycat suicides among youths.

http://news.bbc.co.uk/1/hi/education/4375399.stm
Rise in sales of "Turkey Twizzlers" after Jamie Oliver's critical remarks.

http://www.dailymail.co.uk/news/article-1082571/Sexually-charged-shows-Sex-And-The-City-Friends-blame-rise-teenage-pregnancy.html
Rise in teenage pregnancy rates because of sexually-charged TV series.

http://www.istfin.eco.usi.ch/h_shefrin09.pdf
"Groupthink" leads people in groups to act as if they value conformity over quality when making decisions.

en.wikipedia.org/wiki/Financial_crisis_(2007–present)
The financial crash of 2008.

http://www.guardian.co.uk/media/2012/apr/03/uk-web-advertising-spend
UK internet advertising expenditure.

http://www.go-gulf.com/blog/online-ad-spending/
Online advertising figures and future estimates.

http://slooowdown.wordpress.com/2012/02/05/summary-of-buy-ology-by-martin-lindstrom-summarised-by-paul-arnold-trainer-facilitator-paul_arnoldme-com/
Martin Lindstrom's book "Buyology" – emotions trump rational thought when buying.

http://en.wikipedia.org/wiki/Advertorial
Explanation of the "advertorial".

http://www.broadcastnow.co.uk/news/broadcasters/itv-signs-first-product-placement-deal/5024303.article
ITV signs the first product-placement deal in the UK.

https://www.tai.org.au/documents/downloads/DP57.pdf
Clive Hamilton – ever-increasing needs caused over-consumption in Britain.

en.wikipedia.org/wiki/Greenwashing
Cynical use of green concerns in marketing and advertising.

en.wikipedia.org/wiki/Brand
Concept of a "brand".

www.economist.com/node/10717849
Summary of Nick Davies' book "Flat Earth News".

http://www.corporatewatch.org/?lid=1570
Rise of the global Public Relations industry.

http://www.prweb.com/releases/2012/12/prweb10225468.htm
USA PR industry's revenue.

http://www.prweb.com/releases/2013/3/prweb10507677.htm
British PR industry's revenue.

en.wikipedia.org/wiki/Self-help
Information about the self-help industry.

http://www.dailymail.co.uk/femail/article-2026001/Self-help-books-ruin-life-They-promise-sell-millions.html
UK publishers earn £60 million from self-help books over 5 years.

www.metro.co.uk/news/47896-shoppers-cover-up-for-wrinkle-free-cream
UK – mad rush for "magic" wrinkle cream.

http://www.dailymail.co.uk/health/article-1090752/Anti-ageing-face-creams-dont-work-exercise-good-diet-do.html
University College London – avoid creams; do exercise and eat sensibly instead.

http://www.womansday.com/health-fitness/conditions-diseases/understanding-adult-anorexia-102247
4 out of 5 women dissatisfied with their body.

http://psychcentral.com/blog/archives/2012/06/02/why-do-women-hate-their-bodies/
Women feel they have to be thin at all costs.

http://www.telegraph.co.uk/health/women_shealth/4682209/Anorexic-girls-admitted-to-hospital-rise-by-80-per-cent-in-a-decade.html "009
England – 80% rise of anorexic young girls admitted to hospital from 1997 to 2007.

http://www.webmd.com/mental-health/anorexia-nervosa/features/anorexia-is-hitting-older-women
http://www.guardian.co.uk/lifeandstyle/2008/apr/29/healthandwellbeing.health
UK – more older women suffering from eating disorders.

http://www.consultingroom.com/media/media-stats-display.asp?id=43
Global statistics for cosmetic procedures.

http://www.nhs.uk/Conditions/Cosmetic-surgery/Pages/Introduction.aspx
UK – increase in cosmetic surgery.

http://www.guardian.co.uk/uk/2011/jan/31/cosmetic-treatment-britons-surgery-knife
UK statistics for cosmetic procedures in 2010 – £2.3 billion spent, and £5 million borrowed in 2009 for them.

http://www.guardian.co.uk/world/us-news-blog/2013/jan/30/plastic-surgery-rise-botox-breast-implants
Global and UK figures for cosmetic procedures in 2011.

en.wikipedia.org/wiki/Breast_implant
Information on breast implants.

http://www.plastic-surgery.net/dangers-breast-implants.html
Dangers of breast implants.

http://www.sunbedtips.co.uk/dangers-of-sunbeds.php
Dangers of sunbeds.

http://www.guardian.co.uk/books/2008/oct/02/poetry.pressandpublishing
Felix Dennis says money won't make you happy, it's more likely to make you neurotic.

news.bbc.co.uk/2/hi/business/7481927.stm
UK 2008 – charity report estimates single person needed to earn at least £13,400 before tax for a minimum standard of living.

http://www.clivehamilton.com/opinion/poverty-in-australia/
Incomes rise but people are no happier and believe they need yet more money.

http://www.iisd.ca/consume/harwood.html
"Yearning for Balance" American survey 1995 – 53% said they spent most of their money on "basic necessities".

http://www.alternet.org/hard-times-usa/disturbing-facts-about-state-lotteries-they-prey-poor-and-trash-economy-and-political
Lotteries and other gambling – the poor man's secret tax.

news.bbc.co.uk/2/hi/8481534.stm
2010 UK – rich-poor divide wider than 40 years ago.

http://www.economicshelp.org/blog/310/economics/rising-inequality-in-the-uk/
Earning gap between the top 10% and the bottom 10% of British workers.

http://www.cbpp.org/cms/index.cfm?fa=view&id=3629
Guide to historic trends in income inequality.

http://www.debtbombshell.com/
UK government debt.

www.creditaction.org.uk/assets/PDF/statistics/2008/january-2008.pdf
UK personal debt.

news.bbc.co.uk/2/hi/uk_news/education/3936529.stm
UK student debt.

econ.economicshelp.org/2008/03/problem-of-personal-debt.html
Problems of personal debt in UK.

http://en.wikipedia.org/wiki/Payday_loans_in_the_United_Kingdom
http://www.oft.gov.uk/shared_oft/Credit/oft1481.pdf
UK – growth in the payday loan industry.

http://www.guardian.co.uk/news/datablog/2009/nov/25/gdp-uk-1948-growth-economy
UK Gross Domestic Product since 1955.

http://www.selfstorageblog.com/vital-statistics-of-the-self-storage-industry/
American self-storage industry.

http://www.propertyweek.com/Journals/44/Files/2011/7/14/DriversJonas.pdf
2011– UK self-storage figures.

http://www.ptisecurity.co.uk/files/SSA%20Annual%20Survey.pdf
UK storage industry trend.

http://southtyneside.espresso.co.uk/espresso/clientu/cgi-bin/primary/wdyt/board.pl?b=24&ks=2&l=en
In 2007, 3% of Britons threw about £48 million of unwanted Xmas presents away.

www.guardian.co.uk/uk/2007/dec/31/gifts.lifeandhealth
2007 – UK Xmas gift coupons remain unused.

http://www.huffingtonpost.com/2012/08/21/food-waste-americans-throw-away-food-study_n_1819340.html
USA – 2012 food waste.

http://en.wikipedia.org/wiki/Food_waste
Wasted food globally and UK – £10.2 billion a year.

http://www.guardian.co.uk/news/datablog/2013/apr/26/brie-bin-food-waste-value
In 2011 the average UK household wasted £660's worth of food.

http://www.humanities.manchester.ac.uk/socialchange/publications/working/documents/TheCivicCultureinBritainandAmerica.pdf
Gradual decline in civil engagement in the UK and USA.

http://en.wikipedia.org/wiki/Happy_Planet_Index
Human wellbeing and environmental impact.

Work

http://en.wikipedia.org/wiki/Job_attitude
Information about job attitude.

http://www.sam.kau.se/sociologi/sums/besum.html
Attitudes to work.

http://www.kent.ac.uk/careers/Choosing/career-satisfaction.htm
UK graduate poll to gauge "boredom ratings" for jobs. Occupations listed by satisfaction level.

http://www.independent.co.uk/news/uk/this-britain/strange-island-pacific-tribesmen-come-to-study-britain-401461.html
Tribesmen from Vanuatu unimpressed by British way of life.

http://www2.warwick.ac.uk/fac/soc/economics/staff/academic/oswald/worklifebalance2003.pdf
Analysis of studies concerning attitudes to work/life balance.

www.cbc.ca/quebecvotes2003/features/feature5.html
Canada – reconciling work and family duties.

https://www.gov.uk/holiday-entitlement-rights/entitlement
UK holiday entitlement.

http://www.housepricecrash.co.uk/forum/index.php?showtopic=153821
Predictions in the past about working hours in the future.

http://www.guardian.co.uk/money/2011/dec/08/uk-employees-work-third-longest-hours
2011 UK – 42.7 working hours a week.

http://www.mentalhealth.org.uk/help-information/mental-health-a-z/W/work-life-balance/
UK 2003 – 1 in 6 people worked more than 60 hours a week.

news.bbc.co.uk/2/hi/uk_news/3101597.stm
UK 2003 – 60% of workers were too busy to take all their annual leave.

en.wikipedia.org/wiki/Working_Time_Directive
EU Working Time Directive – maximum of 48 hours in a given 7-day period protects people from stress, depression and illness.

http://thesocietypages.org/socimages/2009/09/07/comparing-hours-at-work-in-select-countries/
Average hours per week/year worked in different countries during 2008.

http://news.bbc.co.uk/1/hi/world/europe/4373167.stm
2005 – France relaxes its 35-hour working week rule.

en.wikipedia.org/wiki/Working_time
Information about working time.

http://www.telegraph.co.uk/health/healthnews/8858191/Commuting-bad-for-health.html
UK 2011 – commuting is bad for workers' health.

http://www.thisismoney.co.uk/money/news/article-2061409/The-average-worker-spends-weeks-year-commuting-statistics-reveal.html
2011 – average UK yearly commuting time.

http://technorati.com/women/article/25-of-employees-are-unhappy-at/
UK 2011 – just 36% of employees happy in their job.

http://www.timesofmalta.com/articles/view/20111008/health-fitness/Unhappiness-at-work-in-UK-on-the-rise.388535
2011 – 1 in 4 British workers were "distinctly unhappy" in their jobs.

http://www.mind.org.uk/news/5053_workers_face_the_sack_for_admitting_they_feel_stressed
Workers' stress levels and employers' attitude.

www.sciencedaily.com/releases/2009/04/090402143503.htm
Sleep essential for long-term memory and finding space for new learning.

www.guardian.co.uk/lifeandstyle/2003/oct/12/health.society
UK – work days lost through stress.

http://www.acas.org.uk/index.aspx?articleid=815
UK – estimated working days lost in 2004/5.

http://www.bbc.co.uk/news/business-11617292
UK 2010 – stress at work causing more days off.

http://www.mirror.co.uk/news/technology-science/science/dvt-warning-for-workers-eating-lunch-1370220
UK – 75% of office workers aged 21 to 30 ate lunch at their desks.

http://www.eupedia.com/forum/showthread.php?24193-Real-productivity-of-European-countries
2005 – real productivity of European countries.

http://www.ir.randstad.com/releasedetail.cfm?ReleaseID=536347
Workers' satisfaction.

http://www.standard.co.uk/news/uk/one-in-three-workers-suffers-from-burnout-8509586.html
2013 UK – 1 in 3 professionals suffering from "burnout".

http://faculty.som.yale.edu/amywrzesniewski/documents/Jobscareersandcallings.pdf
Study about how people view work – as job, career or calling.

http://en.wikipedia.org/wiki/Workaholics_Anonymous
Information on "Workaholics Anonymous".

http://www.eurofound.europa.eu/ewco/reports/TN0502TR01/TN0502TR01.pdf
European study of work-related stress.

http://www.acas.org.uk/media/pdf/7/k/The_future_of_health_and_wellbeing_in_the_workplace.pdf
UK 2012 – ACAS union discussion paper on health and wellbeing in the workplace.

http://www.guardian.co.uk/society/2009/aug/10/nuffield-health-study-laziness
UK – dog owners too tired to walk their pets and most parents being too tired to play with their children or have sex.

http://press.pwc.com/GLOBAL/News-releases/nextgen-global-generational-study/s/376ce2a9-1769-46f2-a228-8b97d252f660
71% of those born between 1980 and 1995 say work demands significantly interfere with their personal lives.

http://www.worklifebalance.com/worklifebalancedefined.html
Definition of work/life balance.

http://blogs.wsj.com/speakeasy/2013/06/16/fathers-day-how-dads-can-achieve-work-life-balance/
Advice for fathers to achieve work/life balance.

http://www.webmd.com/balance/guide/5-strategies-for-life-balance
Strategies for a better work/life balance.

Speed

http://www.slowfood.com/_2010_pagine/com/popup_pagina.lasso?-id_pg=121
The advantages of Slow Food.

http://www.slowmovement.com/slow_cities.php
Slow City movement – up to 50,000 population.

http://www.guardian.co.uk/theobserver/2001/jul/08/life1.lifemagazine8
Alternative and Slow Health treatments.

http://www.ecoliteracy.org/essays/nature-and-purpose-education
Maurice Holt and Slow Education.

http://www.robertfulford.com/2008-07-19-hefner.html
The Slow Sex movement.

https://www.tai.org.au/file.php?file=DP58.pdf
Clive Hamilton – downshifting in Britain.

http://www.telegraph.co.uk/science/science-news/8591919/City-dwellers-more-likely-to-suffer-stress.html
Schizophrenia, anxiety and mood disorders more likely in a city

http://www.ingentaconnect.com/content/brill/beh/1992/00000123/F0020001/art00005
1992 walking speeds correlate with the size of the city.

http://jcc.sagepub.com/content/30/2/178.short?rss=1&ssource=mfc
1999 study – pace faster in colder and more economically productive countries, and in individualistic cultures, causing more coronary heart disease and higher smoking rates.

http://www.livescience.com/10406-fast-walk-predict-long-youll-live.html
How fast you walk may predict how long you'll live.

http://www.thisislondon.co.uk/news/article-7914355-six-of-the-best-friends.do
The average Briton makes and loses 363 friends during their lifetime. Modern technology has created the "silent friend" who is rarely seen face-to-face.

http://www.corporatewatch.org/?lid=2629
Lowered food quality and cost of damage to the environment and human health of agricultural short-cuts to cut costs.

http://www.eateco.org/PDF/EnvDamage.pdf
Global environmental damage from industrial-scale farming and aquaculture.

http://www.ukeof.org.uk/documents/Defra-white-paper.pdf
The UK government plans to protect the environment.

http://www.guardian.co.uk/education/2010/may/12/middle-class-children-too-busy
Middle-class children are too busy.

http://www.kidsbehaviour.co.uk/ChildAnxietyDisorders.html
Child anxiety disorders.

http://www.brainy-child.com/article/childhood.shtml
Hurried children.

http://mret.wordpress.com/
Mobile phone use at bedtime can lead to headaches, confusion and depression.

http://www.dailymail.co.uk/health/article-1205669/Is-multi-tasking-bad-brain-Experts-reveal-hidden-perils-juggling-jobs.html
Multi-tasking is not as efficient and can lead to stress.

http://www.telegraph.co.uk/health/healthnews/5070874/Reading-can-help-reduce-stress.html
Activities that reduce stress.

http://foodmatters.tv/articles-1/7-health-benefits-of-meditation
7 health benefits of meditation.

Information
http://news.usc.edu/#!/article/29360/How-Much-Information-Is-There-in-the-World
University of South Carolina – mankind emits two quadrillion megabytes per year.

http://www.dailymail.co.uk/sciencetech/article-1355892/Each-person-inundated-174-newspapers-worth-information-EVERY-DAY.html
2 quadrillion megabytes a year is equivalent to a person reading 174 newspapers a day.

http://ischool.uw.edu/people/faculty/dmlevy
David Levy warned of information overload in 2006.

http://en.wikipedia.org/wiki/Information_overload
Causes of information overload.

http://iorgforum.org/about-iorg/media-releases/
Information overload has been a problem for workers since the mid-90s.

http://news.bbc.co.uk/1/hi/programmes/click_online/9742180.stm
University of California, San Diego – internet addiction could affect 1 in 10 people.

http://www.economist.com/node/17723028
http://answers.google.com/answers/threadview?id=762490
2010 – the average American supermarket has about 50,000 items, more than 5 times the number in 1975.

http://www.mckinsey.com/insights/organization/recovering_from_information_overload
Always-on, multi-tasking work environments are killing productivity, dampening creativity, and making us unhappy – we need time for reflection.

http://www.guardian.co.uk/lifeandstyle/2012/nov/02/change-you-life-information-overload
Taking back control over your communications.

http://www.infogineering.net/understanding-information-overload.htm
The reasons for and solutions to information overload.

http://boydio.wordpress.com/category/information-overload-research-group/
94% of knowledge workers surveyed have sometimes felt overwhelmed by information to the point of incapacitation.

"Find your Focus Zone: An Effective New Plan to Defeat Distraction and Overload", a book by Lucy Palladino – strategies to deal with information overload.

http://www.economist.com/node/18895468
Coping with information overload.

Technology

http://www.commonsensemedia.org/research/zero-eight-childrens-media-use-america/key-finding-1:-young-children-use-digital-media-frequently
USA – children's media use.

http://stakeholders.ofcom.org.uk/binaries/research/media-literacy/oct2012/Annex_2.pdf
UK 2011 – children's TV viewing figures.

http://www.dailymail.co.uk/health/article-194723/Kids-watch-TV-6-hours-day.html
UK – third of under-threes have a TV in their bedroom.

news.bbc.co.uk/2/hi/health/6944747.stm
Glasgow University – workers feel stressed out by emails.

http://news.bbc.co.uk/1/hi/education/4669378.stm
2006 – third of British children have gadgets worth up to £2,000 in their bedrooms.

http://www.telegraph.co.uk/technology/facebook/8335443/The-unacceptable-face-of-Facebook.html
Edinburgh Napier University – Facebook makes students stressed.

http://www.bbc.co.uk/news/uk-england-birmingham-14121631
Facebook bullying.

http://www.medindia.net/patients/lifestyleandwellness/computer-related-injuries.htm
Health problems from the use of computers.

http://www.prevention.com/health/emotional-health/technology-can-negatively-affect-health-research
Twitter is addictive and Facebook can damage self-esteem.

http://en.wikipedia.org/wiki/Implications_of_nanotechnology
Projected benefits and potential risks of nanotechnology.

http://www.foe.org/pdf/nano_food.pdf
Alienation and physical health dangers from nanotechnology in food.

en.wikipedia.org/wiki/Nanotoxicology
Possible dangers of nanotechnology.

http://www.scientificamerican.com/article.cfm?id=do-nanoparticles-in-food-pose-health-risk
Friends of the Earth – potentially damaging nanoparticles in food have not undergone governmental agency safety checks and are not labelled on products.

http://www.couriermail.com.au/news/national/laser-printers-bad-as-smoking/story-e6freooo-1111114083132
Queensland University of Technology – potentially dangerous laser printers.

http://www.socialanxietysupport.com/forum/f32/ipods-could-make-you-hallucinate-12433/
Whitchurch Hospital, Cardiff – iPods are causing more cases of musical hallucinations.

http://www.telegraph.co.uk/property/3359621/Second-Life-Clicks-and-mortar.html
The imaginary world of Second Life.

http://en.wikipedia.org/wiki/Anshe_Chung
Linden dollars in Second Life made Ailin Graef a real-life millionaire.

www.thisislondon.co.uk/.../article-23919657-how-to-control-your-blackberry-addiction.do
Nomophobia – addiction to smartphones.

http://article.wn.com/view/2008/11/29/Cyber_Terrorism_in_the_UK/
Dangers of cyber terrorism.

georgiaupdate.gov.ge/doc/10006922/CYBERWAR-%20fd_2_.pdf
Cyber attacks by Russia on Georgia before the Russian invasion.

www.aricsigman.com/IMAGES/VisualVoodoo.LowRes.pdf
Dr. Aric Sigman – biological dangers of watching TV.

http://www.dailymail.co.uk/news/article-56282/How-children-Britain-watching-TV.html
British children spend less time playing outdoors than other European children.

http://www.telegraph.co.uk/health/children_shealth/6306858/Australia-ban-TV-for-under-twos.html
Warning over the effects of toddlers watching TV and DVDs.

http://www.sciencedaily.com/releases/2007/08/070808082039.htm
University of Washington – watching DVDs and videos can hinder language learning of babies 8 to 16 months old.

http://www.sciencedaily.com/releases/2009/01/090113074419.htm
Seattle Children's Research Institute – warning about effects of TV and DVDs for under-twos.

news.bbc.co.uk/2/hi/health/3896093.stm
University of Otago NZ – children shouldn't watch more than 2 hours TV a day because they might well become overweight, have high cholesterol and smoke.

http://www.reuters.com/article/2007/10/01/us-children-television-idUSN2822538120071001
Johns Hopkins Bloomberg School of Public Health – advice on toddlers' TV exposure.

http://www.guardian.co.uk/environment/2009/oct/15/which-survey-electric-recycling
People dump old electrical goods rather than recycle them.

http://www.webmd.com/eye-health/eye-fatigue-causes-symptoms-treatment
Computer vision syndrome – eyestrain from watching screens.

http://achebreakapp.com/statistics-for-repetitive-strain-injury.php
Extent of RSI in USA.

http://www.intersperience.com/news_more.asp?news_id=56
Smartphone addiction of British teens.

http://www.bullguard.com/bullguard-security-center/internet-security/social-media-dangers/privacy-violations-in-social-media.aspx
Privacy problems with social media.

http://www.dailymail.co.uk/sciencetech/article-2221822/Take-TV-childrens-bedroom-sleep-properly-say-researchers.html
University of Alberta – children sleep better and live a healthier lifestyle if technology is not in bedrooms.

http://www.dailymail.co.uk/news/article-2209474/Online-banking-fraud-rises-quarter-crime-gangs-target-Britons-phishing-sites.html
Online fraud.

http://apise.org.ar/apise/index.php?option=com_content&view=article&id=67%3Ahow-technology-has-changed-childhood-ten-stats&catid=1%3Alatest-news&Itemid=2
Technology has changed childhood – statistics for 11 different countries.

http://www.computeractive.co.uk/ca/news/1913513/unwanted-gadgets-worth-gbp23bn
2007 UK – usable but unused gadgets in homes.

http://www.gulf-daily-news.com/NewsDetails.aspx?storyid=121840
2005 – estimated collective expenditure on gadgets by the British over their lifetime.

Entertainment
http://www.telegraph.co.uk/culture/tvandradio/5344212/Sir-Michael-Parkinson-delivers-fresh-attack-on-modern-TV-culture.html
Michael Parkinson's attack on modern culture.

www.itfacts.biz/us-tv-watching-by-age-groups/10928
Information about American TV use, and IT facts, including the huge choice.

http://www.statisticbrain.com/television-watching-statistics/
2012 American TV viewing statistics.

http://www.guardian.co.uk/media/2012/jan/24/television-viewing-peaks-hours-day and
http://www.guardian.co.uk/tv-and-radio/2013/mar/18/britons-own-fewer-tvs-research
In 2012 the average Briton watched 4 hrs and 2 mins of TV a day, up from 3 hrs and 36 mins in 2006.

http://www.tvlicensing.co.uk/resources/library/BBC/MEDIA_CENTRE/TVLicensing_TeleScope_2013.pdf
UK 2012 TV use and viewing information.

http://www.dailymail.co.uk/sciencetech/article-1352361/Children-spend-time-computers-TV-exercising-week.html
2011 – British children spent 2hrs 40m watching TV and 1 hr and 50m online.

www.turnoffyourtv.com/turnoffweek/TV.turnoff.week.html
Organisation that promotes time away from TV and other IT.

en.wikipedia.org/wiki/Center_for_SCREEN-TIME_Awareness
Screen-Free Week – an annual event where people are encouraged to turn off screens and "turn on life".

http://en.wikipedia.org/wiki/Books_published_per_country_per_year
Number of books published in various countries.

http://www.guardian.co.uk/books/2011/aug/30/death-books-exaggerated
2001 UK - 162 million books sold. In 2011 it was 229 million.

http://www.bbc.co.uk/blogs/radio4/posts/rajar_listening_figures_for_q3_1
In 2011 10.83 million listeners tuned in to BBC Radio 4.

http://www.mediauk.com/radio/311/bbc-radio-3
Over 2 million listen to BBC Radio 3.

http://well.blogs.nytimes.com/2012/10/17/get-up-get-out-dont-sit/
University of Queensland – an hour of TV reduces lifespan by 22 minutes on average.

http://videogames.procon.org/sourcefiles/Empathy.pdf
Violence in video games and films associated with a stronger pro-violence attitude.

www.thisislondon.co.uk/.../article-23610303-new-anti-obesity-campaign-under-way.do
The "Change4Life" anti-obesity governmental initiative in 2009 involved companies like Coca-Cola, Mars and Nestle.

Education

http://schools-wikipedia.org/wp/e/Education.htm
Definition of education and systems of formal education.

http://news.bbc.co.uk/1/hi/education/7715362.stm
2008 UK – Head Teacher warned that an emphasis on skills could lead to pupils' cultural and intellectual impoverishment.

http://en.wikipedia.org/wiki/History_of_education_in_England
England's education history.

http://www.chomsky.info/interviews/199811--.htm
Noam Chomsky's views on education.

http://news.bbc.co.uk/1/hi/6330631.stm
Philosophy lessons allow pupils to move to a level where informed choice can be made.

http://www.thisislondon.co.uk/news/article-23417830-meditation-classes-can-save-children.do
Meditation caused a drop in violence, depression, suicide and drugs in some of the worst American schools.

http://www.forbes.com/2004/07/15/cx_0715health.html
Music taught to children increases IQ.

http://www.telegraph.co.uk/health/wellbeing/8050394/If-youre-happy-and-you-know-it-raise-your-hand.html
Wellington College's "happiness classes" teach wellbeing and positive psychology.

http://seattletimes.nwsource.com/html/opinion/2002652185_woman29.html
Home-schooled children are more well-adjusted, polite, socially adept and academically advanced.

http://www.telegraph.co.uk/news/uknews/1550221/Children-damaged-by-exam-factories.html
UK Government advisor – children's self-esteem and long-term development undermined by target-driven culture in state schools.

http://www.sec-ed.co.uk/news/warning-over-raising-of-school-leaving-age-to-18
Warning about absenteeism from raising school (or college) education.

http://www.guardian.co.uk/education/2010/mar/09/abolish-50percent-target
Report says abolish Labour's target for 50% of pupils to attend university.

http://www.guardian.co.uk/commentisfree/2011/dec/16/schools-exam-system-not-fit
English pupils are the most tested – and stressed – in the industrialised world.

http://www.dailymontessori.com/montessori-theory/
The Montessori approach to teaching.

news.bbc.co.uk/2/hi/uk_news/education/7234578.stm
Some countries don't have formal school till later than 5 years-old.

http://www.education.gov.uk/popularquestions/schools/buildings/a005553/how-many-schools-are-there-in-england
Number of schools in England.

http://www.humanism.org.uk/education/education-policy/faith-schools-why-not
The humanist arguments against faith schools.

http://www.learning-together.org.uk/docs/creationists.htm
Some schools in the UK are teaching creationism.

http://www.sfs-group.co.uk/2011/09/14/UKprivateschoolclasssizessmallerthanstateschoolsandOECDaverage/
UK – class sizes in private schools are far smaller than those in state schools. Half as many in primary education and a third less in secondary education.

www.archachieve.net/smallschools/Resources/dollars_sense2.pdf
USA – advantages of small schools. They are not less cost-effective than large ones.

http://www.dailymail.co.uk/femail/article-466899/Suspended-teacher-insists-filming-classroom-behaviour-right.html
UK – "Classroom Chaos" filmed in 2005.

http://www.telegraph.co.uk/news/uknews/law-and-order/3901729/Police-called-to-deal-with-40-violent-school-incidents-every-day.html
2008 England - police called to 40 violent incidents in schools each day. Over 65,000 pupils were suspended from school for physical assault.

https://en.wikipedia.org/wiki/School_violence
School violence in UK and many other countries.

news.bbc.co.uk/2/hi/uk_news/education/7995869.stm
2009 England and Wales – the use of cover supervisors (bouncers) in schools.

news.bbc.co.uk/2/hi/uk_news/7259171.stm
England 2008 – 71% of pupils admit to being a bully.

http://www.guardian.co.uk/education/2008/feb/29/schools.uk4
2008 – UK schools worst in Europe for bullying.

http://www.dailymail.co.uk/news/article-1033435/Bird-brained-TV-generation-children-likely-recognise-Dalek-magpie.html
National Trust campaign to get children outdoors to learn about nature.

http://www.independent.co.uk/news/education/education-news/truancy-rate-falls-to-5-8214919.html
2011 – 5% absence rate in England's state schools.

Alienation

http://www.sciencedaily.com/releases/2007/05/070525000642.htm
May 23rd 2007 Earth's population becomes more urban than rural.

en.wikipedia.org/wiki/Urbanization
Process of urbanisation and its causes.

http://seattletimes.nwsource.com/html/living/2004364222_birdnote22.html
Seattle radio station KPLU's "BirdNote" program.

http://www.childrenandnature.org/news/detail/study_finds_access_to_nature_increases_longevity
Health benefits of access to nature.

http://www.theglobeandmail.com/life/the-hot-button/pork-wings-and-chicken-chops-do-you-really-know-what-youre-eating/article1941167/
British public's lack of knowledge about food and where it comes from.

http://www.dailymail.co.uk/news/article-1328869/DIY-dimwits--15-men-change-lightbulb.html
UK survey about lack of DIY ability. 15% of men can't change a lightbulb.

http://expandedramblings.com/index.php/resource-how-many-people-use-the-top-social-media/
Statistics 2013 for social website users.

http://www.labnol.org/internet/youtube-statistics-2012/20954/
YouTube statistics for 2012.

http://www.networkworld.com/weblogs/layer8/week_2005_08_14.html
Intel study – 75% said their mobiles gave them "flexibility" when meeting friends.

http://www.dailymail.co.uk/health/article-1149207/How-using-Facebook-raise-risk-cancer.html
Dr. Aric Sigman claims increased isolation could alter the way genes work, upset immune response and impair mental performance.

http://uk.gamespot.com/pc/rpg/worldofwarcraft/news_6167847.htm
Multiplayer online games statistics.

http://www.guardian.co.uk/lifeandstyle/2011/jan/01/technology-ban-kids-home-experiment
Lady and 3 children offline for 6 months.

http://www.ted.com/talks/richard_wilkinson.html
Richard Wilkinson talks about income inequality and social problems.

http://www.guardian.co.uk/commentisfree/2011/jul/25/britain-rich-poor-in-this-together
2011 article about the growth of income inequality in the UK.

http://www.usatoday.com/news/nation/2002-12-15-gated-usat_x.htm
In 2001, 7 million American households (6% of the total) lived in gated communities.

news.bbc.co.uk/2/hi/uk_news/politics/2518747.stm
Warning about a potential rise in gated communities in UK – will breed hostility and threaten the social cohesion of British cities.

http://www.telegraph.co.uk/news/uknews/1580991/Gadgets-driving-couples-to-sleep-separately.html
Bedroom use as a communications hub is contributing to people sleeping apart.

http://www.dailymail.co.uk/femail/article-1188541/Family-time-We-spare-45-minutes-TV-dinner.html
UK "family-unfriendly culture" – families are together for just 45 minutes in a day and mostly while eating and watching TV.

http://www.independent.co.uk/news/uk/home-news/49-minutes-the-time-each-day-the-average-family-spends-together-1987035.html
49 minutes is the average time that UK families spends together in a day. Family life is being reduced to stress and chaos by time pressures and money worries.

http://www.anxiety-and-depression-solutions.com/articles/news/063006_social.php
The growth of American social isolation.

http://www.ons.gov.uk/ons/rel/family-demography/families-and-households/2011/stb-families-households.html
Statistics for UK households in 2011.

http://www.dailymail.co.uk/femail/article-1126658/Rise-freemale-Number-single-women-doubles-decades.html
The number of single women in UK has more than doubled in 30 years.

http://www.bbc.co.uk/news/uk-england-oxfordshire-16051494
2011 – Xmas loneliness in UK.

http://www.dailymail.co.uk/health/article-1147106/Loneliness-bad-health-smoking-obesity-experts-warn.html
Being lonely is as bad for health as smoking and obesity.

http://www.economist.com/node/18226813
Lonely people at a greater risk of developing illnesses associated with chronic inflammation such as heart disease and certain cancers.

http://news.bbc.co.uk/1/hi/health/6991584.stm
http://news.monstersandcritics.com/health/news/article_1355699.php/Scientists_link_loneliness_to_ill_health
Genes connected to the immune system and tissue inflammation may have something to do with greater ill-health in lonely people.

http://www.upliftprogram.com/h_men.html#h17
Loneliness and health problems of older men might go unseen.

http://www.jrf.org.uk/publications/older-people-vision-long-term-care
Quality of care in US care homes.

http://www.alzheimers.org.uk/statistics
80% of people in UK care homes are suffering from dementia.

http://www.guardian.co.uk/commentisfree/2009/jan/05/youngpeople-mentalhealth
UK – young people's mental health.

www.thisislondon.co.uk/.../article-23600139-all-day-nurseries-can-lead-to-behavioural-problems-says-unicef.do
2008 UNICEF – all-day nurseries can lead to behavioural problems.

http://www.communitycare.co.uk/Articles/2008/06/26/108657/Education-of-children-in-care.htm
Low educational attainment of children in care.

http://www.telegraph.co.uk/news/uknews/3282549/Fathers-prefer-work-to-looking-after-children.html
2008 – British fathers' attitude to home life.

http://www.infed.org/thinkers/putnam.htm
Robert Putnam – less community engagement and trust of authorities in USA.

http://www.eauk.org/culture/statistics/family-life-in-the-uk.cfm
2011 UK household statistics. Of 26.4 million households, 29% consisted of only one person.

http://en.wikipedia.org/wiki/Retirement_community
Details of retirement communities.

http://www.ons.gov.uk/ons/rel/family-demography/families-and-households/2012/stb-families-households.html
UK governmental statistics for 2012 – families and households.

http://www.gallup.com/poll/5392/trust-government.aspx
2009 – lack of trust in US government.

http://www.guardian.co.uk/news/datablog/2012/nov/02/happiness-index-how-much-trust-government
2012 – lack of trust in UK parliament and government, and 2010/11 civic participation.

http://www.ucl.ac.uk/spp/publications/unit-publications/112.pdf
UK 2004 – decline in voting and trust in government.

Fear and Anxiety
http://www.bbc.co.uk/learningzone/clips/human-planet-sustainable-living-korowai-tribe-and-tree-houses/11965.html
2011 BBC film of Papua New Guineans building tree house.

http://www.social-consciousness.com/2010/06/dr-bruce-lipton-biology-of-perception.html?m=1
Bruce Lipton talks about epigenetics.

http://news.bbc.co.uk/1/hi/health/7988310.stm
2009 Mental Health Foundation poll – 77% of Britons found the world more frightening than in 1999.

http://www.guardian.co.uk/money/2010/feb/03/money-worries-britons-stress
UK 2010 – 40 million adults worried about finances, health, work or unemployment.

http://www.ft.com/cms/s/0/310f1920-05cf-11dd-a9e0-0000779fd2ac.html#axzz2WyPIwah5
Luke Johnson – disproportionate amount of bad news stokes up anxiety.

http://www.dailymail.co.uk/news/article-459477/Health-safety-purge-park-benches-3-inches-low.html
Park benches 3 inches too low for old people had to be replaced.

http://www.dailymail.co.uk/news/article-460538/Danger-A-5m-injury-risk-allotment.html
£375 minimum cost of insurance for £10-a-year allotment holders – in case a visitor has an accident.

http://www.dailymail.co.uk/news/article-1257445/Gloucester-cheese-rolling-event-Coopers-Hill-cancelled-200-years.html
http://www.bbc.co.uk/news/uk-22664900
http://www.guardian.co.uk/uk/2013/may/27/gloucestershire-cheese-rolling-race
200-year-old cheese rolling competition cancelled.

http://www.thisislondon.co.uk/news/article-23416471-british-high-streets-facing-christmas-lights-blackout-thanks-to-health-and-safety.do
Christmas lights on Britain's high streets under threat.

http://www.commutebybike.com/2007/07/06/green-transportation-specialist-to-workers-get-off-your-bikes/
Workers ordered not to use bikes to get to work.

www.thesun.co.uk/sol/homepage/news/article1220125.ece
Students banned from throwing mortar boards into air.

http://www.civitas.org.uk/pubs/crimeFear.php
UK – crime rate is 10 times higher than in 1950s.

www.ucl.ac.uk/news/news-articles/0709/09072801
US study - those with a high fear of crime are twice as likely to suffer from depression.

www.guardian.co.uk/society/2007/dec/03/longtermcare
2007 poll – Britons fear old age.

news.bbc.co.uk/2/hi/uk_news/3044625.stm
UK 2003 – 50% of over-75s afraid to leave their homes for fear of abuse or mugging.

http://www.dailymail.co.uk/news/article-555168/25-10-year-olds-allowed-play--Ed-Balls-swings-action.html
25% of 10-year-olds never allowed to play out on their own.

http://www.guardian.co.uk/lifeandstyle/2010/jul/11/cycling-school-child-safety-schonrock
Parents of children cycling 1 mile to school threatened with being reported to social services by headmaster.

http://www.freerangekids.com/why-i-let-my-9-year-old-ride-the-subway-alone/
9-year-old child finds his way home in New York, "ecstatic with independence!"

http://www.playengland.org.uk/news/2012/01/play-england-calls-for-community-action-to-help-children-missing-out-on-outdoor-play.aspx
Statistics for English children playing outside.

http://www.dailymail.co.uk/news/article-409507/Killjoy-officials-accused-nanny-state-madness-childrens-conkers.html
Children stopped from climbing trees to get conkers.

http://www.dailymail.co.uk/news/article-1021517/150-year-old-Monkey-puzzle-tree-facing-chop-council-says-needles-like-syringes.html
Council threatens to chop down "dangerous" 150-year-old monkey puzzle tree.

http://www.thisislondon.co.uk/news/article-23492131-fifty-years-without-an-accident-but-health-and-safety-orders-slide-to-be-taken-down---just-in-case.do
10-foot slide taken down after 50 years because "it could cause serious injury".

http://www.dailymail.co.uk/news/article-1023669/We-need-fingerprints-want-pick-children-nursery-tells-parents.html
A nursery requires a biometric fingerprint to collect children.

http://www.dailymail.co.uk/news/article-1223528/Parents-banned-supervising-children-playgrounds--case-paedophiles.html
Parents banned from watching their children in council recreation areas.

www.guardian.co.uk/commentisfree/2007/oct/14/comment.politics
UNICEF – British children are the unhappiest in the Western world.

www.primaryreview.org.uk/downloads/Childhood_lecture_2.pdf
UK 2008 Childhood Review – the many factors causing primary school children stress.

www.guardian.co.uk/uk/2007/oct/12/politics.schools
Test stress of 7-year-olds.

http://www.nspcc.org.uk/help-and-advice/worried-about-a-child/online-advice/bullying/bullying-a_wda87098.html
Online bullying.

http://zakka.dk/cykelhjelm/cykelhjelm_org_060131_ECF_Helmet_brochure.pdf
Myths about helmets and reasons for more cycling.

en.wikipedia.org/wiki/Shared_space
Shared space can be safer.

http://www.mindpowernews.com/ThoughtsAffectHealth.htm
How your thoughts can affect your health.

http://www.nytimes.com/2010/02/28/magazine/28depression-t.html?pagewanted=all
The upside of depression.

http://www.guardian.co.uk/uk/2006/jan/17/health.healthandwellbeing
Dementia risk lower for those who exercise.

http://en.wikipedia.org/wiki/Insomnia
Insomnia can lead to memory problems, anxiety and even depression

http://www.stressless.com/stressinfo.cfm
USA – anxiety and stress facts and advice.

Mental Illness
http://www.overcomedepression.co.uk/HowCommonDepression.html
WHO 2012 – depression will be the leading cause of the global disease burden by 2030.

http://en.wikipedia.org/wiki/Mental_disorder
WHO – over a third of people in most countries report mental illness problems at some time in their life.

http://www.mentalhealth.org.uk/content/assets/PDF/campaigns/MHF-Business-case-for-MH-research-Nov2010.pdf
2010 UK Mental Health Foundation Report.

http://www.mentalhealthresearchuk.org.uk/background/
Over 1.25 million people used NHS mental services in 2009/10, a 4% increase on the previous year in a continuing upward trend.

http://www.hscic.gov.uk/mentalhealth
1 in 6 Britons suffer from a mental problem. Mental illness costs £105 billion a year

http://www.dailymail.co.uk/news/article-463194/A-million-children-suffer-mental-health-problems.html
UK 2007 - a million children suffered from behavioural and other mental problems.

http://news.bbc.co.uk/1/hi/health/3532572.stm
UK 2004 – rise in teen depression.

http://www.parliament.uk/documents/lords-library/lln-2009-006.pdf
UK – rise in number of children with significant emotional or behavioural difficulties.

www.unicef.org/media/files/ChildPovertyReport.pdf
Unicef 2007 report – UK 24th ranking for child wellbeing.

http://news.bbc.co.uk/1/hi/health/7810902.stm
The Prince's Trust – poll on mental health of young Britons.

http://www.mind.org.uk/help/research_and_policy/statistics_1_how_common_is_mental_distress#howmany
UK mental health statistics.

www.anxietyuk.org.uk/about-anxiety/frequently-asked-questions/
UK – 12.8% rise in mixed anxiety and depression from 1993 to 2007.

http://www.mind.org.uk/help/diagnoses_and_conditions/body_dysmorphic_disorder#How%20common%20is%20BDD
Information on body dysmorphic disorder.

http://www.phobias-help.com/phobia_statistics.html
UK – 2.5 million phobia sufferers.

www.bipolarcentral.com/otherillnesses/hypochondria.php
1% to 14% of patients suffer from hyperchondria.

http://www.phc.ox.ac.uk/news/eating-disorders-in-young-people-are-still-widely-misunderstood
1.6 million people in the UK affected by eating disorders, the majority aged 12 to 20.

http://www.telegraph.co.uk/health/women_shealth/4682209/Anorexic-girls-admitted-to-hospital-rise-by-80-per-cent-in-a-decade.html.
2010 – 80% rise over 10 years in young girls admitted to English hospitals for anorexia.

http://www.huffingtonpost.co.uk/2012/10/12/social-media-anorexia-bulimia-young-people_n_1962730.html
Hospital admissions in the UK for eating disorders rose by 16% in 2011, with the biggest rise of 69% in girls aged 10 to 15.

http://www.guardian.co.uk/lifeandstyle/2008/apr/29/healthandwellbeing.health
UK – anorexia rise in adult women.

http://en.wikipedia.org/wiki/Attention_deficit_hyperactivity_disorder
ADHD explained.

http://www.netdoctor.co.uk/diseases/facts/adhd.htm
Facts about ADHD.

http://www.bbc.co.uk/news/health-20414822
2012 UK – 3% of children diagnosed with ADHD, with about 50% continuing to have the condition in adult life.

http://www.thejournal.ie/junk-food-child-iq-621799-Oct2012/
University of Bristol – junk food lowers IQ and a healthy diet increases it.

http://www.dailymail.co.uk/health/article-2212562/Fast-food-children-develop-lower-IQs--Junk-diet-lasting-effect-warn-experts.html
University of London – socio-economic status linked to fast food and intelligence.

http://archneur.ama-assn.org/cgi/content/abstract/58/3/498
Regular physical activity protects against cognitive decline and dementia.

http://www.nhs.uk/news/2010/04April/Pages/Alzheimers-risk-and-diet.aspx
Mediterranean diet reduces risk of Alzheimer's.

http://www.dailymail.co.uk/health/article-347122/Junk-food-diet-makes-children-badly-behaved.html
Junk food makes children badly behaved. Less processed food improves behaviour

http://www.memory-key.com/problems/dementia/prevention/diet-exercise
People with high scores on Mediterranean diet had a 28% lower risk of developing MCI (mild cognitive impairment) and 48% lower risk for Alzheimer's.

http://www.ncbi.nlm.nih.gov/pubmed/19362278
Sleep duration has an effect on risk of Type 2 diabetes.

http://www.guardian.co.uk/lifeandstyle/2009/aug/04/middle-aged-smokers-risk-dementia
Middle-aged smokers at a higher risk of dementia.

http://psychcentral.com/news/2012/02/28/childhood-stress-may-cause-genetic-changes/35336.html
Childhood stress may cause genetic changes and psychiatric problems in adulthood.

http://www.myaddventure.org.uk/blog/2012/11/27/adhd-statistics-are-a-statistical-nightmare/
2011 – estimated ADHD figures for English and Welsh children and adults.

http://www.guardian.co.uk/society/2012/may/06/ritalin-adhd-shocks-child-psychologists
2012 UK – prescriptions of Ritalin soar fourfold in a decade for ADHD children. 5% to 10% of British children are affected by ADHD.

http://www.mind.org.uk/news/9310_landmark_moment_as_antidepressant_prescriptions_top_50_million
England – anti-depressant prescriptions top 50 million in 2012.

http://www.mentalhealth.org.uk/content/assets/PDF/campaigns/MHF-Business-case-for-MH-research-Nov2010.pdf
UK 2009/10 – estimated annual cost of mental care.

http://www.bbc.co.uk/news/health-12986314
UK 2011 – economic problems may be fuelling a rise in depression.

http://www.guardian.co.uk/science/2006/jan/15/socialcare.food
Poor diet linked to mental health problems like ADHD and depression.

http://www.maternity.net/2008/smart-fats-breast-milk-omega-3s-and-baby-iq/
Higher IQ in babies fed with breast milk because of omega-3 fats.

http://www.bbc.co.uk/science/humanbody/sleep/articles/sleepdisorders.shtml
25% of UK population suffers from some sort of sleep problem.

http://www.calmconnection.com/SubPage.aspx?PageType=Articles&ArticleID=19
Information on anxiety and advice on stopping a panic attack.

Awareness

http://www.guardian.co.uk/society/2011/nov/11/smoking-drinking-pregnancy-harms-babies
UK 2011 – 10,000 babies can suffer brain damage, disability or physical deformity each year from smoking and drinking in pregnancy.

http://en.wikipedia.org/wiki/Deferred_gratification
Delaying gratification and "The Marshmallow Test".

The Way Ahead

http://www.bbc.co.uk/news/health-25576400
2014 – Overseas Development Institute report shows huge global rise in overweight and obese adults since 1980, including a 400% increase in developing countries.

Source Books

Food for a Future. By Jon Wynne-Tyson, published 1976 in Great Britain by Sphere Books Ltd.

Raw Energy. By Leslie and Susannah Kenton, published 1984 in Great Britain by Century Publishing Co. Ltd.

Dynamic Living – how to take charge of your health. By Aileen Ludington MD and Hans Diehl Dr HSc, published 1995 in the USA by Review and Herald Publishing Association.

What to Eat. By Joanna Blythman, published 2012 in Great Britain by 4th Estate.

The Natural Mind. By Andrew Weil, published 1975 in Great Britain by Penguin Books.

The Hundred-Year Lie – how food and medicine are destroying your health. By Randall Fitzgerald, published 2006 in Great Britain by Penguin Books.

American Mania – when more is not enough. By Peter C. Whybrow MD, published 2005 Great Britain by W.W. Norton and Co. Ltd.

Affluenza – the all-consuming epidemic. By John de Graaf, David Wann and Thomas H. Naylor, published 2005 by Berrett-Koehler Publishers, Inc. San Francisco, USA.

Growth Fetish. By Clive Hamilton, published 2004 in Great Britain by Pluto Press.

Walden - and civil disobedience. By Henry David Thoreau, published 1960 in the USA by the New American Library.

Seeing Green – the politics of ecology explained. By Jonathon Porritt, published 1984 in Great Britain by Basil Blackwell Publisher Ltd.

The Spirit Level – why equality is better for everyone. By Richard Wilkinson and Kate Pickett, published 2010 in Great Britain by Penguin Books.

Deschooling Society. By Ivan Illich, published 1973 in Great Britain by Penguin Books.

Flat Earth News. By Nick Davies, published 2008 in Great Britain by Chatto and Windus.

The Power of Now – a guide to spiritual enlightenment. By Eckhart Tolle, published 2005 in Great Britain by Hodder and Stoughton.

A New Earth – create a better life. By Eckhart Tolle, published 2006 in Great Britain by Penguin Books.

Happiness – a guide to developing life's most important skill. By Matthieu Ricard, published 2007 in Great Britain by Atlantic Books.

The Road Less Travelled – a new psychology of love, traditional values and spiritual growth. By M. Scott Peck, published 1990 in Great Britain by Arrow Books.

Six Impossible Things Before Breakfast – the evolutionary origins of belief. By Lewis Wolpert, published 2006 by Faber and Faber Ltd.

Status Anxiety. By Alain de Botton, published 2005 in Great Britain by Penguin Books.

The Drunkard's Walk – how randomness rules our lives. By Leonard Mlodinow, published 2009 in Great Britain by Penguin Books.

Predictably Irrational – the hidden forces that shape our decisions. By Dan Ariely, published 2009 in Great Britain by Harper Collins.

The Disowned Self. By Nathaniel Branden, published 1973 in Great Britain by Bantam Books.

Emotional Intelligence – why it can matter more than IQ. By Daniel Goleman, published 1996 in Great Britain by Bloomsbury Publishing PLC.

The Big Book of Calm. By Paul Wilson, published 1999 in Great Britain by Penguin Books.

You Can Heal Your Life. By Louise L. Hay, published 1984 in the USA by Hay House.

The Genie in Your Genes – epigenetic medicine and the new biology of intention. By Dawson Church, published 2007 in the USA by Elite Books.

Willpower: rediscovering the greatest human strength. By Roy Baumeister and John Tierney, published 2011 in Great Britain by Penguin Books.

The Anxiety Toolbox: the complete fear-free plan. By Gloria Thomas, published 2010 in Great Britain by Thorsons

Quote Authors' Biographies

Adler, Stella (1901-1992) was an American actress and an acclaimed acting teacher who founded the Stella Adler Studio of Acting in New York City.

Bowman, Kristi (?) is the American author of "Journey to One: A Woman's Story of Emotional Healing and Spiritual Awakening", published in 2009, and co-founder of "The Centre for Sacred Movement" in California that promotes greater health in spirit, mind and body through yoga, nature and community.

Carson, Rachael (1907-1964) was an American marine biologist and conservationist, whose writings are credited with advancing the global environmental movement. She is best known for her best-selling book "Silent Spring", which inspired a grassroots environmental movement.

Collins, Judy (1939-) is an American singer and songwriter, known for her eclectic tastes in the material she records. She is also known for her social activism. In 1969 she appeared in support of the Chicago Seven, and was admonished by the prosecutor when she began singing "Where Have All the Flowers Gone" during her testimony.

D'Angelo, Anthony J. (1972-) is an American who sparked a revolution in higher education. He set up a non-profit educational company to empower students throughout the USA. He was the main contributing author of the New York Times best-seller "Chicken Soup for the College Soul".

Didion, Joan (1934-) is an American author best known for her novels and literary journalism which explore the disintegration of American morals and cultural chaos.

Einstein, Albert (1879-1955) was a German-born theoretical physicist who developed "The Theory of General Relativity". He received the Nobel Prize and effected a revolution in physics. After World War 2 he was a leading figure in the World Government Movement. He was offered the presidency of the State of Israel, but declined.

France, Anatole (1844-1924) was a French poet, journalist, and novelist. Ironic and sceptical, he was considered in his day to be the ideal French man of letters. He was a member of the Academie Francaise, and won the Nobel Prize for Literature.

Frisch, Max (1911-1991) was a Swiss playwright and novelist. He concentrated on issues relating to problems of human identity, individuality, responsibility, morality, and political commitment. His use of irony is a significant feature of his post-war publications.

Goldacre, Ben (1974-) is a British science writer, doctor and psychiatrist. He is the author of the Guardian newspaper's "Bad Science" column and a book of the same title published in 2008.

Gordon, James Samuel M.D. (?) is an American author and psychiatrist, and a world-renowned expert in using mind-body medicine to heal depression, anxiety, and psychological trauma. He considers the mainstream "disease model" of health care misguided and that doctors should focus on keeping people well. He advocates health care education in schools as early as possible.

Gregory, Dick (1932-) is a black American comedian, social activist, social critic, writer, and entrepreneur. He was one of the first comedians to perform successfully for both black and white audiences.

Holtz, Lou (1937-) is a retired American football coach, sportscaster, author and motivational speaker.

Honoré, Carl (1967-) is a Canadian journalist who wrote "In Praise of Slow: How a Worldwide Movement Is Challenging the Cult of Speed", about the "Slow Movement".

Kellogg, John Harvey (1852-1943) was an American medical doctor in Michigan. He ran a sanatorium using holistic methods, with particular focus on nutrition, enemas and exercise. He was an advocate of vegetarianism. He is best known for the invention of the corn flakes breakfast cereal with his brother Will Keith.

Kieran, Dan (1975-) is a writer and editor. He is the Deputy Editor of "The Idler", a bi-yearly British magazine, and edited the books "Crap Jobs, Crap Holidays" and "The Book of Idle Pleasures".

Lawton, C. R. (No details available)

Lindbergh, Charles A. (1902-1974) was an American who attained instant worldwide fame in 1927 for the first solo, non-stop flight from the USA to Europe. In his later years he was a prolific and prize-winning author, as well as inventor, explorer, and social activist.

Marquez, Gabriel Garcia (1927-) is a Columbian novelist, short-story writer, screenwriter and journalist, known affectionately as "Gabo" throughout Latin America. He is best known for his novel "One Hundred Years of Solitude" which popularised a literary style known as 'magical realism'.

Millman, Daniel Jay (1946-) is an American author and lecturer in the self-help field. He served as Director of Gymnastics at Stamford University. He trained in Aikido and eventually earned a black belt and studied T'ai Chi and other martial arts. His books are largely to do with the human potential movement. His first book "Way of the Peaceful Warrior" was adapted to a film with Nick Nolte.

Ogunlaru, Rasheed (?) born in England to Nigerian parents, he is a life coach, speaker, and author of "Soul Trader – Putting the Heart Back Into Your Business".

Ornish, Dr. Dean (1953-) is president and founder of the non-profit "Preventative Medicine Research Institute" in California, as well as Clinical Professor of Medicine at the University of California. His research showed that heart disease could be reversed by the adoption of a whole foods, plant-based diet, smoking cessation, moderate exercise, stress management techniques including yoga and meditation, and psycho-social support.

Porritt, Jonathan (1950-) is an English environmentalist and writer. In the 1970s and early 1980s he was a prominent member of the Ecology Party. His first and best-selling book, "Seeing Green", was published in 1984, when he became a director of "Friends of the Earth" in Britain.

Rajneesh, Bhagwan Shree (1931-1990) was an Indian mystic, guru, and spiritual teacher who garnered an international following. His teachings emphasised the importance of meditation, awareness, love, celebration, courage, creativity, and humour – qualities he viewed as being suppressed by the adherence to static belief systems, religious tradition and socialisation.

Ricard, Matthieu (1946-) is a French Buddhist monk, author and photographer who lives in a Napal monastery. His book "Plaidoyer Pour le Bonheur" was translated into English and published in 2006 under the title "Happiness: A Guide to Developing Life's Most Important Skill". He was instrumental in gathering experienced meditators to submit themselves to scientific scrutiny for research into mind training.

Robbins, Tony (1960-), is an American motivational speaker and self-help author of "Unlimited Power: The New Science of Personal Achievement" and "Awaken The Giant Within".

Rogers, Richard (1933-) is a British architect who designs were modernist and functional. He is best known for his work on the Pompidou Centre in Paris, the Lloyds building and Millennium Dome in London, and the European Court of Human Rights building in Strasbourg.

Saint Teresa of Avila (1515–1582) was a Spanish Carmelite nun and mystic who claimed to have experienced a vision of "the sorely wounded Christ". She struggled to create a more primitive Carmelite movement, the "Discalced" (shoeless), and wrote "The Way of Perfection".

Shaw, George Bernard (1856-1950) was an Irish playwright and a co-founder of the London School of Economics. Nearly all his writings addressed social problems, but with a vein of comedy. An ardent socialist, he was angered by what he perceived as the exploitation of the working class.

Siddharta, Gautama (563-483BC) was a spiritual teacher from the Indian subcontinent, on whose teachings Buddhism was founded. After a reputed 49 days of meditation under a papal tree, at the age of 35 he is said to have attained enlightenment. He provided a detailed series of steps that people could follow to eliminate their suffering.

Stoll, Clifford (1950-) is an American astronomer and author. As a systems administrator at the Lawrence Berkeley National Laboratory he tracked down one of the first wave of hackers – detailed in his book "The Cuckoo's Egg". In 1995 he called the prospect of e-commerce "baloney" and questioned the future influence of the Internet on society.

Spurgeon, Charles Haddon (1834-1892) was a British Baptist preacher. He remains highly influential among Christians of different denominations, among whom he is known as the "Prince of Preachers". Over his lifetime he preached to around 10 million people, often up to 10 times a week at different places.

Trotman, Wayne Gerard (1964-) is a Trinidad-born, British independent filmmaker, writer, photographer, composer, and producer of electronic music.

Tzu, Lao (570-490BC) was a philosopher and reputed to be the author of the Tao Te Ching. Born in what is now Henan Province, his name means "old master". He was appointed Keeper of the Imperial Archives by the King of Zhou. He studied the archive's books avidly and his insight grew. Apparently Confucius heard of his wisdom and travelled to meet him.

John Wooden (1910–2010) was an American basketball player and coach, nicknamed "The Wizard of Westwood" because he won ten national championships in a 12-year period. He was renowned for his short, simple inspirational messages to his players, including his "Pyramid of Success". They were often directed at success in life as well as basketball.

Wynne-Tyson, Jon (1924-) is a British author, publisher, activist and pacifist, who founded the Centaur Press. He has written books on vegetarianism and animal rights, in particular "Food for a Future", published in 1979.

Zuboff, Shoshana (1951-) is an author and academic. She was the Charles Edward Wilson Professor of Business Administration at the Harvard Business School. She wrote the celebrated classic "In the Age of the Smart Machine: The Future of Work and Power", published in 1988. It is now considered the definitive study of information technology in the workplace.